DAILY LIFE IN

THE MEDIEVAL

ISLAMIC WORLD

The Greenwood Press "Daily Life Through History" Series*

The Age of Charlemagne
John J. Butt

The Age of Sail
Dorothy Denneen Volo and James M. Volo

The American Revolution
Dorothy Denneen Volo and James M. Volo

The Ancient Egyptians
Bob Brier and Hoyt Hobbs

The Ancient Greeks
Robert Garland

Ancient Mesopotamia
Karen Rhea Nemet-Nejat

The Ancient Romans
David Matz

The Aztecs: People of the Sun and Earth
Davíd Carrasco with Scott Sessions

Chaucer's England
Jeffrey L. Singman and Will McLean

Civil War America
Dorothy Denneen Volo and James M. Volo

Colonial New England
Claudia Durst Johnson

Early Modern Japan
Louis G. Perez

The Early American Republic, 1790–1820:
Creating a New Nation
David S. Heidler and Jeanne T. Heidler

18th-Century England
Kirstin Olsen

Elizabethan England
Jeffrey L. Singman

The Holocaust
Eve Nussbaum Soumerai and Carol D. Schulz

The Inca Empire
Michael A. Malpass

The Industrial United States, 1870–1900
Julie Husband and Jim O'Loughlin

Maya Civilization
Robert J. Sharer

Medieval Europe
Jeffrey L. Singman

The Nineteenth Century American
Frontier
Mary Ellen Jones

The Nubians
Robert S. Bianchi

The Old Colonial Frontier
James M. Volo and Dorothy Denneen Volo

Renaissance Italy
Elizabeth S. Cohen and Thomas V. Cohen

The Soviet Union
Katherine B. Eaton

The Spanish Inquisition
James M. Anderson

Traditional China: The Tang Dynasty
Charles Benn

The United States, 1920–1939: Decades of
Promise and Pain
David E. Kyvig

The United States, 1940–1959: Shifting
Worlds
Eugenia Kaledin

The United States, 1960–1990: Decades of
Discord
Myron A. Marty

Victorian England
Sally Mitchell

The Vikings
Kirsten Wolf

World War I
Neil M. Heyman

*Look for more books in this series in paperback from Hackett Publishing Company.

DAILY LIFE IN

THE MEDIEVAL ISLAMIC WORLD

JAMES E. LINDSAY

Hackett Publishing Company, Inc.
Indianapolis/Cambridge

Printed in the United States of America
22 21 20 19 18   3 4 5 6 7

Hackett Publishing Company, Inc.
P.O. Box 44937
Indianapolis, Indiana 46244-0937

www.hackettpublishing.com

Cover design by Abigail Coyle

Library of Congress Cataloging-in-Publication Data

Lindsay, James E., 1957–
    Daily life in the medieval Islamic world / James E. Lindsay.
       p.   cm.
    Includes bibliographical references and index.
    ISBN 978-0-87220-934-3 (pbk.)
    1. Islamic Empire—Social life and customs.   2. Civilization, Islamic.   I. Title.
    DS36.855.L56   2008
    953′.02—dc22

                                                        2008021557

The paper used in this publication meets the minimum requirements of American National Standard for Information Sciences—Permanence of Paper for Printed Library Materials, ANSI Z39.48–1984.

∞

For my children: Jonisa, Zachary, and Joshua

CONTENTS

ILLUSTRATIONS

PREFACE

Americans know a great deal about the European Middle Ages based on our exposure to popular literature and films depicting King Arthur, Robin Hood, foreboding castles, knights in shining armor, damsels in distress, and of course the collected works of Monty Python. A few are even lucky (or unlucky) enough to have studied Chaucer's *Canterbury Tales* without the benefit of a modern English translation. Despite the romantic and humorous quality of our popular understanding of the European Middle Ages, most Americans possess a range of religious, cultural, political, and even linguistic reference points from which to begin a more serious study of the history of medieval Europe. When we turn our attention to the medieval Islamic world, most of us have few, if any, points of reference at all.

Daily Life in the Medieval Islamic World is intended for such an audience. It is a general introduction to the Islamic world from the point of view of those who lived there when the Islamic world represented much of the best of what human civilization had to offer with respect to political order, military prowess, economic vitality, and civil society, as well as intellectual and scientific inquiry. As such, this book attempts to deal with a broad range of issues relevant to daily life in the many societies and regions that constituted the Islamic world from its origins in seventh-century Arabia to the end of the thirteenth century. I have chosen A.D. 1300 as the rough cut-off point for this study because the Islamic world becomes a very different place in many respects in the wake of the Mongol conquest of Baghdad in 1258, the end of the Crusader enterprise in the Near East in the 1290s, the rise of the Ottoman house in Anatolia and Eastern Europe in the early fourteenth century, and the waning of the Mongol threat by the 1320s.[1]

Because the medieval Islamic world during the seven centuries covered in this study ranged from Spain and West Africa in the west to Central Asia and the Indian Subcontinent in the east, one must make some choices about which regions and subjects to focus one's attention on and which perforce must be given less attention. Since Islam originated in the Arabian Peninsula and established its first cosmopolitan imperial capitals in Damascus, Baghdad, and Cairo, the bulk of our attention will be given to the central Islamic lands between the Nile and Oxus Rivers. Such an approach can give the impression that the central Islamic lands are where one can find "typical" Islamic religion and culture. To a certain extent this was the view of a great many of those who hailed from the region, as evidenced by the extensive literature praising the merits (*fadaʾil*) of one's home province, city, or town that developed during the early centuries of Islamic history. In order to illustrate the continuity as well as the diversity within and among medieval Islamic societies, I will occasionally provide examples from other areas as well.

In an attempt to make daily life in the medieval Islamic world accessible to the general reader, I will also on occasion refer to certain American political, social, and religious values in order to highlight the very real differences between the medieval Islamic world and modern American society. I am well aware that many Americans are conflicted about a host of political, social, and religious values, including the proper relationship between the state and religion, the state and the individual, the state and the family, the individual and the family, and between men and women. Nevertheless, our public debates about these issues inevitably involve some sort of discussion of persons as autonomous individuals and appeal to concepts such as individual rights, individual choice, individual responsibility, privacy rights, private property, and personal fulfillment. Moreover, I would argue that it is this emphasis on the individual and his or her individuality that most distinguishes modern Americans not only from the peoples of the medieval Islamic world, but also from the members of many ancient and medieval civilizations, including those of Greece, Rome, Europe, Iran, India, and China.

The occasionally comparative approach I use in this study is based on the premise that in order to understand daily life in the medieval Islamic world, we must appreciate the fact that many of the religious, political, and social values and expectations of the inhabitants of that world really are fundamentally different from our own. At the same time, we must realize that daily life in the medieval Islamic world actually made as much sense to the people who lived in it as ours does to us today. Therefore, if we are to have any success in this enterprise, we must seek to understand that world as best we can on its own terms as portrayed by its most articulate representatives. In other words, we must accept the proposition that the people who lived in that world were not simply folks like us transplanted into different costumes and who ordered from different menus.[2]

"Major Themes in Medieval Islamic History" is a basic overview of some of the important themes in medieval Islamic history and is intended to provide the necessary background for the remaining five chapters. It deals with some of the problems that historians must confront when trying to understand early Islamic history, the life of Muhammad, the early Islamic conquests, ethnicity in the medieval Islamic world, geography and environment, the political character of medieval Islamic societies, the fragmentation of the caliphate beginning in the mid-ninth century, the development of Islamic law (*shariʿa*), and Islamic mysticism (Sufism; *tasawwuf*).

"Arabia" deals with the world of Islamic origins. It focuses on the geography, environment, and trade of the region as well as the kinship-based social order that was shared by nomad and oasis dweller alike and that is taken for granted in the Qur'an. Although the region was the birthplace of Islam, it soon became peripheral to the political, intellectual, and economic centers of the Islamic empire and emerging Islamic civilization.

"Warfare and Politics" focuses on military technology and institutions in the medieval Islamic world. The chapter begins with a basic discussion of the Islamic concept of jihad, often incompletely translated as "holy war." It then addresses specific developments and changes in military technology and institutions in the medieval Islamic world. The chapter examines these in the context of the early centuries of conquest and consolidation of the Islamic empire, the introduction of military slavery in the ninth century and its subsequent development, and the Crusades in the Near East (1095–1291).

"Cities" focuses on daily life in three major cosmopolitan centers— Damascus, Baghdad, and Cairo. Damascus is one of the oldest continuously inhabited cities in the world and served as the Umayyad imperial capital from 661–750. Baghdad (est. 762) and Cairo (est. 969) were founded as palace cities for new imperial dynasties, the Abbasids (750–1258) and Fatimids (909–1171), respectively. These three imperial capitals represent themes peculiar to the political and religious idiosyncrasies of their rulers and their regions. However, our primary concern here is what they can teach us about more mundane issues of urban life in the medieval Islamic world. That is, what did the residents of these cities buy and sell in their markets? What kinds of goods did they manufacture? What kinds of produce did they grow? What kind of money did they use? How did they travel and transport goods from one city to another? How did Muslims, Christians, and Jews interact in these cities? What kind of homes did people live in? What did they eat and drink? What kinds of irrigation techniques were employed in their agricultural hinterlands?

"Ritual and Worship" focuses on the five requirements upon which the entire edifice of Islam rests: the statement of belief (*shahada*), ritual prayer (*salat*), almsgiving (*zakat*), fasting (*sawm*) during the daylight hours of Ramadan (the ninth month of the Islamic calendar), and the pilgrimage (*hajj*) to Mecca during the twelfth month of the Islamic calendar. Taken together, these five rituals are also the instruments that have for centuries produced the rhythms and the melodies of daily life in all Islamic societies. The chapter also examines the distinctive Shi'i pilgrimages in Iraq as well as other pilgrimages observed in the medieval Islamic world, especially in the sacred territories of Syria and Palestine.

"Curious and Entertaining Information" is modeled on al-Tha'alibi's (961–1038) book by the same title (*Kitab lata'if al-ma'arif*). Like al-Tha'alibi's *Lata'if* the chapter is a bit of a grab bag in its subject matter. That is, it treats a wide range of themes relevant to daily life not dealt with in the first five chapters, in particular those that deal with life cycle and family life issues. Topics addressed in this chapter include the traditional Arabic naming system, Qur'anic admonitions on the role and status of women and men in the family and society, children and childhood, circumcision, clothing and modesty, education, entertainments, and death and the afterlife.

"Suggestions for Further Reading" is by no means comprehensive but does provide some of the major English-language works relevant to the subjects addressed herein. Those interested in further investigating Islamic history or religion should find what they are looking for there. Essential resources for beginners and specialists alike are three encyclopaedias and one historiographical handbook. The best place to begin any study of Islamic history or religion is the *Encyclopaedia of Islam*, new edition, 12 volumes (Leiden: Brill, 1954–2004). A more recent contribution is the *Encyclopaedia of the Qur'an*, 5 volumes (Leiden: Brill, 2000–2005). While the *Dictionary of the Middle Ages*, 13 volumes (New York: Scribner, 1982–1989) emphasizes the European Middle Ages, it also includes many entries pertinent to the medieval Islamic world as well. Finally, R. Stephen Humphreys, *Islamic History: A Framework for Inquiry*, revised edition (Princeton, NJ: Princeton University Press, 1991) is the most comprehensive English-language introduction to the primary and secondary sources for understanding the history of the medieval Islamic world. Anyone familiar with Professor Humphreys' work will easily recognize the influence of the teacher on his student.

I have included a glossary of technical terms and have eliminated most diacritical marks when transliterating Arabic terms. Specialists will know which ones are missing. Nonspecialists will likely be thankful for their absence. I have also included some recipes from medieval Arabic cookbooks, a series of genealogical and dynastic tables, and an explanation of and conversion table for the Christian solar and Islamic lunar calendars.

NOTES

1. For an excellent treatment of the Islamic world in the fourteenth century, see Ross E. Dunn's *The Adventures of Ibn Battuta: A Muslim Traveler of the Fourteenth Century*, rev. ed. (Berkeley: University of California Press, 2005).

2. See especially Patricia Crone, *Pre-Industrial Societies: Anatomy of the Pre-Modern World* (Oxford: Oneworld, 1993).

ACKNOWLEDGMENTS

One incurs many debts over the course of a project such as this. Kevin Ohe invited me to contribute a volume on the medieval Islamic world to Greenwood's "Daily Life Through History" Series. Michael Hermann, Leanne Small, and the team at Apex Publishing shepherded it through to completion. Robert Hoyland graciously allowed me to include several of his photographs of Arabia. Travis Leirer prepared these and other images according to Greenwood's production specifications. Thanks are also due to those who have granted permission to quote from their translations of primary sources. I have tried to contact all copyright holders and would be happy to correct any oversights brought to my attention. My colleagues in the CSU history department faculty seminar provided helpful comments on very early drafts of chapters 1 and 2. Frank Towers provided much appreciated friendship and moral support. Special thanks are due to the readers for Greenwood Press and Jon Armajani, Nathan Citino, Paul Cobb, Rose Gaudio, William Griswold, Marianne Kamp, Suleiman Mourad, Warren Schultz, and Shawkat Toorawa who were kind enough to read a nearly complete draft of the manuscript. Their astute comments and criticisms, while not always followed, have made this a far better book than it would have been otherwise. Of course, any errors are entirely of my own doing.

James E. Lindsay
Fort Collins, Colorado
March 2005

BASIC CHRONOLOGY
OF EVENTS

(All dates are given according to the Gregorian Calendar; for an explanation of the traditional Arabic naming system see chapter 6, pp. 173-78)

ca. 570	Muhammad born to the clan of Hashim, a branch of Quraysh in Mecca, a brackish shrine center in the Hijaz (western Arabia)
ca. 600	Had achieved prosperity and married Khadija (d. 619)
ca. 610	Call to prophethood
ca. 610–622	Lives and preaches in Mecca
619	Death of Khadija and Muhammad's uncle and protector, Abu Talib
622	Hijra (emigration) to Medina; year one of the Muslim calendar
622–624	Organizes new community (*umma*) of faith in Medina
624–627	Internal opposition within Medina, which led to the expulsion of two Jewish clans and the extermination of the adult males of a third
624–630	Conflicts with Mecca
628–632	Consolidation and expansion within Arabia

630	Occupies Mecca
632	Muhammad dies and is buried in Medina; Abu Bakr proclaimed first caliph
632–634	*Ridda* Wars (Wars of Apostasy); rule of Abu Bakr
632–661	Reign of the Four Rashidun "Rightly Guided" Caliphs
638	Occupation of Jerusalem
644	Caliph Umar stabbed; dies one week after appointing a committee to choose his successor; Uthman ibn Affan selected; Qur'an is collected and put in its final form during Uthman's reign
656	Assassination of Uthman ibn Affan and the start of the first civil war in Islam
656–661	First Civil War
661	Assassination of Ali ibn Abi Talib; Mu'awiya ibn Abi Sufyan (r. 661–680) establishes the Umayyad dynasty
661–750	Umayyad caliphate based in Damascus
680	Martyrdom of Husayn at Karbala; model of protest and suffering for Shi'is
680–692	Second Civil War
691	Completion of Dome of the Rock in Jerusalem
705–715	Construction of Umayyad Mosque in Damascus
711	Beginning of Muslim conquest of Spain
732	Battle of Tours; Charles Martel halts the possible expansion of Islam into Western Europe
744–750	Third Civil War; defeat of Umayyads by Abbasids
750–1258	Abbasid caliphate—golden age of Islamic civilization
754–775	Caliphate of al-Mansur, second Abbasid caliph, real founder of the Abbasid state, builder of Baghdad and initiator of the movement to translate Greek philosophical and scientific works into Arabic
756	Establishment of Umayyad amirate in Cordoba, Spain
762	Baghdad founded
765	Death of Ja'ar al-Sadiq, sixth Shi'i Imam and eponym of Ja'fri school of Islamic law. Succession disputed, creat-

	ing split between Isma'ili (Sevener) and Imami (Twelver) Shi'is.
767	Death of Abu Hanifa, eponym of Hanafi school of Islamic law, dominant in Ottoman and Mughal Empires
786–809	Caliphate of Harun al-Rashid, height of Abbasid caliphate
795	Death of Malik ibn Anas, eponym of Maliki school of Islamic law, dominant in Islamic Africa
801	Death of Rabi'a al-Adawiyya, female Sufi mystic credited with fusing asceticism with love of God
820	Death of al-Shafi'i, eponym of Shafi'i school of Islamic law, dominant in Arabic-speaking territories of eastern Mediterranean
833–945	Emergence of regional states within Abbasid territories
836	Abbasid capital temporarily moved from Baghdad to Samarra, where it remained until it was returned to Baghdad in the late ninth century
855	Death of Ahmad ibn Hanbal, eponym of Hanbali school of Islamic law
874	Occultation of Twelfth Shi'i Imam
909–969	Fatimid caliphate in North Africa
929	Andalusian Umayyad caliphate established by Abd al-Rahman III
934–1063	Buyid dynasty in western Iran, Iraq, and Mesopotamia
945	Buyid occupation of Baghdad; end of direct rule by Abbasid caliphs
969–1171	Fatimid caliphate in North Africa, Egypt, and Syria
977–1186	Ghaznavid rule in Khurasan, Afghanistan, and northern India
ca. 1000	Death of the Syrian geographer, al-Muqaddasi
1009	Fatimid caliph al-Hakim orders destruction of Church of the Holy Sepulcher
1030	Death of Sultan Mahmud of Ghana
1031	End of Andalusian Umayyad caliphate
1037	Death of Ibn Sina (Avicenna)
1038–1194	Seljuk dynasty in Iraq and Iran

1058–1111   Life of Abu Hamid al-Ghazali, theologian, legal scholar, and mystic who integrated Sufism into mainstream Sunni thought

1075   Death of the Persian traveler, Naser-e Khosraw

1071   Battle of Manzikert

1095   Pope Urban II calls First Crusade

1099   Crusaders capture Jerusalem, establish Latin Kingdom of Jerusalem

12th Century   Sufi orders begin to provide organizational framework for social movements throughout Islamic world

1143   First translation of Qur'an into Latin commissioned to Robert of Ketton by Peter the Venerable, Abbot of Cluny

1171   Saladin conquers Egypt

1187   Saladin defeats Franks at the Battle of Hattin and reconquers Jerusalem for Islam

1198   Death of philosopher Ibn Rushd (Averröes)

1217   Death of the Andalusian traveler, Ibn Jubayr

1220–1260   Mongol invasions of Muslim territories

1250–1517   Mamluk dynasty in Egypt and Syria

1258   Mongols sack Baghdad

1260   Mamluks defeat Mongols at Ayn Jalut in Palestine

1261–1517   Abbasid caliphate in Cairo

1281–1924   Ottoman Empire

1291   Mamluk conquest of Acre, last Frankish stronghold in Syria

1295–1304   Ghazan—first Mongol khan to convert to Islam

1326   Ottomans take Bursa

1345   Ottomans cross Straits of Gallipoli

1370–1405   Conquests of Tamerlane

1389   Ottoman defeat of Serbians at Battle of Kosovo

1444   Last anti-Ottoman Crusade defeated at Varna

1453   Ottoman conquest of Constantinople

1

Major Themes in Medieval Islamic History

The Middle East in the sixth century was dominated by two imperial powers—Byzantium, or the Eastern Roman Empire to the west, and Sasanian Iran to the east. Neither the Byzantines nor the Sasanians were able to assert direct political or military control over the Arabian Peninsula, and they generally sought to police their southern borders by employing Christian Arabian tribal confederations as clients or buffers between themselves and the peoples of Arabia and each other. The Byzantines were allied with the Banu Ghassan, who resided in what is now southern Jordan; the Sasanians with the Banu Lakhm, who resided in what is now southern Iraq. (None of the modern states or borders in the Middle East existed prior to the twentieth century.) Both served their respective patrons well as long as compensation was regular and to their liking. Although the Arabian Peninsula lay on the periphery of both empires, it certainly was not isolated from either. In fact, Arabia at times was an area of direct competition between both empires in the areas of politics and trade as well as intellectual and religious worldviews.

As the Eastern Roman Empire, the Byzantines were defenders of Orthodox Christianity as well as the preservers of Greek language, learning, and culture (Hellenism). The Sasanians, on the other hand, were heirs to ancient Iranian and Semitic traditions and viewed themselves as the defenders of Zoroastrianism. Despite the official religions of both regimes, each ruled over populations that were diverse in language and culture as well as religion. Large populations of Jews were scattered throughout the region and lived under Byzantine and Sasanian rule. Orthodox Christians,

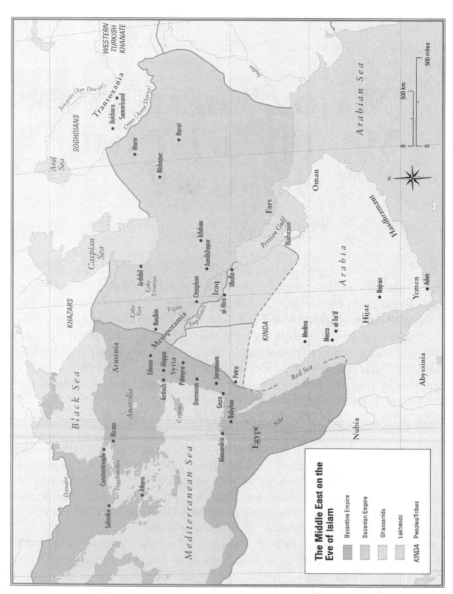

The Middle East on the eve of Islam. *Source:* Adapted from Lapidus, *A History of Islamic Societies.*

The Middle East on the Eve of Islam

- Byzantine Empire
- Sasanian Empire
- Ghassanids
- Lakhmids
- *KINDA* Peoples/Tribes

WESTERN TURKISH KHANATE

SOGHDIANS

Transoxania

Jaxartes (Syr Darya)

Bukhara · Samarkand

Oxus (Amu Darya)

Aral Sea

· Marw

· Herat

· Nishapur

KHAZARS

Caspian Sea

Armenia

Lake Van

Ardabil ·

Lake Urmiya

Nisibin ·

Mesopotamia

Tigris

Euphrates

Ctesiphon ·

· Isfahan

· Jundishapur

Fars

Iraq

al-Hira ·

Ubulla ·

Oman

Persian Gulf

Bahrain

Black Sea

Anatolia

Nicaea ·

Edessa ·

· Aleppo

Antioch ·

Syria

Palmyra ·

Damascus ·

Cyprus

Jerusalem ·

Gaza ·

· Petra

Babylon ·

Constantinople ·

Dardanelles

Athens ·

Salonika ·

Danube

Mediterranean Sea

Alexandria ·

Egypt

Nile

Red Sea

Nubia

Abyssinia

Arabia

KINDA

Hijaz

Medina ·

Mecca · · al-Ta'if

· Najran

Yemen

· Aden

Hadramaut

Arabian Sea

N

0   500 km

0   500 miles

Indus

of course, were favored in Byzantium. However, substantial populations of other Eastern Christian communities (Nestorians, Monophysites, and Armenians) lived under Byzantine rule as well. Nestorians likely constituted the bulk of the Christian population in the Sasanian Empire. Zoroastrians lived primarily under Sasanian control in Iraq, Iran, and the fringes of Central Asia. Finally, although the Muslim sources generally paint a picture of widespread polytheism in Arabia on the eve of Muhammad's mission, it is clear that representatives of all three scriptural traditions (Judaism, Christianity, and Zoroastrianism) lived in Arabia as well, especially in the Yemen and the Hijaz.[1] In fact, Muhammad's relations with the Jewish clans in the oasis settlement of Medina would prove to be especially troubling to him and the new community. Parts of Arabia on the eve of Muhammad's birth were in many ways connected with the major political and economic centers of the Middle East and were informed of the goings on in the region.

According to Islamic tradition, Islam began around the year 610 with a revelation from God to Muhammad ibn Abd Allah in the brackish settlement of Mecca in Western Arabia. By 750, Islam had become the religion of a military and political elite of a vast empire that spanned from Spain in the west to the Indus Valley in the east and parts of Central Asia to the north. Although Anatolia—Constantinople in particular—was a target of Islamic expansion since the late 600s, it did not begin to be incorporated into the Islamic world until the eve of the Crusader period in the eleventh century. It was not brought under complete Muslim political domination until the fall of Constantinople to the Ottoman sultan, Mehmed II, in 1453. Initially, Islam was the religion of a small elite, but by the mid-900s, Islam had become the majority religion in most of the places where Islamic political authority held sway. By the mid-900s as well, the Arabic language had become the preferred language of science and learning for nearly every ethnic and religious group under Muslim rule. Arabic served to unite the educated elites in the Islamic world in much the same way that Latin did in medieval Western Europe or English does in the modern world. That is, in the tenth century, an educated Jew in Baghdad wrote in Arabic (often with Hebrew characters), while he employed Hebrew for religious purposes, and possibly a dialect of Aramaic in everyday speech. An educated Muslim or Zoroastrian in Iran could speak and write Arabic but used a dialect of Persian for everyday speech. Educated Christians in Cairo (many of whom served in bureaucratic positions) were fluent in Arabic but used Coptic for religious purposes and possibly for everyday speech. The same held true for educated Christians in Damascus. They knew Arabic but used a dialect of Aramaic for religious purposes and possibly for everyday speech as well. Similar situations existed among the educated Muslim and non-Muslim populations of Spain, North Africa, Central Asia, and Sind (the Indus River plain).

How is it then that a small—even minor—religious movement in Western Arabia in the early seventh century could be transformed into a

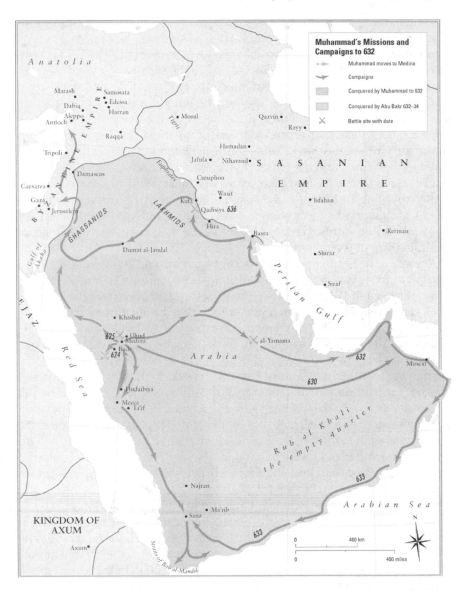

Early Islamic Conquests

far-flung Islamic empire by the early eighth century and a sophisticated Islamic civilization by the tenth century and beyond? In a sense this is the very question that early Muslim historians grappled with. Not surprisingly, Muslim historians—like their Jewish and Christian predecessors—credit God with their success and for the miraculous victories of the early Islamic conquests. What the Muslim historians did is reminiscent of what one finds in the historical books of the Old Testament (or Hebrew Bible), in which God is portrayed as having entered into a covenant relationship between Himself and the Children of Israel, often intervening on their behalf against their enemies. One also finds examples of this in the Acts of the Apostles in the New Testament, in which persecutions of early Christians are portrayed as ordained by God for the purpose of dispersing the community and spreading the Gospel around the Mediterranean basin. Most modern historians do not claim (at least in public) to see the hand of God in history. Ancient Jewish and Christian writers as well as early Muslim writers could not help but see it nor did they hesitate to write about it. Needless to say, caution is required of modern historians, who must rely on accounts that were written by people with worldviews so different from our own.

PROBLEMS FACED BY MODERN HISTORIANS OF EARLY ISLAMIC HISTORY

The societies examined in this volume roughly shared the same time frame as the European Middle Ages, ca. 600–1300. As we progress through these seven centuries, sources become more plentiful and we can begin to speak with greater confidence about what actually occurred. However, before we can begin to discuss daily life in the medieval Islamic world, we need to address the nature of the extant sources for the origins of Islam and assess what we can learn from them. In other words, what can we know about the earliest Islamic societies and how can we know it? As with most questions of this type, the answer is, "it depends"—on the sources, on the time period, on the specific question or questions asked.

The first issue that historians of the earliest and most important period of Islamic history (ca. 600–700) must come to grips with is that while we have an abundance of literary sources that describe the events of the golden age of Islamic history—the life of Muhammad, the early Islamic community (*umma*), the establishment of the caliphate, the Islamic conquests, and so forth—there are few, if any, documentary sources that actually date from the early seventh century. The second is that the bulk of our literary sources for early Islamic history come from within the Islamic tradition itself. That is, Muslim scholars wrote their narratives about Muslims, for Muslims.[2]

The kinds of literary materials that we have can be divided into four basic categories:

1. The sacred text of Islam (*al-Kitab*, The Scripture or The Book; also known as *al-Qur'an*, The Recitation);
2. Commentary on the Qur'an (*tafsir*)

3. Statements attributed to or reports about Muhammad by his companions (*ahadith;* sing. *hadith*);

4. Narrative reports about the events of the early community (*akhbar;* sing. *khabar*).

Muhammad's biographers combined these four distinct types of literature into a biographical genre called *sira,* the earliest example of which is the *sira* of Muhammad compiled by Ibn Ishaq (d. 767). The version of Ibn Ishaq's *sira* that has come down to us is the one edited by Ibn Hisham, who died in 834, two centuries after Muhammad.[3]

The Qur'an, for the vast majority of Muslims, is the eternal uncreated speech of God flawlessly communicated to humankind through His messenger, Muhammad. The revelations Muhammad received and recited to the people of Mecca (ca. 610–22) and Medina (622–32) are referred to as *al-Kitab* (The Scripture or The Book) as well as *al-Qur'an* (The Recitation). The traditional Muslim account places the compilation of the Qur'an into a single manuscript during the reign of the third caliph, or leader of the Muslim community after Muhammad, Uthman ibn Affan (r. 644–56), some two decades after Muhammad's passing. Since according to Muslim dogma, the Qur'an represents God's speech and not Muhammad's human teachings, it is believed to be without error. Therefore, for the believer, the veracity of the Qur'anic text cannot be called into question. Translations, of course, are another matter because, according to Muslim dogma, since God chose to reveal himself in Arabic, the true meaning of the Qur'an is simply untranslatable into another language. Therefore, Muslims refer to all translations of the Qur'an as interpretations of or commentaries on the Arabic text.[4]

There was a heated debate in the early Islamic centuries as to whether the Qur'an represented God's eternal uncreated speech or whether it represented God's speech created at a specific time. The debate was cast in terms of the createdness and the uncreatedness of the Qur'an. In time the majority position embraced the notion that the Qur'an represented God's eternal uncreated speech. While debates about the *meaning* of the Qur'an continue to this day, debates about the nature of the text itself, for the most part, do not. It should be noted that the minority position in favor of the createdness of the Qur'an has seen a bit of a revival among some modern Islamic reform movements such as the Aligarh school in nineteenth- and twentieth-century India.

Debates about the authenticity and reliability of literary sources other than the Qur'an have always been more acceptable, but even so, the basic narratives of these events are rarely called into question by the faithful. Most of the arguments about which sources were reliable and which were unsound were resolved by the end of the third Islamic century (A.D. 900s). That is not to say that disagreements ceased. Accounts of the first Islamic centuries tended to harden along sectarian lines and were recycled and modified within these communities to meet the concerns of later authors who faced the task of writing about more recent events, and not the "settled" issues of the distant, though crucially important, past.

Among non-Muslim scholars no such consensus exists. The reason for this is twofold: 1) modern western scholars tend to be skeptical of "in-house" accounts about anything, especially religious origins and/or dogma and 2) the vast majority of the narrative sources we have for Islamic origins date from several centuries after the events they describe. While not always accepting the traditional account of *how* the Qur'anic text was compiled under Uthman's direction, most western scholars do accept a seventh-century date for the text itself. There are some scholars who date the Qur'an to the second Islamic century. This is a minority view among western scholars (and is, of course, anathema to Muslims); however, its advocates have forced scholars to reassess their approaches to the Qur'an as well as the host of other literary sources for early Islamic history.[5]

The modern historian, therefore, faces a fundamental problem—how does one uncover "what actually happened" without contemporary documentary sources, especially when so many of the literary sources that are available contradict one another? Fred M. Donner, who has written extensively on early Islamic history, pointedly sets forth the problems with these sources as follows:

Chronological discrepancies and absurdities abound, as do flat contradictions in the meaning of events or even, less frequently, on their fundamental course. Many accounts present information that seems clearly anachronistic; others provide ample evidence of embellishment or outright invention to serve the purpose of political or religious apologetic.[6]

What to do with such sources? Some historians have been confident of the sources' general reliability and to a great extent have accepted the basic narrative of events as preserved in the Muslim chronicles. Others have been more skeptical but have argued that if one uses the sources with a critical eye for bias and obvious anachronisms, one can separate some wheat from chaff and uncover a kernel of truth about the past. Others go so far as to say that the literary sources that have come down to us, including the Qur'an, were written so long after the events described and present a narrative of Islamic origins that is so hopelessly confused and partisan that we cannot rely on them at all for reconstructing "what really happened" in early Islamic history. I fall somewhere in the middle category—skeptical, but at the same time optimistic. I am skeptical because there are very real problems involving contradictions among, as well as heavy-handed partisan editing of, the extant sources. Nevertheless, I am optimistic because I believe in the rather old-fashioned notion that it is indeed possible to reconstruct some sort of accurate representation of what actually occurred in the past despite the many problems our sources present.

Non-Muslim scholars' questions and speculations about the date and authenticity of the Qur'an as well as the reliability of the *sira* literature and other accounts of early Islamic history have elicited a wide range of responses from Muslims. Some simply dismiss them as the irrelevant fantasies of unbelievers. Others—as some believing Jews and Christians have done in response to critical approaches to the texts of their own faiths—have sought to find acceptable ways to reconcile their faith with the findings of modern scholarship. Others view them more ominously as dangerous attacks from an enemy designed to undermine the true faith.

Apart from these literary sources, archaeologists have unearthed a variety of sources that historians like to classify under the heading of material culture—such as abandoned settlements, graffiti, inscriptions, coins, pottery, glassware, and even mile markers along caravan routes that shed some light on our understanding of early Islamic history. Unfortunately, for the earliest period, we are still left with very little of even this kind of material that can be confidently dated to the early seventh century. Yet all is not lost. In fact, I would argue that these kinds of issues may be set aside for our purposes here; for it is the traditional narrative of Muhammad's life and early community that serves as the essential story that gives meaning to Islam as a religion and serves, in principle, as the underpinning of the daily life in the medieval Islamic world that will be examined in this study. Let us now turn our attention to that narrative.

THE LIFE OF MUHAMMAD (CA. 570–632)

According to the Islamic sources, Muhammad's prophetic career spanned some two decades, beginning around the year 610 when he was about 40 years old and lasting right up to the year of his death in 632.[7] These sources also agree that Muhammad was a reluctant prophet when the angel Gabriel brought him the first revelation. However, he soon realized that he was a prophet in the mold of the ancient Hebrew prophets, and like Isaiah and Jeremiah of old, he knew that he could not refuse to preach. After all, in a world where people still believed very concretely in the supernatural and were aware of at least the gist of the Biblical stories of God's powerful and miraculous dealings with the Children of Israel and their enemies, one simply could not ignore a summons from the very creator and sustainer of the universe.

As one might expect, Muhammad's biographers tell us far more about Muhammad's career after he received his revelations than about his childhood and early adulthood. Nevertheless, what they do have to say about his early years tells us a great deal about the values of the Arabian kinship-based society into which Muhammad was born, as well as the desire on the part of his biographers to demonstrate that Muhammad was indeed the Messenger of God. Like Abraham, Isaac, Jacob, Moses, and Jesus—to name but a few of the Biblical prophets—Muhammad is portrayed as having a prophetic pedigree. He, too, could trace his lineage to Abraham, though unlike the Biblical prophets, his genealogy went through Abraham's son Ishmael rather than Isaac. In addition to genealogy, Muhammad's biographers include numerous stories in which Christian and Jewish holy men give their stamp of approval to Muhammad's prophethood. What better ways to prove to one's audience that God's chosen messenger was indeed who he claimed to be? Not only did he belong to a long line of prophets, but the very holy men who had access to the special knowledge that only holy men possess agreed that he was in fact who he claimed to be.[8]

Muhammad was born in Mecca around the year 570 to a woman named Amina. Although accounts differ, most indicate that his father, Abd Allah, died before Muhammad was born. Muhammad's mother died while he was a young boy, after which he came under the protection of his father's brother, Abu Talib, the leader of Muhammad's clan, the Banu Hashim—an honorable, though certainly not the most important, branch of the Quraysh.[9] The dominant group in Mecca at the time, the Quraysh derived much of its prestige and wealth from two things. First, it was the custodian of the principal pagan shrine of the town—the Ka'ba—that focused on Hubal, an Arabian god of war. Second, it was involved in regional trade. It is doubtful that Mecca was a major player in long-distance trade at the time, but the Quraysh's trading activities and shrine custodianship did serve as the basis for the group's relations with outlying tribal confederations in the Hijaz and other regions of Arabia.

Muhammad's biographers portray him as a trustworthy young man who participated in the religious and commercial activities of Mecca. In fact, his trustworthiness in business affairs ultimately led to his first marriage (ca. 600) to a wealthy widowed businesswoman named Khadija. Khadija provided significant moral support to Muhammad during the early years of his prophetic career—both after he received his first revelations around the year 610 and especially after he received the revelation to begin his public preaching three years later. She remained his sole wife until her death in 619, the year that his uncle and protector, Abu Talib, also died.

Muhammad's prophetic career can be divided into two roughly equal periods. The first took place in his hometown of Mecca from about 610 to 622. By 622, he had fallen out of favor with the leaders of Mecca and negotiated a move for himself and his followers to the oasis settlement of Medina approximately 250 miles to the north. This move from Mecca to Medina in 622 is referred to as his *hijra* (migration), and is of such importance to his prophetic career that the year 622 of the Gregorian Christian calendar marks the year one of the Muslim calendar.[10] Those early Meccan converts who moved to Medina with Muhammad are referred to as *muhajirun* (emigrants). The people of Medina who embraced Muhammad and his message and who welcomed him to Medina are referred to as *ansar* (helpers). These two groups and their descendants played major roles in the course of Islamic history both during Muhammad's career in Medina as well as after his death in 632.

Muhammad spent his first two years in Medina organizing the settlement into a new community based on the principles of the revelations he had already received and a document that modern historians call "The Constitution of Medina." The year 624 marks the beginning of a series of bloody conflicts between Muhammad and his supporters in Medina and the Quraysh of Mecca. It also marks the beginning of a number of conflicts between Muhammad and three of the major Jewish clans of Medina, which by 627 had resulted in the expulsion of two Jewish clans (the Banu Qaynuqa and the Banu Nadir) and the extermination of the adult males and the enslavement of the women and children of a third (the Banu Qurayza). The conflict with Mecca ended in 630 when the leaders of Mecca agreed to accept Muhammad as the Messenger of God along with his religion and to restore Mecca to its rightful place as a pilgrimage center as established by Adam and Abraham.[11]

Muhammad's agenda during his career in Medina was much like that of the ancient Hebrew prophets. Unlike modern American society—the basis of which is supposed to be a Constitution written by men—Muhammad's principal goal was to create a society that lived in accordance with God's commandments as revealed to his prophet. This was to be achieved by persuasion, coercion and even warfare if necessary. While violence in the name of religion tends to make modern westerners uncomfortable, the idea that it could be an expression of piety was certainly not a new idea at the time, nor was religion expressly seen as separate from the needs of what was essentially a Muslim state. Similar notions can be found in the historical books of the Old Testament, which provide the basis, in part, for a similar approach by Christian religious and political theorists and warriors of the Crusader period.

By the time Muhammad died in 632, he had become the ruler of the Hijaz and had established tributary alliances with a number of the outlying tribes in Arabia. At his death, Muhammad's senior associates reached a consensus about a successor to Muhammad and proclaimed his close friend, early convert, and father-in-law—Abu Bakr—as the head of the community. As such, he enjoyed all of Muhammad's authority except prophethood.

THE EARLY ISLAMIC CONQUESTS (632–750)

Abu Bakr's principal objective during his short reign (632–34) was to subdue a rebellion in Arabia among the tribes who believed that their agreements with Muhammad died with him or who did not think that Abu Bakr was worthy of their allegiance. Abu Bakr and Muhammad's companions obviously disagreed. For them, the tribes' submission to Muhammad during his lifetime was equal to their submission to God;

therefore, they did not have the option of seceding from the new political and religious community. Hence, the wars to subjugate the Arabic-speaking tribes of the peninsula are known as the *Ridda* Wars—or the Wars of Apostasy, although not all of those who were compelled to accept Islam and submit to Muslim political authority were actual apostates. That is, some had never been Muslims nor had they submitted to Muhammad's authority during his lifetime.[12]

In 633, the leaders of Islam mobilized their armies and moved against the lands of the Fertile Crescent. Between 633 and 651, the Arabian Muslim armies conquered the Iranian Plateau, Syria, Egypt, and part of North Africa. During a second wave of conquests beginning in the 670s and lasting until around 750, they conquered Eastern Iran, Afghanistan, Sind, North Africa, and Spain.[13] The point of the conquests—apart from the *Ridda* Wars—was not conversion to Islam. In fact, conversion of the non-Arabian peoples was discouraged in this early phase of Islamic history. While it is likely that most of the soldiers were new converts and probably did not fully understand the religion themselves, the principal reason for this policy is that Islam appears to have been perceived by many at this time as a badge of Arabian identity. In short, many of the conquerors simply did not want to corrupt the bloodlines of their kinship groups. Of course, this attitude would change during the first few centuries of Islamic history as more of the subject population adopted the religion of the conquerors. However, even these conversions were not without conflict.[14]

After the initial conquests, the Arabian Muslims established garrison centers or military bases to control the new territories and maintain Arabian Muslim purity of the military. Some of the most important of these garrison towns were Kufa and Basra in southern Iraq, Fustat in Egypt (near where Cairo would be established in 969), and Qayrawan in modern-day Tunisia. As Americans learn every decade, precise U.S. population figures are impossible to determine even with our modern technology and intrepid census takers. Population figures for the first century of Islamic history are even more difficult to determine with any degree of confidence because we have no reliable contemporary data. Nevertheless, we can guess (based on admittedly rough figures for the Roman Empire and even less reliable ones for Iran) that the population in the areas conquered by the late seventh century possibly totaled somewhere between twenty million and sixty million (hardly precise numbers by any stretch of the imagination).

Based on the conflicting Arabic chronicles we can estimate that by the beginning of the eighth century there were roughly 250,000 to 300,000 troops enrolled in the Umayyad registers. If we multiply the number of troops by a factor of four to account for the troops' dependants as well as provincial administrators, we can estimate that the total number of Arabian Muslims—the soldiers, the administrators, and their dependants—constituted maybe one million persons, or at most 5 percent of the total population. While these figures are extremely imprecise, they do illustrate that during the first century of Islamic history, the Arabian Muslim conquerors were a very small minority in a vast non-Muslim sea.[15]

ETHNICITY

That those who speak a common language, have a common culture, and have a common past (however real or imagined) are necessarily entitled to govern themselves in the form of an independent state is taken as the natural order of things in the modern world. Yet, it is a fairly new idea in the annals of human history. The ancient, medieval, and even early modern worlds were ages in which kings and conquerors founded multiethnic, multireligious, and multilinguistic empires on a grand scale. The empires and lesser states of the medieval Islamic world certainly pursued the business of empire as enthusiastically as their predecessors in Rome and Iran and their contemporaries in China.

By 1500, Islamic political authority had expanded down into sub-Saharan West Africa, along the east African Coast, well into Central Asia, and throughout most of the Indian subcontinent. Even so, it was only in Syria, Egypt, and Iraq that Arabic became the language of everyday speech. Iran retained its own distinctive identity as a largely Persian-speaking area and witnessed a revival of Persian as a language of literature and administration by the tenth century, ironically under regimes of Turkic origin. The third principal language of the pre-modern Islamic world—Turkish—began to be used in much the same way by 1400 after the rise of the Ottoman house in Anatolia and southeastern Europe.

Because of the wide variety of language and cultural groups that became incorporated into the medieval Islamic world, a few comments on conceptions of ethnic identity are in order. Since there are too many groups to discuss each individually, I will limit my remarks to medieval and modern conceptions of Arab identity to illustrate how modern conceptions of ethnicity can cloud our understanding of daily life in the medieval Islamic world. Thus far, I have referred to "Arabian Muslims" or those who could trace their ancestry to the Arabian Peninsula. I have avoided using the term "Arab" because it has meanings today that it simply did not have in the premodern Islamic world. In fact, the sources rarely speak of Arabs as a coherent group with a sense of ethnic identity in the way we think of ethnicity today.

Those who spoke one of the dialects of Arabic did see themselves as distinct from non-Arabic speakers. However, when our sources use the term "Arab," they generally are referring to the pastoral nomads of the Arabian Peninsula; that is, the Bedouin. Since most of the important Arabian actors in early Islamic history hailed from the oasis settlements of the Hijaz, they were not "Arabs" in this sense of the word. In fact, these individuals are primarily identified as members of a host of specific kinship groups

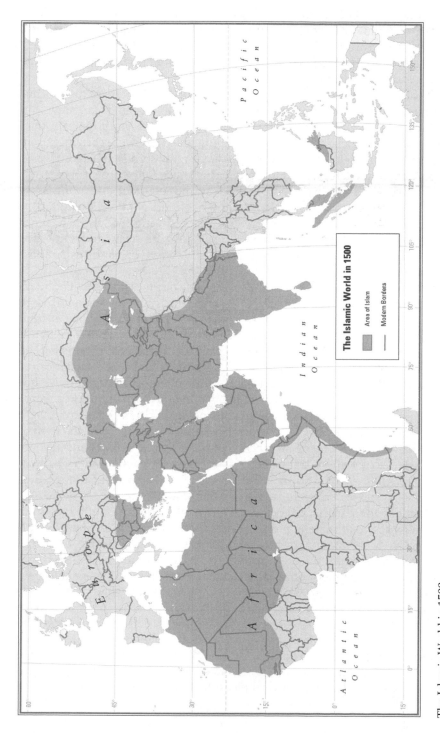

The Islamic World in 1500

such the Banu Hashim, the Banu Abd Shams, the Banu l-Harith, the Banu l-Aws, the Banu l-Khazraj, the Banu Tamim, the Banu Kinda, and so forth. While these groups did share a common language and shared many customs and expectations from life, the primary wellsprings of identity were blood and kinship; that is, family, clan, and tribe.

Throughout the medieval period people were well aware of their ethnic identities and certain groups took great pride in issues of language, literature, and culture, but these issues were in general less important than issues of religion, class, profession, and kinship. They were certainly more important than issues of ethnic identity in the modern sense of the word. According to the late Albert Hourani, "That those who speak Arabic form a 'nation', and that this nation should be independent and united, are beliefs which only became articulate and acquired political strength during the present [twentieth] century."[16] In fact, during the late nineteenth and early twentieth centuries, those who spoke of an Arab identity tended to define only the Arabic-speaking peoples of West Asia and the Arabian Peninsula as Arabs.

To these early Arab nationalist thinkers in Beirut, Damascus, Baghdad, Mecca, and even Cairo, Egyptians had a separate identity altogether (though the majority of the population of Egypt were in fact Arabic speakers), and North Africans were not really even part of the discussion. However, by the time of the establishment of the Arab League in Cairo in 1945, this had all changed, and Egypt had become the recognized center of the "Arab World." Today the Arab League is comprised of 22 members spanning from Mauritania in West Africa, across North Africa, around the horn of Africa to Somalia, across the Red Sea to the Arabian Peninsula, north to Syria, and east to Iraq. Most of the people who live in these countries identify themselves as Arabs, though there are significant populations of Berbers and Jews in North Africa as well as Armenians, Kurds, Turks, Syriacs, Chaldeans, Jews, and others in the East who are self-consciously *not* Arabs even though they may speak Arabic very well, or even as their first language.

Many of the earliest advocates of an Arab identity as distinct from Ottoman, regional, or religious identities were in fact Christians. Not surprisingly, those late-nineteenth- and early-twentieth-century Christian thinkers who advocated an Arab identity based on language also advocated the establishment of modern secular political institutions and civil liberties in the Arabic-speaking lands of the Ottoman Empire. If they were to have any hope of participating in the modern political arena as equals, they needed to find a basis of participation in something other than the religion of Islam. Despite the disproportionate role of Christian thinkers in formulating early Arab nationalist thought, most of the major figures in the debates surrounding Arab nationalism since the late nineteenth century have been Muslims. Nevertheless, it was only during the twentieth century that we could begin to speak of Christian Arabs as opposed to Arabic-speaking Christians in the settled lands of the Middle East.[17]

While one occasionally hears the Jews in the countries of the Arab world referred to as Arab Jews, rarely do Jews define themselves in such terms. Usually, one finds these Jewish communities referred to as Sephardic Jews, the Jews of Arab lands, Arabic-speaking Jews, or Iraqi Jews, Yemeni Jews, Moroccan Jews, and so forth. Some may argue that this digression into conceptions of Arab identity in the modern period is merely an academic quibble over nouns and adjectives. But it is more than that. It illustrates one very important note of caution that historians must heed when writing about the past with the language of the present.

GEOGRAPHY AND ENVIRONMENT

As in the ancient world, access to water was the principal concern of every regime, city, town, village, and pastoral nomadic group in the medieval Islamic world. Since the bulk of the territories under Islamic political authority consisted of mountains, deserts, and semi-arid steppe lands, the overwhelming majority of the population was concentrated in cities, towns, and their immediate hinterlands that had ready access to water. In addition to the narrow coastal areas around the Mediterranean, the southern shores of the Caspian Sea, and the coasts of South Asia, the areas that received significant annual rainfall include parts of Anatolia, the highlands of Yemen in the southern Arabian Peninsula, the Caucasus mountains between the Black and Caspian Seas, the Zagros mountains in western Iran, and the Rif Mountains of northern Morocco. Outside of these areas, there simply was not enough annual rainfall to support agriculture without some sort of sophisticated irrigation practices.

Nevertheless, the bulk of the population lived near the great river systems in the region that had sustained civilizations for millennia. The Nile in Egypt and the Tigris-Euphrates in Iraq are the most famous of these, but the Oxus, the Jaxartes, and the Zarafshan Rivers to the northeast were critical for Central Asia. Of course, the Indus and Ganges had long played similar roles in South Asia and would be crucial to the Islamic regimes there, especially after the establishment of the Delhi Sultanates in the early thirteenth century. In addition to these major river systems were seemingly countless oases scattered throughout the region. Some of these were fed by underground springs, while larger oasis settlements such as Damascus and Isfahan were fed by smaller rivers and streams that emptied into the desert. In Iran and Afghanistan there were long-established and complex irrigation canals that were dug in order to provided access to water stored in natural as well as man-made cisterns.

THE POLITICAL CHARACTER OF MEDIEVAL ISLAMIC SOCIETIES

From the death of Muhammad (632) until the Mongol destruction of Baghdad (1258), Islamic societies looked to the institution of the caliphate for guidance, protection, and inspiration—at the very least for a sense of unity among the community of believers as a whole. Since the institution of the caliphate and debates about it figured into nearly every aspect of Islamic life in the premodern period, it is useful at this point to treat some of the basic issues surrounding the institution as well as make some comments about the nature of medieval Islamic societies in general.

Islam began with a religious and political leader—Muhammad—who was believed to possess a divinely appointed right to govern the community. In fact, the Qur'an contains very little political material at all—it simply envisages a community led by a prophet. Initially, the Islamic community was constituted as a voluntary community. As noted above, after Muhammad's death, the *umma* agreed on the need for a leader and selected Abu Bakr as Muhammad's first successor. The earliest sources refer to the holders of this office by three titles: 1) *Khalifat Rasul Allah* (caliph—deputy or successor of the Messenger of God);[18] 2) *Amir al-Mu'minin* (commander of the believers); and 3) *Imam* (religious leader).

For all intents and purposes, these titles simply emphasize different aspects of the caliph's political, military, and religious authority. Whatever the title, there was a general consensus about the basic responsibilities of the office: 1) the caliph should be the sole leader of the community; 2) all political power was to be invested in this one man; and 3) this office was to be a lifetime office. Most of the major Muslim factions agreed with the above positions. The basic problem was related to the criteria for determining who was qualified to hold this office. While there was and remains a great deal of diversity of opinion within the Muslim community on this issue, three broad groupings—Sunnis, Shi'is, and Kharijis—deserve consideration here.

The Sunnis represent the majority of Muslims in the premodern and modern worlds. The name "Sunni" is derived from the formal title of this group—*ahl al-sunna wa l-jama'a* (people of tradition and community consensus). At the risk of oversimplification, one of the highest values of the Sunni community was the maintenance of the broad unity of the *umma*. As such, the general position that developed among Sunni theorists was that the caliph needed only to be good enough politically to do the job and maintain the unity of the entire community. Hence, the Sunnis are often referred to as "caliphal loyalists."

The second major group is referred to as the Shi'is or the Shi'a. This name derives from the fact that they belonged to the party or faction (*shi'a*) of Muhammad's cousin and son-in-law, Ali ibn Abi Talib. The Shi'is believe that prior to his death, Muhammad designated Ali as his successor; therefore, from the Shi'i perspective the acclamation of Abu Bakr as the first caliph was a perfidious usurpation. There are two basic doctrines that developed among the Shi'is that are worth noting here as well. First, the rightful caliph or imam had to be a lineal descendant of Muhammad, in particular through the line of Ali and Muhammad's daughter, Fatima. The second, and more controversial, is that the caliph or imam was not only the political head of the community, but an infallible religious teacher—guaranteed to be without error in matters of faith and morals. Because of this emphasis on the religious and theological role of the head of the community, Shi'i texts tend to use the title Imam for this office more frequently than Caliph or *Amir al-Mu'minin*.[19]

The third group is referred to as the Kharijis (sing. *khariji*; pl. *khawarij*)—that is, "the seceders." This group disagreed with both the Sunni and the Shi'i positions. They were purists in that their principal criteria for leadership of the community was piety—genealogy did not matter to them nor did the practical consideration of maintaining the unity of the community. For them, moral purity was far more important than temporal political unity. In time, these political groups evolved into separate religious and theological factions within the larger Islamic community.

FRAGMENTATION OF THE CALIPHATE AND PERSO-ISLAMIC KINGSHIP

The political fragmentation of the Islamic empire and of the institution of the caliphate had its beginnings under the Abbasid caliphs (750–1258) in the early ninth century. The Abbasids had come to power by manipulating a Shi'i revolt against their predecessors, the Umayyad caliphs (661–750), in the late 740s, but once the Abbasids took power they began to follow the Sunni paradigm for the caliphate. The Abbasid caliphate never fully recovered from the civil war between Harun al-Rashid's (r. 786–809) two sons, al-Amin (r. 809–13) and al-Ma'mun (r. 813–33). By the 860s and 870s many petty states had established themselves under Muslim rulers in North Africa and Spain to the west and in Iran and lands further east. Some of these had even declared full autonomy from the Abbasid caliphs in Baghdad. By the early 900s, the Abbasid caliphs really only ruled in central and southern Iraq.

In 945, Baghdad was sacked by the Buyids—a group of Shi'i soldiers of fortune from the region of Daylam on the southern shores of the Caspian Sea. From 945 onward, the Abbasid caliphs remained subordinate to a series of Muslim warlord regimes until 1258, when the invading Mongol armies sacked Baghdad and, for all intents and purposes, brought an end to the Abbasid caliphate.[20] In spite of the failure of the political ideal of a single community of believers under the universal government of Muhammad's successors, it was during the tenth through the fifteenth

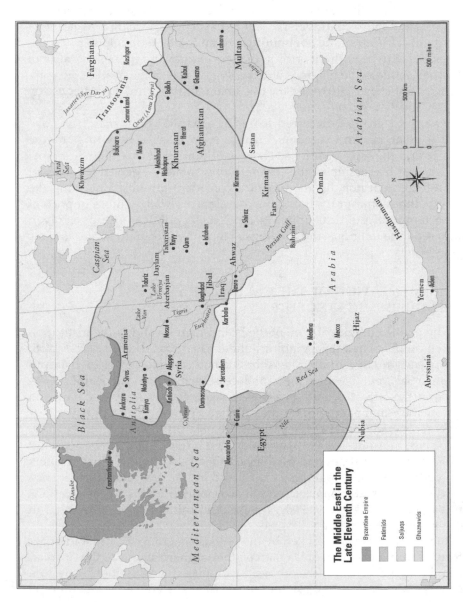

The Middle East in the late eleventh century. *Source:* Adapted from Lapidus, *A History of Islamic Societies.*

centuries that we see Islam's capacity to expand, both geographically as well as in the intellectual, cultural, and economic spheres.

There was an important ethnic shift also, since by the tenth century Islam had begun to lose its close and almost exclusive association with those who traced their lineage to the first Arabian Muslim warriors. In the political realm, people who could trace their lineage to the Arabian Muslim conquests had lost their leading role by 900 as well. Throughout the following centuries (and in fact into the twentieth century), dynasties of Turkic origin dominated the political life of the Islamic world from modern Algeria to India. This Turkish political domination reflected a substantial migration of Turkic peoples from Inner Asia into the Middle East, though only in a few areas did these immigrants come to constitute a majority of the population—Transoxiana (Central Asia north of the Oxus River), Northwestern Iran, and eventually Anatolia. The newcomers did not drive out or assimilate the old Muslim populations in the lands they ruled, and in many respects the Turkic conquerors became the firmest advocates of the established cultural and religious traditions of Sunni Islam.

One faction of these immigrants, named after a man called Seljuk, belonged to the great Oghuzz confederation of Turkic tribesmen. The Seljukids had converted to Islam in the late tenth century and served as irregular cavalry forces in a number of frontier regimes during the early decades of the eleventh century. Under the leadership of two of Seljuk's grandsons—Toghril Beg and Chagri Beg—the Seljukids entered the service of the famed Ghaznavid regime (994–1040).[21] In the late 1030s, they rebelled against their overlords. In 1040, they defeated the Ghaznavids at the Battle of Dandanqan in Afghanistan and established themselves in Afghanistan and eastern Iran.[22]

Leaving his younger brother, Chagri, to administer the family lands in the east, Toghril turned his attention westward. In 1055, Toghril and his ardently Sunni Seljukid Turkoman tribesmen overthrew the equally ardently Shi'i Buyids in Baghdad. The Abbasid caliph conferred on Toghril the title of Sultan, and he and his house ruled from Baghdad in the name of the Abbasid caliphs. In their heyday, the Seljukid sultans ruled an empire that stretched from eastern Iran to the Mediterranean. Although their position in Syria had all but disappeared by the late eleventh century, they did control Baghdad until 1194.

While the Seljukids conquered as Turkomans (that is, as free Muslim Turkish pastoral nomads), they soon sought to establish themselves as rulers of the settled agrarian world of Iran and Iraq. In order to do this, they adopted the trappings of Perso-Islamic kingship employed by the Abbasid caliphs in Baghdad and later by the Abbasids' Buyid overlords. The Seljukid wazir, Nizam al-Mulk (d. 1092), articulates this theory of kingship in his *Book of Government or Rules for Kings*.[23] Composed at the behest of the Seljukid Sultan, Malikshah (r. 1073–92), the first chapter is entitled "On the

Turn of Fortune's Wheel and in Praise of the Master of the World—May God Confirm His Sovereignty." The opening paragraphs outline a vision of kingship in which God in His wisdom chooses the sultan to rule on His behalf. The sultan's duty is to provide justice and maintain order in society. If he does, he and his kingdom will prosper. If he does not, he will lose God's favor, be replaced by another, and the cycle begins anew.

In every age and time God (be He exalted) chooses one member of the human race and, having adorned and endowed him with kingly virtues, entrusts him with the interests of the world and the well-being of His servants; He charges that person to close the doors of corruption, confusion and discord, and He imparts to him such dignity and majesty in the eyes and hearts of men, that under his just rule they may live their lives in constant security and ever wish for his reign to continue.

Whenever—God be our refuge!—there occurs any disobedience or disregard of divine laws on the part of His servants, or any failure in devotion and attention to the commands of The Truth (be He exalted), and He wishes to chasten them and make them taste the retribution for their deeds—may God not deal us such a fate, and keep us far from such a calamity!—verily the wrath of The Truth overtakes those people and He forsakes them for the vileness of their disobedience; anarchy rears its head in their midst, opposing swords are drawn, blood is shed, and whoever has the stronger hand does whatever he wishes, until those sinners are all destroyed in tumults and bloodshed, and the world becomes free and clear of them; and through the wickedness of such sinners many innocent persons too perish in the tumults; just as, by analogy, when a reed-bed catches fire every dry particle is burned also, because it is near to that which is dry.[24]

This theory is cyclical in that God uses the sultan's army to bring the sultan to power, but it is the sultan's responsibility to do God's bidding and provide justice and order on God's behalf. If he does not, God will take away his throne and replace him with another. The rest of Nizam al-Mulk's lengthy treatise is essentially a handbook for how to rule justly and to maintain order in the realm. Nizam al-Mulk's conception of just rule requires the sultan to devote a great deal of attention to creating and maintaining an environment in which trade can flourish. Nizam al-Mulk was particularly concerned with the construction and maintenance of trade routes, caravanserais, and bridges; the appointment of trustworthy market inspectors and tax collectors; and the appointment of spies throughout the realm—policies crucial to rooting out corruption and fostering confidence in local and long-distance trade.

According to Nizam al-Mulk, such just rule necessarily results in prosperity among the agrarian peasants and among the traders in the towns and cities. Such prosperity also results in a full treasury with which the sultan can pay his soldiers, who are absolutely essential to protecting his throne against interlopers as well as maintaining order and economic prosperity in the realm so that his subjects "may live their lives in constant security and ever wish for his reign to continue." While others had articulated similar theories of kingship based on the ancient Persian model, including the Abbasids and the Buyids, Nizam al-Mulk's iteration is one of the most influential and would continue to be used to legitimate regimes for centuries after its composition.

Nizam al-Mulk also advised Malikshah that any kingdom in which women interfere in politics is doomed to failure because women "are wearers of the veil and have not complete intelligence."[25] Based on the negative examples of Eve, Aisha (one of Muhammad's wives and a participant in the first civil war in 656), and others, Nizam al-Mulk argued that "if women had been able to control themselves, [God] would not have set men over their heads. So if anyone places women over men, whatever mistakes and mischiefs occur are his fault, for permitting such a thing and changing the custom."[26] While Nizam al-Mulk's opinions of women's abilities and failings were certainly commonplace in his day, he likely was motivated by more immediate practical concerns as well. After all, Malikshah's own wife, Turkhan (d. 1094), was involved in intrigues against Nizam al-Mulk and wanted her husband to replace him with someone more to her liking.

Nizam al-Mulk's vision of political legitimacy of course had its problems, most notably the fact that it was of little help when the sultan needed it most—when his legitimacy was called into question. Once confidence in the sultan began to wane, and once he suffered defeats on the battlefield, this theory of kingship tended to reinforce his opponents' argument that the sultan was in fact illegitimate and that God would soon replace him with another of His own choosing, namely one of the sultan's opponents. Despite the internal weakness of this theory of political legitimacy, it was embraced by regime after regime for centuries, and rulers continued to commission handbooks for princes that offered advice very similar to that of Nizam al-Mulk for centuries as well.[27]

ISLAMIC LAW (*SHARI'A*)

In addition to the development of political philosophy, this period also witnessed a tremendous deepening of Islamic culture and identity within the old Islamic lands of North Africa and the Middle East. For the great majority of the population in this region, Islam came to provide not only a system of beliefs, but also a framework for social action and cultural expression. It is this era that produced a genuinely "Islamic society" with its own distinctive institutions and ways of life. However, whether in the city or the countryside, the subject populations had wide areas of autonomy in daily life. Still, relations among individuals and relations between individuals and a regime were, in principle, governed by shari'a, one of the many Arabic words that convey the idea of pathway. In fact, *shari'a* is derived from the same root as the Arabic word for street. Although shari'a is sometimes translated as Islamic law, it is not a formal body of legislation in the modern sense; rather, it is an all-encompassing code of behavior worked out over the centuries by religious scholars (*ʿulamaʾ*), who sought to determine how Muslims could best live in accordance with God's will as they understood it. In theory, this was done by examining in detail each category of human behavior in order to see whether it was in agreement with the religious scholars' understanding of God's revelation in the Qurʾan.[28]

The specific commandments and prohibitions derived from the intense study of authoritative sacred texts differ between Islam and Judaism; however, the idea that individual Muslims and Jews should follow a specific set of duties and obligations worked out by scholars or rabbis has much in common. In fact, in the Jewish tradition, this whole body of discussion among the rabbis is referred to as the *halakha*, a Hebrew word that conveys the idea of pathway as well. This similarity between conceptions of shariʿa and *halakha* in Islam and Judaism has led some scholars to argue that Islam and Judaism are concerned primarily with right behavior in obedience to God (orthopraxis), whereas Christianity is concerned primarily with right belief about God (orthodoxy). While this distinction can be useful in clarifying certain similarities and differences in *emphasis* among the three Abrahamic traditions, it is an oversimplification since it implies that Muslims and Jews are not concerned with right theology and that Christians are not concerned with proper behavior. Clearly, all three religious traditions are very much concerned with both.

One of the most common theological doctrines in the Qurʾan is God's mercy and His compassion. In fact, all but one of the 114 chapters of the Qurʾan begin with the same phrase, "In the name of God, the Merciful, the Compassionate." At the same time, one of the most common themes in the Qurʾan is humankind's duty to obey God. Compared to the Old Testament (especially the books of Leviticus and Deuteronomy), the Qurʾan contains very little legal material. While the commandments, prohibitions, and punishments that are in the Qurʾan are quite specific, they do not even come close to covering the many possibilities Muslims might encounter in seventh-century Arabia, let alone the cosmopolitan centers of the Muslim empires in the centuries to come. If the early Muslim community was to determine God's will in every aspect of life after the divine revelations ceased with Muhammad's death, it needed to find authoritative guidance outside the text of the Qurʾan itself. Initially, this was found in the practice or tradition (*sunna*) of the early community. Since the early community (especially the early community in Medina) was seen to be the best community by virtue of its first-hand encounter with the Messenger of God, its example could be used to answer questions that were not specifically addressed in the Qurʾan.

Although assertion of Muhammad's infallibility is nowhere to be found in the Qurʾan, by the late eighth century a doctrine had developed that Muhammad and all the prophets had been protected by God from gross moral error (*maʿsum*). One of the most important early legal scholars, Muhammad ibn Idris al-Shafiʿi (d. 820), argued that because of Muhammad's moral perfection, his sunna was the only reliable guide to right conduct apart from the Qur'an. According to al-Shafi'i, since Muhammad's teachings and example were necessarily preserved from error, all Muslims could confidently rely upon his sunna for guidance.[29] This assertion only begs the question of how to determine what was Muhammad's sunna? According to al-Shafi'i, Muhammad's sunna could be found in those hadiths (reports about what Muhammad said or did) that were determined to be authentic.

Not surprisingly, as the sunna of the early community and Muhammad came to be seen as authoritative, many hadiths were put into circulation that purported to be the words of Muhammad, but were in fact made up out of whole cloth for political and sectarian purposes. In response to these fabrications, scholars devised a methodology for determining which hadiths were authentic and which were fabrications. Scholars began to argue that only those hadiths that were transmitted by an unbroken chain (*isnad*) of reliable transmitters reaching back to Muhammad himself could be deemed authentic.

Scholars were well aware that it was just as easy to fabricate an *isnad* as it was to fabricate a hadith. Nevertheless, by the end of the ninth century there had emerged a general consensus about which hadiths were authentic. By the same time, the followers of a given teacher began to refer to themselves as a *madhhab*, another Arabic word conveying the idea of pathway. *Madhhab* is generally translated as "school of law," in the sense of a "school of thought," not a physical school building. By the eleventh century, there remained only four Sunni *madhhab*s to speak of (Hanafi, Hanbali, Maliki, Shafi'i). Each was named after the scholar whose teaching the *madhhab* ostensibly followed, though none had actually founded a formal school in his lifetime.[30]

The science of working out the shari'a can be divided into two basic categories, and since the Arabic language is fond of agricultural metaphors these categories are referred to as the roots of jurisprudence (*usul al-fiqh*, legal theory) and the branches of jurisprudence (*furu al-fiqh*, practical application). Since knowledge of the Qur'an and the sunna of Muhammad were essential to the sciences of jurisprudence, and since proper jurisprudence was essential to determining what it meant to be a good Muslim, the entire religious educational system of the period was based on memorizing the Qur'an as well as thousands of these hadiths along with their *isnad*s.

Scholars employed (at least in theory) a five-step process to determine whether a given practice was acceptable.

1. If the Qur'an specifically commanded or prohibited something, there really was nothing to discuss; God had spoken.
2. If the Qur'an addressed an issue, but without specific guidance, scholars turned to the sunna of Muhammad for clarification of the

Qur'anic commandment. For example, Muslims are admonished repeatedly in the Qur'an to pray; however, it is only because of the sunna of Muhammad that Muslims know that they are required to pray five times per day, to perform specific ablutions and in which order, and to perform certain prostrations and in which order.

3. Since Muhammad is understood to have been preserved from gross moral error, if an authentic hadith spoke specifically to an issue not addressed in the Qur'an, Muslims could be assured that if they followed the admonition of that hadith, they would be acting in obedience to God.

4. When neither the Qur'an nor the sunna addressed an issue, scholars argued that they had to employ their reason to extrapolate the proper response based on the principles set forth in the Qur'an and the sunna as a whole. Since most aspects of life are in this category, and since this category is most open to interpretation, it is to this category that the scholars devoted most of their energies and their arguments. In fact, they developed a range of classifications of reasoning that could be employed in this enterprise. Not surprisingly, scholars did not always agree on which methods of reasoning (if any) were legitimate.

5. Sunni scholars used the principle of consensus (*ijma'*) to determine whether a doctrine or decision was legitimate in these instances. This principle of consensus is rooted in a hadith in which Muhammad is purported to have said that his community would never agree upon an error. In practical terms, the scholars identified the community as themselves, since whenever there was no scholar of good repute holding a contrary position on a particular issue, the problem was generally considered settled.

Modern western scholars tend to be skeptical about the authenticity of even the hadiths in the authoritative collections. Often, they are skeptical about when or even if the methodology described above was actually employed or whether it was simply used after the fact to legitimate practices and decisions that were really rooted in Arabian tribal custom or in the local practice of Medina, Kufa, Basra, Damascus, Baghdad, or elsewhere. In any case, it is clear that the formal positions of the shari'a reflect the life of the towns and cities in the medieval Islamic world, for it is in the urban centers that the scholars were studying the religious sciences and articulating the details of the shari'a in response to the questions that arose in the urban environments in which they lived.

Moreover, it was in the urban centers that there were actual judges (*qadi*s) and the mechanisms to enforce judges' decisions. In the countryside and among the pastoral nomadic groups, the at times arcane details of the shari'a tended to take a back seat to local custom. In these circumstances, a person was helpless to contest a violation of shariʿa because there was no judge to hear his or her case nor was there anyone to enforce it. If there was an Islamic "scholar" there, he most likely was an ill-educated preacher who was not well versed in the intricate details of Islamic jurisprudence.

Whether or not the methodology of jurisprudence described here was actually employed consistently or even at all is difficult to ascertain. However, the fact that it (or some other methodology ostensibly based on the authoritative scriptures of Islam) was *supposed* to be employed illustrates the importance that Muslims attached to following the dictates of the Qurʾan and the teachings of Muhammad in their daily lives. In short, the shariʿa in all its manifestations gives us insight into daily life and practice in the medieval Islamic world because it was understood to comprise the entire body of duties and obligations incumbent on all believers covering every imaginable aspect of daily life. It is that straight path by which medieval Muslims believed they could (and modern Muslims believe they can) walk according to God's will.

ISLAMIC MYSTICISM (SUFISM; *TASAWWUF*)

Islamic mystics were called Sufis because of their habit of wearing wool (*suf*). The Arabic term for mysticism (*tasawwuf*) is derived from *suf* as well. The development of Sufism, like the development of shariʿa, is rooted in the search for the proper understanding of right religion. At the risk of oversimplification, the shariʿa-minded vision of the religious scholars and jurists defined Islam as a "religion of law" based on the meticulous study of the Qurʾan and hadith. The Sufi-minded vision of the mystics and ascetics defined Islam as a "religion of the heart" based on the individual's direct encounter with and knowledge of God. In other words, the shariʿa-minded and the Sufi-minded sought to answer the question of how knowledge is defined—knowledge *about* God based on what he has revealed of himself through his prophets and messengers; and knowledge *of* God based on one's direct mystical experience.

Thirty years after its initial publication, J. Spencer Trimingham's *The Sufi Orders in Islam* "remains the most useful and comprehensive guide to the Sufi orders of Islam in the premodern era."[31] Trimingham divides the development of Sufism into three broad periods.[32] During the first period, what Trimingham calls the "golden age of mysticism" or *khanaqah* (lodge) period, Sufism was an intellectually and emotionally aristocratic movement. It was characterized by an ad hoc master-disciple (*murshid-murid*) relationship in which masters guided their disciples on a personal quest to experience God directly. Early Sufis often lived itinerant lives, but by the tenth century we begin to see the establishment of informal lodges (*khanaqah*s) and convents (*zawiya*s) where masters and disciples pursued mystical union (*wahda*) with God.

During the second period (ca. 1100–1400) Sufi rituals and practices came to be characterized by more formal and clearly defined devotional "paths" or "ways" (*tariqa*s). Consequently, the emphasis was less on the individual's surrender to God and more on his surrender to a specific rule. It was at the beginning of this "*tariqa* period" that al-Ghazali (d. 1111) composed his magnum opus, *The Revivification of the Religious Sciences.*[33] The third period (ca. 1400–1800) is beyond the chronological scope of this book. But it is worth noting that during the fifteenth century Sufism became an even more organized mass popular movement. Whatever the period or method, the goal of the Sufi remained the same—to know the ecstasy of the direct experience and knowledge of God.

There are separate Arabic words to define the types of knowledge that concern us here. The cognitive or "head" knowledge of the shariʿa-minded religious scholars is known as ʿ*ilm*. The affective or "heart" knowledge of the Sufi-minded mystics is known as *maʿrifa*, or gnosis. Hence, one who knows *about* God based on the study of revelation and religious texts (Qurʾan, hadith, *fiqh*, etc.) is known as an ʿ*alim* (pl. ʿ*ulama*ʾ). One who has direct experience or knowledge *of* God is known as an ʿ*arif*.[34] Of course, it would be incorrect to imagine that the shariʿa-minded and Sufi-minded visions of Islam were mutually exclusive. Rather, they should be seen as emphases, even tendencies, along a broad spectrum of religious experience and practice in the medieval Islamic world.

Nevertheless, it should come as no surprise that extremes of the spectrum did exist. Some religious scholars condemned the more ecstatic mystical strains of Islam as departures from the true faith as defined by the commandments and prohibitions of shariʿa. Some Sufis gave them reason to be suspicious by arguing that shariʿa constrained, even inhibited, their superior existential knowledge of God. The most famous of these is the Sufi icon, al-Hallaj (857–922). Originally from Tus in Iran, al-Hallaj moved to Basra in his early twenties. It was in Basra and Baghdad that he made his mark as a popular ascetic and preacher.

Al-Hallaj's declarations of his burning love of and his claims of mystical union with God ignited popular passions as well as scholarly ire. He is most famous for a brief statement he made one day in Baghdad to the great Sufi master, al-Junayd (d. 910).

It is related that Hallaj met Junayd one day, and said to him, "I am the Truth [*ana al-haqq*]." "No," Junayd answered him, "it is by means of the Truth that you are! What gibbet will you stain with your blood!"[35]

By claiming one of God's titles (*al-haqq*; "The Truth" or "The Ultimate Reality") as his own, al-Hallaj was claiming to be God; that is, that he had no other "I" than God. Many of his opponents viewed his claims as blasphemous. At best, they viewed him as a vile charlatan.

In 913, al-Hallaj was arrested. He remained in a Baghdad prison for nine years where he preached to his fellow prisoners and is said to have healed the sick as well as performed other wonders. In the end, al-Hallaj's supporters within the Abbasid house were unable to protect him. In March 922, he was executed on charges of blasphemy. His modern biographer, Louis Massignon, describes his execution before a great crowd near the Khurasan Gate in Baghdad.

Al-Halladj, with a crown on his head was beaten, half-killed, and exposed, still alive, on a gibbet (*salib*). While rioters set fire to the shops, friends and enemies questioned him as he hung on the gibbet and traditions related some of his replies. The caliph's warrant for his decapitation did not arrive until nightfall, and in fact his final execution was postponed until the next day. During the night there spread accounts of wonders and supernatural happenings. In the morning... those who had signed his condemnation ... cried out: "It is for Islam; let his blood be on our heads." Al-Halladj's head fell, his body was sprinkled with oil and burned and the ashes thrown into the Tigris from the top of a minaret (27 March 922). Witnesses reported that the last words of the tortured man were: "All that matters for the ecstatic is that the Unique should reduce him to Unity."[36]

Al-Hallaj's execution may have curtailed some of the excesses of the Sufis, but his life and teachings continued to inspire Sufis for generations. Based on the teachings of al-Hallaj, al-Junayd, and many other early Sufis, Kalabadhi (d. 995) argued in the late-tenth century that Sufism conforms to the strictest standards of orthodoxy and is in no way heretical. According to Kalabadhi's translator, A. J. Arberry, Kalabadhi's *The Doctrine of the Sufis* blazed "a path which was subsequently to be followed by the Sufi who was the greatest theologian of all: Ghazali (d. 1111), whose [*The Revivification of the Religious Sciences*] finally reconciled scholastic and mystic."[37] Hence, it would be a mistake to argue that Sufis were necessarily anti-intellectual or antinomian as some of their critics charged; rather, the Sufi attitude toward the intellect was that it "is an instrument of servanthood, not a means of approaching lordship."[38] That is, while the intellect is sufficient for determining what human beings, as God's servants, must perform in submission (*islam*) to God (e.g., shari'a), it is insufficient as a guide to existential or mystical knowledge (*ma'rifa*) of God.

In his chapter entitled "Their Doctrine of the Gnosis of God," Kalabadhi argues that "no man knows God, save he who possesses an intellect, for the intellect is the instrument by means of which man knows whatever he may know; nevertheless, he cannot know God of himself."[39] In the same chapter, Kalabadhi illustrates the inadequacies of the intellect with a poem by al-Hallaj:

Whoso seeks God, and takes the intellect for guide,
God drives him forth, in vain distraction to abide;

With wild confusion He confounds his inmost heart,
So that distraught, he cries, "I know not if Thou art."[40]

He appeals to al-Hallaj again as he argues that human beings can only
know God if God chooses to reveal himself to them:

God made us to know Himself through Himself, and guided us to the knowledge
of Himself through Himself, so that the attestation of gnosis arose out of gnosis
through gnosis, after he who possessed gnosis had been taught gnosis by Him
Who is the object of gnosis.[41]

Of course, unless one is mystically inclined, statements such as this are
impenetrably obtuse, even nonsensical. Moreover, as evidenced by al-
Hallaj's fate, they were far too fuzzy and malleable for the tastes of many
of the shariʿa-minded religious scholars.

NOTES

1. See G. R. Hawting, *The Idea of Idolatry and the Emergence of Islam: From Polemic
to History* (New York: Cambridge University Press, 1999), in which the author
argues that there was less polytheism in Arabia than the Islamic sources indicate.

2. Robert G. Hoyland's *Seeing Islam as Others Saw It: A Survey and Evaluation
of Christian, Jewish and Zoroastrian Writings on Early Islam* (Princeton, NJ: Darwin
Press, 1997) represents the most complete treatment of non-Muslim sources for
early Islamic history. While this scattered material can be used as a kind of correc-
tive to the far more plentiful Muslim literary sources, this material is also characterized by religious and sectarian bias.

3. Alfred Guillaume, trans., *The Life of Muhammad: A Translation of Ibn Ishaq's
Sirat Rasul Allah* (Oxford: Oxford University Press, 1955).

4. There are many English translations of the Qurʾan, some more felicitous
than others. I have chosen to use N. J. Dawood, trans., *The Koran*, fifth revised
edition (New York: Penguin Books, 1995) primarily because it is affordable and
available in nearly every major bookstore. For a list of English translations of the
Qurʾan, see "The Qurʾan: Translations and Introductions" in the "Suggestions for
Further Reading" at the back of this book.

5. For an overview of the debates about the nature of the Qurʾan among
western and Muslim scholars, see Toby Lester, "What Is the Koran?," *The Atlantic
Monthly* 283 (January 1999): 43–56. See also Andrew Rippin, "Literary Analysis of
Qurʾan, Tafsir, and Sira: The Methodologies of John Wansbrough," in *Approaches
to Islam in Religious Studies*, ed. Richard C. Martin (Tucson: University of Arizona
Press, 1985), 151–63.

6. Fred M. Donner, *Narratives of Islamic Origins: The Beginnings of Islamic Historical Writing* (Princeton, NJ: Darwin Press, 1998): 4–5. Donner's *Narratives* is by
far the most accessible treatment of the complex historiographical and method-
ological problems faced by the student of early Islamic history.

7. There is a vast biographical literature on Muhammad. Standard Muslim
accounts can be found in Alfred Guillaume, trans., *The Life of Muhammad*; al-
Tabari, *The History of al-Tabari*, vols. 6–9 (Albany: State University of New York

Press, 1985); and Trevor Le Gassick, trans., *The Life of the Prophet Muhammad: A Translation of Ibn Kathir's al-Sira al-Nabawiyya* (Reading, UK: Center for Muslim Contribution to Civilization, 1998). See also Josef Horovitz, *The Earliest Biographies of the Prophet and Their Authors* (Princeton, NJ: Darwin Press, 2002); and F. E. Peters, *Muhammad and the Origins of Islam* (Albany: State University of New York Press, 1994).

8. See pp. 47–51 of this book for examples of how Ibn Ishaq's biography of Muhammad informs us about the kinship values of Arabian society.

9. See "The Banu Quraysh" table in the "Geneaological and Dynastic Tables" section at the back of this book.

10. See "Christian and Islamic Calendars with Conversion Table," pp. 253–80 of this book.

11. See pp. 154–59 of this book for a discussion of Abraham's role in this.

12. See Elias Shoufani, *al-Ridda and the Muslim Conquest of Arabia* (Toronto: University of Toronto Press, 1973); Fred M. Donner, *The Early Islamic Conquests* (Princeton, NJ: Princeton University Press, 1981); Ella Landau-Tasseron, "From Tribal Society to Centralized Polity: An Interpretation of Events and Anecdotes in the Formative Period of Islam," *Jerusalem Studies in Arabic and Islam* 24 (2000): 180–216; and Elizabeth Savage, *A Gateway to Hell, a Gateway to Paradise: The North African Response to the Arab Conquest* (Princeton, NJ: Darwin Press, 1997).

13. On the Islamic conquests in India, see André Wink, *al-Hind: The Making of the Indo-Islamic World, Volume 1: Early Medieval India and the Expansion of Islam in the 7th–11th Centuries* (Leiden: Brill, 1990), 192–218.

14. Richard W. Bulliet, *Conversion to Islam in the Medieval Period: An Essay in Quantitative History.* (Cambridge, MA: Harvard University Press, 1979).

15. For estimates of general population figures, see Charles Issawi, "The Area and Population of the Arab Empire: An Essay in Speculation," in *The Islamic Middle East, 700–1900: Studies in Economic and Social History,* ed. A. L. Udovitch (Princeton, NJ: Darwin Press, 1981), 374–396. For estimates of the numbers of troops in the Umayyad registers, see Hugh N. Kennedy, *The Armies of the Caliphs: Military and Society in the Early Islamic State* (New York: Routledge, 2001), 19–21. See also Khalil 'Athamina, "Arab Settlement during the Umayyad Caliphate," *Jerusalem Studies in Arabic and Islam* 8 (1986): 185–207.

16. Albert Hourani, *Arabic Thought in the Liberal Age, 1798–1939* (New York: Oxford University Press, 1962), 260. While more recent literature on modern Arabic thought and Arab nationalism is legion, Hourani's seminal treatment of the early period remains one of the most astute.

17. Several of the Arabian tribal confederations in the seventh century were Christian; however, most of the members of these confederations converted to Islam during the first few Islamic centuries.

18. Early on they are referred to as *Khalifat Allah* (God's Deputy) as well. See Patricia Crone and Martin Hinds, *God's Caliph: Religious Authority in the First Centuries of Islam* (New York: Cambridge University Press, 1986).

19. See pp. 160–65 of this book for a fuller discussion of the Shi'is.

20. A version of the Abbasid caliphate continued under Mamluk tutelage in Cairo, but it amounted to little more than a means to provide a veneer of legitimacy for the Mamluk sultans.

21. Beg is the Turkish equivalent of amir (commander). It is not the family name of Toghril and Chagri.

22. On the Seljukids, see C. E. Bosworth, *The Ghaznavids: Their Empire in Afghanistan and Eastern Iran, 944–1040* (Beirut: Librairie du Liban, 1973), 206–68. See also A. K. S. Lambton, "The Internal Structure of the Saljuq Empire," in *The Cambridge History of Iran,* vol. 5 (New York: Cambridge University Press, 1968), 203–82; Claude Cahen, "The Turkish Invasion: The Selchükids," in *A History of the Crusades,* ed. Kenneth M. Setton, vol. 1, *The First Hundred Years,* eds. K. M. Setton and M. W. Baldwin (Madison: University of Wisconsin Press, 1969), 135–76; Gary Leiser, ed. and trans., *A History of the Seljukids: Ibrahim Kafesoglu's Interpretation and the Resulting Controversy* (Carbondale: Southern Illinois University Press, 1988); and Kenneth Allin Luther, trans. *The History of the Seljuq Turks from the Jami' al-Tawarikh: An Ilkhanid Adaption of the Saljuq-nama of Zahir al-Din Nishapuri* (Richmond, UK: Curzon Press, 2001).

23. Hubert Darke, trans., *The Book of Government or Rules for Kings: The Siyar al-Mulk or Siyasat-nama of Nizam al-Mulk* (Richmond, UK: Curzon Press, 2002).

24. Ibid., 9. See also R. Stephen Humphreys, "Ideology and Propaganda: Religion and the State in the Early Seljukid Period," in *Islamic History: A Framework for Inquiry,* rev. ed. (Princeton, NJ: Princeton University Press, 1991), 148–68.

25. Darke, *The Book of Government,* 179.

26. Ibid., 186. On Aisha, see p. 68 of this book. For a perceptive analysis of Nizam al-Mulk's views on women and politics, see Denise A. Spellberg, *Politics, Gender, and the Islamic Past: The Legacy of 'A'isha bint Abi Bakr* (New York: Columbia University Press, 1994), 140–49.

27. See R. Stephen Humphreys, "Legitimacy and Political Instability in the Age of the Crusades," in *The Jihad and Its Times,* eds. H. Dajani-Shakeel and R. A. Messier (Ann Arbor: University of Michigan Press, 1991), 5–13.

28. For an overview of the literature on Islamic law through the late 1980s, see R. Stephen Humphreys, "Islamic Law and Islamic Society," in *Islamic History: A Framework for Inquiry,* 209–27. For additional bibliography, see the "Islamic Law" section in "Suggestions for Further Reading."

29. Majid Khadduri, trans., *al-Shafi'i's Risala: Treatise on the Foundations of Islamic Jurisprudence,* second edition (Cambridge, UK: The Islamic Texts Society, 1987). See Wael Hallaq, "Was al-Shafi'i the Master Architect of Islamic Jurisprudence?" *International Journal of Middle East Studies* 25.4 (1993): 587–605 for a reassessment of al-Shafi'i's role in the development of Islamic law.

30. On the formation of the Sunni schools of law, see especially Christopher Melchert, *The Formation of the Sunni Schools of Law, 9th–10th Centuries C.E.* (Leiden: Brill, 1997). See also Nimrod Hurvitz, "From Scholarly Circles to Mass Movements: The Formation of Legal Communities in Islamic Societies," *American Historical Review* 108.4 (October 2003): 985–1008.

31. John O. Voll in his foreword to the new edition of J. Spencer Trimingham, *The Sufi Orders in Islam* (New York: Oxford University Press, 1998 [1971]), xv.

32. Trimingham, *The Sufi Orders in Islam,* 103.

33. English translations of excerpts from al-Ghazali's *The Revivification of the Religious Sciences* (*Ihya 'ulum al-din*) have been published by The Islamic Texts Society. See the "Sufism" section in "Suggestions for Further Reading."

34. Dozens of English-language primers on Sufism of varying quality have been published over the years. See the "Sufism" section in "Suggestions for Further Reading."

35. Louis Massignon, *The Passion of al-Hallaj: Mystic and Martyr of Islam*, 4 vols. (Princeton, NJ: Princeton University Press, 1982), 1:127.

36. Louis Massignon, "al-Halladj," in *Encyclopaedia of Islam*, New Edition, 12 vols. (Leiden: Brill, 1954–2004), 3:99–104.

37. A. J. Arberry, trans. *The Doctrine of the Sufis* (New York: Cambridge University Press, 1935), xiv. See also W. Montgomery Watt, trans. *The Faith and Practice of al-Ghazali* (London: George Allen and Unwin, 1953), which includes al-Ghazali's account of his intellectual and spiritual journey to Sufism, *al-Munqidh min al-dalal* (*Deliverance from Error*), 19-85.

38. Arberry, *Doctrine of the Sufis*, 51.

39. Ibid., 54–55. Arberry uses the Greek work "gnosis" for mystical knowledge (*ma'rifa*) throughout his translation.

40. Ibid., 52.

41. Ibid., 54.

2

ARABIA

Since Islam originated in the brackish shrine center that was Mecca and the agricultural oasis of Medina in the Hijaz (northwestern Arabia), it is appropriate to begin this examination of daily life in the medieval Islamic world in the Arabian Peninsula. The language, culture, and values of pre-Islamic Arabia informed the religion of Islam at its inception and continued to do so long after the establishment of a vast and cosmopolitan Islamic empire. While reference will be made to areas outside the Hijaz, the world of the Hijaz in the seventh century will be the principal focus of this chapter. It will examine the geography, environment, and trade of the region as well as the kinship-based social order that was shared by nomad and oasis dweller alike and that is taken for granted in the Qur'an. Although the region was the birthplace of the religion of Islam, it soon became peripheral to the political, intellectual, and economic centers of the Islamic empire and emerging Islamic civilization. But first a few comments about the sources for this chapter are in order.

SOURCES

Christian historians divide human history into two distinct periods with Easter as the watershed event between the two, for according to Christian theology it is the death, burial, and especially the resurrection of Jesus Christ that gives meaning to the basic claims of Christian theology. St. Paul summarizes this theological position very succinctly in his statement, "And if Christ has not been raised, your faith is futile; you are still in your sins"

(1 Corinthians 15:17).[1] Muslim historians divide human history into two distinct periods as well. Of course, since Muslim theology does not accept the Christian account of Jesus' crucifixion and resurrection, the Easter story cannot serve as the dividing line. Rather, history is divided into that which came before and that which came after the Angel Gabriel delivered the first revelation from God to Muhammad. The first period is generally referred to as the *jahiliyya* (the age of ignorance, especially moral ignorance); that is, the period before the truth of God's revelation in the Qur'an was made known through his messenger Muhammad. This Qur'anic conception of *jahiliyya* and Islam is juxtaposed in Qur'an 48:26, "And while bigotry—the bigotry of ignorance [*jahiliyya*]—was holding its reign in the hearts of the unbelievers, God sent down His tranquility on His apostle and on the faithful and made the work of piety binding on them, for they were most worthy and deserving of it. God has knowledge of all things."[2]

Although the period of the *jahiliyya* represents the height of rebellion against God—the antithesis to true submission (*islam*) to him—the term itself can be used to represent more than just pre-Islamic Arabia. In fact, some modern Muslim thinkers have argued that the regimes in the modern Islamic world are in fact *jahili* regimes. That is, they are not merely corrupt Muslim regimes in need of reform; they are *jahili* regimes that must be destroyed.[3] Despite the rhetoric of division between *jahiliyya* and Islam, few early Muslim scholars consigned everything from this period to the ash heap of infidel ideologies. The most obvious thing that was preserved and studied with care was the Arabic language itself. In fact, early grammarians and especially lexicographers spent a great deal of time collecting as much information on Arabic in all its complexities, turns of phrase, obscure words, and multiple meanings as they could, for a precise knowledge of the language was absolutely essential to a proper understanding of the Qur'an and the teachings of Muhammad. Muslim scholars' efforts in the scientific study of the Arabic language during the first Islamic centuries have preserved for us a broad range of literary sources that give us insight into the values of daily life in seventh-century Arabia.

One of the most important sources for this transitional period is the principal art form of the *jahiliyya*, the *qasida* or ode. While the *qasida* was valued for its beauty and as the epitome of Arabic poetry, it was also venerated because, apart from the Qur'an itself, it represented the Arabic language at its purest. Apart from its literary qualities, this poetry provides the modern historian with a window (however opaque) onto the values and customs of Arabian tribal society, especially the critically important role that kinship played in every aspect of that society. In addition to poetry, we will also draw on the Qur'an and the extensive biographical literature (*sira*) on the life of Muhammad as well as historical chronicles for our understanding of Arabian tribal society.

Because contemporary documentary evidence for the earliest decades of Islamic history, especially in the Arabian Peninsula, is very slight, we have no choice but to draw on the literary sources that date from 150 and more years after the fact, but which purport to preserve material from the *jahiliyya* as well as the first decades of Islamic history. Whether these sources necessarily provide us with specific and reliable evidence for what actually occurred in all that they claim to represent is a vigorously debated point among modern historians that need not be belabored here.[4] However, many of the events described in these sources were debated with equal passion among competing factions in early Islamic history, especially those events that had direct implications for such crucial issues as doctrine, ritual practice, law, the role and status of women, and political legitimacy. Since our purpose is to convey a sense of Arabian life, we can set aside the task of *resolving* these and many other thorny issues that to a certain degree remain unresolved even among Muslims today. Since these topics were so hotly contested (at times to the point of open conflict), we will revisit some of them in subsequent chapters since the early community's values and expectations ostensibly inform the values and practices of the medieval Islamic world.

GEOGRAPHY AND ENVIRONMENT

While the Arabian Peninsula (*Jazirat al-ʿArab* or "Island of the Arabs") is named after the ʿ*Arab*s; that is, the nomads or Bedouin who lived there and in the deserts that extend northward into Syria and Iraq (and even into the Sinai and Egypt east of the Nile), the vast majority of the population of the region, even in antiquity, have always lived some sort of settled existence.[5] These settled populations lived in disparate environments and supported themselves in a variety of ways, determined to a great extent on the availability of water. Yemen (the *Arabia Felix* or "Happy Arabia" of the classical geographers) was exceptional in just about everything. Unlike the Bedouin, who lived in tents, or the residents of the oasis settlements of the Hijaz, who lived in dwellings that we might call simple adobe huts, many of the people of Yemen lived in villages and towns made up of multistory tenements. Moreover, the people of Yemen built dams in the valleys in order to catch the annual monsoon rains.

In the highlands that reached as high as 10,000 feet they built extensive terraces for the same purpose. As the rains poured down these terraces, the water soaked deep into the soil and deposited nutrients that it brought with it from terrace to terrace. Such water catchment practices produced an agricultural bounty of wheat and barley as well as fruits, vegetables, dates, and grapes that was simply impossible elsewhere in the peninsula. In addition to agricultural wealth, the ancient kingdoms in Yemen benefited from trade in precious stones and metals mined there as well as the locally harvested aromatic gum resins such as frankincense and myrrh that were so desired in the ancient Near East. One of these ancient kingdoms was that of the Sabeans in Yemen, the earliest mention of which is in the Biblical account

The Harra, Jabal Says in southeastern Syria. *Source:* Felix Ng.

of the Queen of Sheba's visit to King Solomon (ca. 955–935 B.C.), during which "she gave the king 120 talents of gold, large quantities of spices, and precious stones. Never again were so many spices brought in as those the Queen of Sheba gave to King Solomon" (1 Kings 10:10).

The sparse annual rainfall in the rest of the region (no more than eight to ten inches, and in most areas fewer than four) was simply nowhere near sufficient to sustain the extensive agriculture practiced in the south. The largely date palm agriculture that was practiced in much of the rest of the region was dependent on natural springs or wells that were dug in order to tap underground reservoirs. Eastern Arabia along the Persian Gulf coast benefited greatly from its extensive underground reservoirs. It produced the ancient kingdom of Dilmun, which achieved legendary status in ancient Mesopotamian literature as the origin of the world as well as the place where the gods retired Ziasudra/Utnapishtim, the Mesopotamian Noah, to live for eternity after the flood.[6] Parts of the Hijaz in northwest Arabia had sufficient water to cultivate a range of crops as well as irrigate massive palm groves with thousands of trees. However, many oasis settlements throughout the region were extremely small and could only sustain a handful of people.

Whereas the ancient Hebrew, Assyrian, Mesopotamian, Greek, and Latin sources speak positively of the kingdoms of ancient Yemen in the south and of Dilmun in the east, their regard for the people of the rest of the region reflects the generally negative attitudes of the settled peoples

Mud brick house in Old Marib, Yemen. *Source:* Robert G. Hoyland.

toward the nomads. For example, while the Old Testament speaks glowingly of the Queen of Sheba and her visit to king Solomon, it depicts the residents of North Arabia and their nomadic ways in the time of Gideon (ca. 1100 B.C.) with contempt:

Whenever the Israelites planted their crops, the Midianites, Amalekites and other eastern peoples invaded the country. They camped on the land and ruined the crops all the way to Gaza and did not spare a living thing for Israel, neither sheep nor cattle nor donkeys. They came up with their livestock and their tents like swarms of locusts. It was impossible to count the men and their camels; they invaded the land to ravage it (Judges 6:3–5).

CAMELS AND TRADE

Although the majority of the population of Arabia did not live the life of a nomad, it is the nomad—the ʿ*Arab*—that gave the region its name, and

Marib Dam. *Source:* Robert G. Hoyland.

it is the nomad, his camel, and his tent that figure into many Americans' images of the region. Since the one-humped camel or dromedary was the camel found throughout Arabia and North Africa, it is appropriate that we begin our discussion of Arabian life with a few comments about the one-humped camel, its suitability to Arabia, as well as its virtues as a means of transportation and as a source of meat, milk, and wealth. (The two-humped or Bactrian camel is much better suited to the colder climates of Asia.)

One of the many myths about camels is that they store water in their humps. While they do store fat in their humps, they do not store water there or anywhere. As Richard Bulliet demonstrates in his *The Camel and the Wheel*, what camels do is *conserve* water remarkably well and in many ways.

Efficient kidneys allow for a high concentration of impurities in liquid waste; dehydration affects bodily fluids other than the blood; immense quantities of water [up to 30 gallons] can be consumed in one watering and the water consumed, which is normally equal to the level of loss from dehydration, is distributed throughout the body tissues within forty-eight hours. Most important, however, for camels living in very hot climates is their capacity to absorb heat by allowing their blood temperature to rise, without ill effect, over six degrees Fahrenheit in the course of a hot day before beginning to perspire. In this way water loss through perspiration is greatly minimized. During the chilly desert night the animal's body temperature falls to its base level ready to begin a new rise the next day.[7]

That the camel had long been domesticated in Arabia prior to the coming of Islam is clear from the Biblical passages about the Midianites and the Queen of Sheba cited above. However, the nomads of Arabia did more

The Du'an Valley of Hadramawt at the time of the summer rains. *Source:* Robert G. Hoyland.

than just enter the settled lands of the Middle East like "swarms of locusts" seeking to ravage farmers' fields or serve as camel drivers for caravans. Some nomads raised sheep and goats as well, but since they need better water and fodder than camels, the nomads who tended sheep and goats necessarily lived in closer proximity to the oasis settlements. In fact, there were some kinship groups that had members who practiced all of these ways of life at the same time—some lived in oasis settlements as agriculturalists or as merchants, others raised sheep and goats nearby, and still others were able to venture further afield as camel breeders. Camels, like sheep and goats, were bred as sources of milk, meat, and wool, but also as indicators of wealth and status. In fact, in the southern deserts and across the Bab al-Mandab straits in Somalia, most of the camel herders bred their beasts primarily for their milk, and few actually used them intensely for transportation or as beasts of burden. But it is the nomads of north Arabia that concern us here.

One of the distinctive aspects of camel breeding in north Arabia is the development (sometime between 500 B.C. and 100 B.C.) of what scholars imaginatively call the "North Arabian Saddle," which enabled the camel herders to use their beasts more effectively for riding, transport, and even military purposes. This saddle is composed of two large inverted V's that are situated on a pad in front and on a pad behind the hump. These two V's are connected by wooden braces of some sort, creating a frame over the hump. Over this frame is placed a pad for the rider, whose weight is borne by the camel's rib cage. When used as a pack saddle, the weight is tied in relatively equal amounts on either side of the saddle.

Because of its location between the Mediterranean world, Africa, Mesopotamia, and India, Arabia inevitably served as a transit point for trade among these regions. Urban settlements along the northern fringes of the desert such as the Hatrans of Hatra in what is now northern Iraq, the Palmyrenes of Palmyra (Tadmor) and the Emesenes of Emesa (Homs) in what is now Syria, and the Nabateans of Petra in what is now southern Jordan benefited considerably from trade because of their proximity to Arabia as well as to Rome and Sasanian Iran. (None of the modern states or borders in the Middle East existed prior to the twentieth century.)

They also received much better treatment in the ancient literature than the nomads. While such communities are referred to as Arabs in these sources, they had largely abandoned the kinds of nomadic practices described above in favor of the benefits of cosmopolitan trade as well as political alliances with the major powers of the region. For example, by the first century A.D. the Emesenes had settled at their capital of Emesa and Rome had recognized the leading Emesene family as kings and had even granted them citizenship.

The critical importance of the camel to all of these trading cities is evidenced by the fact that in A.D. 137, the Palmyrenes passed a law that imposed an exorbitant tariff on all goods brought in by cart. Clearly the Palmyrenes were determined to protect their economic position in the long-distance camel caravan trade in their city from any and all outsiders from the settled areas of Syria where wheeled carts were used. There are other examples of such legislation during late antiquity, but what is important for our purposes is that sometime between the third and sixth centuries A.D., the camel replaced wheeled transport throughout nearly all of the Middle East and North Africa.

The primary reason for this appears to be the greater efficiency and economic viability of the camel as a means of transportation. Not only could camels go long periods without water (up to one month in the winter), they could eat just about anything. Fully loaded, camels could cover 20 to 25 miles per day;[8] they did not need paved roads at all, could ford shallow rivers easily, and did not need to be shod. Moreover, most camels could carry roughly 600 pounds and a single driver could take care of several camels by himself. Compare this with the need for paved roads to operate a cart, the "wasted" weight and expense of the cart itself, the greater needs of water and fodder for oxen, donkeys, mules, or horses to pull a cart, as well as the fact that it usually took at least one person to operate each cart and team. As one might expect, this near total lack of wheeled transportation throughout much of the medieval Islamic world had major political, social, and economic implications for daily life—especially with respect to urban planning, travel, trade, and the general lack of extensive networks of paved roads (although bridges still needed to be built).

Because of their water and agricultural wealth, a number of the oasis settlements in the Hijaz (including Medina) were able to sustain populations that included artisans, merchants, religious leaders, and others who were not directly involved in agricultural production. Mecca, however,

Limestone relief from a sarcophagus in the camp of Diocletian, Palmyra, depicting two caravan leaders with a camel. *Source:* Palmyra Museum.

possessed neither the quantity nor the quality of Medina's water. Nevertheless, according to the Islamic tradition, Mecca did serve as a local cult center prior to the advent of Islam for its own population as well as that of the surrounding oases and even for some of the nomads in the region. It also participated in some local trade, apparently trafficking primarily in hides. In time, of course, Mecca became the center of the Islamic universe and the geographic focus of Muslim ritual prayer. Moreover, pilgrimage to Mecca and its environs became obligatory for every Muslim who was able to make the journey during his or her lifetime.

Although groups such as the Nabateans and Palmyrenes had been major players in large-scale international caravan trade in antiquity, by the time of Islam's rise in the seventh century they and others were just memories. In fact, even in antiquity most of the peoples of Arabia were not involved in such trade, though out of necessity they as well as their seventh-century descendants participated to some degree in local trade. It is from this local trade as well as its status as a shrine center that Mecca appears to have derived much of its wealth. It is also in this local trade that we see most clearly where the settled met the nomadic. Bedouin came to oasis settlements throughout Arabia to trade milk, clarified butter, wool, hides, and skins from their flocks and herds for the produce of the oases such as grains, dates, oil, clothing, wine, arms, cooking pots, and other items that their smiths produced.

While such bartering could take place at any time of the year, lucrative trade fairs were established throughout the peninsula at specified times of the year. Since these trade fairs were crucial to the welfare of all parties who traded at them, security of person and property was absolutely essential. The security of some fairs was guaranteed by the holiness of the site where the fair took place; others were protected by the strength and prestige of the tribe that administered it; while others, like the fair of Ukaz in the Hijaz (in which Mecca participated each spring), were held during a holy month. Fairs held during a holy month were especially popular because their duration provided safety of travel to the fair and back, but they also promoted a kind of festival atmosphere among the participants from far and wide. One of the most popular events at these fairs was the poetry competition among the leading poets of the clans present. For to the best poet went not only a financial reward, but his entire clan benefited from the prestige of his poetic prowess.

In addition to such economic opportunities and poetic rewards, there was a very mundane but crucially important benefit to seasonal trade fairs as well as smaller-scale trade between the nomads and oasis dwellers. That is, as the nomads' flocks and herds feasted on the fodder left in the farmers' fields after a harvest, their droppings fertilized these fields for the next agricultural cycle. Relations between the nomadic and the settled populations in Arabia were not always so amicable or mutually beneficial. In fact, during the more hostile encounter of a raid (*razzia*) against an agricultural settlement, nomads often simply allowed their own animals to graze on the settlement's crops before they made off with whatever booty they could get their hands on—gold, silver, jewels, livestock, and so on.

Although the Arabic sources indicate that Mecca's wealth was derived from small-scale local trade, western scholars have long argued that Mecca derived its wealth from large-scale international trade in spices and luxury goods. More recent western scholarship, however, indicates that this appears to be more a projection of ancient Arabian trading practices onto the seventh century than an accurate representation of trade in seventh-century Mecca. In fact, since Mecca had no port on the Red Sea at this time, it could not easily benefit from seaborne trade around the peninsula—whether to the west with East Africa, along the southern coast of the peninsula to Oman, or to Iran and places further east. Moreover, Mecca does not appear to have been on any *major* caravan route between Yemen, about 600 miles to the south and Syria, about 600 miles to the north.

So how did Mecca derive its wealth? According to Patricia Crone, who has written extensively on this topic,

… such information as we have leaves no doubt that [the Meccans'] imports were the necessities and petty luxuries that the inhabitants of Arabia have always had to procure from the fringes of the Fertile Crescent and elsewhere.… The Meccans, in short, are presented as having exchanged pastoralist products with those settled agriculturalists within their reach.... Meccan trade was thus trade generated by Arab needs, not by the commercial appetites of the surrounding empires, and it is as traders operating in Arabia rather than beyond its borders that the Meccans should be seen.[9]

While the camel was necessary to the success of the lucrative caravan trade in antiquity and the lesser trade of Mecca and elsewhere in seventh-century Arabia, it was the horse that received the greater praise as an object of beauty in poetry and as an essential element of warfare. In antiquity, the Palmyrenes maintained a camel corps to protect their caravans en route, but their army was made up primarily of cavalry. It should be noted that while lances and swords were eventually used from atop camels, the principal military purpose for the camel was as a pack animal, because it was simply no match for the cavalry charge of a warhorse. Thus, the nomads' tactics against cavalry dictated that they either dismount and fight as infantry or (as was preferable) that they bring a warhorse along on campaign and use it in battle.

In the seventh-century Hijaz, we see the importance of horses for military purposes in two early conflicts between Muhammad's Meccan opponents and Muhammad and his supporters in Medina. At the Battle of Badr in 624, Muhammad and the Medinese had two horses, while the Meccans had 100. At the Battle of Uhud the next year, the Medinese had no horses while the Meccans had 200. This disparity reflects, in part, the alliances with outlying tribal groups that the Meccans were able to bring to bear against Muhammad at this early stage of his career in Medina. Nevertheless, by 630, Mecca and her allies had submitted to Muhammad's authority.

HOUSING

As noted above, to most outsiders, the residents of Arabia were simple, even rapacious, Bedouins who lived in tents. The prophet Jeremiah, in one of his many fiery pronouncements against the enemies of ancient Israel, describes the "tent-dwelling" people of Kedar as "a nation that has neither gates nor bars; its people live alone. Their camels will become plunder, and their large herds will be booty" (Jeremiah 49:31–32). Jeremiah's perception and similar ones by Arabia's settled neighbors are incomplete and unrepresentative of Arabia's inhabitants as a whole. Certainly, nomads resided in tents made of camel hair or leather; however, many also built residential compounds (*qasr*) made of stone or mud-brick, which were very similar to those used by the settled peoples of oases such as Mecca or Medina.

Although little physical evidence has survived from this period, because of the limitations of geography, environment, and building materials one can presume that the kinds of structures found in many oasis settlements or along caravan routes in seventh-century Arabia differed little from those described by the twelfth-century Andalusian traveler, Ibn Jubayr.

In May 1184, after completing the annual pilgrimage, he and his companions were traversing Arabia from Mecca to Kufa in southern Iraq when they "alighted at Zarud, which is a depression in a stretch of land covered with sand. It has a large enceinte containing small houses, and resembles a stronghold, being called in these parts al-Qasr [The Castle]. The water here comes from brackish wells."[10]

Intrepid European travelers such as John L. Burckhardt (1784–1817), Sir Richard F. Burton (1819–1890), Charles M. Doughty (1843–1926), Alois Musil (1868–1944), and others described their Arabian journeys in far greater detail, in part because Arabia was a more exotic and foreign world for their readers than it was for Ibn Jubayr's, many of whom had already or would in the future make the pilgrimage themselves.[11] Doughty described a *qasr* he observed during his travels in Arabia in the 1870s:

The high-walled *qasr* of this ground was a four-square building in clay, sixty paces upon a side, with low corner towers. In the midst is the well of seven fathoms to the rock, steyned with dry masonry, a double camel-yard, and stalling for kine and asses; chambers of a slave-woman caretaker and her son, rude store-houses in the towers, and the well-driver's abode.... An only gateway into this close was barred at nightfall. Such redoubts, impregnable in the weak Arabian warfare, are made in all outlying properties. The farm beasts were driven in at the going down of the sun.[12]

Such descriptions portray the *qasr* as more than a mere residential dwelling. Rather, it was a walled compound that served as domicile, corral, warehouse, and fortress all at the same time.

The courtyard also served as a common area and kitchen for all who resided within or outside its walls. Burckhardt's description of his Bedouin companions' primitive bread-making practices during his travels in Arabia in the early nineteenth century presumably differs little from the Bedouin practices of the seventh century as well. According to Burckhardt, his companions began by encircling a fire with stones. Once the stones had been heated, and the embers removed, dough was set on the stones, and covered with the embers and ash until the bread was cooked. The result was a coarse, flat, hard loaf that was clearly edible and provided basic nourishment.[13] However, it was a far cry from the fine breads and cuisine that would later characterize the opulent kitchens of the caliphs and other notables in the cosmopolitan cities of the medieval Islamic world.

According to Islamic tradition, Muhammad declared that the rather simple traditional Arabian dish called *tharid* (small pieces of meat cooked in broth with dried bread crumbled over it at the end of the stewing process) was the most excellent of foods, just as his wife, Aisha, was the most excellent of women. Consequently, *tharid* became a celebrated dish among Muslims. The *tharid* prepared in the better kitchens of the medieval Islamic world was made with a wide range of vegetables and choice cuts of lamb, kid, beef, or chicken. The bread broken over it was of a finer quality as well.

Zafar, in the highlands of Yemen. *Source*: Robert G. Hoyland.

KINSHIP

American literature, film, and music are full of images glorifying the individual. Novelists and Hollywood directors have made fortunes portraying cowboys, frontiersmen, soldiers, and even intrepid CIA officers who, against incredible odds, are able to defeat perfidious enemies—Indians, Nazis, Russians, drug kingpins, Islamic terrorists, and even space aliens of all types. In films and novels of a more recent vintage we increasingly find that women are equally capable of such deeds of derring-do. And then there is Frank Sinatra's famous hymn to himself, "My Way." Americans know full well that such glorification of the individual is largely the stuff of fiction; nevertheless, we still like to dream of ourselves as capable of such heroics.

Seventh-century Arabians, of course, produced neither novels nor films. What they did produce is a very rich tradition of poetry that conveys conceptions of manhood and womanhood that are very different from the American ideals of the rugged individualist, the self-made man, the solitary high plains drifter, or the autonomous woman who has sole control of her body and her sexuality. In *jahili* and early Islamic poetry we find men, women, and children who defined themselves not as individuals, but as kin. In short, whether one was an oasis dweller, a resident of the highlands of Yemen, a pastoral nomad, or someone whose way of life fell somewhere between settled and nomadic, it was kinship—one's family, one's clan, one's tribe—that defined who one was. The issue of kinship remained important even in the cosmopolitan urban worlds of medieval

Damascus, Baghdad, Cairo, and elsewhere. It continues to be important in many Islamic societies today.

In seventh-century Arabia, this concern with kinship entailed more than just knowing the identity of one's parents, grandparents, uncles, aunts, and cousins. The bonds of kinship provided the means by which a family's position in relation to its clan, a clan's position in relation to its tribe, and a tribe's position in relation to other tribes were made clear. In short, one's name and the genealogy that it contained located a person in a complex pecking order of overlapping relationships immediately among one's siblings, and more broadly within a potentially huge tribal confederation.

In American society, family connections are certainly important, and the study of genealogy and individual quests for one's "roots" have long occupied many Americans for reasons of religion as well as simple curiosity. However, there are numerous institutions outside the family in which individuals can make names for themselves. In addition, there are layers of federal, state, county, and local governmental institutions to which individuals can appeal in order to resolve disputes and seek protection.

In the Arabian Peninsula and the neighboring areas to the north, such an individualistic approach to life was for the most part unthinkable. There were few states or state institutions to which to appeal for aid in times of need. Moreover, the physical environment of the region was simply too harsh to strike out on one's own; and if one did, the likelihood of falling victim to thieves or worse was nearly absolute. Such virtual statelessness did not, however, result in unchecked anarchy. In fact, the need for protection against a myriad of potential threats from neighbors as well as from the harsh physical environment fostered cooperation and only served to strengthen the bonds of kinship, at least on the local level. Because there was no state police or state judicial system to which one could appeal, it necessarily fell to one's kin to provide sustenance, protection, and arbitration of disputes. Moreover, since these relationships between families and groups were negotiated on the basis of kinship, ensuring the honor and the purity of the family tree was critical.

Some of the most common themes that we find in *jahili* and early Islamic poetry deal with the courage and physical prowess in battle among the men of a family, clan, and tribe as well as the beauty and sexual purity of the women. The following are two poems that date from this period. While the names of the groups and individuals in the poems are important to poetry scholars, the poems are reproduced here merely to illustrate some of the values of Arabian tribal society. Sir Charles J. Lyall (1845–1920), the translator of these poems, employed an archaic English style in an attempt to convey the meter of the original Arabic. Although certain words and phrases may be unfamiliar to the reader, the general sense of the poems and the values they describe should be clear.

The first poem was composed by a certain Abd al-Malik, son of Abd al-Rahman of the Banu l-Dayyan clan, the chief family of the Christian Banu l-Harith tribal confederation of Najran in the Arabian Peninsula.[14] Abd al-Malik composed his verse in response to a woman who had belittled the Banu l-Dayyan because it was relatively small. As the poet sings the praises of his kin, he challenges any and all to find another that can equal the Banu l-Dayyan's honor, prowess, purity, and generosity despite their small numbers.

> She cast blame on us that our number was little to count and few:
> I answered her—Yea: the count of noble men is little.
> But not few canst thou call those whose remnants are like to us
> —young men who vie with the old in the quest of glory.
> It hurts us naught that we be few, when our friend by us
> is safe, though the friends of most men beside be trampled; ...
> A folk are we who deem it no shame to be slain in fight,
> though that be the deeming thereof of Salul and 'Amir;[15]
> Our love of death brings near to us our days of doom,
> but their dooms shrink from death and stand far distant.
> There dies among us no lord a quiet death in his bed,
> and never is blood of us poured forth without vengeance....
> Pure is our stock, unsullied: fair is it kept and bright
> by mothers whose bed bears well, and fathers mighty.
> To the best of the Uplands we wend, and when the season comes,
> we travel adown to the best of fruitful valleys.
> Like rain of the heaven are we: there is not in all our line
> one blunt of heart, nor among us is counted a niggard.
> We say nay whenso we will to the words of other men:
> but no man to us says nay when we give sentence....
> Our Days are famous among our foeman, of fair report,
> branded and blazed with glory like noble horses.
> The children of ad-Dayyan are the shaft of their people's mill:
> around them it turns and whirls, while they stand midmost.

The second poem, by Kurait son of Unaif of the Banu l-Ambar, was written after a group of men from a rival clan, the Banu Shaiban, had attacked Kurait's herds and made off with thirty of his camels.[16] When Kurait, according to Arabian custom, called upon his kinsmen from the Banu l-Ambar to help him get them back, they turned a deaf ear to his pleas. He then turned to the men of another clan, the Banu Mazin, who agreed to help him. So Kurait and they went and made off with 100 of the Banu Shaiban's camels. The Banu Mazin not only gave him these 100 camels, but guarded him and the camels until he returned to his tribe. In the poem that commemorates these events, Kurait sings the praises of the Banu Mazin, who unlike the Banu l-Ambar, are honorable, valiant, and live up to the code of kinship.

Had I been a man of Mazin, there had not plundered my herds
the sons of the Child of the Dust, Dhuhl son of Shaiban![17]
There had straightway arisen to help me a heavy-handed kin,
good smiters when help is needed, though the feeble bend to the blow:
Men who, when Evil bares before them his hindmost teeth,
fly gaily to meet him, in companies or alone.
They ask not their brother, when he lays before them his wrong
in his trouble, to give them proof of the truth of what he says.
But as for my people, though their number be not small,
they are good for naught against evil, however light it be.
They requite with forgiveness the wrong of those that do them wrong,
and the evil deeds of the evil they meet with kindness and love;
As though thy Lord had created among the tribes of men
themselves alone to fear Him, and never one man more.
Would that I had in their stead a folk who, when they ride forth,
strike swiftly and hard, on horse or on camel borne!

It cannot be overemphasized that kinship is the glue that held Arabian society together, nomadic or settled. As these two poems illustrate, one's identity was subordinate to the honor (or shame) of one's kin, whether immediate family, clan, or tribe. According to Abd al-Malik, his clan, the Banu l-Dayyan, were honorable because the young men vied with the old in quest for glory, because they were eager to fly into battle and confront death, because the purity of their lineage was preserved by "mothers whose bed bears well, and fathers mighty," because they grazed their flock wherever they wished without opposition from any other group, because they were open-handed and hospitable, because they were subordinate to no clan but their own, and because their prowess was known far and wide as witnessed by the statement, "The children of ad-Dayyan are the shaft of their people's mill: / around them it turns and whirls, while they stand midmost."

While there certainly were groups who would have disagreed with the poet, and may have even thought that his song in praise of his kin was sheer poppycock, his glorification of his kin's independence, honor, open-handedness, military prowess, and sexual purity bespeaks the values of Arabian tribal society at large. All we need to do is examine the second poem by Kurait, son of Unaif, to see the shame he felt as a member of the Banu l-Ambar. According to Kurait, his was a clan that had no honor because they did not come to his aid in his time of need. As far as he was concerned, he would have rather traded in his clan for the Banu Mazin, who lived by the same values espoused by Abd al-Malik. Unfortunately for Kurait, he just had to make do with his bad luck of having been born to the Banu l-Ambar.

A single couplet in the middle of Abd al-Malik's poem highlights one of the most important values of Arabian society during this transitional period—generosity and its companion, hospitality:

Like rain of the heaven are we: there is not in all our line
one blunt of heart, nor among us is counted a niggard.

To be known as generous and hospitable brought a person and his or her kin tremendous honor and praise and guaranteed immortality in the memories of friend and foe alike for generations to come. Being "counted a niggard" brought immortality as well; however, it was the immortality of shame and dishonor that stained one's kin as stingy and inhospitable for generations.

Poets were fond of stories about men who slaughtered herds of camels to provide stupendous feasts to win the love of a woman, to celebrate a great victory in battle, or simply to demonstrate one's open-handedness. However, some of the most memorable of these are tales of those who slaughtered their last camel to feed a stranger or even an enemy who happened to pass by their tents. While in many of these stories, such generosity resulted in the host's utter destitution, glorious poems were composed to honor him and his kin. And as these poems were recited around campfires far and wide, it was the exceedingly charitable and benevolent who were immortalized as exemplars of the enduring values of generosity and hospitality.[18]

In addition to poetry, we see these kinship values throughout the biographical literature on the life of Muhammad in the context of sojourns in Mecca (ca. 570–622) and Medina (622–32). Seven brief examples should be sufficient to illustrate this point.

1. The most obvious instance of the values of kinship in Arabia is that Muhammad's biographers went to great lengths to establish a genealogy for him that went back to Abraham through Ishmael to demonstrate that not only did Muhammad come from *honorable* stock, he, like Abraham and the other ancient prophets, came from *prophetic* stock.

2. When Muhammad was orphaned as a young boy, he was taken in and raised by his uncle, Abu Talib. While it may seem perfectly normal to us that a family member would provide assistance in such circumstances, in Muhammad's case it is significant that it was his *father's* brother, Abu Talib, who took him in. Since Abu Talib was the leader of the Banu Hashim clan, it was his protection that made Muhammad's early prophetic career possible. (See "The Banu Quraysh" in the "Genealogical and Dynastic Tables" section at the back of this book.)

3. Muhammad's public preaching as an adult was replete with condemnations of the religious and moral values of Meccan society, especially its polytheism, its idolatry, and its maltreatment of the poor and downtrodden. Not surprisingly, Muhammad's criticisms upset the town's leaders very much. From their point of view, if Muhammad were successful in gaining converts, the leaders could very well lose everything that they had built. However, there was little they could actually do to stop Muhammad as long as his uncle, Abu Talib, afforded him the Banu Hashim's protection. As in the poems above, according to the kinship values of Arabia, any

offense against one member of a clan was an offense against every member of that person's clan.

While the Banu Hashim were not the most powerful clan in Mecca, they were prestigious enough that the leaders of Mecca could not simply act against Muhammad with impunity. Their only viable option at that point was to approach Abu Talib and ask him to intervene on their behalf. They asked him to inform Muhammad that they were willing to give him wealth and position if he would only cease his preaching. Concerned that things were becoming dangerous for his nephew, Abu Talib passed along their offer to him. Muhammad responded with a resounding no. "O my uncle, by God, if they put the sun in my right hand and the moon in my left on condition that I abandoned this course, until God has made it victorious, or I perish therein, I would not abandon it."[19]

4. The importance of a clan's protection is also seen in how Muhammad's followers in Mecca were treated. Muhammad did have some converts who were members of important clans in Mecca, but many of his followers at that stage of his career fell outside this kinship system. And since the leaders of Mecca could not afford to hurt Muhammad or their own kin who had accepted his call, they began to persecute (and even kill) those of his converts—slaves, orphans, and outcasts of various sorts—who did not have a clan's protection. Because he could not protect his followers, Muhammad sent those without the protection of a clan on what is called the first *hijra* to seek the protection of the Christian Negus (or king) of Abyssinia.

Some of the Meccans went to Abyssinia to retrieve Muhammad's followers, and in their negotiations with the Negus they argued that those to whom he had given refuge were in fact slaves and rebels. The Negus said that he was willing to return the slaves as he would expect them to return his, if the situation were reversed; however, he was uncomfortable about returning free persons. The Meccans sought to strengthen their case by arguing that the refugees were also rebels in religion, which led to a long theological discussion between the refugees and the Negus. In the end, the Negus was impressed with what Muhammad's followers had to say and told them that they could stay under his protection as long as they needed.

The reason that Muhammad sent them on this *hijra* was that he simply could not protect those who had no kin to protect them. However, the story serves another purpose and parallels many other stories in which a person of religious authority (usually a Jew or Christian) vindicates Muhammad's message—in this case, it was none other than the great Christian Negus of Abyssinia, who by the end of the story appears to have secretly embraced Muhammad's message as well.

5. After Abu Talib's death in 619, leadership of the Banu Hashim passed to his brother, Abu Lahab, who had little sympathy for Muhammad's preaching and was less inclined to extend the protection of the clan to this troublesome nephew. In the same year, Khadija, Muhammad's wife and great source of encouragement, died as well. In this context Muhammad began to search for a new place to preach. In the end, after sending many of his followers on ahead of him, he made his way to Medina in 622. Even the circumstances of Muhammad's *hijra* to Medina were rooted in the values of kinship. Since there was no effective state in the Hijaz to which one could appeal for the resolution of disputes or conflicts, it was customary for the leaders of the clans to which the disputants belonged to negotiate a compromise. However, when the clans could not reach an agreement among themselves, they often turned to an outsider as arbiter.

Medina was being torn apart by a long-standing blood feud among the two major clans of the town—the Banu l-Aws and the Banu l-Khazraj. Unable to resolve this conflict, the two clans' leaders approached Muhammad hoping that he could successfully arbitrate their dispute. In the end, Muhammad agreed to go to Medina with his followers on the condition that the Medinese accept him as the Messenger of God and his authority as the final arbiter of all their disputes, while agreeing to take up arms on his behalf to protect him, for war with Mecca would be inevitable.

That the Medinese agreed to his conditions indicates the depth of their despair when it came to resolving their disputes on their own. As in the case of the first *hijra* to Abyssinia, this negotiation illustrates the values of kinship and vindicates Muhammad's prophethood—this time by reinforcing one of the many Biblical themes emphasized by Muhammad's biographers—that a prophet is without honor in his own country, for Muhammad clearly had greater prestige among the warring clans of Medina than he did in his hometown of Mecca.

6. Muhammad left Mecca for Medina just in time to avoid a plot to kill him, and even the story of this plot reflects the values of kinship. According to Ibn Ishaq, each of the leading clans opposed to Muhammad was supposed to contribute "a young, powerful, well-born, aristocratic warrior; then ... each of them should strike a blow at him and kill him."[20] The genius of this plot was that if each of the clans was responsible for Muhammad's death, his clan would be vastly outnumbered and therefore unable to fight all the clans who were parties to the murder. Muhammad's kin would have to accept blood-money; Muhammad's opponents would be rid of him, and they would also avoid a blood feud. But according to Ibn Ishaq, the angel Gabriel warned Muhammad not to sleep in his bed that night; he was spared and made his way to Medina.

7. Once Muhammad reached Medina, and in his role as the Messenger of God and the arbitrator of all affairs, he established a
new social order that is described in what modern scholars call
the "Constitution of Medina." The key to membership in this
new community (*umma*) in Medina was right belief, not kinship.
In particular, the *muhajirun* (those Meccan converts who immi-
grated to Medina) were to be equal to the *ansar* (Muhammad's
Medinese supporters), not clients under the *ansar*'s protection as
was customary in such circumstances. While Muhammad sought
to replace the bonds of *blood* kinship among his followers with
the bonds of *spiritual* kinship, one of the opening passages of the
Constitution of Medina makes clear that the new order in Medina
embraced the fundamental values of vengeance, retribution, and
mutual aid so common in Arabian society:

A believer shall not take as an ally the freedman of another Muslim against him.
The God-fearing believers shall be against the rebellious or him who seeks to
spread injustice, or sin or enmity, or corruption between believers; the hand of
every man shall be against him even if he be a son of one of them. A believer shall
not slay a believer for the sake of an unbeliever, nor shall he aid an unbeliever
against a believer. God's protection is one, the least of them may give protection
to a stranger on their behalf. Believers are friends one to the other to the exclusion
of outsiders. To the Jew who follows us belong help and equality. He shall not
be wronged nor shall his enemies be aided. The peace of the believers is indivis-
ible. No separate peace shall be made when believers are fighting in the way of
God. Conditions must be fair and equitable to all. In every foray a rider must take
another behind him. The believers must avenge the blood of one another shed in
the way of God. The God-fearing believers enjoy the best and most upright guidance. No polytheist shall take the property or person of Quraysh under his protection nor shall he intervene against a believer. Whosoever is convicted of killing a
believer without good reason shall be subject to retaliation unless the next of kin
is satisfied (with blood-money), and the believers shall be against him as one man,
and they are bound to take action against him.[21]

This new order was a genuine departure from the norm and would prove
very costly to some, for it meant that they now had an absolute duty to
support their fellow Muslims come what may, even against their own kin
who had rejected Muhammad's message.

Because of his charismatic personality and standing as the Messenger of
God in the eyes of his followers, Muhammad's vision of a community in
which the bonds of right religion superseded the bonds of blood kinship
remained largely intact during his lifetime. It would continue to be the
ideal that Muslim scholars have long venerated as well. However, as the
sources make clear, the tug of blood kinship remained very strong throughout Muhammad's prophetic career. In spite of Muhammad's message of
unity, the early community plunged immediately into intertribal strife as

the *ansar* of Medina argued with the *muhajirun* of Mecca for leadership of Muhammad's community even while his corpse was being prepared for burial. In the end, the Meccans prevailed. Abu Bakr was proclaimed the first caliph, and all the subsequent caliphs in Islamic history traced their ancestry to one of the clans of the Meccan Quraysh. Nevertheless, tensions within and among the various kinship groups in early Islamic history led to many a conflict, at times breaking out in open civil war.[22]

Arabia was the birthplace of Islam, and the society and values of the seventh-century Hijaz informed every aspect of the early Muslim community, yet within a generation of Muhammad's death, his followers had been deeply split by civil war. By that time, the political, military, and economic centers of the Islamic world had shifted out of the peninsula to the garrison towns of Kufa and Basra in southern Iraq and to Damascus in Syria, and within a little more than a century, the geographic reach of the new Islamic empire had expanded phenomenally.

Despite the fact that Arabia was now on the political, economic, and even intellectual periphery of the Muslim world, the final ten years of Muhammad's career in Medina served as a model for the faithful in all aspects of daily life and as the quintessential example of the ideal society in the medieval Islamic world. Regimes throughout Islamic history have sought to portray themselves as the preservers of that order; dissenters and reformers have legitimated their opposition by asserting that only they and their visions of right religion and society could restore the pristine community of Muhammad at Medina. While in many instances such arguments favoring or opposing existing regimes can be understood in terms of the political and material self-interests of many factions, the ideal of Islam's golden age under the leadership of the Messenger of God remained a powerful force in the imagination of Muslims throughout the premodern world and continues to be persuasive to this very day.

Essential to the achievement of such a society is the pious adherence to Muhammad's example in every facet of daily life. The most obvious of these is the proper observance of the fundamental religious rituals of Islam, what Muslims call the five pillars of Islam. But such piety also includes the meticulous emulation of Muhammad's example in areas ranging from the mundane private rituals of personal hygiene to the complex public rituals of social etiquette, especially with respect to relations between men and women. The precedent for this wide range of behaviors is rooted in the early Muslim scholars' accounts of the life and practice of Muhammad and the early Muslim community in seventh-century Mecca and especially Medina.

NOTES

1. All biblical citations are from the *Holy Bible: New International Version* (Grand Rapids: Zondervan Bible Publishers, 1978). Used by permission.

2. All Qur'anic citations are from N. J. Dawood, trans., *The Koran*, 5th rev. ed. (New York: Penguin Books, 1995). Used by permission.

3. Much has been written on modern advocates of this vision of Islam. See especially Richard P. Mitchell, *The Society of the Muslim Brothers* (New York: Oxford University Press, 1969); Emmanuel Sivan, *Radical Islam: Medieval Theology and Modern Politics* (New Haven, CT: Yale University Press, 1985); William Shepard, *Sayyid Qutb and Islamic Activism: A Translation and Critical Analysis of Social Justice in Islam* (Leiden: Brill, 1996); Seyyed Vali Reza Nasr, *Mawdudi and the Making of Islamic Revivalism* (New York: Oxford University Press, 1996); and Gilles Kepel, *Jihad: The Trail of Political Islam* (Cambridge: Harvard University Press, 2002).

4. See pp. 5–8 of this book.

5. My discussion of geography, environment, camels, and trade in Arabia is based largely on Richard W. Bulliet, *The Camel and the Wheel* (Cambridge, MA: Harvard University Press, 1975); Fred M. Donner, *The Early Islamic Conquests* (Princeton, NJ: Princeton University Press, 1981); idem, "The Role of Nomads in the Near East in Late Antiquity (400–800 C.E.)," in *Tradition and Innovation in Late Antiquity*, eds. Frank M. Clover and R. Stephen Humphreys (Madison: University of Wisconsin Press, 1989), 73–88; Patricia Crone, *Meccan Trade and the Rise of Islam* (Princeton, NJ: Princeton University Press, 1987); and Robert G. Hoyland, *Arabia and the Arabs: From the Bronze Age to the Coming of Islam* (New York: Routledge, 2001).

6. *The Epic of Gilgamesh* (New York: W. W. Norton & Company, 2001).

7. Bulliet, *The Camel and the Wheel*, 31. Bulliet's study is one of the most important works on the role of the camel throughout human history and is the source for most of our discussion of camels.

8. There are reports that couriers who were unencumbered by heavy loads or by women and children could cover far greater distances in a single day. According to D. R. Hill, such riders could cover up to "100 miles in one day, 400 miles in a week, and 700 miles in a fortnight." See D. R. Hill, "The Role of the Camel and the Horse in the Early Arab Conquests," in *War, Technology and Society in the Middle East*, eds. V. J. Parry and M. E. Yapp (London: Oxford University Press, 1975), 34.

9. Crone, *Meccan Trade and the Rise of Islam*, 150–51.

10. R. J. C. Broadhurst, trans., *The Travels of Ibn Jubayr* (London: J. Cape, 1952), 215.

11. John L. Burckhardt, *Notes on the Bedouins and Wahabys* (New York: Johnson Reprint, 1970); Richard F. Burton, *Personal Narrative of a Pilgrimage to al-Madina and Meccah*, 2 vols. (New York: Dover Publications, 1964); Charles M. Doughty, *Travels in Arabia Deserta*, 2 vols. (Cambridge: Cambridge University Press, 1888); and Alois Musil, *The Manners and Customs of the Rwala Bedouins* (New York: American Geographical Society, 1928).

12. Doughty, *Travels in Arabia Deserta*, 2:417. Cited in Hoyland, *Arabia and the Arabs*, 170.

13. Burckhardt, *Notes on the Bedouins and Wahabys*, 58. Cited in David Waines, "Bread, Cereals and Society," *Journal of the Economic and Social History of the Orient* 30.3 (1987): 269.

14. I have reproduced an abridged version of Lyall's translation here. For his complete translation, see Charles J. Lyall, *Translations of Ancient Arabian Poetry, Chiefly Pre-Islamic, with an Introduction and Notes* (Westport, CT: Hyperion Press, Inc., 1986), 20–22. The Hyperion edition is a reprint of the 1930 Columbia University Press edition.

15. According to the Islamic tradition, the Banu l-Harith had numerous conflicts with the Banu Amir. The Salul were a brother tribe of the Banu Amir. Lyall, *Translations*, 22.

16. Ibid., *Translations*, 1–2.

17. According to Lyall, the phrase "the Child of the Dust" refers to a "foundling—one whose parentage is unknown and who is as it were picked up out of the dust." In the context of this poem, the "Child of the Dust" is the mother of the family of Dhuhl ibn Shaiban. See Lyall, *Translations*, 2.

18. For an excellent treatment of the importance of generosity and hospitality in Arabian society, see Gert Jan van Gelder, "Early Poetry: Feeding as Good Breeding," in *God's Banquet: Food in Classical Arabic Literature* (New York: Columbia University Press, 2000), 7–21. See also al-Jahiz, *al-Bukhala'*, translated by R. B. Serjeant as *The Book of Misers: al-Bukhala'* (Reading, UK: Garnet Publishing, 1997). According to one of the most important Jahiz scholars, Charles Pellat, *The Book of Misers* represents "an analysis of avarice the equivalent of which is not to be found anywhere in Arabic literature." Charles Pellat, "al-Djahiz," in *Encyclopaedia of Islam*, New Edition, 12 vols. (Leiden: Brill, 1954–2004) 2:386.

19. Alfred Guillaume, trans., *The Life of Muhammad: A Translation of Ibn Ishaq's Sirat Rasul Allah* (Oxford: Oxford University Press, 1955), 119.

20. Ibid., 222.

21. Ibid., 232.

22. See F. E. Peters, *Muhammad and the Origins of Islam* (Albany: State University of New York Press, 1994) for a more complete treatment of the life of Muhammad.

3

WARFARE
AND POLITICS

By the time Muhammad died in 632, he had become the ruler of the Hijaz and had established tributary alliances with a number of the outlying tribes in Arabia. Islamic historical sources indicate that Muhammad achieved his goal of establishing a society that lived in accordance with God's commandments in part by persuasion, but also by coercion and even warfare. While violence in the name of religion tends to make modern westerners uncomfortable, the idea that brutality could be an expression of piety was neither new nor unique to the seventh-century Near East.

The Bible is replete with stories in which the ancient Israelites slaughtered their enemies in the name of God. The Prophetess Deborah eulogized Jael, the wife of Heber the Kenite, as "the most blessed of tent-dwelling women" because she gave refuge to the Canaanite general, Sisera, and then drove a tent stake through his head as he slept in her tent (Judges 5:24–27). Samson killed a thousand Philistines with the jawbone of an ass, and even more as he pulled the Philistine temple down upon himself and his captors in his final act (Judges 15:15–16; 16:30). It fell to the prophet Samuel to hew to pieces the Amalekite King Agag because the Israelite King Saul, in his disobedience to God, had spared him (1 Samuel 15:33). David's victory against Goliath and the Philistines was immortalized by the women of Israel "with singing and dancing, with joyful songs and with tambourines and lutes. As they danced, they sang: 'Saul has slain his thousands, and David his tens of thousands'" (1 Samuel 18:6–7).

While the Bible tells us that it upset King Saul to see such dancing in the streets in praise of the young David's military exploits, David's military victories against Goliath and the Philistines, against the Jebusites at Jerusalem, and against others ultimately led to the establishment of the ancient kingdom of Israel under his kingship ca. 1000 B.C. In addition, these and other military victories (and defeats) of the ancient Israelites so vividly depicted throughout the historical books of the Old Testament inspired many Christian religious and political theorists and warriors during the Crusader period in the Near East some two thousand years later (A.D. 1095–1291). Given the long and rich tradition of warfare as an expression of right religion in the histories of ancient Israel and Christianity, it should come as no surprise that we find it among Islam's founding generation and throughout its history as well.

This chapter begins with a discussion of the basic arguments for the Islamic concept of jihad, often incompletely translated as "holy war." It then addresses specific developments and changes in military technology and institutions in the medieval Islamic world. The chapter examines these in the context of the early centuries of conquest and consolidation of the Islamic empire, the introduction of military slavery in the ninth century and its subsequent development, and the Crusades in the Near East.

JIHAD

Jihad is an Arabic noun that conveys the idea of struggle or striving. In the Qur'an jihad is often used as part of the phrase, *jihad fi sabil Allah* (striving in the path of God). While most Muslim scholars regarded jihad as obligatory on all able-bodied Muslims, some even referred to it as a sixth pillar of Islam. As such, jihad in its various forms is essential to understanding daily life in the medieval Islamic world.[1] The principal textual authorities for the Islamic doctrine of jihad are the Qur'an and the hadiths, or statements attributed to Muhammad about the subject. Hence, the doctrine of jihad is rooted in the life and practice of Muhammad and the early Islamic community in Medina.

The principal Qur'anic material on jihad is in the ninth chapter, which speaks of jihad as *offensive* warfare against idolaters, polytheists, and infidels (Qur'an 9:5), but also as *defensive* warfare against those who fight against Muhammad, his followers, and right religion in general (Qur'an 9:13–14).[2] While Jews and Christians are lumped in the category of polytheists at times—and hence are fair game—other passages in the Qur'an speak favorably of those among the Jews and Christians who shall see paradise (Qur'an 9:29–30).[3] Finally, the Qur'an also informs us that the rewards awaiting those who strive in the path of God include "gardens watered by running streams, in which they shall abide forever" (Qur'an 9:87–88). In addition to these and other Qur'anic passages, Muslim scholars also appealed to a host of statements attributed to Muhammad that extolled the merits of jihad against the enemies of right religion (however defined) and the rewards that awaited those engaged in it.

Since Muhammad found himself at war with the Meccans and others after his *hijra* to Medina, it is easy to see the relevance of these and other statements to his immediate situations. After Muhammad's death, his followers used these texts and others like them to form the basis for an ideology of jihad in the medieval Islamic world. They inspired many of the faithful during the Islamic conquests of the seventh century even as others were undoubtedly inspired merely by booty and glory in battle. Once the frontiers of the new Islamic empire were more or less stabilized, from Spain in the west to the Indus River in the east, the caliphs maintained an expansionist jihad ideology by leading or ordering raids along the Syrian Byzantine frontier. Many caliphs and sultans strengthened their own religious *bone fides* by leading raids themselves. The Abbasid Harun al-Rashid (r. 786–809) is one of the most famous to have done so.

As Islamic scholars honed their understanding of right religion, they divided the world into two broad spheres—the Abode of Islam (*dar al-Islam*; lit., the Abode of Surrender or the Abode of Submission) and the Abode of War (*dar al-harb*)—in an effort to clarify the role of jihad and warfare in Islam. The Abode of Islam was comprised of those territories under Islamic political domination. The Abode of War was everywhere else. Now this division of the world into two spheres did not mean that all Muslims were at all times engaged in a state of open warfare against the Abode of War. Formal truces did exist. Moreover, for purely practical reasons of inertia, military capability, and political calculation, expansion of the borders of Islam waxed and waned over time.

Nevertheless, throughout the Middle Ages Muslim armies did what all armies are supposed to do—they fought. At times they engaged in jihad to expand the borders of the Islamic world in Central Asia, India, Africa, Anatolia, and Europe. At other times Muslim armies went to war against other Muslim armies within the Islamic world in order to implement a particular vision of proper Islamic religion and government. This was the case in the civil wars that plagued the early Muslim community during the Rashidun (632–61) and the Umayyad caliphates (661–750). We see this also in the Abbasid Revolution in the late 740s that established the Abbasid caliphate, which endured until the Mongols sacked Baghdad in 1258. The Almoravids (1062–1147) and the Almohads (1130–1269) represent two major revivalist movements that employed the ideologies of jihad against what they viewed as corrupt Muslim regimes in North Africa and Spain, and against the Christian monarchs in Spain as well.

Whether the motivation for the jihads fought throughout the medieval Islamic world met medieval Muslim scholars' standards for religious purity in every instance is beyond our ken. We do know, however, that some of those ostensibly engaged in jihad against the external enemies of Islam and internal schismatics and heretics (however defined) were little more than bandits, thugs, and soldiers of fortune—at least they are portrayed as such by many of the Muslim scholars and historians who wrote the extant sources.

In contrast to these modes of thought and action, some Muslims, especially followers of the mystical (Sufi) traditions and other more piety-minded scholars, argued that there were two types of jihad. For them, the greater jihad was that internal struggle within oneself against temptation and evil. This greater jihad is also known as the jihad of the tongue or the jihad of the pen; that is, the jihad of piety and persuasion. According to this position, military jihad was the lesser jihad, or the jihad of the sword. But it was the military vision of jihad that predominated and that concerns us here.[4]

WARFARE IN EARLY ISLAMIC HISTORY

The year after his arrival in Medina, Muhammad engaged in a number of small-scale raids (*razzias*) against Meccan caravans, most of which were unsuccessful. The purpose of these raids appears to have been to obtain booty for the emigrants to Medina, but also to annoy, even provoke a fight with, his enemies in Mecca for their rejection of him and his message. Since Muhammad fought far too many battles during his ten years in Medina to be adequately examined here, three of these military conflicts will be analyzed in this section—the Battle of Badr (mid-March 624), the Battle of Uhud (mid-March 625), and the Battle of the Trench (late March 627).[5] These battles illustrate how Muhammad used warfare against Mecca to consolidate his position in Medina among his followers, his opponents (especially the Jews), and the undecided. The Qur'anic statements on jihad need to be understood with these and similar events in mind.

Muhammad's first break with the Jews of Medina and the change in the direction (*qibla*) of prayer from Jerusalem to Mecca occurred in February 624.[6] March of 624 brought with it Muhammad's first full-scale battle against the Meccans. His decision to attack a Meccan caravan at the wells of Badr (11 miles southwest of Medina on the coastal road between Syria and Mecca) upon its return from Gaza appears to have been the culmination of the earlier smaller raids he and some of his followers had undertaken in the previous year. The leader of this enemy caravan of some 50,000 dinars worth of goods borne by some 1,000 camels was Abu Sufyan, one of the leaders of the Umayyad branch of the Quraysh and a long-time opponent of Muhammad. Muhammad's forces numbered some 300 men. By the time his forces confronted the Meccan caravan, it had been reinforced by some 950 men. In the end, Muhammad's outnumbered forces were victorious and made off with a great deal of booty and prisoners, many of whom embraced Islam.

This victory for Muhammad and his outnumbered followers was hailed as a vindication of the righteousness of his cause and religion. It also strengthened his position in Medina with respect to his opponents and doubters. In this context, he took his first action against one of the Jewish clans in the town, the Banu Qaynuqa. Apart from the fact that the Jewish clans of Medina in general did not accept Muhammad's claims to prophethood, his targeting of the Banu Qaynuqa in particular made sense for two reasons. They had long been allied with one of Muhammad's strongest opponents in Medina, a certain Abu Abd Allah ibn Ubayy; they also were silversmiths who controlled much of the commerce in Medina where the immigrants from Mecca were still in need of economic support. After a market dispute that left one Jew and one Muslim dead, Muhammad ordered the execution of the entire Banu Qaynuqa. Abu Abd Allah ibn Ubayy intervened on behalf of his allies. Muhammad stayed their execution but had them expelled from the city and their property confiscated. Initially they moved north to a nearby Jewish community in Wadi l-Qura, and then about a month later they moved north to Syria.

The next year, 625, we find Muhammad at war with the Meccans in mid-March again. This time, the Meccans, under the leadership of Abu Sufyan, sought to avenge their loss at Badr and at several other skirmishes. Again, the Meccans outnumbered Muhammad and his followers. The battle initially went in Muhammad's favor, but by the end of the day the Meccan cavalry, under the leadership of Khalid ibn al-Walid, turned the tide. The Medinese took refuge in the lava flows near the hill of Uhud north of Medina where the Meccans' horses and camels could not pursue them. Muhammad and some of his followers defended themselves from atop the hill until the Meccans disbursed. Muhammad sustained some injuries and Hamza, his uncle and hero of early Islam, was killed. Muhammad's daughter, Fatima, was one of the women who cared for the wounded that day.

The ambivalent outcome of the Battle of Uhud stood in stark contrast to the near-miraculous victory at Badr. Muhammad sought to strengthen his position in Medina in two ways. First, he called on the faithful to redouble their commitment to the true faith, since according to accounts of Muhammad's declarations, he stated that had their faith been stronger they would have been victorious. Second, he targeted for expulsion the wealthiest of the Jewish clans in Medina, the Banu l-Nadir, who are portrayed as having rejected Muhammad's prophethood and having plotted against him. In addition, scholars generally agree that after Uhud, the Qur'an begins to emphasize increasingly the differences between Muhammad's followers and the Jews, who are portrayed as perfidious because they had rejected their own prophets in days past. Other passages admonish Muhammad's followers not to take Jews (or Christians) as friends because they are untrustworthy. As had been the case with the Banu Qaynuqa, the Banu l-Nadir were expelled, this time to the oasis of Khaybar where there was a large Jewish population. Their lands were then divided among the Muslims.

The competition between the two towns continued for the next two years and culminated in the Meccans laying siege to Medina again in late March 627. While Muhammad's forces now numbered some 3,000, they were still vastly outnumbered, for Abu Sufyan had been able to rally some 10,000 Meccans and their allies to lay siege to Medina, once again from the north. Because of the trench that Muhammad ordered dug as a defensive measure against the siege, this conflict is known as the Battle of the Trench. Since the Meccans possessed neither the equipment to fight a siege battle nor the will to fight a war of attrition, after about three weeks of insults and occasional skirmishes they abandoned their siege and went home. In the wake of this battle, Muhammad sought to rid Medina of the last vestiges of opposition to his rule—the remaining Jewish clan of note, the Banu Qurayza. They are depicted as having collaborated with the Meccans in the hope of ridding themselves of Muhammad and his followers. There would be no exile this time. In a bold, though certainly not unusual, move in seventh-century Arabia, the men of the Banu Qurayza were executed, while the women and children were enslaved.

What can be learned from these three battles about politics and warfare during this early period in Islamic history? First, they clarify some of the political issues that Muhammad had to address in consolidating his new position in Medina. That is, although he had been invited to Medina to arbitrate a dispute between the Aws and Khazraj and to bring peace to the town, not everyone was willing to abide by the terms of the agreement. While some opposed his political authority, others (especially the Jews of Medina) simply could not accept his religious authority or his claim to prophethood. As such, it is understandable, though tragic, that he sought to eliminate his opposition within Medina by exiling the Banu Qaynuqa and the Banu l-Nadir, and finally by executing the men of the Banu Qurayza and enslaving the clan's women and children. Despite having secured his position in Medina, the situation between Mecca and Medina remained stalemated until 630 when Muhammad was finally able to occupy his hometown and establish himself as the direct ruler of Mecca and Medina.

Second, and most important for our purposes, these battles provide lessons about the nature of warfare in early Islamic history, including the role of raiding (*razzias*), camels, horses, infantry, weapons, women in battle, siege warfare, exile, and even the execution of one-time allies. Since the literary sources for early Islamic history are so late, it is difficult to speak with absolute certainty about warfare, weapons, terminology, and tactics. Therefore, while we will use accounts of these three battles as starting points, we will also draw on later information of which we are more certain.[7]

WEAPONS AND TACTICS IN EARLY ISLAMIC HISTORY

It would be an overstatement to refer to a *razzia* as a battle, or even an act of open warfare. As we saw in Kurait son of Unaif's lament in chapter

2, raiding caravans or encampments and running off with another's live-stock and possessions was a simple fact of life in the nomadic societies of Arabia.[8] The goal of the *razzia* was not to kill or destroy an enemy; in many ways it was a kind of sport where the stronger and more prestigious clans took flocks, herds, wells, and other booty from the weaker, while they sought alliances with others for protection. Actual full-scale battles were indeed bloody confrontations but tended to be rare in any case.

According to Ibn Ishaq, Muhammad's forces fouled nearly all the wells at Badr in order to provoke a clash with the Meccans, who had little choice but to fight for the remaining water on their return from Gaza. As was customary, the two sides faced each other. Muhammad's Meccan opponents sent out three champions—Utba ibn Rabi'a, his brother Shayba ibn Rabi'a, and Utba's son al-Walid. Muhammad sent three Medinese *ansar* (Helpers) to meet them, but Utba, Shayba, and al-Walid were offended on the grounds that these *ansar* were not their equals. Muhammad then sent forth three Meccan *muhajirun* (Immigrants)—his uncle Hamza, his cousin Ali ibn Abi Talib, and a man named Ubayda ibn Harith—all of whom were acceptable to the Meccans. When combat ensued, "it was not long before Hamza slew Shayba and Ali slew al-Walid."[9] The battle between Ubayda and Utba continued to the point of stalemate with Ubayda losing a leg. Hamza and Ali then turned on Utba, killed him, and carried their fallen comrade back to camp, where he expired. After the clash of the champions, the archers and infantrymen of both sides engaged one another, and at the end of the day, Muhammad's outnumbered forces were victorious.

Whether in relatively minor raids, in pitched battles among archers, infantry, cavalry, or when one side laid siege to another as the Meccans did unsuccessfully during the Battle of the Trench, combatants generally were outfitted with similar body armor and weapons. The sources employ a range of vocabulary to describe military equipment, which included coats of mail, helmets, shields, swords, spears, lances, knives, iron maces, bows, arrows, and (after being on the receiving end of it during the naval siege of Constantinople in the 670s) Greek or liquid fire (*naft*).[10] Of course, since each person was expected to provision himself, only the wealthiest were outfitted completely. For example, despite its critical role as body armor, only a small percentage of soldiers could actually afford a coat of mail given the great expense and craftsmanship involved in producing one. In fact, seven decades after Muhammad's death (704), the province of Khurasan in northeastern Iran had a military force of some 50,000 men, but only 350 coats of mail.[11]

Helmets were crucial for protection as well. Many were constructed with pieces of mail or other fabric that hung down from the back to protect the neck. There is even the occasional mention of helmets with nose guards. It should come as no surprise that some fought without helmets for reasons of expense; some fought without them for other reasons. Before he met his fate as a Meccan champion at Badr, Utba ibn Rabi'a "looked for a helmet to put on his head; but seeing that his head was so big that he could not find in the army a helmet that would contain it, he wound a piece of cloth he had round his head."[12] Husayn ibn Ali is said to have met his demise at the battle of Karbala in 680 without any armor at all. Others are said to have followed his example in preparation for their own martyrdom.

Swords were the principal weapons employed at that time. They were straight, hilted, and carried on straps around the shoulder or waist. The earliest evidence of curved swords or scimitars is from the ninth century and among the soldiers in Khurasan. A great deal is made of swords in early Arabic literature; the best swords came from India, followed by those made in Yemen and Syria after the Indian fashion. Given the number of stories of severed legs, arms, hands, and heads, these swords appear to have been put to use effectively. Very few early Islamic swords have actually survived, but those that have correspond to the descriptions in our sources as about thirty-seven inches in length, two and one-half to three inches in width, and three pounds in weight.

As is the case in other literatures, the swords of famous people were given names. One of Muhammad's most famous swords (which he took as booty after Badr) was called Dhu l-Faqar because of the presence of *fuqra* (notches or grooves). Muhammad gave the sword to his cousin and son-in-law, Ali ibn Abi Talib, who fought with it at the battle of Uhud. According to Islamic tradition, Dhu l-Faqar also bore an inscription, which contained the phrase, "No Muslim shall be slain for an unbeliever." In iconographic and artistic representations, Dhu l-Faqar is commonly depicted with two points—possibly to indicate its mythical or magical character; possibly to better put out the eyes of the enemy. Fine swords were inscribed with phrases extolling its unique virtues. It also became an important symbol of Ali and his descendants. Some parents (primarily among Shi'is) even gave Dhu l-Faqar as a name to their sons.

Most battles were fought among infantry and archers, in part because of the general paucity of horses. However, it is clear that horses were critically important to those who had them, as was the case for the Meccans at Uhud. Because of their scarcity and importance, horses tended to be led to battle and only mounted when hostilities broke out. Horses were outfitted with some sort of protection as well, but it is not clear what it was at this early stage. We do know that in the Umayyad period (661–750) a heavy felt armor was widely used, but there is no evidence that horses were outfitted with mail or any other sort of metallic armor until the tenth century along the Byzantine frontier (by both Byzantine and Muslim forces), and even then it was quite rare. Given the scarcity of coats of mail among soldiers, one can assume that it was even more expensive to outfit one's horse in such a fashion at that early date.

In the process of the early Islamic conquests, Muslim armies captured far more horses than were available to them in Arabia. They also adopted new equipment as a result of their encounters. One of the principal innovations borrowed from the Persians in the late seventh century was the iron stirrup. Leather loop stirrups were not unknown in Arabia, and mounted archers were very effective even without the benefit of stirrups at all. In any case, as Hugh N. Kennedy argues, the adoption of the iron stirrup in the late seventh century "gave the mounted warrior greater stability and encouraged the widespread use of the mounted archer and the replacement of infantry by cavalry as the dominant force on the battlefield by the early third/ninth century."[13]

Siege warfare was not unknown in seventh-century Arabia, but as the Battle of the Trench demonstrates, the residents of the Hijaz were not very good at it and preferred to fight in the open. For example, while Muhammad's forces successfully laid siege to Ta'if (southeast of Mecca) in 630 with primitive siege technology, several of his warriors were not even present because "they were in Jurash learning the use of the testudo [a protective tortoise-shell-like covering], the catapult, and other instruments."[14] In fact, it is the weapons of open warfare that are extolled in the poems composed in commemoration of Muhammad's victory there. One poem praises the "finest blood horses" and "sharp cutting swords ... tempered by Indian smiths;" another praises their warriors' "light mail" and "sharp swords." A third praises "our unmailed men ... fully armed glittering with death-dealing weapons," while a fourth extols the imposing beauty of

> ...long armour which whenever it is donned
> Is like a shimmering pool ruffled by the wind;
> Well-woven armour which reaches to our sandals
> Woven by David and the family of Muharriq.[15]

The early Muslim armies laid siege to cities and even took refuge behind fortifications such as the trench dug by Muhammad at Medina in 627 However, during the conquest period as well as during the Umayyad and early Abbasid caliphates, many preferred to fight in the open and found that fighting from behind walls was too restrictive. Others even deemed it dishonorable to seek refuge behind walls. When the early Muslim armies actually deployed siege engines and other techniques of siege warfare, it tended to be against non-Muslim fortresses along the frontiers, though there were two major sieges of Baghdad in the ninth century during the civil war between Harun al-Rashid's (r. 786–809) two sons, al-Amin (r. 809–13) and al-Ma'mun (r. 813–33).[16]

WOMEN AND WARFARE IN EARLY ISLAMIC HISTORY

Women were frequently present at battles in seventh-century Arabia. While women occasionally took up arms themselves, more often they served as the moral voice of the tribe, beating tambourines and drums to incite their men to battle. For example, Ibn Ishaq records that prior to the

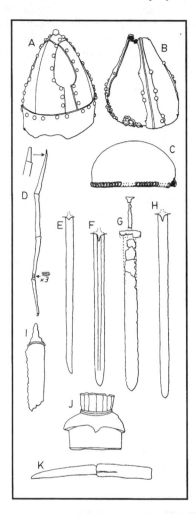

Early Islamic armaments. *Source:* David Nicolle, *Yarmuk A.D. 636,* 41.

Key:
A. Late Sasanian-early Islamic segmented helmet from Nineveh, 5th-7th centuries.
B. Late Sasanian-early Islamic segmented helmet from Nineveh, 7th century.
C. One-piece iron helmet from Varaghsah, Transoxiana, early 8th century.
D. One-piece reed "Bow of the Prophet Muhammad," traditionally mid-7th century.
E. "Sword of the Caliph Uthman" with later hilt, traditionally mid-7th century.
F. "Sword of the Caliph Umar" with later hilt, traditionally mid-7th century.
G. Late Sassanian or early Islamic sword from Oman, 5th-7th century.
H. "Sword of Khalid ibn al-Walid" with later hilt, traditionally mid-7th century.
I. Iron dagger with bronze guard from Pella, early-mid-8th century.
J. Iron sword guard from al-Rabadhah, 7th-8th centuries.
K. Iron knife with wooden grip from Qasr Ibrim, Nubia, 8th-9th centuries.

battle of Uhud, the Meccan leader Abu Sufyan sought to encourage the men of the Banu Abd al-Dar to go to battle:

"O Banu 'Abdu'l-Dar, you had charge of our flag on the day of Badr—you saw what happened. Men are dependent on the fortunes of their flags, so either you must guard our standard efficiently or you must leave it to us and we will save you the trouble (of defending) it."[17]

Needless to say, the Banu Abd al-Dar resented the implication of Abu Sufyan's words and eagerly accepted his challenge.

Ibn Ishaq then states that Abu Sufyan's wife, Hind bint Utba, and the women who were with her arose, took their tambourines, and beat them to incite the men to battle as Hind taunted them with the following anti-*Lysistrata* verses:

> On ye sons of 'Abdu'l-Dar,
> On protectors of our rear,
> Smite with every sharpened spear!
> If you advance we hug you,
> Spread soft rugs beneath you;
> If you retreat we leave you,
> Leave and no more love you.[18]

Hind was particularly concerned that the Meccans should defeat Muhammad's forces at Uhud, because her father, the helmetless Utba ibn Rabi'a, and her brother al-Walid ibn Utba were two of the three Meccan champions killed by Hamza and Ali at Badr the previous spring. According to Ibn Ishaq, an Abysinnian slave named Wahshi who was skilled with the javelin was offered his freedom in exchange for Hamza's life. Wahshi fulfilled the terms of the bargain at Uhud as his javelin pierced Hamza's body and exited between his legs. Hamza staggered forward toward Wahshi, fell to the ground, and died.

The Battle of Uhud illustrates two additional ways in which women were involved in warfare in early Islamic Arabia. After the battle, Hind and the other Meccan women mutilated the bodies of Muhammad's companions, the enemies who had murdered their kinsmen. They cut off the ears and noses of the dead and made necklaces and anklets out of them as trophies. Hind gave her trophies to Wahshi in appreciation for his avenging of her father's death. She also cut out Hamza's liver and chewed it, but since she could not swallow it, threw it away.[19] At the same time, in the midst of severed limbs and impaled warriors, Muslim women cared for their own wounded kinsmen as did Muhammad's daughter, Fatima, who tended to her father and other wounded Medinese. Hind's behavior is often portrayed as typically pagan and vengeful; Fatima's as typically Islamic and compassionate.

Of all the women in battle in the early Islamic period, few are more memorable than Aisha bint Abi Bakr. She was the daughter of Muhammad's close companion, Abu Bakr, the first caliph. She was betrothed to Muhammad at age nine and is the only one of his wives who was not a widow when she married him, a virginal virtue of which she reminded her fellow wives often. She was also accused of adultery when she was fourteen, but exonerated by divine intervention. Finally, because of Aisha's closeness to Muhammad, she is one of the most revered transmitters of hadiths or anecdotes about Muhammad's teachings and behavior. Despite being admired as a transmitter of hadiths about her husband, attitudes about Aisha were ambivalent in the Middle Ages and remain so today, in large part because she was one of the principal figures on the losing side in the first civil war (*fitna*) that broke out in the wake of the assassination of the third caliph, Uthman, and the contested succession of Ali ibn Abi Talib.

The best example of Aisha's opposition to Ali is her participation in the Battle of the Camel in 656. Her presence there can be viewed as an example of a woman inciting her clan's men to victory. Rather than beating a tambourine, Aisha was there in a closed litter atop her camel, around which the fiercest fighting occurred (hence the name of the battle). In the end, Ali's forces were victorious that day. Two of Aisha's allies—Talha and al-Zubayr—were killed. Aisha's life was spared, but she spent the rest of her days at her home in Medina, quietly transmitting hadiths about her husband.[20]

Since Aisha was not the only woman present at the Battle of the Camel and since the sources indicate that there were other women at subsequent battles as well, what offended later commentators was not so much the fact that women per se were present that day. Rather, they were offended that Aisha—a wife of Muhammad—had inserted herself in the politics of succession and had violated the Qurʾanic injunction that Muhammad's wives should remain in their homes (33:28–34). As Denise A. Spellberg demonstrates, many later commentators used Aisha's involvement in the Battle of the Camel to argue that women should never participate in the community's political life.[21] Some accounts actually portray Aisha on her deathbed acknowledging the error of her ways and expressing regret that she ever participated in the Battle of the Camel.

Even Zubayda, the wife of the Abbasid caliph Harun al-Rashid (r. 786–809), refused to intervene after her son, the caliph al-Amin (r. 809–813), was killed in the civil war between himself and his half brother, al-Maʾmun (r. 813–33).[22] In September 813, after the residents of Baghdad awoke to find al-Amin's head suspended from the city gate, Zubayda was urged to follow Aisha's example and avenge her son on the battlefield. According to al-Masʿudi (d. 956), she responded by rejecting Aisha's example as she echoed the sentiments of Aisha's detractors:

Aisha in a litter atop her camel. *Source:* Image
catalog number OR 2936 313R 04E00755R.
Reproduced by permission of The British
Museum.

"What do women from among the believers have to do with seeking vengeance
and taking the field against warriors?" Then she withdrew and went into deep
mourning.[23]

As the wife of the Abbasid caliph, Zubayda was obviously not one of
Muhammad's wives and was not governed by any Qur'anic instruction
specifically directed to them. Nevertheless, by the early ninth century she
(or at least al-Mas'udi a century later) had embraced the idea that a good
Muslim woman should have nothing to do with warfare or politics. Of

course, there were women who did play important public and political roles in the medieval Islamic world, but they were by far the exception.

MILITARY SLAVERY—THE MAMLUK INSTITUTION

By the early ninth century, cavalry had replaced infantry as the dominant force on the battlefield in the Islamic world. Infantry units continued to be used and used effectively, but it was the mounted archer that was now and would continue to be the core of any effective fighting force. Also, by the early ninth century the mamluk institution was established as a means of recruiting and training elite cavalry units, largely comprised of mounted archers who had been enslaved as young boys and raised to the profession of arms.

While there is evidence that some mamluks of Iranian origin were employed in the late Umayyad and early Abbasid periods, the Abbasid caliph al-Mu'tasim (r. 833–42) is credited with establishing the first effective mamluk corps with the encouragement of his brother al-Ma'mun (r. 813–33).[24] He purchased some of his mamluks in the slave markets of Baghdad, while the Samanids in Samarqand supplied him with others, primarily Turks from along the Central Asian frontier. By the end of al-Ma'mun's reign, al-Mu'tasim had a force of 3,000–4,000 troops who were intensely loyal to him, their master or *ustadh*. Al-Mu'tasim was able to use them to convince al-Ma'mun to set aside his own son's accession and designate him as his successor. When al-Ma'mun died on a campaign against the Byzantines in 833, al-Mu'tasim became caliph with more than the usual rumblings among those who had been favored under the previous regime.

Al-Mu'tasim's predominantly Turkish mamluk troops represent a major change in the Abbasid military structure. No longer would the military be comprised largely of men who could trace their lineage to the Arabian Peninsula. Rather, it would increasingly be the preserve of ethnic minorities such as Turks, Berbers, Armenians, Daylamis, and others recruited from the fringes of the empire. Al-Mu'tasim even built a new city—Samarra—to house his new troops. Located some 80 miles north of Baghdad on the Tigris, Samarra served as the Abbasid capital to the late ninth century. Recent studies have begun to shed more light on this crucial early period, but far more is known about the institution in its later incarnations.[25]

But what is a mamluk? Where did they come from? How were they trained? What did they do? As with any institution that endured for centuries there are many ways to answer these questions. Even defining the status of a mamluk is rather tricky, for not all those referred to as mamluks were actually enslaved persons. In general, even when a mamluk was manumitted, he was still identified by the term *mamluk*. Others who had never been enslaved at all, but were still part of the elite corps, are identified as mamluks in the sources. What follows is a general attempt to answer the above questions and to convey a sense of the importance of the mamluk institution as well as the contribution of the mounted warrior of Central Asian origin to the history of the medieval Islamic world.

While *mamluk* is an Arabic word that means "one who is owned," it is almost always used as a technical term for a particular type of military slavery designed to produce an elite force of mounted warriors. '*Abd* and *khadim* are the words generally used to describe field hands and domestic servants, which evoke images of slavery and servitude that more closely resemble the history of slavery in the agrarian slave societies of the southern United States. In fact, there is plenty of evidence that the kinds of abuses that are equated with slavery in the United States were inflicted on field hands and domestic servants in Islamic history as well.

In the medieval Islamic world, however, having been enslaved as a young boy and raised to the profession of arms was anything but degrading. In fact, mamluks served in a number of important offices on behalf of the ruler—personal attendants, cup bearers, officers charged with attending to and training the ruler's horses and hunting falcons, even as provincial governors. Moreover, being a mamluk was a position of privilege that opened the door to many avenues of wealth and status in society, even to the highest offices in the regime. It appears that in the ninth through eleventh centuries, it was not required for mamluks who rose to such high positions to be manumitted. Thereafter, it was much more common that they were.

While the preferred route for developing mamluk regiments was to purchase boys and to train them in barracks apart from the rest of society in the sciences of horsemanship, warfare, and religion, some adults were incorporated into mamluk regiments, especially during the early years of the institution. According to Islamic law, a free person could only be enslaved if he was a non-Muslim and resided outside the Abode of Islam; that is, in the Abode of War. Hence, military slaves were recruited from peoples who lived on the fringes of the Abode of Islam—sub-Saharan Africans, Eastern Europeans, Greeks, Armenians, Circassians, Indians, and so forth. However, the preferred practice was to purchase boys from the slave markets along the Central Asian frontier north of the Oxus River. While these boys were generally referred to as Turks, many were not actually ethnic Turks in the modern sense of the word. Nevertheless, the term *Turk* functioned as a kind of shorthand for anyone who was a pastoral nomad from the Central Asian steppe, and it was this steppe that served as a vast military reservoir for many of the regimes in the medieval Islamic world.

The Ottomans (ca. 1300–1923) took non-Muslim slaves from neighboring Russia and the Caucasus region as well. However, they also undertook a policy that was a dramatic departure from the traditional practice of slave procurement; in the late fourteenth century they began to levy a rather peculiar tax on their (primarily) Balkan Christian subjects, which involved drafting Christian children into service to the sultan. This tax, called the *devshirme,* produced the elite janissary corps as well as so many high government officials in the Ottoman regime that there are instances where Muslim families in the Balkans presented their own children as Christians so that they too might benefit from such prestigious and lucrative opportunities.[26]

From the outset, purchasing Turkish boys had at least three advantages for their *ustadh.* First, given the high rates of infant mortality in the pre-vaccination age of the medieval Islamic world, to purchase children at a younger age was simply a bad investment. However, once a boy had reached ten to twelve years of age, had survived his childhood diseases, and had built up considerable immunities, he was very likely to live a relatively long and healthy life. Second, since these boys were taken from their homes and families at such young ages, they were still quite amenable to the kind of training designed to produce an elite force of mounted warriors with a high level of esprit de corps and intense loyalty to their *ustadh.* Finally, it was widely believed at the time that Turks were by nature tough and loyal, but also superior horsemen and archers. Therefore, since the goal was to produce elite mounted warriors, purchasing Turkish boys who already were quite skilled in horsemanship and archery by the time they were ten to twelve years old was a pragmatic policy and saved an *ustadh* considerable effort and expense with respect to basic training in the necessary skills.

In his essay, "The Merits of the Turks and of the Imperial Army as a Whole,"[27] the prolific ninth-century author, al-Jahiz (777–869), argued that al-Mu'tasim knew what he was doing when he recruited Turks, for Turks have four eyes (two in front and two in back), are experts with a lasso, are inveterate hunters, are skilled in all aspects of horsemanship, can withstand extreme weather conditions, and are superb archers who can shoot their arrows while their horses race at full gallop in any direction. In addition, "the Turk is at one and the same time herdsman, groom, trainer, horse-dealer, farrier and rider: in short, a one-man team."[28] Turks also carry two or three bows and everything they might need on their horses, can ride for days, sleep in the saddle, change mounts at a full gallop, and over the course of their lifetimes spend more time in the saddle than with their feet on the ground. According to al-Jahiz, the Turks are to warfare what the Greeks are to philosophy and the Chinese to craftsmanship. Of course, al-Jahiz is engaging in a bit of hyperbole here—at least the part about the four eyes. But his essay conveys very eloquently the dominant sentiment that there is no better horseman than a Turk.

Since horse societies did not exist in sub-Saharan Africa, the military slaves recruited there for the North African regimes tended to serve as infantry and are referred to as *'abid,* while *mamluk* was a term reserved for cavalry. Not surprisingly, al-Jahiz (whose family may well have been of east African origin) had much to say about sub-Saharan Africans as well. In contrast to his essay on the Turks, al-Jahiz did not speak of blacks as a race of warriors in his essay "The Superiority of Blacks [al-Sudan] to Whites [al-Bidan]."[29] He did, however, mention the exploits of several individual blacks in early Islamic military history such as Wahshi, the Abyssinian slave who not only killed Muhammad's uncle, Hamza, with his javelin, but later, after his conversion to Islam, used the same javelin to kill Musaylima, one of the false prophets who arose during the latter stages of Muhammad's career.[30]

When speaking specifically about the superiority of blacks as a race, al-Jahiz emphasized qualities other than military prowess. "There is general agreement that among no other people is generosity so widespread and deep-rooted as it is among blacks. This is a characteristic feature of nobility."[31] In addition, al-Jahiz argued that black people have a natural sense of rhythm, dance and drum beat.[32] Moreover, according to al-Jahiz blacks are by nature better singers, more eloquent, physically stronger, and generally more happy-go-lucky than whites. Al-Jahiz's essay demonstrates that certain stereotypes about sub-Saharan Africans long antedated the trans-Atlantic African slave trade, though al-Jahiz enumerated these qualities as evidence of the *superiority* of blacks rather than as evidence of their inferiority.

In addition to their military prowess and horsemanship, Turkish slaves were renowned for their beauty, which served some in good stead in their service as pages, personal attendants, and occasional bedfellows.[33] Turkish slave girls were prized as singing girls and concubines. We learn from the geographer Ibn Hawqal (fl. 943–77) just how much folks were willing to pay for the very best Turkish slaves—male and female—in the tenth-century:

The most valuable slaves are those which come from the land of the Turks. Among all the slaves in the world, the Turks are incomparable and none approach them in value and beauty. I have not infrequently seen a slave boy sold in Khurasan for 3000 dinars; and Turkish slave girls fetch up to 3000 dinars. In all the regions of the earth I have never seen slave boys or girls which are as costly as this, neither Greek nor one born in slave status.[34]

Mamluks frequently referred to their *ustadh* as father, and it was not unusual for an *ustadh* to feel a bond of kinship with his mamluks and make them his heirs. Even when manumitted, the mamluk's loyalty to his *ustadh* remained strong since, despite his manumission, he remained a part of the *ustadh*'s family. In addition to the sciences of warfare, the mamluks were taught the sciences of the Islamic religion. Many learned to speak Arabic; some even learned to read and write it as well. One of the clear strengths of the mamluk system was that it produced superb cavalry forces who were intensely loyal to one another as well as to their *ustadh*.

This strength also proved to be a weakness, in large part because the loyalty that mamluks felt toward their *ustadh* did not always transfer to his sons upon his death. For while it was the *ustadh* who made the mamluks, in many fundamental ways it was the mamluks who made the son. An early and dramatic example of this was when some of the Abbasid Turkish troops assassinated the Abbasid caliph al-Mutawakkil in December 861 because they felt that their positions of privilege under al-Mutawakkil's father (al-Muʿtasim) were threatened.

In the wake of al-Mutawakkil's assassination, a range of petty states were established in North Africa and Spain to the west and in Iran and lands further east. Some of these declared full autonomy from the Abbasids, while others represented themselves as clients. Many of these outlying regimes employed mamluks as well, the most notable of which were the Samanids in Transoxiana (819–1005), from whom al-Muʿtasim had purchased some of his own mamluks, and the Ghaznavids in eastern Iran and Afghanistan (994–1040), who began as mamluks under the Samanids.

Some Turkish mamluks were employed in North Africa and Spain also. However, the Ismaʿili Shiʿi Fatimids, who presented themselves as the true caliphs in North Africa (909–969), came to power with the assistance of local Kutama Berber tribesmen from the Little Kabylie Mountains in eastern Algeria. After they moved to their new palace city in Cairo (969–1171), they too employed Turkish mamluks but relied primarily on the Kutama Berbers as well as sub-Saharan and Armenian troops. The Armenian wazir, Badr al-Jamali, is certainly one of the most famous of these and was the de facto ruler of the Fatimid state (1074–94) as wazir to the Fatimid caliph, al-Mustansir (r. 1036–94). In 945, the Buyids, a group of Shiʿi soldiers of fortune from Daylam on the southern shores of the Caspian Sea, occupied Baghdad and placed the Abbasid caliphs under house arrest and ruled as the Abbasids' deputies. They also developed their own Mamluk regiments.

SELJUKIDS AND MAMLUKS ON THE EVE OF THE CRUSADES

The ethnic shift within the Abbasid army that began under al-Muʿtasim's largely Turkish mamluk experiment in the early ninth century moved into high gear in the late tenth century as free Muslim Turkish pastoral nomadic warriors (Turkomans) migrated into the eastern territories of the caliphate. One faction of these Turkomans was the Seljukids, led by Toghril Beg and his younger brother, Chagri Beg. As noted in chapter 1, the Seljukids defeated the Ghaznavids at the Battle of Dandanqan (1040) in Afghanistan and established themselves in Afghanistan and eastern Iran. Toghril then left Chagri to administer the family lands in the east, while he turned his attention westward, conquering Baghdad in 1055.[35]

Toghril and his successors determined early on that if they were to administer a thriving urban and agrarian society in Iraq and Iran they would need a disciplined standing army. Toghril's successor, Sultan Alp

Arslan (r. 1063–73), pursued an aggressive policy of removing the fiercely independent Turkomans and replacing them with his own mamluks, or *ghulam*s (boys), as the Seljukids called them. No regime could afford to rely entirely on mamluk regiments. Hence, the bulk of most regimes' troops in the medieval Islamic world consisted of irregular Turkish and non-Turkish cavalry, infantry, and archery units. In fact, Nizam al-Mulk (d. 1092) strongly advocated in his *Book of Government or Rules for Kings* that the most effective military was one comprised of troops of different races because "when troops are all of one race dangers arise; they lack zeal and they are apt to be disorderly."[36] As is often the case in Nizam al-Mulk's work, Mahmud of Ghazna (r. 998–1030) set the standard of excellence by employing "troops of various races such as Turks, Khurasanis, Arabs, Hindus, [as well as] men of Ghur and Dailam."[37]

The benefits of such disparate groups in the military were twofold. Pitting one against another stirred up each group's racial pride so that when battle was joined "each race strove to preserve their name and honour, and fought the more zealously lest anyone should say that such-and-such race showed slackness in battle. Thus all races endeavored to surpass one another."[38] Another benefit was that fostering internal competition and division among various groups meant that no single one could become large enough to pose a threat to the ruler himself, yet another pragmatic reason for the Seljukids to drive off the Turkomans.

Some of the Turkomans migrated north and east; others migrated to the northwest and pursued their nomadic raiding practices along the Byzantine frontier. For the Byzantines, these Turkomans were nothing but bandits and genuinely threatened their territory and subjects. The Turkomans, on the other hand, legitimated their raiding and pillaging in eastern and central Anatolia as the righteous work of holy warriors (*ghazi*s) engaged in jihad against the Byzantines. After all, from the Turkomans' point of view, they were merely striving in the path of God (*jihad fi sabil Allah*) against the preferred infidel enemy of Islam since the days of Mu'awiya in the mid-seventh century. Things came to a head in 1071 as the Byzantine emperor Romanus Diogenes (r. 1068–71) led several Byzantine columns eastward to deal with this Turkish menace once and for all.

Already on campaign in Syria, Alp Arslan turned his forces north to come to the aid of his fellow Turkomans and fellow Muslims. A pitched battle between the two sides took place at Manzikert, near Lake Van, in the summer of 1071. Alp Arslan's forces were victorious and Romanus Diogenes was taken captive. He was ultimately ransomed and deposed. The Battle of Manzikert marks the beginnings of the process by which Anatolia became Turkey.

In 1095, Pope Urban II preached a sermon in Clermont, France, in which he called on the interminably feuding nobility of Western Europe to turn their energies to the cause of Christ and his Church. Urban was by no means the first to call on them to use their military skills in aide of their Byzantine

Seljukid Period horsemen, twelfth–thirteenth centuries. *Source:* David Nicolle, "Saljuq Arms and Armour in Art and Literature," 255.

Christian brothers who, since the Battle of Manzikert, were increasingly threatened by Muslim Turkish marauders in eastern and central Anatolia. In fact, Pope Gregory VII had proposed that he himself lead a force of some 50,000 men to liberate their Eastern brethren in 1074. More importantly, however, Urban called on the Frankish nobility to take up the cross of Christ and make an armed pilgrimage to Jerusalem in order to redeem their Lord's patrimony, which had been stolen by the infidel Saracens some four centuries earlier. By the summer of 1099, Jerusalem was in the hands of the Crusaders. Unfortunately for Pope Urban II, he died shortly after Jerusalem was taken, but before word reached Western Europe.[39]

WARFARE IN THE ERA OF THE CRUSADES

In 1092, the Seljukid wazir, Nizam al-Mulk, was murdered by Nizari Isma'ilis (better known in the west as the Assassins). A month later, the Seljukid Sultan Malikshah died under suspicious circumstances. Two years later, "the year of the death of caliphs and commanders," brought with it the death of al-Mustansir, the Fatimid caliph in Egypt, and his wazir Badr al-Jamali. In Baghdad, the Abbasid caliph al-Muqtadi died in 1094 as well.[40] Consequently, Egypt, Syria, and Iraq were largely devoid of effective political leadership during the last decade of the eleventh century. While there is no evidence that the Franks had been briefed on the disarray in Syria when they responded to Urban's call, they could not have arrived at a more auspicious time.

There is evidence that some Syrian preachers and scholars decried the loss of Jerusalem and even undertook missions to Baghdad for assistance

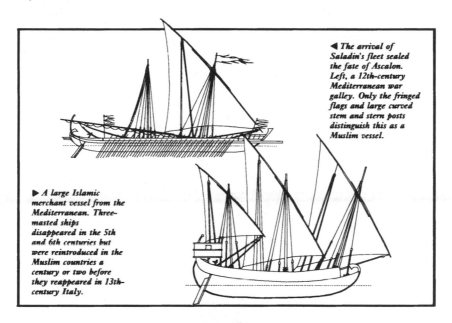

◀ *The arrival of Saladin's fleet sealed the fate of Ascalon. Left, a 12th-century Mediterranean war galley. Only the fringed flags and large curved stem and stern posts distinguish this as a Muslim vessel.*

▶ *A large Islamic merchant vessel from the Mediterranean. Three-masted ships disappeared in the 5th and 6th centuries but were reintroduced in the Muslim countries a century or two before they reappeared in 13th-century Italy.*

Ships. *Source:* David Nicolle, *Hattin 1187*, 81.

from the Abbasid caliphs and Seljukid sultans. But neither was in a position to respond favorably to such requests. It was not until 1144 when a Turkish commander named Zengi (d. 1146) captured the Frankish city of Edessa (ostensibly on behalf of his Abbasid overlords) that the first successful Muslim counteroffensive against the Franks took place. His son Nur al-Din (d. 1174), after occupying Damascus in 1154, was able to unite the Muslim controlled areas of Syria and undertook his own jihad against the Franks as well as against the domestic enemies of Sunni Islam—the Shiʻi Fatimids in Egypt and their coreligionists in Syria. But his successor and Kurdish protégé, Saladin (d. 1193), was finally able to bring an end to the Fatimid Caliphate in Cairo in 1171. He also dealt the Franks a decisive defeat at the Battle of Hattin in 1187 and retook Jerusalem shortly thereafter.

Under Saladin's leadership, Egypt and Syria were ruled as a family confederation, with members of his extended family administering various provinces throughout the realm. Named after Saladin's father, Ayyub (Job), the Ayyubid family confederation ruled Syria and Egypt from Saladin's death in 1193 until the Egyptian branch of the family was overthrown in 1250 by some of its mamluks. Ten years later, the Mamluk Sultanate defeated the Mongols at Ayn Jalut in Palestine, absorbed the Ayyubid holdings in Syria, and began the process of driving the Franks from the region. Had such an effective military regime been in place in the late eleventh century, it is doubtful that the Frankish knights would have

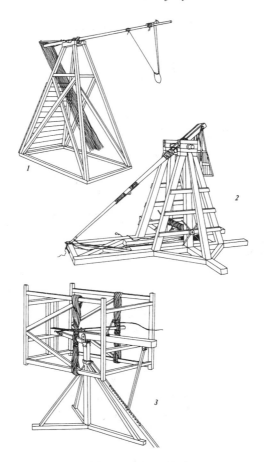

Siege weapons. *Source:* David Nicolle, *Hattin 1187,* 4.

reached Jerusalem, let alone succeeded in their mission to reclaim their Lord's patrimony from the Saracens in 1099.

While the styles of weapons varied according to region and time period, the warriors of the Crusader era generally employed many of the same types of weapons used during the first Islamic centuries—coats of mail, helmets, shields, swords, spears, lances, knives, iron maces, lassos, bows, arrows, and *naft* (or Greek fire). Although the Fatimid navy in Egypt was able to acquit itself fairly well in the early twelfth century, there was essentially no naval resistance to the Franks from Syria.[41] A century later, however, Saladin's navy proved essential to his victory at Ashkelon.

In the end, what distinguished the Muslim forces from the Franks during the Crusader era was the absolutely crucial role of Muslim cavalry forces (both freeborn and mamluk regiments) and the Muslims' improved techniques of siege warfare.[42] Moreover, the changed international political realities in the wake of the establishment of the Mamluk Sultanate and the Mongol defeat at Ayn Jalut allowed Baybars (r. 1260–77) and his successors to pursue a more active policy of extirpation of the Franks, in contrast to the more accommodationist policies of their Ayyubid predecessors. For reasons of space, this discussion will be limited to Saladin's victory against the Franks at Hattin and Jerusalem (1187); the very brief tenure of Shajar al-Durr, one of the few Muslim women who held real political authority in the medieval Islamic world (1250); and the emergence of the Mamluk Sultanate in Egypt and Syria.

SALADIN, SHAJAR AL-DURR, AND THE MAMLUK SULTANATE

Saladin's cavalry numbered some 12,000 with possibly the same number of irregulars at the Battle of Hattin on July 4, 1187. The Franks are said to have mustered roughly the same numbers, maybe even more. Saladin was clearly the better commander that day as he maneuvered the fractious Franks into unfavorable conditions on the plain of Hattin overlooking the northwestern shores of the Sea of Galilee. According to Ibn al-Athir (d. 1233), as the battle commenced,

[t]he Muslim archers sent up clouds of arrows like thick swarms of locusts, killing many of the Frankish horses. The Franks, surrounding themselves with their infantry, tried to fight their way toward Tiberias in the hope of reaching water, but Saladin realized their objective and forestalled them by planting himself and his army in the way. He himself rode up and down the Muslim lines encouraging and restraining his troops when necessary. The whole army obeyed his command and respected his prohibitions. One of his young mamluks led a terrifying charge on the Franks and performed prodigious feats of valour until he was overwhelmed by numbers and killed, when all the Muslims charged the enemy lines and almost broke through, slaying many Franks in the process.... One of the volunteers set fire to the dry grass that covered the ground; it took fire and the wind carried the heat and smoke down on the enemy.[43]

Trapped, the Franks attacked, but Saladin's forces held their ground. Later, the Franks scrambled for the hill of Hattin in an attempt to seek refuge, but no refuge was to be found that day. Hattin was an unqualified success for Saladin and an abject and utter defeat for the Franks. It was also an opportunity for Saladin to taste revenge against his nemesis, Reynald of Chatillon, who had tried to attack Mecca and Medina, had plundered the pilgrimage caravan of Saladin's sister, and had violated numerous truces. After the battle, Saladin had King Guy and Reynald brought to his tent. He gave King Guy some water, who in turn shared it with Reynald. Needless to say, Saladin did not approve, and said, "This godless man did not have my permission to drink, and will not save his life that way." Saladin then turned on Reynald, "casting his crimes in his teeth and enumerating his sins. Then he rose and with his own hand cut off the man's head." Saladin spared King Guy, but the Knights of the Temple and the Knights of the Hospital were rounded up and given the opportunity to accept Islam or die; 200 of them rejected the offer and were beheaded.[44]

On July 5 Tiberias surrendered; Acre surrendered on July 9 and Ashkelon on September 5. By the end of September all the ports south of Tripoli had fallen except for Tyre, the sole location where reinforcements from Europe could be received. Many of the outposts in the hinterland had surrendered as well. Saladin's next target was Jerusalem. While Jerusalem surrendered easily enough on October 2, and Saladin was hailed as a conquering hero of Islam, his decision to move against Jerusalem rather than the strategically more important Tyre proved to be a major blunder. Nevertheless, things looked particularly bleak for the Franks as Saladin and his forces laid siege to Tyre in November 1187. Unfortunately for Saladin, his irregular troops decided that the summer campaigning season had come to an end (a recurring problem for medieval Muslim commanders of all stripes). They returned home, and shortly thereafter, Frankish ships reinforced Tyre with men and matériel. Although they were unable to retake the holy city of Jerusalem, the Frankish states were given new life. A golden opportunity was lost, for had Saladin been able to continue his siege of Tyre, the Franks may well have been driven from Syria by the end of the twelfth century rather than at the end of the thirteenth.

While Saladin's Ayyubid successors did have some success against the Franks, the nearly six decades after his death were characterized by a series of shifting alliances and accommodations among various Ayyubid and Frankish princes. Not until the Egyptian branch of the Ayyubid house was overthrown in 1250, and Qutuz's (r. 1259–60) forces defeated the Mongols at Ayn Jalut on September 3, 1260, did the policy of accommodation with the Franks begin to change.[45] The transition from the Ayyubid family confederation to the Mamluk Sultanate took a good decade to complete. One of the more fascinating aspects of this transition is the brief tenure of Shajar al-Durr, the widow of Sultan al-Salih Ayyub, as Sultana in her own right.

Overcome by illness, Sultan al-Salih Ayyub died in the midst of Louis IX's invasion of Egypt on November 21, 1249. His only living son and successor, Turanshah, was in northern Iraq as governor of Hisn Kayfa at the time. Shajar al-Durr kept her husband's death a secret from all save his commander-in-chief, Fakhr al-Din ibn al-Shaykh, and a few others. They held things together until Turanshah reached Egypt to assume the Sultanate. By the time he arrived on February 23, 1250, Fakhr al-Din had been killed in battle with the Franks and things looked bleak. He had, however, arrived in time to lead a victory over Louis IX and even captured the French king on April 6. In a "last will and testament" letter to Turanshah, the sick Sultan al-Salih Ayyub advised his son to stay away from alcohol and to be generous to his father's mamluks. As sons often do, Turanshah chose to ignore his father's wise counsel and sought to replace his father's mamluks with those of his own. In the end, his disloyalty cost him his life as his father's mamluks killed him on May 2, 1250. But what to do now that al-Salih Ayyub and his only surviving son were gone?

Enter Shajar al-Durr, who became Sultana in May 1250, one of the few Muslim women who held real political authority in pre-modern Islamic history.[46] The minting of coins (*sikka*) and the invocation of the ruler's name in the Friday sermon (*khutba*) were two of the most important symbols of political legitimacy in the medieval Islamic world. Hence, Sultana Shajar al-Durr's name was invoked in Friday sermons and coins were minted in her name. The coins referred to her as the Queen of the Muslims; they also declared her fealty to the Abbasid caliph in Baghdad. However, her sultanate was neither popular in Cairo nor was it acceptable to the caliph, who offered to send a man from Baghdad to rule the country if none could be found in Egypt. So in July 1250, she abdicated in favor of her new husband, al-Salih Ayyub's former food-taster, Izz al-Din Aybak al-Turkomani, chosen primarily because of his apparent malleability. Five days later, he was replaced by an Ayyubid child prince, al-Ashraf Musa, whom he served as *atabeg;* that is, as guardian of the prince and as commander of the army. It would take another decade and the defeat of the Mongols at Ayn Jalut before the Mamluk Sultanate was firmly established in Egypt and Syria under Sultan Baybars and his successors.

As R. Stephen Humphreys has demonstrated, Sultan Baybars (r. 1260–77) aggressively pursued a remarkably effective, multifaceted foreign policy to achieve his goals of fending off renewed Mongol incursions and removing the Franks from Syria.[47] He cultivated good relations with the Golden Horde branch of the Mongol empire in Russia, which controlled the reservoir for the regime's new mamluk recruits and also served as a counter to the Mongol Il-Khans in Iraq and Iran with whom the Golden Horde and the Mamluks were frequently at war.[48] He concluded a commercial treaty with Genoa, whose merchants held a near monopoly on trade in the Black Sea. The treaty supplied the Mamluk Sultanate with new recruits who could no longer be transported by land through Il-Khan territory, but it had the added benefit of strengthening the Genoese in their competition with the Venetians. In addition, he established a commercial treaty with the Byzantine Empire, which controlled access from the Black Sea to Alexandria via Constantinople. It too had an added benefit for the Mamluk Sultanate in that it served as a counter to the Papacy's efforts to support the Franks in Palestine. In the end, the Mamluks were able to drive the Franks from Acre in 1291, thus ending nearly two centuries of Frankish presence in the Near East. By the end of the twelfth century the Il-Khans had converted to Islam and by the 1320s were no longer a major threat to the Mamluk regime in Syria and Egypt.

NOTES

1. On jihad in medieval Islamic history, see Rudolph Peters's collection of primary texts in translation, *Jihad in Classical and Modern Islam* (Princeton, NJ: Markus Wiener, 1996), especially chapters 1–5. See also Ella Landau Tasseron, "Jihad," in *Encyclopaedia of the Qur'an* (Leiden: Brill, 2003), 3:35–43; Reuven Firestone, *Jihad: The Origin of Holy War in Islam* (New York: Oxford University Press, 1999); and David Cook, "Muslim Apocalyptic and *Jihad*," *Jerusalem Studies in Arabic and Islam*

20 (1996): 66–104. Carole Hillenbrand provides a nuanced treatment of jihad in the context of the Crusades in her *The Crusades: Islamic Perspectives* (Edinburgh: Edinburgh University Press, 1999), 89–256. See also Emmanuel Sivan, *L'Islam et la Croisade* (Paris, 1968). On modern reinterpretations of jihad, see Emmanuel Sivan, *Radical Islam: Medieval Theology and Modern Politics* (New Haven, CT: Yale University Press, 1985); Gilles Kepel, *Jihad: The Trail of Political Islam* (Cambridge: Harvard University Press, 2002); and Malise Ruthven, *A Fury for God: The Islamist Attack on America* (Granta Books, 2002).

2. The ninth chapter of the Qur'an is known as "The Chapter of Repentance [*surat al-tawba*]," and is the only chapter of the Qur'an's 114 chapters that does not begin with the phrase, "In the name of God the Merciful, the Compassionate." Some scholars have argued that this is because of its rather grim content.

3. Fred M. Donner examines the relevant Qur'anic passages on Jews and Christians in "From Believers to Muslims: Confessional Self-Identity in the Early Islamic Community," in *The Byzantine and Early Islamic Near East*, vol. 4, *Patterns of Communal Identity*, ed. Lawrence I. Conrad (Princeton, NJ: Darwin Press, forthcoming).

4. See Suleiman A. Mourad and James E. Lindsay, "Rescuing Syria from the Infidels: The Contribution of Ibn 'Asakir of Damascus to the *Jihad* Campaign of Sultan Nur al-Din," in *Crusades* 6 (2007): 37–55.

5. For accounts of Muhammad's wars with the Meccans and others after his *hijra*, see Alfred Guillaume, trans., *The Life of Muhammad: A Translation of Ibn Ishaq's Sirat Rasul Allah* (Oxford: Oxford University Press, 1955); al-Tabari, *The History of al-Tabari*, vol. 7, *The Foundation of the Community*, trans. M. V. McDonald and annotator W. Montgomery Watt (Albany: State University of New York Press, 1987); al-Tabari, *The History of al-Tabari*, vol. 8, *The Victory of Islam*, trans. Michael Fishbein (Albany: State University of New York Press, 1997); W. Montgomery Watt, *Muhammad at Medina* (Oxford: Clarendon Press, 1956); Hugh N. Kennedy, *The Prophet and the Age of the Caliphates: The Islamic Near East from the Sixth to the Eleventh Century* (New York: Longman, 1986); and F. E. Peters, *Muhammad and the Origins of Islam* (Albany: State University of New York Press, 1994).

6. See pp. 143–144 of this book.

7. My discussion of warfare, weapons, and tactics in the early Islamic history is based largely on Robert Elgood, ed., *Islamic Arms and Armour* (London: Scholar Press, 1979); Fred M. Donner, *The Early Islamic Conquests* (Princeton, NJ: Princeton University Press, 1981); Hugh N. Kennedy, *The Armies of the Caliphs: Military and Society in the Early Islamic State* (New York: Routledge, 2001); and the many works of David Nicolle (see the "Jihad and Military History" section in "Suggestions for Further Reading").

8. See pp. 47–48 of this book.

9. Guillaume, trans., *The Life of Muhammad*, 299.

10. When the Byzantines hurled Greek fire or "liquid fire" onto the ships of their enemies it burst into flames on contact. Since it was believed that this liquid fire could not be extinguished and even burned on water, it sowed panic and dread among the Byzantines' enemies. See the works of David Nicolle listed in the "Jihad and Military History" section in "Suggestions for Further Reading" for Angus McBride's detailed illustrations of arms and armor of the period.

11. Kennedy, *The Armies of the Caliphs*, 169–70.

12. Guillaume, trans., *The Life of Muhammad*, 298–99.

13. Kennedy, *The Armies of the Caliphs*, 173.

14. Guillaume, trans., *The Life of Muhammad*, 587.

15. Ibid., 587, 588, 591, 592. The family of Muharriq refers to Amr ibn Hind, the ruler of Hira west of the Euphrates in southern Iraq. According to Qur'an 34:10–11, David was the first to whom God taught the skills of iron working. "On David We bestowed our bounty. We said: 'Mountains, and you birds, echo his songs of praise. 'We made hard iron pliant to him. 'Make coats of mail and measure their links with care. Do what is right: I am watching over all your actions. '"

16. Kennedy, *The Armies of the Caliphs*, 183.

17. Guillaume, trans., *The Life of Muhammad*, 374.

18. Ibid., 374. *Lysistrata* is a play by the Greek playwright Aristophanes, in which the women of ancient Athens prevailed on their husbands to stop making war in Peloponnesia by withholding sex from them.

19. Guillaume, trans., *The Life of Muhammad*, 385.

20. For multiple accounts of the Battle of the Camel, see al-Tabari, *The History of al-Tabari*, vol. 16, *The Community Divided*, trans. Adrian Brockett (Albany: State University of New York Press, 1997).

21. For a wide-ranging analysis of Aisha in medieval Islamic literature, see Denise A. Spellberg, *Politics, Gender, and the Islamic Past: The Legacy of 'A'isha bint Abi Bakr* (New York: Columbia University Press, 1994). See also the earlier study by Nabia Abbott, *'A'isha: The Beloved of Mohammed* (Chicago: University of Chicago Press, 1942).

22. On the civil war between al-Amin and al-Ma'mun, see al-Tabari, *The History of al-Tabari*, vol. 31, *The War between Brothers*, trans. Michael Fishbein (Albany: State University of New York Press, 1992). See also Hugh N. Kennedy, *The Early Abbasid Caliphate* (London: Croom Helm, 1981), 135–63; and Tayeb El-Hibri, *Reinterpreting Islamic Historiography: Harun al-Rashid and the Narrative of the Abbasid Caliphate* (New York: Cambridge University Press, 1999), 59–94.

23. Spellberg, *Politics, Gender, and the Islamic Past*, 138.

24. On the mamluk system in general, see R. Stephen Humphreys, "Mamluk," in *The Dictionary of the Middle Ages* (New York: Scribner, 1982–1989), 8:68–69; David Ayalon, "Mamluk," in *Encyclopaedia of Islam*, New Edition, 12 vols. (Leiden: Brill, 1954–2004), 6:314–21; and Robert Irwin, *The Middle East in the Middle Ages: The Early Mamluk Sultanate, 1250–1382* (Carbondale: Southern Illinois University Press, 1986), 1–25. For a broad overview of slave elites in Islamic history, see the essays in *Slave Elites in the Middle East and Africa: A Comparative Study*, eds. Miura Toru and John Edward Philips (New York: Kegan Paul International, 2000). The most complete bibliography on mamluks in Islamic history is the searchable database of primary and secondary sources called *Mamluk Bibliography Online*, an ongoing project of the University of Chicago's Middle East Document Center—http://www.lib.uchicago.edu/e/su/mideast/mamluk/.

25. See especially Matthew Gordon, *The Breaking of a Thousand Swords: A History of the Turkish Military of Samarra*, A.H. *200–275/815–889* C.E. (Albany: State University of New York Press, 2001), which engages two earlier studies—Patricia Crone, *Slaves on Horses: The Evolution of the Islamic Polity* (New York: Cambridge University Press, 1980) and Daniel Pipes, *Slave Soldiers and Islam: The Genesis of a Military System* (New Haven, CT: Yale University Press, 1981).

26. See V. L. Ménage, "Devshirme," in *Encyclopaedia of Islam*, New Edition, 2:210–13.

27. Charles Pellat, trans., *The Life and Works of al-Jahiz* (Berkeley: University of California Press, 1969), 91–97.

28. Ibid., 94.

29. Jim Colville, trans., *Sobriety and Mirth: A Selection of the Shorter Writings of al-Jahiz* (London: Kegan Paul, 2002), 25–52.

30. For the statement attributed to Wahshi, "If I killed him [Musaylima], then I have killed the best man after the apostle [Hamza] and I have also killed the worst man [Musaylima]," see Guillaume, trans., *The Life of Muhammad*, 377. See a slightly different version in Colville, trans., *Sobriety and Mirth*, 27. Charles Pellat does not include this statement in his abridged translation of al-Jahiz's essay in *The Life and Works of al-Jahiz*, 195–198.

31. Colville, trans., *Sobriety and Mirth*, 35.

32. Ibid.

33. Everett K. Rowson, "Two Homoerotic Narratives from Mamluk Literature: al-Safadi's *Law'at al-shaki* and Ibn Daniyal's *al-Mutayyam*," in *Homoeroticism in Classical Arabic Literature*, eds. Jerry W. Wright and Everett K. Rowson (New York: Columbia University Press, 1997), 158–91. See also Robert Irwin, "'Ali al-Baghdadi and the Joy of Mamluk Sex," in *The Historiography of Islamic Egypt, c. 950–1800*, ed. Hugh N. Kennedy (Leiden: Brill, 2001), 45–57.

34. Cited in Clifford E. Bosworth, *The Ghaznavids: Their Empire in Afghanistan and Eastern Iran, 994–1040* (Beirut: Librairie du Liban, 1973), 209.

35. On the Seljukids, see pp. 19–21 of this book.

36. Hubert Darke, trans., *The Book of Government or Rules for Kings: The Siyar al-Mulk or Siyasat-nama of Nizam al-Mulk* (Richmond, Surrey: Curzon Press, 2002), 100.

37. Ibid., 100.

38. Ibid., 101.

39. On the Crusaders' activities in Europe and the Near East, see Jonathan Riley-Smith, *The Crusades: A Short History* (New Haven, CT: Yale University Press, 1987) and idem, ed., *The Oxford Illustrated History of the Crusades* (New York: Oxford University Press, 1995).

40. My discussion of the Crusader period in the Near East is based largely on Carole Hillenbrand's magisterial *The Crusades: Islamic Perspectives* (Edinburgh: Edinburgh University Press, 1999) and P. M. Holt, *The Age of the Crusades: The Near East from the Eleventh Century to 1517* (New York: Longman, 1986).

41. See Yaacov Lev, *State and Society in Fatimid Egypt* (Leiden: Brill, 1991), 93–121.

42. On the weapons of the Crusader period, see David Nicolle, *Arms and Armour of the Crusading Era, 1050–1350* (London: Greenhill Books, 1999); idem, *Saladin and the Saracens: Armies of the Middle East, 1100–1300* (London: Osprey Publishing, 1986); and Hillenbrand, *The Crusades: Islamic Perspectives*, 329–430. See also Paul Cheveddin, "The Invention of the Counterweight Trebuchet: A Study in Cultural Diffusion," *Dumbarton Oaks Papers* 54 (2000): 71–116.

43. Francesco Gabrieli, *Arab Historians of the Crusades* (New York: Dorset Press, 1989), 121.

44. Ibid., 124.

45. On the Ayyubids, see R. Stephen Humphreys, *From Saladin to the Mongols: The Ayyubids of Damascus, 1193–1260* (Albany: State University of New York Press, 1977).

46. On the assassination of Turanshah and the brief career of Shajar al-Durr, see Humphreys, *From Saladin to the Mongols*, 300–307; Irwin, *The Middle East in the Middle Ages*, 19–27; and L. Ammann, "Shadjar al-Durr," *Encyclopaedia of Islam*, New Edition, 9:176. See Fatima Mernissi, *The Forgotten Queens of Islam* (Minneapolis: University of Minneapolis Press, 1993), for other examples.

47. R. Stephen Humphreys, "Ayyubids, Mamluks, and the Latin East in the Thirteenth Century," *Mamluk Studies Review* 2 (1998): 1–17.

48. Reuven Amitai-Preiss, *Mongols and Mamluks: The Mamluk-Ilkhanid War, 1260–1281* (New York: Cambridge University Press, 1995).

4

CITIES

While the Islamic religion had its origins in the oases of western Arabia, what historians call Islamic civilization began to emerge in the new garrison towns established during the Islamic conquests of the seventh century, especially in Basra (est. 637) and Kufa (est. 638) in southern Iraq, and in Fustat (est. 642) in Egypt near where Cairo would be established in 969.[1] In the wake of the conquest of Syria, Muslim forces established camps at Ramle in central Palestine and at the old Ghassanid capital, al-Jabiya, in the Golan. However, both were quickly replaced by Damascus as the administrative center of Syria. Initially, these and other garrison towns were little more than military bases and administrative centers for the conquering forces. Over time they developed into full-fledged urban centers with governors, military commanders, soldiers and their families, mosques, markets, merchants, craftsmen, and scholars as well as religious strife, political dissent, beggars, gangs, and what we would call organized crime.

For reasons of space and in an attempt to provide a broad chronological framework for our discussion of daily life in the medieval Islamic world, the bulk of this chapter will be devoted to three major cosmopolitan centers—Damascus, Baghdad, and Cairo—and their respective provinces of Syria, Iraq, and Egypt. Whereas Damascus is one of the oldest continuously inhabited cities in the world, Baghdad (est. 762) and Cairo (est. 969) were founded as palace cities for new imperial dynasties—the Abbasids (750–1258) and Fatimids (909–1171), respectively. While these three capitals represent themes peculiar to the political and religious idiosyncrasies of their rulers and regions, they also represent more common and mundane themes of urban life in the Middle Ages whether in the early garrison settlements or in a host of other urban centers from Cordoba in the west to Delhi in the east.[2]

Daily life in the medieval Islamic world revolved around its markets and its mosques—two institutions essential to the hustle and bustle of daily life in every city and town. For it was in the local markets that goods were manufactured and food was bought and sold. In the major cities such as Damascus, Baghdad, Cairo, and others everything imaginable from all over the Abode of Islam and beyond could be found as well. The main congregational mosque—the center of official religious and political life—was always located within or next to a market. In those instances where congregational mosques were constructed in new garrison towns such as Basra and Kufa or in new palace cities such as Baghdad and Cairo, new markets soon sprang up adjacent to the principal gathering place for the faithful.

As we work our way through Syria, Iraq, and Egypt in this chapter considerable attention will be devoted to the markets of Damascus, Baghdad, and Cairo and how people went about their daily lives in these cities. What kinds of goods did they manufacture? What kinds of produce did they grow? What kind of money did they use? How did folks travel and transport goods from one city to another? How did Muslims, Christians, and Jews interact in these cities? What kinds of homes did people live in? What did they eat and drink? What kinds of irrigation techniques were employed in their agricultural hinterlands? But before we turn our attention to these themes, a note on some of the sources for this chapter is in order.

SOURCES

The sources for the early centuries of Islamic history pose a distinctive set of problems that we will not rehearse here.[3] However, once historians get past the first few centuries of Islamic history the sources are much more plentiful and provide a very good sense of daily life, at least public life, in the medieval Islamic world. In particular, modern historians are fortunate to have detailed accounts of travelers, geographers, gazetteers, and local historians that describe the physical layouts of Damascus, Baghdad, and Cairo, as well as many other towns and cities during the Middle Ages.[4] In addition we have the *fadaʾil al-buldan* (merits of places) literature, in which scholars brought together much of the available (often legendary) material on a given city or region with the expressed intent of extolling the merits of their hometowns or regions. Of particular interest for our purposes is the fascinating *fadaʾil al-quds* (merits of Jerusalem) and *fadaʾil al-sham* (merits of Syria) literature, which provide a window onto daily life, especially religious life in the Biblical Holy Land during the Islamic Middle Ages.[5]

Finally, another very rich source for daily life are the some 250,000 Hebrew documents in the Cairo Geniza. According to Jewish custom, documents on which the personal name of God is written should not be destroyed. Hence, the Egyptian Jewish community placed such documents in a storeroom (*geniza*) in the Ibn Ezra synagogue in Fustat until they were supposed to be buried. The documents from this particular geniza were never buried and were eventually discovered quite by accident in the nineteenth century. These documents (most of which date from 1002 to 1266) are particularly useful for understanding daily life among greater Cairo's Jewish community; however, as S. D. Goitein has so ably demonstrated, these documents can also be used to construct a very detailed picture of daily life in Egypt, the Mediterranean world, and beyond.[6]

As we explore the sacred as well as the profane in our investigation of daily life in Syria, Iraq, and Egypt we will draw heavily (but not exclusively) on the works of three men—the tenth-century Syrian geographer al-Muqaddasi (ca. 945–ca. 1000), the eleventh-century Persian traveler Naser-e Khosraw (d. ca. 1075), and the twelfth-century Andalusian traveler Ibn Jubayr (1145–1217), all of whom were educated men who traveled extensively throughout the Abode of Islam. It is difficult to ascertain whether their urge to travel was a result of fulfilling the ritual obligation to undertake the pilgrimage to Mecca or whether their desire to make the pilgrimage was rooted in their own wanderlust. Whatever their true motivations, al-Muqaddasi, Naser-e Khosraw, and Ibn Jubayr began their travels with the expressed intent of making the pilgrimage, and each left for posterity a detailed record of his travels. As one might expect, their respective professions and interests color what they thought important to record from their travels throughout the region.

The details of al-Muqaddasi's life are fairly sketchy.[7] Most of what we know about him is derived from his pioneering work in the fields of physical, economic, political, and human geography. We do know that he undertook the pilgrimage in 966 and spent the next 20 years traveling. As he criss-crossed the Islamic world from Morocco to the frontiers of Sind, he made the pilgrimage two more times—in 977 and 987. He is careful to record material praising the merits (*fada'il*) of each province and is fond of detailed descriptions of their topography and climate as well as the agricultural produce, manufactured goods, and items imported to and exported from their markets. As a native of Jerusalem (*Bayt al-Muqaddas* or *Bayt al-Maqdis*; hence the *nisba* al-Muqaddasi), his descriptions of his hometown and province and the province of Syria are especially detailed.[8]

The particulars of Naser-e Khosraw's life are scanty as well. We do know that in the fall of 1045 he had a dream that convinced him that he was on the wrong path. He left his career as a civil administrator in Khurasan and undertook a personal quest for truth, which involved making the pilgrimage to Mecca. His conversion to Isma'ilism probably coincided with his desire to undertake the pilgrimage, for although he eventually made it to Mecca, he took a circuitous route to the Hijaz. He avoided most of the major cities of his day (including Damascus) but visited many Isma'ili outposts along his journey. Of particular concern for our purposes are his sojourns in Cairo, the capital of the Isma'ili Fatimid caliphate, and Jerusalem, which was nominally under Fatimid control at the time. In addition, Naser-e Khosraw's civil administrator's eye for detail resulted in an account full of meticulous descriptions of the markets, civil infrastructure, and public ceremonies he observed during his seven-year trip.[9]

Although Ibn Jubayr's journey only lasted two years, he covered far more territory than did Naser-e Khosraw. As was the case with al-Muqaddasi and Naser-e Khosraw, Ibn Jubayr's sojourns in Syria, Iraq, and Egypt were linked to the purpose of his pilgrimage. He departed from his home in Granada in February 1183, sailed across the Mediterranean to the port of Alexandria in Egypt, and traveled down the Nile to Cairo and eventually to the Egyptian Red Sea port of Aydhab. He then crossed the Red Sea with his fellow pilgrims to the west Arabian port of Jiddah on his way to Mecca. He arrived in Mecca in September 1183, where he waited until the annual pilgrimage commenced in mid-March 1184. After undertaking the pilgrimage, Ibn Jubayr then traveled northeast across the Arabian Peninsula to Baghdad and up the Tigris to Mosul. He then traveled west to Aleppo in northern Syria and south to Damascus where he spent four months (July to October 1184).

He then traveled to the port of Acre, which he departed in October 1184, and sailed westward across the Mediterranean. After a number of detours along the way, he finally reached his home in Granada in May 1185. Although Ibn Jubayr's avoidance of Jerusalem may simply have been a case of his desire to reach home after an already long and arduous trip, it may have had more to do with the fact that in 1184, Jerusalem was still the capital of the Crusader kingdom. The invocation with which Ibn Jubayr begins his brief description of Acre leaves no doubt as to his sentiments towards the Crusaders, "May God destroy (the Christians in) it and restore it (to the Muslims)."[10] Unfortunately from Ibn Jubayr's point of view, since the Crusaders controlled many of the port cities along the Syrian coast at the time, he had little choice but to either depart from a Crusader port or make the long overland trek to the port of Alexandria.

SYRIA AND DAMASCUS

As the administrative center of Syria after the initial conquests in the 630s and as the seat of the Umayyad caliphate (661–750), Damascus oversaw the consolidation and continued expansion of the Islamic empire and the development of many of the administrative policies and institutions that would be employed by the Umayyads' successors. With the conclusion of the first civil war (656–61) and Mu'awiya's consolidation of his position in Syria, Islamic expansion was renewed—in Iran to the east as

The Dome of the Rock, Jerusalem, ca. 1870. *Source:* The Middle East Documentation Center, The University of Chicago.

well as in North Africa and Spain in the west. During this early period, the Umayyads also initiated a number of policies to consolidate their administrative control over the new empire. Most notable are the reforms undertaken by Abd al-Malik (r. 685–705) to issue a distinctive currency and to establish Arabic as the principal administrative language of the regime. It was under Abd al-Malik's direction that the Dome of the Rock in Jerusalem was constructed as a symbol that the new Islamic regime had permanently replaced that of the Byzantines. Abd al-Malik's son, al-Walid (r. 705–15), continued with this theme as he transformed the Cathedral of St. John the Baptist in Damascus into the great Umayyad Mosque in the center of the city. He also refurbished and rebuilt Muhammad's mosque in Medina.

Throughout the Middle Ages and even until modern times, nearly every traveler's account of his sojourn in Syria describes at considerable length the architectural wonders of the Dome of the Rock and the Umayyad Mosque as well as the beauty, geographical diversity, and agricultural bounty of the province as a whole. By the time the Andalusian traveler Ibn Jubayr arrived in Damascus on 5 July 1184, the Umayyad caliphs had been out of office for more than four centuries. However, the Dome of the Rock in Jerusalem and the Umayyad Mosque in Damascus remained enduring testimonies to nearly a century of Umayyad rule from Damascus. What struck Ibn Jubayr immediately upon his arrival in Damascus, however,

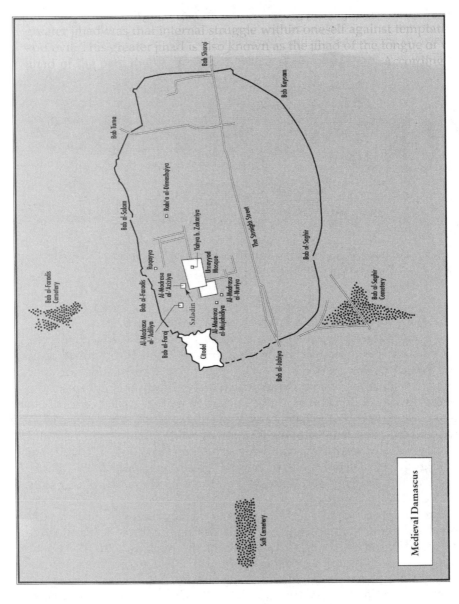

Medieval Damascus. *Source:* Adapted from Meri, *The Cult of Saints among Muslims and Jews in Medieval Syria.*

The Umayyad Mosque, Damascus, ca. 1865. *Source:* The Middle East Documentation Center, The University of Chicago.

was not so much her monumental architecture, but the radiant beauty of her gardens.

An account of the city of Damascus—may God Most High protect it. She is the paradise of the Orient, the place where dawned her gracious and radiant beauty, the seal of the lands of Islam where we have sought hospitality, and the bride of the cities we have observed. She is garnished with the flowers of sweet-scented herbs, and bedecked in the brocaded vestments of gardens. In the place of beauty she holds a sure position, and on her nuptial chair she is most richly adorned.[11]

Ibn Jubayr continues in the spirit of the well-established *fada'il al-sham* (merits of Syria) literary tradition and cites a number of Damascus's virtues—that Mary and Jesus took refuge there from Herod (as opposed to the New Testament account in which they fled to Egypt, Matthew 2:13–18), its "superfluity of water, so that it yearns even for a drought," and its green Ghuta (the lands surrounding the city) that stretch "as far as the eye can see, and wherever you look on its four sides its ripe fruit hold the gaze."[12] For Ibn Jubayr, these and many other merits of Damascus vindicate the truthfulness of those who say, "If Paradise is on earth then Damascus without a doubt is in it. If it is in the sky, then it vies with it and shares its glory."[13]

Ibn Jubayr then turns his attention to "one of the most celebrated mosques of the world," located in the center of the city.[14] Initially constructed in 375 as the Cathedral of St. John the Baptist by Emperor Theodosius I, the church had long been a place of veneration and pilgrimage for Christians, since the main building housed the tomb of John the Baptist. In the early 700s, al-Walid ibn Abd al-Malik (r. 705–15) appropriated the Cathedral and transformed it into a congregational mosque symbolizing Umayyad and Islamic supremacy. However, in the years between the Islamic conquest of Damascus (635) and al-Walid's reign, the Cathedral of St. John the Baptist had served as a place of worship for both the majority local Christian population and the relatively few Islamic forces.

Legend has it that the early Islamic armies conquered Damascus from the west and the east. Abu Ubaydah ibn al-Jarrah (the general in charge of the conquest of Syria) had made peace with the city's Christians prior to entering the city and the church from the west. However, Khalid ibn al-Walid (hero of the *Ridda* Wars and early Islamic conquests) had made no such peace and conquered the city and the church from the east. Henceforth, the eastern part of the cathedral belonged to the Muslims; the western part to the Christians. The cathedral's gradual transition to cathedral/mosque and then to mosque illustrates the degree to which Syria's early Muslim rulers were required to accommodate the majority local Christian population until their own position was solidified by Abd al-Malik and his son, al-Walid.

As one might expect, Ibn Jubayr's account of al-Walid's construction of the new cathedral mosque paints Islam and al-Walid in the best possible light. According to Ibn Jubayr, al-Walid initially asked the Christians for the church in exchange for compensation. When they refused his generous offer, he seized the building by force and razed it. When he began to rebuild it anew as a mosque, al-Walid wrote to the "king of Rum at Constantinople ordering him to send twelve thousand craftsmen from his country, offering threats in case he should delay."[15] Of course, the Byzantine Emperor submissively obeyed the caliph and complied. The details of this story have long been disputed, especially the nature of the cathedral's joint use and whether the Christians were fairly compensated for it or whether it was seized by force. Whatever the actual truth of the details, al-Walid's mosque in Damascus is an impressive example of early Islamic monumental architecture. It soon became an object of veneration and pilgrimage for Muslims of the Middle Ages and remains so to this day.[16] Subsequent to al-Walid's transformation, it took on even greater importance as an Islamic pilgrimage site because the head of al-Husayn ibn Ali (the prophet Muhammad's martyred grandson) was buried in the eastern side of the courtyard after he was killed at Karbala, Iraq, in 680.[17]

While the Syria of the medieval Muslim geographers and travelers included the modern state of Syria, it also included the modern states of Lebanon, Jordan, Israel, and the Palestinian territories of the West Bank

Interior of the Umayyad Mosque, Damascus, ca. 1870. *Source:* The Middle East
Photograph Archive, The University of Chicago.

and Gaza Strip—that is, everything north of the western Arabian Peninsula. In addition, they rarely used the word *Syria* to describe the region;
rather, they generally referred to it as *al-Sham.* Al-Muqaddasi explains the
meaning of *al-Sham:*

It has been said that Syria is called "Shâm" because it lies on the left of the Ka'bah,
and also because those who journey thither (from the Hijaz) bear to the *left* or
north; or else it may be because there are in Syria so many Beauty-spots, such as
we call *Shâmât*—red, white, and black—(which are the fields and gardens held to
resemble the moles on a beauty's face).[18]

The rather mundane directional etymology of *al-Sham* is certainly correct.
Nevertheless, the fact that al-Muqaddasi takes the trouble to include his
fanciful "beauty-spot" etymology is indicative of the lengths that scholars
were willing to go in order to praise the merits of their home provinces or
cities. That is not to say that Syria was devoid of beauty spots. In fact, as
al-Muqaddasi, Naser-e Khosraw, Ibn Jubayr, and others described at great
length, Syria was particularly blessed with verdant gardens and abundant
agricultural produce.

Al-Muqaddasi divides the region of Syria into four north-south zones with brief descriptions of its land, water resources, and major towns and cities: 1) The first zone is comprised of the plains along the Mediterranean coast, "the sandy tracts following one another, and alternating with the cultivated land." The major cities include the coastal port cities of Ashkelon, Jaffa, Acre, Tyre, Sidon, Beirut, and Tripoli as well as Ramle, roughly 10 miles inland. 2) East of the coastal plain is the "mountain-country, well wooded, and possessing many springs, with frequent villages and cultivated fields." The major towns of this zone range from Jerusalem and Nablus in the south to Antioch in the north. 3) East of the second zone is the Jordan Valley "wherein are found many villages and streams, also palm-trees, well cultivated fields, [bananas], and indigo plantations." The major towns of the Jordan Valley include Jericho, Beit Shean, Tiberias, and Baniyas. 4) East of the third zone there are the mountains that border the Arabian Desert that reaches to the north of the Fertile Crescent. Despite its bleak climate, "it has many villages, with springs of water and forests of trees." The main towns along the edge of the desert include Amman, Damascus, Hims (Emesa), Tadmur (Palmyra), and Aleppo, all of which benefit from springs or rivers that flow down the eastern slopes of the mountains and empty into the desert.[19]

After describing Syria's four zones, al-Muqaddasi then turns his attention to Syria's climate, which is generally temperate, but because of its mountains and valleys it is also subject to the extremes of bitter cold and debilitating heat. Ba'alabakk in the mountains of Lebanon qualifies as the coldest place in Syria, while the Jordan Valley ranks as the hottest. In the tenth century, al-Muqaddasi could not have known that the Dead Sea, just south of Jericho in the Jordan valley, is the lowest place on the planet (1,349 feet below sea level). However, he was well aware that the Jordan Valley rift stretched south past the Hijaz and that it was a "Wâdy of heat and of palm-trees."[20]

As a good geographer al-Muqaddasi is rather fond of lists. A list of particular importance for our purposes is his list of the agricultural bounty and other goods produced in Syria. For it is from his list (arranged according to region and town) that we can know what people ate in tenth-century Syria and what they manufactured and sold in their local markets. Many of these foodstuffs and manufactured goods were purchased by merchants and other middlemen for sale in Damascus, but also in the markets of Cairo and Baghdad. Some may have even been purchased by long-distance traders for sale in the markets of Cordoba in Andalusia, Isfahan in Iran, and even Constantinople, the capital of the Byzantine Empire.

Al-Muqaddasi's list of Jerusalem's produce is the longest and most detailed. As one might expect, some of his hometown's produce is celebrated, excellent, and without equal.

From Jerusalem come cheeses, cotton, the celebrated raisins of the species known as 'Ainûnî and Dûrî, excellent apples, bananas—which same is the fruit in the form of a cucumber, but when the skin is peeled off, the interior is not unlike the water-melon, only finer flavored and more luscious—also pine-nuts of the kind called 'Kuraish-bite,' and their equal is not found elsewhere; further mirrors, lamp-jars, and needles.[21]

Elsewhere, al-Muqaddasi reports that Palestine was known for olives, dried figs, raisins, the carob-fruit, textiles of mixed silk and cotton, soap, and kerchiefs; Jericho for excellent indigo; Amman for grain, lamb, and honey; Tiberias for carpet stuffs, paper, and cloth; Beit Shean for indigo, dates, and rice; Tyre for sugar, glass beads, as well as cut and blown glass vessels; Aleppo for cotton, clothes, dried figs, dried herbs, and a red chalk called *al-maghrah* (that is, the mineral *Rubrica Sinopica*). Al-Muqaddasi's list for Damascus is fuller, though not as long as his list for his hometown. "From Damascus come all these: olive-oil fresh-pressed, the *Bal'īsiyyah* cloth, brocade, oil of violets of an inferior quality, brass vessels, paper, nuts, dried figs, and raisins."[22]

In addition to the wide variety of foodstuffs produced in Syria, al-Muqaddasi's list illustrates very nicely the types of local manufactured goods found in Syria—various types of textiles made from locally grown silk and cotton, soap, carpets, cotton paper, glassware, brass vessels, and *al maghrah*. Similar types of manufactured products dominated the lists of goods produced in Iraq and Egypt as well. Of particular importance for our purposes is the extensive presence of a range of textiles, cotton paper, and *al-maghrah*. Textiles were important staples of trade in the medieval Islamic world. Paper production exploded in the medieval Islamic world after the introduction of paper-making technology in the eighth century.[23] Finally, the red chalk called *al-maghrah* was thought to have curative powers for a range of liver disorders and is an example of the type of medicine employed in large part on the recommendation of Galen (d. A.D. 203) and other ancient medical practitioners whose works had been translated into Arabic between the eighth and tenth centuries under the patronage of the Abbasids.[24] In the medieval Islamic world, textiles, paper, and medicines were particularly attractive to long-distance traders because of their great value and the relative ease with which they were transported by ship as well as overland by camel caravan.[25]

IRAQ AND BAGHDAD

Despite their many successes, including extensive conquests in North Africa, Spain, Sind, and Central Asia, the Umayyad caliphate (661–750) was riddled with internal divisions by the 740s. In the end, the Umayyad house was toppled by a clandestine revolutionary movement, which operated in the name of "the approved one from the house" of Muhammad. During a Friday sermon in late October or early November 749, Abu l-Abbas Abd Allah ibn Muhammad al-Saffah publicly declared himself

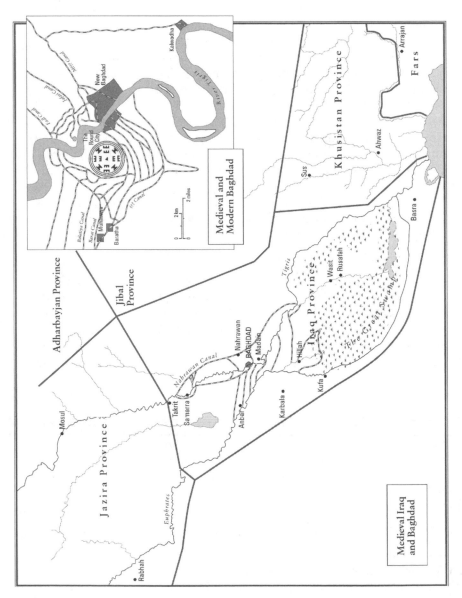

Medieval Baghdad and Iraq. *Source:* Adapted from Le Strange, *Baghdad during the Abbasid Caliphate.*

"the approved one from the house" in the main congregational mosque in Kufa in Iraq. Al-Saffah (r. 749–54) and his Abbasid successors based their claims principally on their kinship with Muhammad since they were descendants of his paternal uncle, Abbas.[26] In January 750, shortly after al-Saffah's public declaration, Abbasid forces defeated the last Umayyad caliph, Marwan II, at the battle of Zab, named after a northern tributary of the Tigris River where the battle took place. As Abbasid forces pursued Marwan through Syria and Egypt, Syrian and Egyptian towns submitted to Abbasid authority. In August 750, Marwan and his few remaining followers were finally caught and killed at Busir in southern Egypt. As was customary, Marwan's severed head was sent back to al-Saffah as proof that the mission had been accomplished.

Whereas Syria was the home province of the Umayyad caliphate and Damascus its capital, the Abbasids found their center of gravity in Iraq. While the political discontent of Kufa had proved advantageous during the revolutionary phase of the movement, al-Saffah's brother and successor, al-Mansur (r. 754–75), determined that the movement's consolidation phase required the establishment of a new palace city in more stable surroundings. Al-Mansur searched along the Tigris River for the ideal location from Jarjaraya in the south to Mosul in the north. In 762, he settled on the site of the ancient Persian village of Baghdad. According to one report preserved by al-Tabari (839–923), when al-Mansur settled on Baghdad, he said,

This is a good place for an army camp. Here's the Tigris, with nothing between us and China, and on it arrives all that the sea can bring, as well as provisions from the Jazira, Armenia and surrounding areas. Further, there is the Euphrates on which can arrive everything from Syria, al-Raqqah, and surrounding areas. The caliph therefore dismounted and pitched his camp on the Sarat Canal. He sketched a plan of the city and put an army commander in charge of each quarter.[27]

Elsewhere we are told that al-Mansur personally supervised the construction of his new round city, the layout of which is given in detail in al-Khatib al-Baghdadi's (1002–71) *History of Baghdad*.[28]

As the home of the ancient biblical prophets, Syria clearly had an advantage with respect to its unique sanctity. But Iraq was not without its own merits. After all, it was the birthplace of Abraham, and legend had it that after Noah's ark came to rest he founded the town of Thamanin in northern Mesopotamia. In addition, al-Tabari records a story about the founding of Baghdad that is reminiscent of the story in which a Christian monk found predictions of Muhammad's prophethood in his sacred books while Muhammad was still a young boy.[29] According to al-Tabari, after al-Mansur had decided on the site for his new city, he spotted a Christian monk nearby. Al-Mansur called to him and asked him if any of his books recorded that a city would be built at this site. The monk replied that they did indeed contain such a prediction and that "a certain Miqlas is to build it." Al-Mansur immediately exclaimed that Miqlas had been his nickname as a child to which the monk replied, "Then you're the man for it!"[30] In another version of this story, the monk replied that the person who would build the city in this spot would be a certain king named Abu Dawaniq, to which al-Mansur replied, "I, in fact, am Abu Dawaniq [The Penny Pincher]."[31]

A keen devotee of astrology, al-Mansur consulted his astrologers to ensure that the heavens agreed with the Christian monk's assessment. According to al-Khatib al-Baghdadi, after the city was completed al-Mansur had Ibrahim ibn Muhammad consult the stars. The astrologer obeyed and was pleased to inform his caliph that the horoscope was indeed auspicious; the city would be long-lived, it would be the home of a great civilization, and the world and its people would gravitate to it. Moreover, he said, "May God honour you, O Commander of the Faithful. I bring you good tidings of yet another gift indicated by the stars. No Caliph shall ever die in the city."[32] Needless to say, Ibrahim's pronouncement greatly pleased al-Mansur.

Al-Khatib al-Baghdadi further enhances Baghdad's prestige with a poem by the ninth-century poet Umara ibn Aqil, extolling Baghdad's unique merits (*fadaʾil*).

> Have you seen in all the length and breadth of the earth
> A city such as Baghdad? Indeed it is paradise on earth.
> Life in Baghdad is pure; its wood becomes verdant,
> While life outside of it is without purity or freshness.
> The lifespan in it is long; its food
> Is healthful; for some parts of the earth are more healthful than others.
> Its Lord has decided that no Caliph shall die
> In it; indeed he determines what he wishes for his creatures....[33]

By the time Ibn Jubayr arrived in Baghdad in May 1184, times had changed. Caliphs had died in Baghdad, and the Abbasid caliphs were little more than symbolic figureheads of the Sunni Islamic world. For all intents and purposes, a series of military dictatorships had kept them under house arrest since the Shiʿi Buyids conquered Baghdad in 945. The Seljukid sultanate, which had ruled Baghdad since 1055, was a mere shell of its former self and would be toppled 10 years after Ibn Jubayr's visit. According to Ibn Jubayr,

Baghdad is an ancient city, and although it has never ceased to be the capital of the ʿAbbaside Caliphate and the pivot of the Qurayshite, Hashimite, Imams' claims, most of its traces have gone, leaving only a famous name. In comparison with its former state, before misfortune struck it and the eyes of adversity turned towards it, it is like an effaced ruin, a remain washed out, or a statue of a ghost. It has no beauty that attracts the eye, or calls him who is restless to depart to neglect his business and to gaze. None but the Tigris which runs between its eastern and its western parts like a mirror shining between two frames, or like a string of pearls between two breasts. The city drinks from it and does not thirst, and looks into a polished mirror that does not tarnish. And the beauty of its women, wrought between in its waters and its air, is celebrated and talked of through the lands, so that if God does not give protection, there are the dangers of love's seductions.[34]

By the time Ibn Jubayr visited Baghdad, the single virtue that remained in the great city of al-Mansur, Harun al-Rashid, al-Ma'mun, and their successors was the life-giving Tigris. Since only God could provide refuge from the seductions of Baghdad's devastatingly beautiful women, it is not clear if Ibn Jubayr actually viewed them as a virtue. Nevertheless, it is clear that he certainly took great pleasure in viewing them. Ibn Jubayr has nothing more to say about Baghdad's women, but his description of the Tigris brings us to the issue of Iraq's geography and the importance of the Tigris and the Euphrates Rivers to the life of Iraq in the Middle Ages.

Unlike medieval Syria, which encompassed much more than the modern state of Syria, medieval Iraq was far smaller than modern Iraq. Medieval geographers divided the land between the Tigris and Euphrates Rivers (Mesopotamia) into two broad regions that roughly corresponded to the ancient designations of Lower and Upper Mesopotamia. Generally, when medieval geographers spoke of Iraq, they meant Lower Mesopotamia—the land between the Tigris and Euphrates Rivers south of the town of Tikrit. The territory between the two rivers north of Tikrit (Upper Mesopotamia) was generally referred to as the Jazira (The Island). Finally, the phrase, "the two Iraqs," was commonly used in the early period to refer to the new garrison towns of Basra, where the Tigris and the Euphrates met, and Kufa, on the Euphrates near the terminus of the ancient caravan route from the Hijaz. Ibn Jubayr took this very route from the Hijaz to Iraq in 1184. By Ibn Jubayr's day, when folks referred to "the two Iraqs" they ordinarily meant Lower Mesopotamia (Iraq) and Upper Mesopotamia (the Jazira).

The importance of the two rivers to the wealth and agricultural bounty of the Abbasid caliphate cannot be overstated, nor can the site of its capital, situated in the center of a bountiful country. Al-Muqaddasi records a variant of the story recorded by al-Tabari in which the locals who knew well the advantages of the region encouraged al-Mansur to build his city near the site of the ancient village. They encouraged him to divide his city into four districts—two on the eastern bank of the Tigris and two on the west. Not only could he live near palms and water, but if one district's crops failed or were late, another's would likely be bountiful. Finally, the city's location on the Sarat Canal would prove a boon to its economy since Baghdad would essentially become a wealthy and secure inland port city.

Provisions will be brought thither by the boats of the Euphrates, and by the caravans through the plains, even from Egypt and Syria. Hither, up from the sea will come the wares of China, while down the Tigris from Mosul will be brought goods from the Byzantines' lands. Thus shall thy city be safe standing between all these streams, and thine enemy shall not reach thee, except it be by a boat or by a bridge, and across the Tigris or the Euphrates.[35]

Not surprisingly, al-Muqaddasi's description of Iraq and the Jazira focuses on the Tigris and Euphrates Rivers and how they affected agriculture and daily life from the Sea of China (Persian Gulf) to their headwaters in Eastern Anatolia. According to al-Muqaddasi, the waters of the Tigris are "feminine, pleasant and excellent, favorable to jurists.... Indeed, two-thirds of the charm of Baghdad derives from this river."[36] The Euphrates, on the other hand, "is a masculine river: it has a hardness about it."[37] An ancient network of canals from the Euphrates had long watered the fertile black (*sawad*) agricultural lands between the rivers that gave Lower Mesopotamia its other name—the Sawad. In the region of Baghdad a network of four canals (including the Sarat Canal) connected the Euphrates to the Tigris. South of Kufa, the Euphrates winds its way toward Wasit where it begins to disperse into a vast marshland. The waters of the Tigris were used to irrigate the lands to its east, primarily by means of the ancient Nahrawan Canal that ran from Tikrit in the north and reconnected to the Tigris about 50 miles north of Wasit in the south. By the time the rivers converged at Basra, they had so intermixed with the sea tides and waste that drinking water had to be brought from upriver by boat. According to al-Muqaddasi, there was a saying that the water in Basra "is one-third seawater, one third tidewater, and one third sewage. This is because at ebb tide the canal banks are laid bare and people relieve their bowels there: then the tide coming in carries the excrement with it."[38]

Textiles, fish, luxuries, dates, and figs are what caught al-Muqaddasi's eye in Iraq. Basra was renowned for its silks and linens, 24 varieties of fish, for pearls, gems, antimony, cinnabar, verdigris, litharge of silver, and for 49 types of dates, which were exported along with henna, silk, essence of violet, and rose water. Kufa was renowned for silk turbans, essence of violet, and *azadh* dates; Hulwan for figs; Wasit for fish and draperies; Nu'maniyya for "superb garments and cloths of wool the colour of honey;" Baghdad for strong cloth, silks, fine apparel, and mats, as well as "shawls and turbans of special *yakanaki* fabrics."[39] The Jazira, whose climate is similar to northern Syria's, was a land of far greater agricultural diversity and was especially renowned for horses, soap, chains, leather straps, cotton, balance scales, and a preserve called *qubbayt* made from locust fruit and nuts. More specifically, Mosul was renowned for grains, honey, dried meats, coal, fats, cheese, honeydew, sumac, pomegranate seeds, pitch, iron, metal buckets, knives, arrows, salted fish, and chains; Nasibin for chestnuts, dried fruits, scales, inkstands, and rods for fulling carpets; Raqqa for soap, olive oil, and reed pens; Harran for *qubbayt*, honey, earthen wine jars, cotton, and balance scales; Mal'athaya for dairy products, coal, grapes, fresh fruit, cannabis seeds, hemp, and dried meat.[40]

Once again al-Muqaddasi's lists illustrate the importance of textiles (cotton, silks, linens, garments, fine apparel, and draperies) to the economy of the medieval Islamic world. Although al-Muqaddasi does not mention paper, the first paper mill in the Islamic world was established in Baghdad in 794–95 during the reign of Harun al-Rashid. Paper's production and its many uses spread from Baghdad throughout the region and ultimately, via Muslim Spain, to Europe.[41] Antimony, cinnabar, verdigris, and litharge of silver were minerals thought to have special medicinal powers. And finally, dates, salted fish, dried meats, dried fruits, and nuts were easily preserved and exported well beyond the regions where they were produced.

EGYPT AND CAIRO

In the wake of a clandestine revolutionary movement among the Berbers of North Africa, Ubayd Allah al-Mahdi proclaimed himself the first Fatimid Imam in 910.[42] Despite the similarities between the methodology and rhetoric of the Fatimids and that of the Abbasids, the Fatimid Imams belonged to the Isma'ili branch of Shi'i Islam, which was openly hostile to the Sunni Abbasid caliphate in Baghdad. In fact, the Fatimids' intent had long been to use North Africa as a staging ground for their ultimate goal of conquering Baghdad and unseating the Abbasids. To that end, and after several failed attempts, Fatimid forces finally conquered Egypt in 969. Almost immediately, the Fatimid general, Jawhar, began laying the foundations for the new palace city, al-Qahira (Cairo). The Fatimids never were able to overthrow the Abbasid caliphs, but under their tutelage Egypt and its new capital became one of the wealthiest and most important cosmopolitan way stations for international trade and culture in the Mediterranean world, southwest Asia, and the Indian Ocean. Saladin brought an end to the Fatimid caliphate in 1171, but Cairo and Egypt continued to flourish under his leadership and that of his Ayyubid successors (1171–1250) and of the Mamluk Sultans (1250–1517).

Egypt, too, played an important role in Islam's sacred past. It was the land of the evil Pharaoh and the beautiful Joseph. It was the land in which Moses performed many of his miracles; it was the land of prophets, the wilderness, and Mount Sinai; and the land where Mary took refuge with her son Jesus (a claim made by Damascus as well). Despite al-Muqaddasi's great affection for his home province, as far as he was concerned, "Syria, with all its greatness, is just a rural district of [Egypt]; and [the] Hijaz, with its inhabitants, depends on it."[43] There are a number of legends about the founding of al-Qahira and the etymology of its name. Unlike Baghdad, a Christian monk did not discover Cairo's founding predicted in his sacred texts. However, according to one legend astrologers were on hand at the groundbreaking.

According to the legend, Jawhar had staked out the perimeter of the city with wooden stakes and ropes with bells on them, but he wanted to wait to break ground until the astrologers determined the most propitious time. When a crow lit on one of the ropes, the workmen took the sound of the ringing bells as the signal to begin their work. Although the astrologers determined that Mars (al-Qahir, the Ruler) was in the ascendant—a

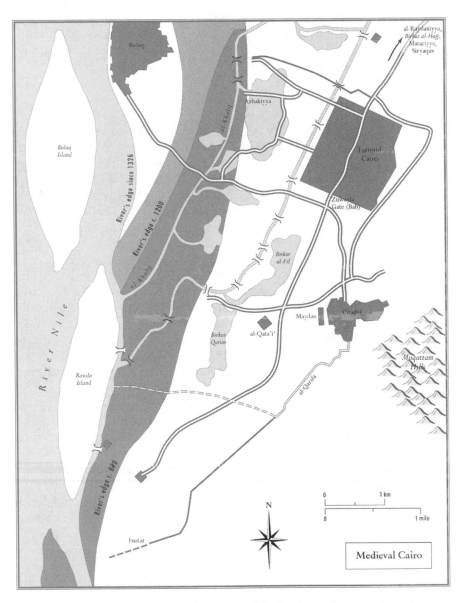

Medieval Cairo. *Source:* Adapted from Petry, *The Cambridge History of Egypt.*

Main entrance to the Azhar Mosque, Cairo, ca. 1870. *Source:* The Middle East Documentation Center, The University of Chicago.

bad sign—work commenced nevertheless. Another legend relates that the Fatimid Imam, al-Mu'izz, had instructed Jawhar before he left North Africa to build a new walled city and call it al-Qahira, for it would rule the world. According to yet another legend, the city was first called al-Mansuriyya (the Victorious; the name of the Fatimid capital in North Africa), but al-Mu'izz changed it to al-Qahira after his arrival four years later. Whatever the truth of these stories, Jawhar built the new Fatimid capital on a sandy plain north of Fustat where it was protected on the east by the Muqattam Hills and on the west by a canal (*khalij*) running along the east bank of the Nile.

Al-Muqaddasi has very little to say about Cairo, for it had not yet become the cosmopolitan city that Naser-e Khosraw would visit in 1047 nor the one Ibn Jubayr would see in 1183.

Courtyard of the Azhar Mosque, Cairo, ca. 1870. *Source:* The Middle East Documentation Center, The University of Chicago.

Al-Qahira (Cairo) is a town which Jawhar the Fatimid built after he had conquered Egypt, and subjugated [*qahara*] its inhabitants. It is large and well-built, with a splendid mosque [al-Azhar]. The imperial palace stands in its center. The town is well fortified, having iron-plated gates. It is on the main road to Syria, and no one may enter al-Fustat except through here, as both places are situated between the mountains and the river. The *Musalla* (place of prayer), where public prayers in connection with the two festivals [Ghadir Khumm and Ashura] are said, is beyond the town, while the burial grounds are between the metropolis and the mountain.[44]

In al-Muqaddasi's day, Fustat was still the principal city of Egypt and the center of commerce and culture. According to al-Muqaddasi, "It has superceded Baghdad, and is the glory of Islam, and is the marketplace for all mankind. It is more sublime than the City of Peace [Baghdad]. It is the storehouse of the Occident, the entrepot of the Orient, and is crowded with people at the time of the Pilgrimage festival."[45] Fustat's markets were without equal, its baths were the peak of perfection, its mosques were crowded with the faithful, and its teeming population lived in four- and five-story tenements, which housed as many as 200 people. In addition, "Victuals

Village near Pyramids at Giza during flood season, ca. 1865. *Source:* The Middle East Documentation Center, The University of Chicago.

here are most appetizing, their savories superb. Confectionaries are cheap, bananas plentiful, as are fresh dates; vegetables and firewood are abundant. The water is palatable, the air salubrious. It is a treasury of learned men; and the winter here is agreeable."[46] Clearly, in al Muqaddasi's mind, there was no finer city in the entire Islamic world.

He was particularly struck by the abundance of ships plying their trade along the Nile and those anchored at Fustat's port. When a man asked al-Muqaddasi where he was from, he told him that he was from Jerusalem. The man proceeded to tell him that if the vessels along the shore of Fustat were to go to Jerusalem, they could carry away all its people and all their possessions, as well as all the stones and timbers that constituted the city; such was the capacity of the ships at Fustat that when they were full, nothing of Jerusalem would remain. One gets the impression that this man told a version of this story to many a stranger, but al-Muqaddasi relates it to convey his sense of wonder about Egypt's teeming economic prosperity in the tenth century.

Many of these ships were small ferries for local use. Some sailed north to the Mediterranean ports of Alexandria and Damietta. Others traveled south to Aswan where they took on goods that had been transported across the desert from the Red Sea port of Aydhab. Still others were ships that plied the waters of the Mediterranean Sea and had sailed down the Nile to offload their goods and passengers—pilgrims, traders, artisans, Muslims, Christians, and Jews—from throughout the Mediterranean world. Some of these Mediterranean ships flew Muslim flags; others flew Byzantine, Genoese, Venetian, and Frankish flags. Clearly, political sensibilities were not to interfere with business in Fatimid Egypt. The abundance brought to Fustat by these many ships can be seen in Naser-e Khosraw's glowing description of one of the markets near the mosque of Amr ibn al-As, named after the general who conquered Egypt and became its first Muslim governor in 642.

On the north side of the mosque is a bazaar called Suq al-Qanadil [Lamp Market], and no one ever saw such a bazaar anywhere else. Every sort of rare goods from all over the world can be had there: I saw tortoise-shell implements such as small boxes, combs, knife handles, and so on. I also saw extremely fine crystal, which the master craftsmen etch beautifully. [This crystal] had been imported from the Maghreb, although they say that near the Red Sea, crystal even finer and more translucent than the Maghrebi variety had been found. I saw elephant tusks from Zanzibar, many of which weighed more than two hundred maunds. There was a type of skin from Abyssinia that resembled a leopard, from which they make sandals. Also from Abyssinia was a domesticated bird, large with white spots and a crown like a peacock's.[47]

The frontiers of medieval Syria and Iraq were different than their modern counterparts; medieval Egypt, however, basically corresponds to modern Egypt. Al-Muqaddasi divides Egypt into seven districts. He begins with the settled areas along the Mediterranean coast of the Sinai Peninsula, then lists three districts in the Nile Delta region ranging westward from modern day Suez to Alexandria; the fifth region is immediately south of the delta, the capital of which is Fustat. The sixth district is the Sa'id or Upper Egypt, which lies to the south of Fustat, and its capital is Aswan, just north of the first cataract on the Nile. The seventh district is the desert and its oases.

Al-Muqaddasi devotes a great deal of attention to the Nile, its annual rise and fall, the public ceremonies held each year to break the dykes when it reached the appropriate level, as well as canals and water wheels used to irrigate farmers' fields and bring water to villages. He was particularly impressed with the crocodile, which looked like a lizard, was terrifyingly dangerous, was invulnerable to all weapons, and could snatch a whole person in its mouth. Even more impressive, though far less dangerous, were the lighthouse at Alexandria and the Pyramids at Giza, Sakkara, and elsewhere along the Nile.

But most important of all for al-Muqaddasi was the produce, since Egypt was a country of commerce as well as agriculture. Its goods included incomparable reed pens and their vitriol, vinegar, wool, canvas, cloth, flax, linen, leather, shoes, leggings, geese, plantains, bananas, sugar cane, dies, apparel, spun yarn, water skins, and fish. In particular, Fustat was renowned for its fine leather, leggings, and cloth made from a three-ply yarn of camelhair and goat's wool; Upper Egypt was known for rice, wool, dates, vinegar, and raisins; Tinnis for multicolored cloth; Damietta for sugarcane; Fayyum for rice and inferior linen; Busir for shrimp and superior cotton; Farama and its villages for fish, baskets, fine ropes, fine white cloth, wraps, canvas, mats, grains, jasmine, and other oils.[48]

Once again, we see the importance of textiles (dies, canvas, spun yarn, cloth, linen, wool, and fine white and multicolored cloth) to international trade in the medieval Islamic world. Paper was also produced in Egypt by al-Muqaddasi's day, having by then largely replaced parchment and papyrus.[49] Although al-Muqaddasi focuses his attention on Egypt as a center for the production of textiles, leather, grain, and other foodstuffs, Egypt had long been a major center for the production of metal works (gold, silver, copper, tin, and lead) and fine glass products, as well as pottery.[50]

TRAVEL AND TRANSPORTATION

Most modern forms of transportation require wheeled vehicles of some sort. The notable exceptions, of course, are traveling by foot, boat, or beasts of burden. However, those who use beasts as their primary means of transportation usually employ them to pull wheeled buggies, carts, carriages, or wagons. Flat tires and broken axles essentially render these as well as cars, trucks, trains, bicycles, and motorcycles useless as modes of transportation. Air travel, too, would be impossible without the wheels necessary for planes to take off and land. (Pontoon planes, ski planes, and some helicopters are the exceptions here.) Compared to the medieval Islamic world, or any premodern era or region, modern modes of transportation are the epitome of ease, speed, and comfort.

Since wheeled transport had disappeared throughout the Middle East and North Africa prior to the Islamic conquests, the peoples of the medieval Islamic world traveled from one city to another on the back of a donkey or mule, as part of a camel caravan in desert regions, or by ship. Many could not afford to travel by any other means than by foot. Unlike the Romans who built extensive networks of paved roads and elaborate gridlike cities with wide throughways, medieval Islamic rulers had little use for such massive expenditures. Donkeys, mules, horses, and camels simply did not need paved roads in order to traverse the trade routes that crisscrossed the Islamic world and beyond. Medieval Muslim rulers did, however, devote a great deal of attention to the construction of bridges so that people, camels, horses, donkeys, and other animals could cross rivers, wadis, gullies, and washes that were either too deep or too swift to ford, especially during flood seasons. Baghdad, in particular, was famous for its pontoon bridges that spanned the Tigris River.

While the camel caravans that traversed the Sahara between North Africa and the trading towns along the Niger River as well as across the Sahara from Morocco to Egypt played vitally important roles in the international trade networks of the Islamic world, merchants, traders, pilgrims, and others who hailed from Spain (viz. Ibn Jubayr) or the port cities along the southern shores of the Mediterranean preferred to travel by ship whenever they could. The winds and waters of the Mediterranean were relatively calm, especially compared to the Indian Ocean where travel was much more dangerous. Of course, the Nile, Tigris, and Euphrates Rivers were the primary highways and preferred means of travel in Egypt and Iraq.

Whatever the means of transportation, travelers were always susceptible to raiders, brigands, and pirates. Consequently, only a fool would travel alone. In fact, it was considered bad form, even disgraceful, to allow a friend or relative to travel even short distances without a *rafiq*, or traveling companion. A famous Arabic proverb, "the companion is more important than the route taken" clarifies that the dangers, discomforts, and duration of travel in the medieval Islamic world necessitated the careful selection of a *rafiq* who was resourceful, trustworthy, and hopefully a pleasant conversationalist.[51]

Since medieval merchants and travelers—like their counterparts in antiquity—required places to provision themselves and their beasts, hostelries or inns were constructed along trade networks, pilgrimage routes, in small towns, and in major cities. Major trading cities often had dozens, even hundreds of them within their walls. *Funduq*, the Arabic term for inn, is derived from the Greek word *pandocheion*, which had been employed throughout the pre-Islamic Mediterranean world.[52] Medieval European travelers and merchants used *fondaco*, a cognate derived from *funduq*. Terms such as *caravansarai* and *khan* were also used to describe inns and hostelries throughout the medieval Islamic world, often interchangeably.

In the eleventh century, Naser-e Khosraw recorded that in Cairo, "there are no end of caravanserais [Persian, *karawansaray*], bathhouses, and other public buildings—all property of the sultan...."[53] Around 1150, the geographer al-Idrisi reported that there were 970 (!) *funduq*s in the Spanish port of Almería.[54] Three decades later, Ibn Jubayr described the customs house in Damascus at the other end of the Mediterranean as "a *khan* prepared to accommodate the caravan."[55] In the tenth century, al-Muqaddasi observed that "taxes in Syria are light, except for those levied on the caravanserais, in which case they are absolutely oppressive...."[56] Whether in Damascus, Baghdad, Cairo, Almería, or elsewhere, *funduq*s, *khan*s, and caravanserais were extremely important tax revenue producers for rulers throughout the medieval Islamic world.

Because of the importance of travel and trade to the international economies of the medieval Islamic world, Muslim rulers took it upon themselves to ensure that the trade routes that passed through their territories were well protected and dotted with secure inns for what they hoped would be many travelers and merchants. In the eleventh century, Nizam al-Mulk emphasizes the importance of such initiatives in his description of a just ruler as one who devotes his attention to that which advances civilization, such as:

constructing underground channels, digging main canals, building bridges across great waters, rehabilitating villages and farms, raising fortifications, building new towns, and erecting lofty buildings and magnificent dwellings; he will have inns [*ribats*] built on the highways and schools for those who seek knowledge; for which things he will be renowned forever; he will gather the fruit of his good works in the next world and blessings will be showered upon him.[57]

Nizam al-Mulk advises the construction of inns [*ribats*] on the highways to facilitate trade in the realm, but also to protect merchants and travelers from brigands and highway robbers. It should be noted that while *ribat* can be used in lieu of *funduq, khan,* or caravanserai, by the later Middle Ages *ribat* tended to be used exclusively to describe a dwelling for mystics or a fortified retreat along the frontier for ghazi warriors (many of whom were mystics as well).

The nuances of terminology for inns and hostelries based on geography and chronology are beyond the scope of our discussion here. What is important for our purposes is that medieval travelers could expect to find a great deal of similarity among *funduqs, khans,* and caravanserais throughout the medieval Islamic world. Architecturally, they tended to be rectangular buildings with a solitary entrance. Inside the building was a central courtyard surrounded by porticos or stalls where travelers could refuel their beasts and store them and their goods overnight. They could also find food and lodging for themselves. *Funduqs* also provided charitable services such as indigent housing, soup kitchens, even medical care. Most *funduqs* in towns and cities were near a mosque. Those located on the overland travel routes between cities had a mosque built into the structure or nearby. Some *funduqs* in Cairo or in the ports of the Mediterranean served Jewish or Christian merchants and contained or were built near to synagogues and churches. In addition, there were opportunities for travelers, merchants, and pilgrims to worship at other altars, since *funduqs* often served as taverns and brothels as well.

MONEY AND MARKETS

Essential to the economic prosperity of the far-flung medieval Islamic world was a degree of political stability, traders' confidence that their persons and property would be generally secure along caravan and sea routes, and a stable currency with which they could buy and sell their goods.[58] In the wake of the Islamic conquests, Muslim rulers and their subjects continued to employ the currency already in use in the conquered Byzantine and Sasanian territories. New coins were struck as well. Many of

Arab-Sasanian *drahm*. *Source:* American Numismatic Society.

these early issues were produced in Iraq and Iran and incorporated Sasanian motifs, language, and imagery. Others were more clearly "Islamic" in style. Coins from Basra and Kufa have been found with the image of an imam flanked with two worshipers, a depiction similar to Sasanian coins with a fire altar and attendants. Others from Damascus show a standing caliph with a sword.

Abd al-Malik's (r. 685–705) coinage reforms departed from the use of human images and Sasanian motifs and incorporated Arabic legends with specifically Islamic themes. These new coins, together with Abd al-Malik's construction of the Dome of the Rock and his efforts to make Arabic the required language of administration throughout the empire, represent a degree of religious self-confidence as well as political strength. His son and successor, al-Walid's (r. 705–15), transformation of the Cathedral of St. John in Damascus into the Umayyad Mosque and his refurbishing of Muhammad's mosque in Medina illustrate similar self-confidence and strength. These monetary, linguistic, and architectural reforms illustrate very nicely what became two of the most important symbols of political legitimacy in the medieval Islamic world—the authority to mint coins (*sikka*) and to have one's name invoked in the Friday sermon (*khutba*) in the congregational mosque (often built by the ruler himself).

Medieval Islamic rulers minted three types of coins. For the most part a gold coin was called a *dinar,* a silver coin was called a *dirham,* and a base metal coin (usually copper) was generally called a *fals.* There were other regional (even slang) names for the coins, but *dinar, dirham,* and *fals* were the customary terms used throughout the medieval Islamic world. Despite the common vocabulary, it would be a gross exaggeration to assert that

Umayyad *dinar*. *Source:* American Numismatic Society.

a *dirham* minted during Abd al-Malik's day had much in common with *dihrams* minted in eleventh-century Cairo, twelfth-century Damascus, or thirteenth-century Nishapur. Basically, the only thing they had in common was that they were (generally) all made from the same type of metal. However, unless one actually has the opportunity to examine a specific *dinar* (or *dirham* or *fals*), there is no way to know the quality of the metal used, the weight of the individual coin, or its value relative to other coins in circulation at the time.

Since at any given time one could find merchants from Damascus, Baghdad, Cairo, Cordoba, Isfahan, Tashkent, Bukhara, Delhi, Constantinople, Genoa, and a host of other Afro-Eurasian cities in the markets of the medieval Islamic world, one of the most important men in any market was the *sayrafi*, usually translated as money-changer. But his job entailed far more than simply making change; it was also to determine the precise value of a coin, especially foreign coins that traveling merchants needed to exchange for Islamic issues. The standard way for a *sayrafi* to determine the value of a coin was to measure its bullion content by weighing the coin itself. According to Claude Cahen, medieval Islamic jurisprudence (*fiqh*), which was "established in an age of pluralism and monetary fluctuation, commanded that coins not be taken at face value, but according to weight (allowing for alloyage), in order to assure honesty, as one would deal in any other form of merchandise."[59]

Because weighing individual coins was a rather tedious and time-consuming affair, it was standard practice for coins to be bought and sold in purses that were sealed by a government assaying office or a local merchant with the exact weight indicated on the outside. It should be noted that while the seal on a purse might indicate that its value was 76 *dinar*s, it

Abbasid *dirham*. *Source:* American Numismatic Society.

did not necessarily follow that the purse held 76 gold coins. It could very well contain 80 *dinars*, some of which were worn, gouged, cut, nicked, and so forth, reducing the purse's total weight (and hence its value) by four *dinars*.[60]

Like the *sayrafi*, the *muhtasib,* or market inspector, was essential to the smooth functioning of markets, long-distance trade, and the overall economy in any given region. His job was to ensure that the weights and measures in the market (including those used by the *sayrafi*) were correct and that business was transacted honestly, but also that public morality in the very public space of the market was upheld.[61] Nizam al-Mulk (d. 1092) emphasizes all three roles in his advice to the Seljukid Sultan Malikshah (r. 1073–92):

In every city a [market inspector] must be appointed whose duty is to check scales and prices and to see that business is carried on in an orderly and upright manner. He must take particular care in regard to goods which are brought from outlying districts and sold in the bazaars to see that there is no fraud or dishonesty, that weights are kept true, and that moral and religious principles are observed.[62]

According to Nizam al-Mulk, maintaining the integrity of the marketplace is "one of the foundations of the state and is itself the product of justice."[63] For if the sultan does not give his full support to his market inspectors and ensure the integrity of the markets in his realm, the poor will suffer, merchants will buy and sell as they see fit without regard to honesty, "sellers of short weight will be predominant; iniquity will be rife and divine law set at naught."[64] Nizam al-Mulk's moral vision of the market place with its emphasis on the importance of honest weights and mea-

Shops on a Cairo street. *Source. Lane, Manners and Customs*, 314.

sures is strikingly reminiscent of the Biblical admonitions that "the LORD abhors dishonest scales, but accurate weights are his delight" (Proverbs 11:1) and that "The LORD detests differing weights, and dishonest scales do not please him" (Proverbs 20:23).

Another of the market inspector's many responsibilities was to remove or repair anything that might hinder the free passage of goods, beasts, merchants, and customers throughout the market. The absence of wheeled vehicles contributed to the warrens of relatively narrow streets and alleys of the medieval Islamic world's bazaars and neighborhoods. While some streets were wide, most only needed to be wide enough for two fully loaded camels, horses, or donkeys to pass one another. Needless to say, traffic jams, filthy streets, and open sewage were the bane of merchants in the medieval Islamic world as much, if not more so, as they are today. Rainstorms, floods, bad weather, and natural disasters created obvious traffic flow problems that were beyond the control of any market inspector. Man-made congestion was another story. In fact, market inspectors had to maintain constant vigilance against shop owners who were fond of arranging their wares well outside their storefronts, making the streets impassable for beasts of burden and sometimes even fellow merchants and customers.

Nizam al-Mulk wrote his *Book of Government* in a time when no ruler could even imagine the kind of inspection and enforcement tools that modern Americans take for granted. Hence, the only way that a sultan could ensure that his markets were honest was to appoint market inspectors who were beyond reproach and who could not be bought off. The best candidates for such jobs in Nizam al-Mulk's mind, of course, were the kinds of men that Mahmud of Ghazna (r. 998–1030) had selected. A nobleman was a good candidate, but even better would be a "eunuch or an old Turk, who having no respect for anybody, would be feared by nobles and commoners alike."[65]

Nizam al-Mulk illustrates the near absolute authority of the market inspector and the importance of public morality in the medieval Islamic world with a story. Mahmud and several of his boon companions had been up all night drinking together. When morning came, Ali Nustigin, who was still feeling giddy with drink, decided that it was time for him to go home. He asked Mahmud if he could take leave of the sultan, but Mahmud advised him that he should stay indoors until he had sobered up because it was inappropriate to go out in public intoxicated. "If the [market inspector] sees you like this in the bazaar, he will arrest you and give you the lash. You will be put to shame, and I shall be very embarrassed and unable to help you."[66]

Since Ali was a general in the sultan's army and a military hero, he assumed that no market inspector would dare approach him in public no matter how drunk he might be. As luck would have it, when he was in the middle of the bazaar, the market inspector appeared with a hundred men. The market inspector, who was an old and venerable Turkish eunuch, ordered his men to drag Ali off his horse. The inspector then dismounted his own horse and proceeded to beat Ali 40 times with a stick until he fell to the ground while everyone silently watched. When the market inspector left, Ali's men carried him home. The next day Mahmud asked him if the market inspector had seen him. When Ali showed him the stripes on his back, he laughed and said, "Now repent and resolve never to go outdoors drunk again."[67]

JEWS AND CHRISTIANS *(AHL AL-KITAB;* PEOPLE OF THE BOOK)

Full membership and participation in the medieval Islamic world was based on religion—an absolutely universal idea in the premodern world, whether in Byzantium, Sasanian Iran, or fifteenth-century France. That is, if one had any hopes of being a full participant in Byzantine society, he had to be an Orthodox Christian; if one had any hopes of being a full participant in Sasanian Iranian society, he had to be Zoroastrian; if one had any hopes of being a full participant in fifteenth-century France, he had to belong to the Latin rite of Christianity.

Relations between Muslims and non-Muslims were ostensibly governed by Qur'anic pronouncements and hadiths about Muhammad's words, deeds, and attitudes towards non-Muslims, as well as the practice of the early Muslim community. Together, they provide the basis for the Islamic concept of *dhimma,* a term "used to designate the sort of indefinitely renewed contract through which the Muslim community accords hospitality and protection to members of other revealed religions, on condition of their acknowledging the domination of Islam."[68] Muslim scholars considered Jews, Christians, Zoroastrians (Magians), Samaritans, and Sabeans to be adherents of "other revealed religions"; that is, *ahl al-kitab* (People of the Book). As such, only they were afforded *dhimmi* status. As Muslim armies conquered new territories and for reasons of political expediency, other groups such as Buddhists in Central Asia and Hindus in India were afforded de facto *dhimmi* status. However, Buddhism and Hinduism were not considered de jure revealed religions.

The Qur'an venerates Noah, Abraham, Moses, David, Solomon, Jesus, and other Biblical figures as prophets who preached the same monotheistic message that Muhammad proclaimed to his kinsmen and followers in Mecca and Medina.[69] While the Qur'an concedes that there are some individual Jews and Christians who are righteous, it condemns Jews and Christians in general as willfully errant communities of faith. "Had the People of the Book accepted the Faith, it would surely have been better for them. Some are true believers, but most of them are evil-doers" (Qur'an 3:111)

Jews are condemned in the Qur'an for having corrupted the *Tawrah* (Torah) given to Moses, for having killed God's prophets, and for falsely claiming to have crucified Jesus:

When We made a covenant with them We raised the Mount above them and said: "Enter the gates in adoration. Do not break the Sabbath." We took from them a solemn covenant. But they broke their covenant, denied the revelations of God, and killed the prophets unjustly.... They denied the truth and uttered a monstrous falsehood against Mary. They declared: "We have put to death the Messiah, Jesus the son of Mary, the apostle of God." They did not kill him, nor did they crucify him, but they thought they did. (Qur'an 4:154–57)

Christians are condemned for having corrupted the *Injil* (Gospel) given to Jesus, for claiming that Jesus is God's son, and especially for the doctrine of the Trinity, which the Qur'an describes as polytheism, the worst of all sins:

People of the Book, do not transgress the bounds of your religion. Speak nothing but the truth about God. The Messiah, Jesus the son of Mary, was no more than God's apostle and His Word which He cast to Mary: a spirit from Him. So believe in God and His apostles and do not say: "Three." Forbear, and it shall be better for you. God is but one God. God forbid that He should have a son! (Qur'an 4:171)

In spite of the Qur'an's veneration of Abraham, Moses, and Jesus, its attitude toward the People of the Book is explicitly aggressive and hostile:

Fight against such of those to whom the Scriptures were given [*ahl al-kitab*] as believe neither in God nor the Last Day, who do not forbid what God and His apostle have forbidden, and do not embrace the true Faith, until they pay tribute [*jizya*] out of hand and are utterly subdued. (Qur'an 9:29)

Accordingly, once the People of the Book were properly subdued and had paid the *jizya* (tribute or poll tax, essentially protection money), there was no need to continue to fight them.

As one might expect, how these and other texts were interpreted by jurists and applied by rulers varied according to time period and region. Nevertheless, in exchange for their humble submission and tribute, all members of these communities were supposed to be afforded protection of life and property as well as limited religious freedoms, at least in those areas such as marriage, divorce, and inheritance where their activities did not impinge on the ruling Muslim classes. Certain disabilities were imposed on them as well, including distinctive dress, restrictions on the construction of new places of worship, even prohibitions against riding horses.

According to *The Book of the Islamic Market Inspector,* compiled in the twelfth century by the Syrian jurist al-Shayzari (d. ca. 1193),

The *dhimmi*s must be made to observe the conditions laid down for them in the treatise on *jizya* written for them by 'Umar b. al-Khattab, and must be made to wear the *ghiyar* [a distinctive piece of cloth]. If he is a Jew, he should put a red or a yellow cord on his shoulder; if a Christian, he should tie a *zunnar* [distinctive girdle] around his waist and hang a cross around his neck; if a woman she should wear two slippers, one of which is white and the other black. When a protected person goes to the baths, he must wear a steel, copper or lead neckband to distinguish him from other people.[70]

As a manual for market inspectors, al-Shayzari's admonitions are more prescriptive of what should be enforced rather than descriptive of what actually occurred. There is plenty of evidence that specific restrictions on *dhimmi*s differed according to time, place, regime, and class. Sometimes they were not enforced at all; at other times, they were enforced with draconian cruelty.

Some of the most famous examples include the arbitrary policies of the Fatimid caliph al-Hakim (r. 996–1021), who was thought to be mad, and the Almohad regime in North Africa and Spain (1130–1269), which was especially brutal to Jews and Christians, but also to Muslims who did not conform to its particularly strict version of Islam. (It was because of Almohad repression that the great Jewish philosopher and physician, Moses Maimonides, left his native Spain and took up residence in Egypt.) However *dhimma* regulations were enforced, their purpose was twofold: 1) to ensure that, as commanded in the Qur'an, the People of the Book properly submitted to Islamic authority and paid the *jizya* and 2) to demonstrate publicly the superiority of Islam and Muslims to the inferior *dhimmi* religions and communities.

In light of Muhammad's conflicts with the leading Jewish clans of Medina (the Banu Qaynuqa, the Banu Nadir, and the Banu Qurayza), hadiths such as the following were favorites of jurists who supported strict enforcement of *dhimma* regulations: "You will fight the Jews to such a point that if one of them hides behind a rock, the rock will say: Servant of God, here is a Jew behind me! Kill him."[71] So too were Qur'anic passages that declare that those who broke the Sabbath and opposed God would be turned into apes and pigs. According to Qur'an 5:60, those among the People of the Book who will receive a worse reward from God are "those whom God has cursed and with whom He has been angry, transforming them into apes and swine...." Some commentators interpreted this and other passages to mean Jews and Christians respectively; others were more equitable in that they argued that both Jews and Christians could be transformed into apes as well as swine.[72]

In addition, the prolific ninth-century author, al-Jahiz (777–869), marshaled many of the standard Muslim arguments against Jews and Christians in his vituperative anti-Christian polemic, *al-Radd ʿala l-nasara* (Contra Christianorum).[73] He begins his treatise with an account of why, despite their perversions and Trinitarian polytheism, Christians are "more trustworthy, more sociable, less pernicious, lesser infidels and generally, less of a torment, than Jews."[74] His basic arguments against Jews are based on Muhammad's negative encounters with the Jews of Medina. According to al-Jahiz, because the Christian Arabian tribes and the lands of Christendom were far removed from Mecca and Medina, Christians "never resorted to intrigue, vilification and open hostility against Muslims. This is the principal reason why Muslim opinion became set against Jews but remains tolerant of Christians."[75] Nevertheless, "the Christian is at heart, a foul and dirty creature. Why? Because he is uncircumcised, does not wash after intercourse and eats pig meat. His wife does not wash after intercourse, either, or even after menstruation and childbirth, which leaves her absolutely filthy. Furthermore she, too, is uncircumcised."[76]

Jewish and Christian attitudes towards Muslims and towards each other were equally contemptuous. After all, all three religions claimed to possess the sole revealed truth. Polemics aside, demographic realities neces-sitated intercommunal contact between the superior Muslim community and the inferior Jewish and Christian communities. It should come as no surprise that the history of Muslim/non-Muslim relations varied consid-erably from the first Islamic centuries when the Muslim military and rul-ing elite represented such a small minority of the population to the later centuries after the majority of the local population had converted to the religion of the conquerors. We see this transition illustrated by the Cathe-dral of St. John the Baptist in Damascus discussed above. After the initial Muslim conquest of Damascus, the church was used as a place of worship for both the local Christian population and the Muslim rulers. However, in the early eighth century, al-Walid ibn Abd al-Malik (r. 705–15) trans-formed it into the great Umayyad Mosque in the center of the city, exclu-sively for Muslim worship.

In addition, Muslim rulers had little choice but to retain non-Muslim peoples (Christians but also Jews in the formerly Byzantine lands; Zoro-astrians and some Christians and Jews in the formerly Sasanian lands) in bureaucratic positions such as revenue collectors and administrators of various types. In fact, one of al-Jahiz's reasons for writing his "Con-tra Christianorum" was the presence of influential Christians and Jews in Baghdad in his day. Christians and Jews continued to be employed in gov-ernment service during the Fatimid (969–1171) and Ayyubid (1171–1250) periods in Egypt as well. According to S. D. Goitein, it was the "unattrac-tiveness of government service which made it available to non-Muslims at a time when plenty of other outlets for economic activity were open to Muslims. This explains why [working with hot melted metals in] the mints in most Muslim states remained largely a domain of the Jews even in later periods."[77] However, during the thirteenth century, when the economies of the Islamic world became increasingly monopolized by the state, Muslims began to seek government posts at the expense of Chris-tians and Jews.

Despite their inferior status, Jews and Christians were not consigned to ghettos as Jews were in parts of medieval Christian Europe. Jews, Christians, and Muslims often lived in the same neighborhoods and in adjoining properties. Muslims and non-Muslims rented apartments, ware-houses, and market stalls from one another. Jewish and Christian congre-gations even occasionally rented space from Muslim landlords to use as synagogues or churches in order to circumvent the laws against the con-struction of non-Muslim places of worship. Occasionally, other legal ruses were used to permit the construction of new churches and synagogues. Muslims and non-Muslims entered into business transactions with one another, whether in the local market or long-distance trade. In fact, the Geniza records indicate that Jews owned many of the ships that operated in the Mediterranean Sea, the Nile, and the Indian Ocean, though there is little evidence that Jews actually piloted very many of them.

The frequency and type of such intercommunal contacts does not mean that the medieval Islamic world was a model of religious diversity and toleration in the modern American sense. Again, according to al-Shayzari,

The *muhtasib* [market inspector] must take the *jizya* from them according to their social status. Thus, at the beginning of the year a poor man with a family pays one dinar, while someone of middling wealth pays two dinars and a rich man pays four dinars. When the *muhtasib* or his agent comes to collect the *jizya*, he should stand the *dhimmi* in front of him, slap him on the side of the neck and say: "Pay the *jizya*, unbeliever." The *dhimmi* will take his hand out of his pocket holding the *jizya* and present it to him with humility and submission.[78]

As the Geniza records make abundantly clear, the poll tax (*jizya*) was the *dhimmi*'s inescapable burden and clear marker of inferiority in any and all relations with Muslims. Hence, religious diversity in the medieval Islamic world was characterized by Jewish and Christian communities that essentially functioned as separate nations within the Abode of Islam, and which tolerated their situation only because they had little choice but to accept the terms of their inferior status.

Since each person was responsible for paying the poll tax annually, it was the first priority for Jews and Christians of all economic classes and professions. If a person died before he paid the poll tax, his family was still required to pay it on his behalf. Fathers were held accountable for sons; brothers for brothers, even for brothers-in-law. No *dhimmi* could legally travel anywhere in the medieval Islamic world without documents certifying that he had paid the poll tax for that year. In addition, travelers were required to pay the poll tax in their home country even if they were away for years at a time—a common occurrence.

The documents of the Cairo Geniza also make it abundantly clear that Jews were involved in extensive and profitable long-distance trade throughout the Mediterranean Basin, East Africa, India, and even as far as Indonesia in Southeast Asia.[79] S. D. Goitein discusses one case in which an Egyptian Jewish merchant had died in India after a nine-year sojourn there. After the merchant's death, his brother paid his poll tax for the whole nine years. He and others had little choice. Failure to pay the poll tax could result in beatings and/or imprisonment, where one faced starvation and even death. Needless to say, people of modest means found the poll tax particularly onerous. Wealthy Jews and Christians, of course, could more easily afford to pay it. In fact, petitions to wealthy Jews and/ or to the head of the local Jewish community for assistance in paying the poll tax represent one of the most common themes in the many letters preserved in the Cairo Geniza.[80]

Finally, al-Muqaddasi's brief comment that "most of the assayers, the dyers, [*sayrafis*], and tanners in [al-Sham] are Jews; while the physicians and the scribes are generally Christians" brings us to the important issue of the role of the *dhimmi* physician in the medieval Islamic world.[81] In keeping with the general distrust of Jews and Christians, Muslim jurists argued that Muslims should abstain from using the services of Jewish and Christian doctors or pharmacists on the grounds that an unbeliever might prescribe medicines that would do them physical or spiritual harm. However, there is probably no *dhimma* regulation that was more frequently ignored than this. Jewish and Christian prohibitions against consulting physicians who did not belong to their own faith communities were widely ignored as well.

Many Muslims, Christians, and Jews (like many modern Americans) were far less concerned with their physician's religion than with his medical knowledge and the quality of his practice. As evidenced by the prominence of Jewish and Christian physicians in Ibn Abi Usaybʻiah's (d. 1270) ʻUyun al-anbaʼ fi tabaqat al-atibbaʼ [The Sources of Information on the Classification of Physicians], it was the medical profession in particular that transcended religious boundaries in the medieval Islamic world.[82] According to S. D. Goitein, physicians were "the torchbearers of secular erudition, the professional expounders of philosophy and the sciences.... [They] were the disciples of the Greeks, and as heirs to a universal tradition formed a spiritual brotherhood that transcended the barriers of religion, language, and countries."[83]

HOUSING

Housing in the medieval Islamic world included tents, mud huts, reed huts, single-story residences, multistoried tenements, and elaborate palaces. In the deserts of Arabia, Syria, Iraq, Iran, and North Africa, tents predominated among the pastoral nomadic populations. These were generally made from the hair, wool, and leather of the nomads' herds and flocks, whether sheep, goats, or camels. In the settled oases of the region, most homes were built from mud or reeds simply because wood and stone were rarely available in sufficient quantities to be practicable. Homes tended to be huts built of mud bricks in Muhammad's hometown of seventh-century Mecca, whereas in other oases, reed huts were more common. In the highlands of Yemen many of the residents lived in villages and towns made up of multistory tenement buildings.

In the major cities such as Damascus, Baghdad, and Cairo, wood, stone, and brick were the preferred building materials in part because they were more readily available but also because they are far more durable than tents and mud or reed huts. While some residents lived in single-story homes, many lived in multistoried apartment buildings. The tenth-century geographer al-Muqaddisi records that Fustat's (Old Cairo's) teeming population lived in four- and five-story tenements, which housed as many as 200 people.[84] Medieval Muslim rulers also built elaborate stone palaces, mosques, madrasas, caravanserais, bathhouses, and hospitals. Depending on the locale, some of the stones and columns used in con-

Exterior of homes in Cairo. *Source:* Lane, *Manners and Customs*, 5.

structing such examples of monumental architecture were recycled from Pharaonic, Roman, and Sasanian ruins or from Christian churches and monasteries. Some of the buildings constructed during the Middle Ages still bear the graffiti and other inscriptions from earlier eras.

Typical of many dwellings at the time was a central courtyard or common area of some sort around which salons, bedrooms, and kitchens were constructed. Only the wealthy could afford indoor plumbing or ovens as part of their residences. Outhouses or outdoor latrine facilities of some sort were the order of the day. Men often simply urinated in a street or alley in a manner reminiscent of the Biblical euphemism for men as those "who pisseth against the wall" (1 Samuel 25:22, 34).[85] Public baths were essential to every city. If there was only one bathhouse in a town, certain days or parts of days were designated for women and others for men.

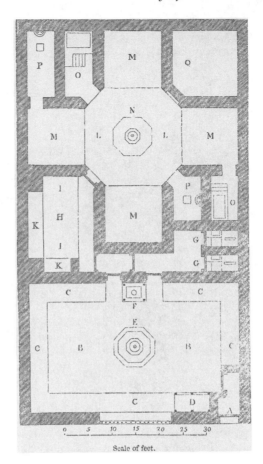

Bathhouse floor plan. *Source:* Lane, *Manner and Customs*, 338–339.

Key:
A. General entrance and vestibule
B. Open courtyard
C. Raised floor
D. Bath keeper's station
E. Cold water fountain
F. Coffee stall
G. Latrine
H. First warm room
I. Raised floor
K. Raised seat
L. Principal warm room
M. Raised floor
N. Hot water fountain
O. Chamber containing a tank of warm water
P. Room with hot and cold water taps
Q. Fire place, over which is the boiler

Larger cities had women's bathhouses, which were usually physically separate from the men's bathhouses.

One's home in the medieval Islamic world served as a sanctuary or refuge from the primarily male-dominated public world of the market and the mosque. Most men who were not part of the ruling classes or military spent much of the day outside the home working, studying, or at prayer in

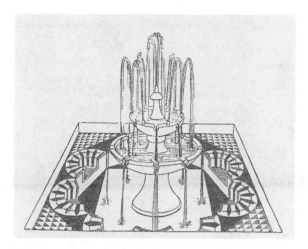

Fountain. *Source:* Lane, *Manners and Customs,* 13.

the mosque with other men. Women (especially respectable women) spent a great deal of their time at home with their children and other women. Women generally performed their ritual prayers at home. Literate women were usually educated at home, often by their fathers, uncles, brothers, or male cousins. If their mothers or other female relatives were educated, they often studied with them as well. Women who worked for a wage generally labored at home doing piecework as seamstresses, weavers, or makers of other handicrafts.

In addition to serving as a refuge from the outside world, the courtyard was a common area shared by the whole family (or families) who lived around it. Among rural and nomadic populations the courtyard might also serve as a corral for livestock. Women tended to prepare hot meals over a fire in such courtyards or in common neighborhood cooking areas. Meals that required an oven were prepared at home and then taken to a local bake house to be cooked. In the residences of the wealthy and the palaces of the ruling classes, courtyards were often quite elaborate. Many were equipped with fountains, gardens, and sophisticated canopies and trellises that allowed in light, but also provided a cooling shade from the often blistering sun.

The courtyard also served as the public space of the home where guests were welcomed and entertained. In addition to the courtyard there was often a salon that served the same purpose. In either case when male guests were involved, the courtyard or the salon became extensions of the outside world in that such gatherings generally were male-only affairs, especially among the wealthy classes. Since hospitality and generosity were notable virtues throughout the Islamic world, food and beverages were served in such instances. In the medieval Islamic world, few things could ruin one's reputation more than being known as stingy or inhospitable.

Courtyard of a house in Cairo. *Source:* Lane, *Manners and Customs,* 10

Because of the strict rules pertaining to sexual segregation every dwelling had an inviolable space (harem) that was separate from the rest of the house where the women retreated when male guests were present. In palaces and the homes of the wealthy this took the form of well-appointed women's quarters or harems which only women, children, male kin, and eunuchs were allowed to enter. The women of less-well-to-do families retreated to a room or an area separated from the rest of the dwelling by a curtain or some sort of partition that served as a harem only when guests were present but was generally used for other purposes such as cooking, sewing, making handicrafts, study, or sleeping.

Sketch of a guest chamber. *Source:* Lane, *Manners and Customs,* frontispiece.

Whether one lived in a courtyard house or in a multistory tenement, a frequent concern was how best to encourage air exchange and cooling breezes in the often stifling summer heat and at the same time preserve the sanctity and privacy of the home's interior space. One common means of achieving both ventilation and privacy is what is known as *mashrabiyya*— a wooden grill or grate that was used to cover windows or balconies. The grills or lattice work were usually made of turned wood that was joined together with carved blocks or spheres of wood to create intricate patterns. (In the homes of the very wealthy or for use in public buildings, the screen was occasionally made of metalwork.) Another means of ventilation was the wind catcher, or *malqaf*. A wind catcher functioned as a kind of reverse chimney/swamp cooler in that it was composed of a shaft that rose above the building's roof. The opening of the shaft was positioned to catch the prevailing winds of the region and force them down into the building, often flowing over pools of water or screens that were dampened with wet fabrics.

While furnishings in the medieval Islamic world did include chairs with legs and beds with frames, it was far more common that homes were furnished with pillows, mattresses, and sofas. That is, domestic life in the medieval Islamic world was generally conducted rather close to the ground. Families did not sit in chairs around a dining room table at mealtime. Nor did they eat from individual plates. Rather, meals were served on large serving trays that were set on the floor or on a low stand. Guests then sat on a carpet, pillow, or very low seat around the serving tray and ate directly from it. They generally ate many dishes with their hands and flat breads; however, utensils (especially knives and spoons) were used for cutting meats and for eating soups.

Woodworkers and smiths did construct benches and chairs that were comparable in height to modern chairs and benches, but these were generally for use outside the home and generally were used to indicate the higher rank and status of the person (ruler, scholar, family patriarch, or other person of high status) who sat on them in relation to those who were seated below him. Sitting on sofas, large pillows, pillows stacked on one another, or anything that might elevate a person over others could just as easily serve the same purpose of reflecting the hierarchy of status and rank.

The heights and kinds of beds people slept on as well as the kinds of material used to make beds, pillows, and sofas were indications of status and wealth also. Beds with legs and frames were a sign of the highest status. Beds without them were a step down, sleeping on a mat or carpet a step further, and sleeping on the bare floor was for the poorest as well as for the mendicant Sufis, who considered themselves as God's poor ones (*fuqara' Allah*).

FOOD AND WATER

The diet of even the lowliest peasant in the medieval Islamic world was generally varied and quite healthy, certainly far healthier than what most classes had access to in medieval Europe. The staple grains in most areas were wheat and in areas with more saline soil, barley. Sorghum was grown widely as well, but it appears that only the lower classes used it as a food crop for both themselves and their animals. Rice could only be cultivated in those areas where there was an abundance of water, such as the southern shores of the Caspian Sea, in parts of Spain, in the Nile Delta and along the Nile in Egypt, along the lower Euphrates in southern Iraq, and even along the Jordan River near Beit Shean. In such areas it competed with wheat and sorghum as a staple. However, in many other areas it was an imported luxury that only the wealthier could afford.

Along the Mediterranean coastlands, olive orchards were as thick on the ground as they had been in antiquity. Vineyards were cultivated as well; however, after the Islamic conquests, they gradually became less important to the local diet than they had been in late antiquity as more and more of the population converted to Islam and adopted the Islamic prohibition against the consumption of wine. Nevertheless, grapes continued to be used in Bilad al-Sham to produce raisins (*zabib*) and molasses (*dibs*), which were staples of the local diet, especially in the winter months. Ba'alabakk was famous for its molasses and Darayya (southeast of Damascus) for its grapes and raisins.

Some of the oasis settlements of Arabia as well as some of the settlements along the rivers in Iraq and Egypt cultivated vast date palm groves.

A wide array of fruits and vegetables native to the region were cultivated along with others such as bananas, citrus, sugarcane, eggplants, watermelons, and mango trees that entered the Middle East from India and Africa in late antiquity or during the early Islamic period. Precisely how these foods spread westward across the Mediterranean to Spain is difficult to ascertain. There are numerous stories about rulers who encouraged the cultivation of exotic foods in their palace gardens and orchards. I mention but three examples here. Abd al-Rahman I (r. 756–88), one of the few Umayyads to survive the Abbasid revolution, surrounded his palace in Spain with trees from around the world, including date palms and pomegranate trees ostensibly brought to Spain by men he had sent to Syria for the purpose of bringing back all sorts of seeds and plants to be grown in his garden.

The Abbasid caliph, al-Ma'mun (r. 813–33), is said to have brought sour orange trees from northeastern Iran to Rayy near modern Tehran. A century later, the Abbasid caliph al-Qahir (r. 932–34) reportedly had sour orange trees brought to Baghdad from India via Yemen. Whether or not rulers were the *principal* agents for the transfer of such foods from region to region, it is clear that the extensive overland and seaborne trade networks of the vast medieval Islamic world facilitated their transfer. Many foods likely began to be cultivated in new regions simply because a traveling merchant or scholar developed a taste for them in his travels and brought some plants or seeds home with him.[86]

Essential to the flourishing cities and states of the medieval Islamic world were the sophisticated and varied irrigation technologies that made it possible to grow crops, such as sugarcane, bananas, mangos, rice, and cotton. These and other crops that originated in tropical or semitropical climes required intensive irrigation, especially during the summer months, for the simple reason that in much of the region (as in southern California and the American southwest) it rained only during the winter months. Consequently, one of the major expenditures of any regime was for the construction and maintenance of irrigation technologies.

Dams were built to contain rainwater in lowlands or to divert rivers and streams. Trenches and canals were dug to channel rainwater to aboveground reservoirs as well as underground cisterns. Some canals were made of brick and stone, others were elaborate aqueducts, and still others included pipes made of tile or lead. Underground aquifers were tapped by digging wells, creating new springs, and in some places (especially in parts of Iran and Afghanistan) by carving tunnels that ran for miles through the bedrock. Each of these methods employed gravity to move water from higher ground to lower.

Whereas gravity-driven water transport requires little human labor beyond initial construction, raising water to higher ground is generally far more labor-intensive than the routine maintenance of a trench, canal, aqueduct, or cistern. Lifting water from a well with a bucket on the end

Shadhuf. Source: Description de l'Egypte, 22 vol. Paris, 1809–1929.

of a rope is hard work, and variations on this bucket and rope theme had been employed since antiquity. Pulling the rope through a pulley made the job much easier. So too did attaching a bucket to a pole with a weight on the other end (*shadhuf*) to counterbalance it. The early nineteenth-century image above from the Napoleonic scientific expedition depicts *shadhuf*s being used to lift water some 18 to 20 feet from the Nile as it receded.[87]

The Archimedes Screw or Archimedes Snail, ostensibly invented by Archimedes (287–212 B.C.) himself, had been used since antiquity as well. An Archimedes Screw is composed of a screw placed inside a cylinder. The lower end is placed in water and as the screw is turned water is raised to the top.[88] Another important means of raising water was the water wheel, which had the labor-saving advantage of being powered by the current of the river on which it was built. None of this technology was really new, but it certainly was improved upon by the hydrologists of the medieval Islamic world.

As can be seen from al-Muqaddisi's lists, the diversity of fruits, vegetables, grains, and meats available in the medieval Islamic world is truly impressive. Markets throughout the medieval Islamic world were full of local fruits, vegetables, meats, and fish as well as preserved foods that had been brought from afar. Some of these were preserved by cooling as well as drying. The most common method of preservation, however, was to pickle them in vinegar and salt along with a range of condiments, including honey, sugar, lemon juice, olive oil, mustard, nuts, and all sorts of spices and herbs. While any meat can be made into sausage, sausages made from mutton and semolina were preferred. Muhammad is said to have been particularly fond of milk, but given the difficulties of preserving fresh milk, it was converted into a wide variety of soft and hard cheeses.

In the countryside women generally ground the flour. In the cities, there were mills that ground flour for sale. Some urban marriage contracts have survived that specify that the bride (usually from a wealthy family) was to be exempt from grinding flour. Since only the wealthiest individuals could afford to have an oven built into their residences, foods prepared at home had to be taken to a local bake-house to be cooked. In addition, there were shops that sold breads, pastries, and sweetmeats, as well as restaurants where one could purchase all sorts of prepared dishes.

Islamic dietary laws are limited to but a few items, including blood, meat from animals that are not slaughtered properly, carrion, pork, and animals that have been consecrated to pagan gods. While there are many similarities between Islamic and Jewish dietary laws, Islamic dietary laws are generally less restrictive than Jewish ones. (Most Christian traditions abandoned Jewish dietary laws in their entirety.) A general rule of thumb is that nearly everything that is permissible (kosher) for Jews to eat is permissible (*halal*) for Muslims to eat. The major exception to this rule is that while wine is kosher and is absolutely essential to Jewish ritual and practice, it is explicitly forbidden in the Qur'an.

However, many things that are *halal* are not kosher. For example, all seafood is permissible (*halal*) for Muslims to eat; however, only fishes with fins and scales are permissible (kosher) for Jews—shellfish, lobster, shrimp, and so forth, are forbidden. In addition, certain meat dishes made with milk or yogurt are said to have been some of Muhammad's favorites and hence are permissible for Muslims to eat. However, Jewish kosher regulations state that meat may not be cooked in or eaten with any milk product. An obvious example of a meat dish that is not kosher is the ubiquitous American cheeseburger.

Dietary regulations are more restrictive for pilgrims to Mecca as well. In order to remain in a state of ritual purity (*tahara*) during the pilgrimage, pilgrims must abstain from killing or eating game (though seafood is permissible) and of course from those foods and drinks that are always forbidden. It should be noted that while the Qur'an specifically forbids the above foods and drinks, the pragmatic side of most schools of Islamic law recognizes exigent circumstances when one might involuntarily or even forcibly be compelled to eat or drink forbidden things.

Although scholars generally extended the Qur'anic prohibition on wine to all alcoholic beverages, it is clear that there were a range of near-beers and other "soft" or lightly fermented fruit drinks that could be commonly found throughout the medieval Islamic world. As such, a great deal of ink was spilled defining which types of drinks were in fact "soft" (lightly fermented) and permitted and which were "hard" (real intoxicants) and forbidden. As one might expect, water was an essential drink, though the quality of water was often determined by how much one was willing and or able to pay a water seller who carried water around in a jug on his back for sale in the market. The wealthiest even purchased snow from snow vendors who brought in snow from afar and kept it in storehouses. Fruit juices mixed with water were very common, including drinks made from lemons, oranges, apples, tamarinds, dates, grapes, and pomegranates.

Various coffees can be found throughout the modern Islamic world, and Arabica beans are a favorite in American coffee houses. However, coffee was only introduced to the Islamic world from Yemen and east Africa in the fifteenth century. There are several legends about who was the first to bring coffee beans to Yemen, and most of them revolve around one or more Sufis (Islamic mystics) who praised the drink as an inhibitor of sleep and an aide to mystical devotional rituals. Tea is ubiquitous in the modern Islamic world as well but was introduced from India even later, and often by European merchants. For example, it was a French merchant who had business dealings in East Asia who first introduced tea to Morocco around 1700.[89]

While the Islamic religion had its origins in the oases of western Arabia, it was in the cities of the medieval Islamic world that what historians call Islamic civilization truly took root and prospered, whatever the political fortunes of the rulers. Damascus was the capital of the Umayyad caliphate for less than a century (661–750); however, Syria (al-Sham) continued to be a significant center of commerce, scholarship, and Muslim, Christian, and Jewish sanctity long after the Abbasid revolution. Baghdad, too, fell on hard times after its heyday in the seventh and eighth centuries. Nevertheless, it and Iraq continued to be the seat of the Abbasid caliphate and Sunni unity (however symbolic) down to the Mongol conquests in 1258. Egypt and its new capital, Cairo, became one of the wealthiest and most important cosmopolitan way stations for international trade and culture in the Mediterranean world, southwest Asia and the Indian Ocean under the Fatimid caliphs (969–1171). Cairo and Egypt continued to flourish under their Ayyubid (1171–1250) and Mamluk successors (1250–1517). In fact, Cairo's continued magnificence inspired the fourteenth-century historian, Ibn Khaldun (1332–1406), to refer to her as the "Mother of the World" (*umm al-dunya*).

As the accounts of al-Muqaddasi, Naser-e Khosraw, Ibn Jubayr, and others demonstrate, cities and towns were closely linked to their agricultural hinterlands. Elaborate and sophisticated irrigation systems produced an agricultural bounty that sustained vibrant cities. Caravan routes and shipping lanes (sustained by networks of hostels and caravanserais) served as the arteries of economic and intellectual exchange throughout the Islamic world and beyond. Finally, it was in these cities and others like them that Jews, Christians, and other People of the Book learned how to manage, succeed, and even flourish as important economic, intellectual, scientific, and occasionally political actors in a world in which they were constantly reminded of their inferior, though protected (*dhimmi*), status.

NOTES

1. While the sources agree on the founding date for Fustat, they do not agree on the precise founding dates for Basra and Kufa, though they tend to agree that Basra was established before Kufa. They are equally imprecise for the conquest of southern Iraq. Donner suggests that the conquest of southern Iraq occurred between A.D. 635 and 642. See Fred M. Donner, *The Early Islamic Conquests* (Princeton, NJ: Princeton University Press, 1981), 212–20; 226–30.

2. For the theoretical literature in the concept of the "Islamic City," see the "Cities" section in "Suggestions for Further Reading."

3. See pp. 5–8 of this book.

4. See the medieval geographical and travel literature translated by C. E. Bosworth, R. J. C. Broadhurst, Basil Collins, Nikita Elisseeff, H. A. R. Gibb, Jacob Lassner, Guy Le Strange, and Wheeler M. Thackston in the "Geography and Travel" section of "Suggestions for Further Reading."

5. On the *fada'il al-quds* and *fada'il al-sham* literature, see Amikam Elad, *Medieval Jerusalem and Islamic Worship: Holy Places, Ceremonies, Pilgrimage* (Leiden: Brill, 1995) and Paul M. Cobb, "Virtual Sacrality: Making Muslim Syria Sacred before the Crusades," *Medieval Encounters: Jewish, Christian and Muslim Culture in Confluence and Dialogue* 8.1 (2002): 35–55. See also Josef W. Meri, *The Cult of Saints among Muslims and Jews in Medieval Syria* (New York: Oxford University Press, 2002).

6. S. D. Goitein, *A Mediterranean Society: The Jewish Communities of the World as Portrayed in the Cairo Geniza*, 6 vols. (Berkeley: University of California Press, 1967–93). See also Jacob Lassner, *A Mediterranean Society: An Abridgement in One Volume* (Berkeley: University of California Press, 1999).

7. See al-Muqaddasi, Basil Collins, trans., *The Best Divisions for Knowledge of the Regions: Ahsan al-taqasim fi ma'rifat al-aqalim.* (Reading, UK: Garnet Publishing, 2001).

8. For an explanation of *nisba* and the traditional Arabic naming system see pp. 173–78 of this book.

9. See Naser-e Khosraw, *Naser-e Khosraw's Book of Travels (Safarnama)* Wheeler M. Thackston, trans. (Albany: State University of New York Press, 1986), ix–xii.

10. R. J. C. Broadhurst, trans., *The Travels of Ibn Jubayr*, (London: J. Cape, 1952), 318.

11. Ibid., 271.

12. Ibid., 271–72.

13. Ibid.

14. Ibid., 272.

15. Ibid.

16. See Finbarr Barry Flood, *The Great Mosque of Damascus: Studies on the Makings of an Umayyad Visual Culture* (Leiden: Brill, 2001).

17. See pp. 161–62 of this book for a discussion of the martyrdom of al-Husayn ibn Ali.

18. Guy Le Strange, trans., *Palestine under the Moslems: A Description of Syria and the Holy Land from A.D. 650 to 1500* (Beirut: Khayats Oriental Reprints, 1965 [1890]), 14; al-Muqaddasi, *The Best Divisions for Knowledge of the Regions,* 129.

19. Le Strange, *Palestine under the Moslems,* 15; al-Muqaddasi, *The Best Divisions for Knowledge of the Regions,* 156–57.

20. Le Strange, *Palestine under the Moslems,* 15; al-Muqaddasi, *The Best Divisions for Knowledge of the Regions,* 150.

21. Le Strange, *Palestine under the Moslems,* 18; al-Muqaddasi, *The Best Divisions for Knowledge of the Regions,* 151.

22. Le Strange, *Palestine under the Moslems,* 19; al-Muqaddasi, *The Best Divisions for Knowledge of the Regions,* 151. It is not clear what *bal'îsiyyah* cloth is.

23. Jonathan M. Bloom, *Paper before Print: The History and Impact of Paper in the Islamic World* (New Haven, CT: Yale University Press, 2001), 46–89.

24. Dimitri Gutas, *Greek Thought, Arabic Culture: The Graeco-Arabic Translation Movement in Baghdad and Early 'Abbasid Society (2nd–4th/8th–10th centuries)* (New York: Routledge, 1998).

25. Efraim Lev, "Trade of Medical Substances in the Medieval and Ottoman Levant *(Bilad al-Sham),*" in *Towns and Material Culture in the Medieval Middle East,* ed. Yaakov Lev (Leiden: Brill, 2002), 159–84.

26. On the early Abbasid caliphate, see Elton Daniel, *The Political and Social History of Khurasan under Abbasid Rule, 747–820* (Minneapolis: Bibliotheca Islamica, 1979); Jacob Lassner, *The Shaping of Abbasid Rule* (Princeton, NJ: Princeton University Press, 1980); Hugh N. Kennedy, *The Early Abbasid Caliphate* (London: Croom Helm, 1981); and Moshe Sharon, *Black Banners from the East: The Establishment of the Abbasid State, Incubation of a Revolt* (Jerusalem: Magnes Press, 1983).

27. al-Tabari, *The History of al-Tabari,* vol. 28, *Abbasid Authority Affirmed,* trans. Jane Dammen McAuliffe (Albany: State University Press of New York, 1995), 238.

28. For the sections of al-Khatib al-Baghdadi's *History of Baghdad* that deal with the topography of the city, see Jacob Lassner, trans. *The Topography of Baghdad in the Early Middle Ages: Texts and Studies* (Detroit, MI: Wayne State University Press, 1970).

29. Alfred Guillaume, trans., *The Life of Muhammad: A Translation of Ibn Ishaq's Sirat Rasul Allah* (Oxford: Oxford University Press, 1955), 79–81.

30. al-Tabari, *The History of al-Tabari,* 28:244.

31. Ibid., 246. Abu Dawaniq was a nickname al-Mansur earned because of his notorious stinginess. *Dawaniq* is the plural of *daniq*—an accounting fraction of the *dirham,* somewhat akin to the modern "mill."

32. Lassner, trans., *The Topography of Baghdad,* 46–47.

33. Ibid., 47.

34. Broadhurst, trans., *The Travels of Ibn Jubayr,* 226.

35. Guy Le Strange, trans., *Baghdad during the Abbasid Caliphate from Contemporary Arabic and Persian Sources* (New York: Barnes and Noble, 1972 [1900]), 14; al-Muqaddasi, *The Best Divisions for Knowledge of the Regions,* 100.

36. al-Muqaddasi, *The Best Divisions for Knowledge of the Regions,* 103.

37. Ibid., 104.

38. Ibid., 108.

39. Ibid., 107–8.

40. Ibid., 123.

41. Bloom, *Paper before Print*, 48.

42. On this revolutionary phase, see Farhad Daftary, *The Isma'ilis: Their History and Doctrines* (New York: Cambridge University Press, 1990), 144–255; Heinz Halm, *The Empire of the Mahdi: The Rise of the Fatimids*, trans. Michael Bonner (Leiden: Brill, 1996); James E. Lindsay, "Prophetic Parallels in Abu 'Abd Allah al-Shi'i's Mission among the Kutama Berbers, 893–910," *International Journal of Middle East Studies* 24.1 (1992): 39–56; idem; "The Fatimid Da'wa in North Africa: Excerpted and Translated from al-Qadi al-Nu'man's (d. 974 A.D.) *Kitab iftitah al-da 'wa*," *Graeco-Arabica* 7–8 (1999–2000): 283–310; and Paul E. Walker, *Exploring an Islamic Empire: Fatimid History and Its Sources* (London: I. B. Tauris, 2002), 17–39.

43. al-Muqaddasi, *The Best Divisions for Knowledge of the Regions*, 163.

44. Ibid., 169. See pp. 160–65 of this book for a discussion of Ghadir Khumm and Ashura, the two festivals at the heart of Shi'i Islam.

45. al-Muqaddasi, *The Best Divisions for Knowledge of the Regions*, 166–67.

46. Ibid., 167.

47. Thackston, trans., *Naser-e Khosraw's Book of Travels*, 53.

48. al-Muqaddasi, *The Best Divisions for Knowledge of the Regions*, 171–72.

49. Bloom, *Paper before Print*, 74. See also Goitein, *A Mediterranean Society*, vol. 1, *Economic Foundations*, 111–15.

50. Goitein, *A Mediterranean Society*, 1:108–111.

51. Ibid., 348.

52. See Olivia Reme Constable, *Housing the Stranger in the Mediterranean World: Lodging, Trade, and Travel in Late Antiquity and the Middle Ages* (New York: Cambridge University Press, 2003).

53. Thackston, trans., *Naser-e Khosraw's Book of Travels*, 45.

54. Cited in Constable, *Housing the Stranger*, 68.

55. Broadhurst, *The Travels of Ibn Jubayr*, 317.

56. al-Muqaddasi, *The Best Divisions for Knowledge of the Regions*, 159.

57. Darke, Hubert, trans., *The Book of Government or Rules for Kings: The Siyar al-Mulk or Siyasat-nama of Nizam al-Mulk* (Richmond, UK: Curzon Press, 2002), 10.

58. My discussion of money in the medieval Islamic world is based on S. D. Goitein, "Money, Banking, and Finance," in *A Mediterranean Society* (Berkeley: University of California Press, 1967), 1:229–65; Michael Bates, *Islamic Coins* (New York: American Numismatic Society, 1982); and Warren C. Schultz, "The Monetary History of Egypt, 642–1517," in *The Cambridge History of Egypt*, ed. Carl F. Petry (New York: Cambridge University Press, 1998), 1:318–38.

59. Claude Cahen, "Monetary Circulation in Egypt at the Time of the Crusades and the Reform of al-Kamil," in *The Islamic Middle East, 700–1900: Studies in Economic and Social History*, ed. A. L. Udovitch (Princeton, NJ: Darwin Press, 1981), 326. Cited in Schultz, "Monetary History," 322.

60. Goitein, *A Mediterranean Society*, 1:231.

61. On the importance of maintaining public morality in the medieval Islamic world, see Michael A. Cook's magisterial *Commanding the Right and Forbidding Wrong in Islamic Thought* (New York: Cambridge University Press, 2000) and the epitome of this work for nonspecialists, *Forbidding Wrong in Islam: A Brief Introduction* (New York: Cambridge University Press, 2003). See also R. P. Buckley, trans.,

The Book of the Islamic Market Inspector: Niyayat al-rutba fi talab al-hisba (The Utmost Authority in the Pursuit of Hisba) by 'Abd al-Rahman b. Nasr al-Shayzari (New York: Oxford University Press, 1999), a twelfth-century market inspector's manual.

62. Darke, trans., *Book of Government,* 45.

63. Ibid.

64. Ibid.

65. Ibid.

66. Ibid.

67. Ibid., 46.

68. Claude Cahen, "Dhimma," in *Encyclopaedia of Islam,* New Edition, 12 vols. (Leiden: Brill, 1954–2004), 2:227–31. For an overview of the literature on non-Muslims in Islamic history, see R. Stephen Humphreys, "Non-Muslim Participants in Islamic Society," in *Islamic History: A Framework for Inquiry,* rev. ed. (Princeton, NJ: Princeton University Press, 1991), 255–83. See also A. S. Tritton, *The Caliphs and Their Non-Muslim Subjects: A Critical Study of the Covenant of Umar* (London: Frank Cass, 1970 [1930]); S. D. Goitein, *A Mediterranean Society;* Yohanan Friedman, *Tolerance and Coercion in Islam: Interfaith Relations in the Muslim Tradition* (New York: Cambridge University Press, 2003); and Richard Fletcher, *The Cross and the Crescent: Christianity and Islam from Muhammad to the Reformation* (New York: Viking, 2004).

69. See Brannon M. Wheeler, *Prophets in the Qur'an: An Introduction to the Qur'an and Muslim Exegesis* (London: Continuum, 2002).

70. Buckley, trans., *The Book of the Islamic Market Inspector,* 121–22.

71. M. Muhsin Khan, trans., *Sahih al-Bukhari: The Translation of the Meanings of Sahih al-Bukhari,* 9 vols. (Riyadh: Darussalam Publishers, 1997), vol. 4, book 52, num. 176. See pp. 60–62 of this book for an account of Muhammad's relations with the Jews of Medina.

72. Qur'an 2:65; 5:60; 5:78; 7:166. Uri Rubin, *Between Bible and the Qur'an: The Children of Israel and the Islamic Self-Image* (Princeton, NJ: Darwin Press, 1999), 213–15.

73. Jim Colville, trans., *Sobriety and Mirth: A Selection of the Shorter Writings of al-Jahiz* (London: Kegan Paul, 2002), 71–94.

74. Ibid., 73.

75. Ibid.

76. Ibid., 79.

77. Goitien, *A Mediterranean Society,* 2:375.

78. Buckley, trans., *The Book of the Islamic Market Inspector,* 122–23.

79. Goitein, trans., *Letters of Medieval Jewish Traders* (Princeton, NJ: Princeton University Press, 1973). See also Amitav Ghosh, *In an Antique Land* (New York: Alfred A. Knopf, 1993).

80. Goitein, *A Mediterranean Society,* 2:380–94.

81. al-Muqaddasi, *The Best Divisions for Knowledge of the Regions,* 153.

82. See especially Shawkat M. Toorawa, "The *Dhimmi* in Medieval Islamic Society: Non-Muslim Physicians of Iraq in Ibn Abi Usayb'iah's *'Uyun al-anba'fi tabaqat al-atibba'* [The Sources of Information on the Classification of Physicians]," *Fides et Historia* 26 (1994): 10–20.

83. Goitein, *A Mediterranean Society,* 2:24–241.

84. al-Muqaddasi, *The Best Divisions for Knowledge of the Regions,* 167.

85. *Holy Bible*, Authorized or King James Version (1611). Most modern English translations prefer to replace the Hebrew euphemism with "men."

86. Andrew M. Watson, *Agricultural Innovation in the Early Islamic World: The Diffusion of Crops and Farming Techniques, 700–1100* (New York: Cambridge University Press, 1983), 87–90.

87. Ibid., 103–11.

88. Archimedes (287–212 B.C.), a native of Syracuse, was a Greek mathematician and inventor. See Reviel Netz, ed. and trans., *The Works of Archimedes: Translated into English* (New York: Cambridge University Press, 2004).

89. See Ralph S. Hattox, *Coffee and Coffeehouses: The Origins of a Social Beverage in the Medieval Near East* (Seattle: University of Washington Press, 1985).

5

RITUAL AND WORSHIP

On the authority of Abu 'Abd al-Rahman 'Abdullah, the son of 'Umar ibn al-Khattab (may God be pleased with them both), who said: I heard the Messenger of God (may blessings and peace of God be upon him) say:

Islam has been built on five [pillars]: testifying that there is no god but God and that Muhammad is the Messenger of God, performing the prayers, paying the *zakat*, making the pilgrimage to the House, and fasting in Ramadan.[1]

As this hadith indicates, Muslim scholars have long described the five basic ritual practices of Islam in architectural terms. They refer to them as five pillars (*al-arkan al-khamsa*); the supports that define one's submission (*islam*) to God. The five pillars upon which the entire edifice of Islam rests are: the statement of belief (*shahada*), ritual prayer (*salat*), almsgiving (*zakat*), fasting (*sawm*) during the daylight hours of Ramadan (the ninth month of the Islamic calendar), and the pilgrimage (*hajj*) to Mecca during the twelfth month of the Islamic calendar. Islam as a religion comprised of five pillars (for some, jihad was a sixth pillar) is an idea that was developed and implemented by scholars and jurists decades or more after Muhammad's death. Nevertheless, these five pillars are the instruments that for centuries have produced the rhythms and the melodies of daily life in all Islamic societies.[2]

As with most issues concerning the first Islamic centuries, when precisely each of the five pillars began to be practiced in a way recognizable to us and to medieval Islamic scholars is a matter of some debate and conjecture. It is clear that each developed in its own way and had its own history. It is also clear that the sources allow us to speak with greater confidence about Islamic ritual practices by the time we get to the third Islamic century. As we turn our attention to each of the five pillars, we will have something to say about how each developed in the early period. But the bulk of our attention will be devoted to how these five pillars were observed in the medieval Islamic world, especially after A.D. 800 or so. As is the case with any religious tradition, there is a broad spectrum of religious practices and rituals in Islam beyond the core elements shared by all Muslims. Hence, this chapter will also examine the distinctive Shi'i pilgrimages in Iraq as well as other pilgrimages observed in the medieval Islamic world, especially in the sacred territories of Syria and Palestine.

SHAHADA—STATEMENT OF FAITH

The first of the five pillars, the *shahada* or statement of belief, is a simple two-part statement that is at the center of Islamic belief, ritual, and worship. This statement declares: *la ilaha illaʾllah* (there is no god but God); *Muhammadun rasul Allah* (Muhammad is the Messenger of God). Both of these statements are in the Qurʾan, but not side by side as in the *shahada* formula. Nor does the Qurʾan treat them as *the* defining statement of what it means to be a Muslim. According to Fred M. Donner, what was of greatest concern, at least in the early years of Muhammad's career in Medina, was belief in the one God and the Last Day.[3] Nevertheless, versions of both phrases begin to appear on coins in the late seventh century. Since we do not find the *shahada* formula per se on earlier coins, it appears that the *shahada* had not been officially established as a ritual statement of faith until the end of the first Islamic century.

The inscriptions on the Dome of the Rock in Jerusalem (est. 692) provide additional early examples of the sentiments of the *shahada*, though again not the specific *shahada* formula per se. One overtly anti-Trinitarian, hence, anti-Byzantine Christian inscription reads, "There is no god but God alone; He has no partner with Him; Muhammad is the messenger of God." Another reads, "Muhammad is the servant of God and His messenger whom He sent with the guidance and the religion of truth. ..." This latter phrase is the same one embossed on Umayyad coins after the reign of Abd al-Malik (r. 685–705), the Umayyad caliph who built the Dome of the Rock.

When precisely the *shahada* became a widespread ritual formula used by Muslims is not clear and for our purposes really not important. Despite the fact that the specific formulaic expression of the *shahada* is missing from the earliest Islamic coins and the first major example of monumental

The Dome of the Rock as seen from the Mount of Olives, ca. 1870. *Source:* The Middle East Documentation Center, The University of Chicago.

architecture in Islamic history, it is clear that the sentiments of the *sha-hada*—that there is no god but God and that Muhammad is His messenger—were very much part of the Qur'an and Islamic doctrine from the earliest period.

While the *shahada* is the simplest of the five pillars to perform because of its brevity, it is arguably the most important of all. For to recite the *shahada* publicly with proper intent in front of Muslim witnesses is to accept one's obligation to perform the remaining four as well. Moreover, the *shahada* is the very wellspring from which the remaining four flow. That is, without belief in the one God and that Muhammad is His messenger, the remaining four pillars are without meaning. Now, while one need recite the *sha-hada* but once to be a Muslim, in practice, observant Muslims recite the *shahada* throughout the day and on all manner of occasions.

The *shahada* is an absolutely crucial part of each of the five daily ritual prayers. It is also used in an abbreviated form (*la illaha illa'llah*) to invoke God's blessing, aid, protection, and so forth throughout the day in any and all circumstances. It is customary for a father to whisper it in the ear of his newborn child, and children are often taught to recite the *shahada* as soon as they are able to speak. Of course, neither a newborn nor a small child is expected to understand the words let alone the meaning of the *shahada* at such young ages. But the act of reciting and hearing is what is important as much for the parent as for the child.

SALAT—PRAYER

While one can make the case that the *shahada* is the most important of the five pillars, in practice, it is the *salat*—the ritual prayer performed five times per day—that is the ubiquitous symbol of Islamic ritual and piety. Qur'an 4:104 is but one of many passages in which the faithful are commanded to perform the *salat*.

Attend to your prayers so long as you are safe: for prayer is a duty incumbent on the faithful, to be conducted at appointed hours.

Qur'an 11:14 provides general guidance as to when and how often one should perfom the salat: "Attend to your prayers, morning and evening, and in the night-time too." What we do not find in the Qur'an are instructions that one should perform the *salat* five times per day (rather than three), the precise hours of the day in which the *salat* should be performed, the ablutions necessary to make one ritually clean (*tahara*) so that one's prayers can be valid, the words that should be said in the ritual prayers, or the prostrations that should be performed. Rather, we learn these things—and in great detail—from the biographical literature about Muhammad's life and teachings.

For example, one of the most famous episodes in these biographies is Muhammad's night journey, during which Muhammad was taken from Mecca to Jerusalem on a winged horse named Buraq. From Jerusalem he was taken up to the seventh heaven where God informed him that his community would be required to perform fifty prayers per day. According to Ibn Ishaq, Muhammad described his return journey as follows:

On my return, I passed by Moses and what a fine friend of yours he was! He asked me how many prayers had been laid upon me and when I told him fifty he said, "Prayer is a weighty matter and your people are weak, so go back to your Lord and ask Him to reduce the number for you and your community." I did so and He took off ten. Again I passed Moses and he said the same again; and so it went on until only five prayers for the whole day and night were left. Moses again gave me the same advice. I replied that I had been back to my Lord and asked Him to reduce the number until I was ashamed, and I would not do it again. He of you who performs them in faith and trust will have the reward of fifty prayers.[4]

Ibn Ishaq's account of Muhammad's negotiations with God to reduce the number of prayers from fifty to five is reminiscent of Abraham's heated argument with God to reduce the number of righteous men necessary to save Sodom from fifty to ten (Genesis 18:22–30). More importantly, Ibn Ishaq's account provides a powerful narrative explaining why the faithful should perform the ritual prayer five times per day.[5] Elsewhere in the biographical literature we learn at what time of day these five ritual prayers should be performed as well as which ablutions, prostrations, and words are required.

Mihrab and *Minbar* in the Aqsa Mosque, Jerusalem, ca. 1870.
Source: The Middle East Documentation Center, The University of Chicago.

Prior to his *hijra* to Medina, Muhammad had instructed his followers to pray toward Syria, which was understood to mean toward Jerusalem. He continued this practice after his arrival in Medina as well. We are given few details about Muhammad's specific relations with the Jews of Medina during this very early period, but according to Ibn Ishaq, when Muhammad received a revelation to change the direction (*qibla*) of prayer toward Mecca "at the beginning of the seventeenth month after the apostle's arrival in Medina" (February 624), a number of the leading Jews of Medina asked him why he had done so. They told him that if he changed it back to Jerusalem, they would follow him. Ibn Ishaq continues by stating that they only did this "to seduce him from his religion."[6] This theme of deceit and perfidy characterizes the subsequent portrayal of the three leading Jewish clans in Medina, resulting in the expulsion of the Banu Qaynuqa in

624 and the Banu l-Nadir in 625, while in 627 the men of the Banu Qurayza were executed and the women and children were enslaved.[7] The importance of determining the direction of Mecca is evidenced by the fact that each mosque has a *mihrab*, which usually takes the form of a niche in a wall to indicate the direction (*qibla*) of Mecca. Near the *mihrab* is a *minbar*, or elevated pulpit, from which the sermon (*khutba*) is preached.

According to shari'a, the day begins at sunset. Hence, the first of the five designated prayer times is technically the evening prayer, followed by the night, morning, noon, and afternoon prayers.[8] However, as far as many (if not most) Muslims are concerned, the day begins with the crack of dawn, and the morning prayer is the first prayer of the day. Each of the five prayers (if possible) is to be performed during specific periods determined according to the position of the sun, not a time on the clock. Thus, the evening prayer can be performed at any time after sunset and before the disappearance of the last light over the horizon; the night prayer at any time between the end of the time period for the evening prayer and beginning of the time period for the morning prayer, which begins with the crack of dawn and ends at sunrise; the noon prayer when the sun is at its mid-point, not at noon. The afternoon prayer is usually performed when an object's shadow is slightly longer than itself.

While each prayer is valid during its appointed time frame, it is best to perform the *salat* shortly after the call to prayer (*adhan*) itself. The person who performs the call to prayer is a muezzin (Arabic, *mu'adhdhin;* he who performs the *adhan*). It should be noted that if one is unable to perform a specific prayer at its designated time it is permissible to perform it later in the day, as long as one fulfills the five daily prayers prior to the night prayer and going to bed (an argument that the morning prayer should be considered the first prayer of the day). In fact, it is common among those for whom it would be extremely inconvenient to pause from their work to perform the ablution and prayer (day laborers, farmers, and so forth) to defer the noon and afternoon prayers until after the evening prayer. The night prayer is said before one retires for the night.

The five daily prayers may be recited in the privacy of one's home (the customary practice among women), though it is more meritorious to say them with others in a mosque, especially on Friday. While the Arabic word for mosque (*masjid*) literally means "place of prostration," its function was essentially the same as a synagogue or church in the ancient world; that is, it was a place for the formal worship and assembly of the community of faith. In early Islamic history, the entire male Muslim population was required to worship together during the Friday noon prayer in its local congregational mosque (*masjid al-jami'a*).

The origins of Friday as the Muslim day of congregational worship are rather cloudy. Some have argued that the choice of Friday is rooted in some sort of effort to distinguish the new Muslim community from the Jews, who worshiped on Saturday, and Christians, who worshiped on

Sunday. This is a reasonable speculation in light of Muhammad's deteriorating relations with the Jews of Medina during his second year there, as well as the abundance of polemical arguments against the theology and practices of Jews and Christians in later sources. However, as S. D. Goitein argues, Muhammad most likely chose Friday for purely practical reasons.[9] Goitein bases his argument on accounts in which Muhammad instructed his followers in Medina (prior to his own *hijra* there) to hold the public worship service on the day when the Jews bought their provisions for their Sabbath; that is, Friday.

The practical reason for choosing Friday (long known in Arabic as *yawm al-jum'a;* day of assembly) was that it was the major market day in Medina and, as such, the bulk of the local population already gathered there for purposes of commerce.[10] The choice of the hottest part of the day in one of the hottest climates in the world for the congregational prayer has a practical explanation also. Since the bulk of the population was already in town on Fridays, and since the day's trading was largely completed by noon because of the heat, holding the congregational worship at that time made perfect sense from a practical standpoint, despite the numerous anecdotes of people dozing off during sermons because of the heat. Of course, since the authors of most of the available sources were, in fact, religious scholars of some sort, they may have had reason to attribute drowsiness to heat rather than the occasionally less-than-impressive sermon by one of their colleagues.

It should be noted that unlike in Judaism and Christianity, the day for weekly congregational prayers was not established as a day of rest in Islam nor was it treated as such in the medieval Islamic world. In fact, as we see in Qur'an 62:9–11, the Friday congregational prayers were established as a break in the business day in which believers were to focus their attention on God:

Believers, when you are summoned to Friday prayers [lit., to prayer on the day of assembly; *yawm al-jum'a*], hasten to the remembrance of God and cease your trading. That would be best for you, if you but knew it. Then when the prayers are ended, disperse and go your ways in quest of God's bounty. Remember God always, so that you may prosper. Yet no sooner do they see some commerce or merriment afoot than they flock eagerly to it, leaving you [Muhammad] standing all alone. Say: "That which God has in store is far better than any merriment or any commerce. God is the Most Munificent Giver."

The sources make it clear that from the earliest times the Friday prayers involved more than religious observance and more than the pious taking a break from commerce to focus attention on the Most Munificent Giver. To participate in the Friday service demonstrated one's adherence to the new community, as did the invocation of God's blessing on the ruler during the Friday sermon (*khutba*). While Friday was not a formal day of rest, it did take on an air of sanctity similar to that associated with Saturday in Judaism and Sunday in most Christian traditions as evidenced by admonitions that Muslims should take care to bathe completely on Fridays, wear their best clothes, perfume themselves, and eat special dishes.

Though one could find slight differences from region to region and among the various factions within the Islamic tradition, the rituals and requirements of the five daily prayers were practiced in much the same fashion throughout the medieval Islamic world whether in Cordoba, Cairo, Damascus, Baghdad, or Delhi. In Islamic countries today and with the benefit of modern audio technology, one can hear a muezzin's voice begin to sound forth from one mosque, then another, and another, until there is a chorus of voices and loudspeakers calling the faithful to prayer throughout an entire city.

The muezzin begins by proclaiming four times that "God is greater" (*Allahu Akbar*). The next five lines are repeated twice each: "I bear witness that there is no god but God; I bear witness that Muhammad is the messenger of God. Hurry to the *salat*. Hurry to salvation. God is greater." The last line, "There is no god but God," is said only once. In the morning call to prayer, the muezzin usually adds the phrase, "prayer is better than sleep" after the phrase, "hurry to salvation." The call to prayer according to the Shi'i tradition is the same as that described above, but concludes with, "Hasten to the best of deeds." According to the Shi'i tradition, the second caliph Umar (r. 634–44), whose religious authority the Shi'is do not accept, arbitrarily changed the original wording of the call to prayer by deleting this phrase.[11] Shi'is also add the phrase, "I bear witness that Ali is truly the friend of God" (*wali Allah*). Obviously, muezzins in the medieval Islamic world did not have access to powerful loudspeakers, but one certainly could hear the call to prayer (*adhan*) in the precincts surrounding the central congregational mosque in any town or city. In fact, a congregational mosque usually had more than one muezzin calling the faithful to prayer from different stations at the same time.

Before one can actually perform the *salat*, he or she needs to perform a series of major or minor ablutions in order to enter into a state of ritual purity (*tahara*). Therefore, it was essential that medieval mosque complexes at the very minimum had access to clean water; some had simple water faucets, others had elaborate and ornate fountains, while still others even housed complete bathing facilities. The major ablution (*ghusul*) is required when one is in a state of major ritual impurity in which one cannot perform the *salat* nor should he or she enter a mosque or even touch a Qur'an. Activities that required a man or woman to perform a major ablution in order to be restored to a state of ritual purity include sexual intercourse and touching a human corpse. In addition, men must perform a major ablution after any emission of semen; women must do so after menstruation and after childbirth. The major ablution requires that one bathe from head to foot, making sure that every part of one's body is made wet.

Ablution vessels. The storage vessel with tap is about 18 inches tall. *Source:* Lane, *Manners and Customs,* 69.

The minor ablution (*wudu*) is less complete but is required after one has entered a state of minor ritual impurity from a range of unavoidable daily activities such as sleeping, relieving oneself, and passing gas. The minor ablution involves washing certain body parts with water in the following order: hands, mouth, nose, right forearm, left forearm, face, head, ears, right foot, left foot. Both the major and the minor ablution can be performed with sand or with a stone in those instances where one has no access to clean water or if one should not touch water for medical or other reasons.

Once one has performed the appropriate ablution he or she is ready to perform the *salat.* The act of ritual prayer is the same whether one performs it by oneself or with others. It consists of a series of precise bowings and prostrations, which together are called a *rak‘a* (lit., bowing) or prayer cycle. In a congregational setting, those performing the *salat* line up behind an imam (prayer leader) in straight rows facing the direction (*qibla*) of Mecca. Hence, those performing the *salat* in Syria face south; in Yemen they face north; in India they face west; and in Morocco they face east. Men line up behind the imam; if women are present, they line up at the back of the mosque behind the men or in an antechamber of some sort. Following the imam's lead, the worshipers stand erect and recite the *Fatiha* or opening chapter of the Qur'an:[12]

In the name of God the Compassionate the Merciful. Praise be to God, Lord of the Universe, the Compassionate, the Merciful, Sovereign of the Day of Judgment!

The prostrations of prayer, 1. *Source:* Lane, *Manners and Customs,* 76.

You alone we worship, and to You alone we turn for help. Guide us to the straight path, the path of those whom you have favored, not of those who have incurred Your wrath, nor of those who have gone astray. (Qurʾan 1:1–7)

After a minute or so they briefly bow at the waist with their back straight (roughly 90 degrees) and their hands on their knees; they then stand erect again, and almost immediately place their knees, hands and forehead on the ground. They hold this position for a few moments and then assume a sitting position. They then prostrate themselves a second time, all the while reciting short prayers. This completes the first *rakʿa,* after which they stand erect and begin the cycle all over again for as many times as required for each daily prayer. The evening prayer consists of three *rakʿa*s, the night four, the morning two, the noon four, and the afternoon four. After the final *rakʿa* is performed the worshipers remain seated and turn to their right and to their left and say *al-salam ʿalaykum* (peace be upon you).

Those who are unable to perform the *salat* because of a physical malady should perform those aspects of the *salat* that they can and recite the appropriate passages at the appropriate times. The five daily *salat*s represent the *required* ritual prayers in Islamic ritual and worship. They do not represent the full extent of prayer in Islamic practice. Additional passages from the Qurʾan may be recited during the *salat* and additional greetings and blessings may be said. Supererogatory *salat*—that is, additional

The prostrations of prayer, 2. *Source:* Lane, *Manners and Customs*, 77.

rakʿas—are highly recommended as expressions of piety and devotion as well. In addition to the ritual prayer of the *salat*, more open-ended supplications are part of Muslim worship. However, such petitions are referred to as *duʿat* and do not fall under the rubric of *salat*, nor do they require the performance of a *rakʿa*. Additional types of prayer are also found as part of the Shiʿi and Islamic mystical (Sufi) traditions.

ZAKAT—THE GIVING OF ALMS

Despite its frequent admonitions to give alms, the Qurʾan does not specify what percentage of one's wealth should be given as *zakat* beyond that one should give "what you can spare" (Qurʾan 2:219). The Qurʾan does, however, set forth who the legitimate recipients of alms are.

Alms (*zakat*) shall be only for the poor and the destitute, for those that are engaged in the management of alms and those whose hearts are sympathetic to the Faith, for the freeing of slaves and debtors, for the advancement of God's cause (lit., *fi sabil Allah*), and for the traveler in need. That is a duty enjoined by God. God is all-knowing and wise.[13] (Qurʾan 9:60)

Since the very concept of the five pillars of Islam was worked out by scholars and jurists decades or more after Muhammad's death, it reflects the vision of right religion as understood by educated and relatively well-to-do individuals. As the scholars and jurists extrapolated from the Qur'an and the hadiths what the specific obligations of the *zakat* were for the faithful, they determined that they only applied to those Muslims who possessed wealth and that the *zakat* should be paid from one's profit, not necessarily the totality of one's wealth. Consequently, the poor and destitute are under no obligation to give it. A consensus also emerged that the portion of one's profit that should be given as *zakat* can range anywhere from 2.5 percent of one's gold, silver, or merchandise to 10 percent of one's crops to be paid at harvest time. How the *zakat* was actually collected and/ or distributed is difficult to ascertain. While the Qur'an speaks of giving *zakat* to those "engaged in the management of alms," individuals could legitimately give their *zakat* directly to the deserving recipients.

It should be noted that throughout Islamic history there have been occasions when one regime or another sought to take control of the collection of *zakat* ostensibly as a means of enhancing its own religious *bona fides*, but also as another means of collecting revenue for the state. Some scholars and reformers have even argued that the *zakat* was the only legitimate form of taxation of Muslims. However, regimes that sought to rely solely on *zakat* collections soon learned that they needed to impose other kinds of taxes as well.

SAWM—FASTING

Fasting as an integral part of religious observance certainly was not new with Islam in seventh-century Arabia. It had long been part of the religious observances of ancient Rome, Greece, Babylon, Egypt, and India.[14] Moreover, it is abundantly clear from even a cursory examination of the Bible that it was essential to the religious life of Ancient Israel and the early Christian Church as an act of repentance, contrition, atonement, mourning, prayer, supplication, and devotion. According to the Bible, Moses, Elijah, and Jesus each fasted 40 days prior to supernatural encounters. Moses fasted for 40 days on Mt. Sinai before God gave him the Ten Commandments on "two stone tablets inscribed by the finger of God" (Deuteronomy 9:9–10). Elijah fasted for 40 days until he reached Horeb, the mountain of God, where "the word of the LORD came to him" (1 Kings 19:7–9). Jesus fasted for 40 days in the desert, after which "the tempter came to him" and put him through a series of three trials and temptations. In the end,

Jesus said to him: "Away from me, Satan! For it is written: 'Worship the Lord your God, and serve him only.'" Then the devil left him, and angels came and attended him. (Matthew 2:1–11)

Fasting remained a crucial religious observance in post-Biblical Judaism and various Christian churches, especially on the Day of Atonement among Jews and during Lent in preparation for Easter among Christians. In addition, fasting and vows of abstinence of various sorts including abstaining from certain foods and beverages, sexual relations, and even from cutting one's hair and bathing were practiced in pre-Islamic Arabia.

While the precise relationship between these pre-Islamic practices and fasting in Islamic ritual practice is a matter of some debate and conjecture, there is evidence that the fasting practices of the Jewish clans of Medina did influence the establishment of Ramadan as the designated month for Islamic fasting. Some Qurʾanic passages from the Meccan phase of Muhammad's career have been interpreted as possibly indicating some sort of fast. However, it is during the Medinan phase of his career (when Muhammad encountered a large Jewish community that practiced fasting) that Qurʾanic passages commanded the new Muslim community to fast. Qurʾan 2:183–87 is the only (and rather long) passage that addresses the establishment of Ramadan as the time for the Muslim fast.

Believers, fasting is decreed for you as it was decreed for those before you; perchance you will guard yourselves against evil. Fast a certain number of days, but if any one among you is ill or on a journey, let him fast a similar number of days later; and for those that cannot endure it there is a ransom: the feeding of a poor man. He that does good of his own accord shall be well regarded; but to fast is better for you, if you but knew it. In the month of Ramadan the Koran was revealed, a book of guidance for mankind with proofs of guidance distinguishing right from wrong. Therefore whoever of you is present in that month let him fast. But he who is ill or on a journey shall fast a similar number of days later on. God desires your well-being, not your discomfort. He desires you to fast the whole month so that you may magnify God and render thanks to Him for giving you His guidance. When My servants question you about Me, tell them that I am near. I answer the prayer of the suppliant when he calls to Me; therefore let them answer My call and put their trust in Me, that they may be rightly guided. It is now lawful for you to lie with your wives on the night of the fast; they are a comfort to you as you are to them. God knew that you were deceiving yourselves. He has relented towards you and pardoned you. Therefore you may now lie with them and seek what God has ordained for you. Eat and drink until you can tell a white thread from a black one in the light of the coming dawn. Then resume the fast till nightfall and do not reproach them, but stay at your prayers in the mosques. These are the bounds set by God: do not approach them. Thus He makes known His revelations to mankind that they may guard themselves against evil.

Since this is the only passage that deals with the establishment of the Ramadan fast, it has fostered a great deal of commentary as to its precise meaning. We will only deal with a few issues here to clarify some basic points as to how the Ramadan fast functions as a pillar of Islamic ritual and worship.

According to the biographical literature, the phrase "those before you" is said to mean the Jews and refers to how Muhammad had originally prescribed that his followers in Medina fast on the day of Ashura, as did the Jews; that is, on the Jewish Day of Atonement. Muhammad did this in part to emphasize his prophetic closeness to Moses. In fact, Moses and Muhammad's closeness to him is one of the dominant themes in the Qur'an.[15] Scholars have argued that after his break with the Jews and the change in direction (*qibla*) of prayer from Jerusalem to Mecca, Muhammad began to emphasize a fast distinct from the one during Ashura. According to this argument, it was after the break with the Jews that Ramadan was established as the distinctive period of Muslim fasting, the duration of which was by that time one lunar month.

Ramadan came to take on a special sanctity in Islamic religious practice as well. According to Qur'an 2:185, it was during the month of Ramadan that Muhammad received his first revelation. This correlation between revelation and fasting parallels the connection between the giving of the tablets to Moses on Mt. Sinai and the fast on the Jewish Day of Atonement. The connection between fasting and repentance is made explicit in a well-known hadith, according to which Muhammad declared that "all previous sins are forgiven to one who keeps Ramadan in faith and for God's sake."[16] This linkage between Ramadan, revelation, fasting, and repentance in Islamic sacred history is further enhanced in a hadith that asserts that Abraham, Moses, David, and Muhammad all received their revelations during Ramadan.

The Messenger of God (May God bless him and grant him peace) said: The Scriptures [*al-suhuf*] were revealed to Abraham on the second night of Ramadan, the Psalms [*zabur*] were revealed to David on the sixth, the Torah to Moses on the eighteenth of Ramadan, and the Qur'an [*al-furqan*] to Muhammad (May God bless him and grant him peace) on the twenty-fourth of Ramadan.[17]

Hadiths such as this not only enhance the sanctity of the month of Ramadan, they also vindicate the prophethood of Muhammad as the legitimate successor to a long line of prophets before him.

Based on Qur'an 2:183–87 and the biographical tradition, Muslim scholars developed lengthy and elaborate treatises that addressed a host of questions regarding the Ramadan fast, including how and when it was to be performed, who should perform it, what exempted one from it, which behaviors and consumable products were to be avoided, and what invalidated one's fast. Scholars argued that the fast was obligatory for all adult Muslims (generally defined as those who had fully entered into puberty) who were in good physical and mental health. For one's fast to be valid, one is required to begin each day by declaring one's intention to abstain from those things which are forbidden from that point when "you can tell a white thread from a black one in the light of the coming dawn" until nightfall. Many Muslims break their fast each evening by eating dates, which according to Islamic tradition was how Muhammad used to break his fasts.

During the fast, one should abstain from all food and drink, even swallowing spittle that could be expectorated. Since one drinks (*sharaba*) rather than smokes tobacco in Arabic, when tobacco was introduced to the Islamic world well after the time period of this book, it was also prohibited. As specified in Qur'an 2:187, sexual relations with one's spouse are forbidden during this period. Deliberate seminal emission, menstruation, and bleeding in the wake of childbirth all invalidate one's fast. Those who could not perform it because of illness, travel, warfare, or other exigent circumstances should make up the fast at a later time; the same applies to women who are pregnant or nursing. Those who simply break the fast without good reason are required to fast for two months to make up for each day. The *moral* importance of the fast as an act of worship and piety is amplified by a hadith according to which Muhammad said, "Five things break the fast of the faster—lying, backbiting, slander, ungodly oaths, and looking with passion."[18] Here it is engaging in morally reprehensible activities that are always forbidden, rather than failing to temporarily abstain from things normally permitted, that invalidates one's fast.

Ramadan begins on the first day of the ninth month of the Islamic lunar calendar; that is, when the new crescent moon is sighted. The Ramadan fast, of course, begins the following morning. It ends with the Festival of Fast Breaking ('*Id al-Fitr*) when the next crescent moon is cited at the beginning of the tenth month, Shawwal. Since lunar months generally last 29 or 30 days, if the skies are too cloudy to see whether there is in fact a crescent moon, the first of Ramadan is deemed to be 30 days after the first of the preceding month. Those accustomed to the 365-day Gregorian Christian solar calendar tend to find the 354-day Islamic lunar calendar rather frustrating since the Islamic calendar does not employ any mechanism to ensure that it coincides with the four seasons of the year. According to the Gregorian calendar, the ninth month (September) always straddles the end of summer and the beginning of autumn. According to the Islamic calendar, the ninth month (Ramadan) *can* correspond to September. But since Ramadan comes eleven days (give or take a day) earlier each year, it would take another 33 years or so before it would correspond with September again. (See "Christian and Islamic Calendars with Conversion Table,"pp. 253–79, for a more detailed comparison of the Christian and Islamic dating systems.)

HAJJ—PILGRIMAGE

What ultimately became the rituals of the Islamic *hajj* represent a combination of several pre-existing Arabian practices associated with Arafat and Mina, two uninhabited sacred pilgrimage areas outside of Mecca; visitations to the Ka'ba in Mecca were later added to these rituals. Other pre-Islamic pilgrimage practices that were incorporated into the Islamic *hajj* include the inviolability of the pilgrim, particular dress called the *ihram*, performances of certain rituals and sacrifices, and commerce. In time, these rituals came to be associated with Abraham who, according to Qur'an 2:127, built the Ka'ba with his son Ishmael.[19]

Whatever the process of how the *hajj* came to be organized or how the various rituals became identified with Abraham, the annual pilgrimage differs from the first four pillars in terms of location, timing, participation, and scope. That is, it takes place in and around the precincts of Mecca and it begins on the eighth and ends on the thirteenth day of the last lunar month of the Islamic calendar, Dhu l-Hijja (The *Hajj* Month). The annual *hajj* is incumbent upon *only* those Muslims who are able to undertake it and can withstand the many physical and financial hardships required of the pilgrims who come from the entire Islamic world. Nevertheless, this communal pilgrimage rite is the single act of devotion that best represents the egalitarian nature that Islam claims for itself.

In addition to the required annual *hajj*, many Muslims perform another pilgrimage (*'umra*), which can be performed at any time of the year. While the *'umra* is considered praiseworthy, it is neither obligatory nor is it considered a substitute for the *hajj*. During the Middle Ages, stations were established along the major arteries well outside of Mecca where pilgrims (after months, even years in transit) removed their regular clothes, performed the necessary ablutions, and donned a special garment consisting of two rectangular pieces of unstitched white cloth, called an *ihram*. (Today, pilgrims who fly usually put on the *ihram* before boarding the plane or in transit.) The men wrap one piece of cloth around their waists. This piece should be large enough that it reaches to the ankles. The second piece of cloth is wrapped around the torso and draped over the left shoulder.

The eleventh-century Persian traveler Naser-e Khosraw describes this procedure in his *Book of Travels* as follows:

> For people who have come from faraway places to perform the minor pilgrimage, there are milestones and mosques set up half a parasang away from Mecca, where they bind their *ehram*. "To bind the *ehram*" means to take off all sewn garments and to wrap an *ezar*, or seamless garment, about the waist and another about the body. Then, in a loud voice, you say, *"Labbayk, allahomma, labbayk,"* [Your servant, O Lord, has answered your call] and approach Mecca.[20]

The *ihram* is worn throughout the entire *hajj*. Pilgrims either go barefoot or wear sandals without heels. Instead of two pieces of unstitched white cloth, women's *ihram* consists of clean, modest, and plain clothes. While women cover their heads, they are not required to wear a face veil as is the custom in some of their home countries.

Upon entering Mecca, the pilgrim enters the Haram mosque and performs a series of prescribed rituals. According to Naser-e Khosraw,

> Having come into the city, you enter the Haram Mosque, approach the Ka'ba, and circumambulate to the right, always keeping the Ka'ba on your left. Then you go

The Ka'ba, ca. 1870. *Source:* The Middle East Documentation Center, The University of Chicago.

to the corner containing the Black Stone, kiss it, and pass on. When the Stone is kissed once again in the same manner, one *tawf*, or circumambulation, has been completed. This continues for seven *tawfs*, three times quickly and four slowly.[21]

According to the Qur'an, Abraham and his son Ishmael built the Ka'ba. It covers the Black Stone, which is about 12 inches across. Today, because it is fractured, the Black Stone is held together in a silver setting. However, in Muhammad's day the Ka'ba housed the deities venerated by the Meccans. In 630, when Muhammad occupied Mecca, he cleansed the Ka'ba of its idolatrous trappings and restored it to its original purpose, much as Judah Maccabee cleansed the temple in Jerusalem when the city was under Seleucid control (ca. 164 B.C.), an event that is commemorated in the Jewish holiday of Hanukah.[22]

Today the Ka'ba is an irregular cube that stands some 50 feet high and is in the center of the massive courtyard of the Haram mosque that was refurbished in the late twentieth century in order to accommodate the millions of pilgrims who (because of the ease of modern transportation and greater security) are now able to make the pilgrimage. In Naser-e Khosraw's day the entire Haram structure was much smaller, though more elaborate than the simple structure that existed in Muhammad's day. According to Naser-e Khosraw,

The Ka'ba stands in the middle of the courtyard and is rectangular, with the length on a north-south axis. It is seventeen cubits long, thirty [high], and sixteen wide. The door is toward the east. Entering the Ka'ba, you find the Iraqi corner on the right, the Black Stone corner on the left, the Yemeni corner at the southwest, and the Syrian corner at the northwest. The Black Stone is set in a large stone in one corner of the Ka'ba at about the height of a man's chest.[23]

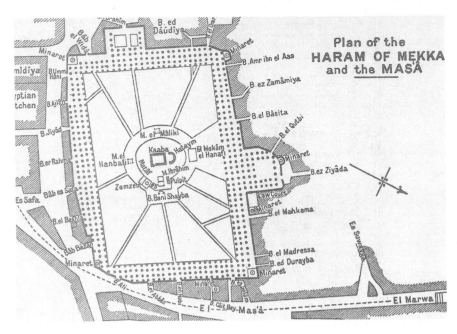

The Haram of Mecca. *Source:* Rutter, *The Holy Cities of Arabia.*

After completing the seven circumambulations, the pilgrim proceeds to the *Maqam Ibrahim* (Station of Abraham), which is opposite the Ka'ba. Standing behind the station, the pilgrim performs two *rak'a*s, which in this case are called the circumambulation prayer. After completing the two *rak'a*s, he or she then goes to the well of Zamzam, drinks some of the water, and performs additional ablutions. Despite the well's brackish water, the waters of Zamzam are believed to possess special healing qualities. According to Islamic tradition, at Zamzam the Angel Gabriel miraculously brought forth water for Hagar and Ishmael after Abraham had left them at Mecca and headed into the desert. The Bible records a similar story; however, according to Genesis 21:8–21, Hagar and Ishmael's exile, their thirst, and the angel of God's miraculous provision of water occurred in the wilderness near Beersheba in the northern Negev desert of modern Israel.[24]

Next, the pilgrim leaves the Haram complex through the southeastern gate and proceeds to a small hill called Safa and then he or she runs or jogs about a quarter mile to another rise called Marwa. The pilgrim repeats this seven times, all the while reciting prayers in commemoration of Hagar's frantic search for water. Today, pilgrims run between Safa and Marwa in an enclosed causeway. In Naser-e Khosraw's day, pilgrims ran the length of the bazaar.

Coming down from Marwa the last time, you find a bazaar with about twenty barber-shops facing each other. You have your head shaven and, with the minor pilgrimage ['*umra*] completed, come out of the Sanctuary.[25]

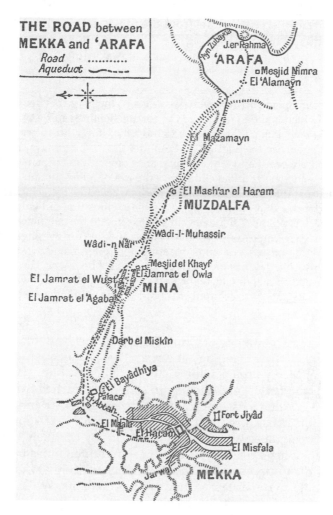

The road between Mecca and Arafat. *Source:* Rutter, *The Holy Cities of Arabia.*

Those performing the *hajj* have only just completed the preliminary rituals. Instead of having their hair cut, they leave the Haram complex and find their lodgings, for there are many more journeys and rituals that must be completed.

First, pilgrims travel east through the desert some four miles to Mina where they spend the night on the eighth day of Dhu l-Hijja. They set out the next day for the plain of Arafat, about seven miles further east. While the wealthy could afford to hire camel transport, most walked the whole way. Some even walked barefoot as an act of piety. Despite the sanctity and inviolability of the pilgrimage month, it was not unusual for Bedouin raiders to plunder the procession. Ibn Jubayr's pilgrimage in mid-March

1184 was interrupted by bandits from the Shuʿbah tribe. But Uthman, the ruler of Yemen who was making the pilgrimage that year, came to the rescue of Ibn Jubayr and his fellow pilgrims. According to Ibn Jubayr, Uthman advanced

with all his companions bristling with weapons, to the gorge between Muzdalifah and ʿArafat, which is the place where the road is hemmed in by two mountains from one of which, being that which is to the left of him who goes to ʿArafat, the Shuʿbah descend upon the pilgrims and plunder them. The Emir raised a pavilion in this gorge between the two mountains, after one of his companions had gone before (to reconnoiter) and had climbed to the top of the mountain on his horse. The mountain is difficult of ascent, and we marvelled at his achievement, and even more so at that of his horse which was able to climb that difficult slope that [a gazelle?] could not climb. All the pilgrims felt secure in the company of this Emir who earned two rewards; one for the holy war, and one for the pilgrimage, since the safeguarding of those who came in deputation [pilgrimage] to Great and Glorious God on such a day, has the merit of the greatest holy war. The ascent of the people continued all that day, all night, and all Friday so that there was assembled on ʿArafat a multitude whose numbers could not be counted save by Great and Glorious God.[26]

At noon on the ninth day of Dhu l-Hijja, pilgrims begin the part of the *hajj* that is called "The Standing" at Arafat. That is, they keep vigil around the Mount of Mercy until sundown, all the while reciting, "What is Your command? I am here!" and listening to sermons preached from the summit where, according to Islamic tradition, the first man, Adam, had prayed and Muhammad had preached his farewell sermon. At sunset, the pilgrims pack up and begin their return to Mecca. By tradition, the pilgrims wait until they have reached Muzdalifa, some three miles behind them towards Mina, to perform their evening prayers. Those who are physically able to do so run as fast as they can to Muzdalifa. While most of the pilgrims sleep at Muzdalifa overnight, women, children, and the infirm can continue the trip to Mina.

At Mina on the tenth of the month, the pilgrims perform a series of rituals in remembrance of God's instruction to Abraham to sacrifice a ram instead of his son:

And when they had both submitted to God's will, and Abraham had laid down his son prostrate upon his face, We called out to him, saying: "Abraham, you have fulfilled your vision." Thus do We reward the righteous. That was indeed a bitter test. We ransomed his son with a noble sacrifice and bestowed on him the praise of later generations. "Peace be on Abraham!" (Qurʾan 37:103–109)

There was disagreement among the earliest commentators as to whether the son in question was Isaac or Ishmael, but majority opinion came to be that (unlike the biblical account in Genesis 22) it was Ishmael.[27]

At Mina three stone pillars are located east to west along the valley. The first ritual act at Mina is for pilgrims to throw pebbles at the westernmost pillar. This "stoning of the devil" symbolically identifies the pilgrim with Abraham, who threw stones at the devil as he sought to convince Abraham not to sacrifice his son as God commanded. After the stoning, the pilgrim then purchases a goat or a sheep (or a camel if he or she can afford it) to sacrifice. The pilgrim turns the face of the animal towards Mecca and then slits its throat as Abraham did. Slitting the animal's throat is the final act of the *ihram* phase.[28] The pilgrim then finds one of the many barbers present at Mina and has his head shaved, or at least has some of his hair cut. After this, he is free to put on his regular clothes. He then returns to Mecca where he circumambulates the Ka'ba once again. In the remaining days of the *hajj*, pilgrims return to Mina to throw pebbles at all three pillars, sacrifice additional animals, and enjoy the festivities with fellow pilgrims. At Mina during Ibn Jubayr's *hajj*, things got a bit out of hand, as he observed

dissension and riot between the negro inhabitants of Mecca and the Turks of 'Iraq in which there were some hurts. Swords were drawn, arrow notches were put to the bow-string, and spears were thrown, while some of the goods of the merchants were plundered. Mina in those days is one of the greatest of markets, and in it are sold wares ranging from precious jewels to the cheapest strings of beads, together with other articles and various merchandises of the world, for it is the meeting place of men from all lands. God preserved us from the evils of this disturbance, and speedily brought calm. Thus ended this successful standing upon 'Arafat, and the faithful had ended their pilgrimage. Praise be to God, Lord of the Universe.[29]

At the end of each *hajj*, the old fabric covering of the Ka'ba (*kiswa*) was removed and replaced with a new one, a pilgrimage practice that has pre-Islamic origins as well. In Islam's early years, it became customary for the caliph to supply the new *kiswa* each year. According to Ibn Jubayr,

On Saturday, which was the Day of Sacrifice, the *Kiswah* ['Robe' or covering] of the holy Ka'bah was conveyed on four camels from the encampment of the 'Iraqi Emir to Mecca. Before it walked the new Qadi, wearing the black vestment given to him by the Caliph, preceded by banners and followed by rolling drums.... The *Kiswah* was placed on the venerated roof of the Ka'bah, and on Tuesday the 13th of the blessed month the Shaybites were busily employed in draping it. It was of a ripe green colour, and held the eyes in spell for its beauty. In its upper part it had a broad red band (that ran around the Ka'bah), and on the side that faces the venerated Maqam [Station of Abraham], the side that has the venerated door and that is blessed, there was written on this band, after the Bismillah [the invocation "In the name of God"] the words "Surely the first Sanctuary appointed for mankind (was that at Bekkah [Mecca])" [Koran III, 95]. On the other side was written the name of the Caliph with invocations in his favour. Running round the band were two reddish zones with small white roundels containing inscriptions in fine characters that included verses from the Koran as well as mentions of the Caliph.[30]

Before the pilgrims depart for home, they return to Mecca to perform a farewell circumambulation as their final ritual act. Although it is not required, many (if not most) pilgrims also make the trek northward to Medina to visit Muhammad's mosque there before returning home. While one must be in Mecca and its surroundings to perform the annual *hajj* rituals, markets in villages, towns, and cities throughout the medieval Islamic world teemed with animals in the days leading up to the day on which pilgrims sacrificed to Mina as Muslims prepared to sacrifice and feast in solidarity with their brothers and sisters in the Arabian desert. In addition, as the Islamic conquests vastly expanded the territories under Islamic political authority, the *hajj* caravans from the furthest reaches of the Islamic world proved to be indispensable to Islamic learning and international commerce.

SHIʿI PILGRIMAGE

Veneration of the imams and visitation (*ziyara*) to their tombs were essential to Shiʿi piety as well. When these and other practices became part of the Shiʿi tradition is not entirely clear but we do know that after the Shiʿi Buyids conquered Baghdad in 945, they encouraged the open and public performance of three public rituals that were fundamentally important to daily life in Shiʿi Islam—the commemoration of Ghadir Khumm, the commemoration of the martyrdom of Husayn ibn Ali, and visitation to the Shiʿi imams' tombs. The Ismaʿili Fatimids in Egypt (969–1171) encouraged the public performance of these rituals also.

Since the Buyids belonged to the Twelver or Imami branch of the Shiʿi tradition and the Fatimids belonged to the Sevener or Ismaʿili branch, a few words to explain the differences between these two groups are in order.[31] There are two basic doctrines that developed among the Shiʿis. First, the rightful caliph or imam had to be a lineal descendant of Muhammad, in particular through the line of Ali ibn Abi Talib and Muhammad's daughter, Fatima. The second, and more controversial, is that the caliph or imam was not only the political head of the community, but an infallible religious teacher—guaranteed to be without error in matters of faith and morals. Because of this emphasis on the religious and theological role of the head of the community, Shiʿi texts tend to use the title Imam for this office more frequently than Caliph (*Khalifa*) or Commander of the Believers (*Amir al-Muʾminin*). The Twelver and the Sevener Shiʿis agree on these two doctrines; where they disagree is over the identity of the seventh Imam.

The Shiʿi doctrine of the imamate is based on the events of 18 Dhu l-Hijja A.H. 10 (16 March A.D. 632). According to the biographical literature, Muhammad stopped at a place called Ghadir Khumm (Pool of Khumm) on his way back to Medina after he had made his final pilgrimage to Mecca. His followers gathered in a grove of trees to escape the suffocating heat and to perform the noon prayers. At the conclusion of the prayers,

Muhammad raised Ali's hand in front of the assembly and asked them if they recognized that he, Muhammad, had a claim on each of the believers that supercedes any claim they might have on themselves. They, of course, responded in the affirmative. He then took Ali's hand again and said, "Of Whomsoever I am Lord [*Mawla*], then 'Ali is also his Lord. O God! Be Thou the supporter of whoever supports 'Ali and the enemy of whoever opposes him." Umar ibn al-Khattab then said to Ali, "Congratulations, O son of Abu Talib! Now morning and evening [i.e. forever] you are the master of every believing man and woman."[32]

Since the version cited above comes from Ibn Hanbal's (d. 855) *Musnad*, a Sunni hadith collection, it is clear that the Sunni tradition does not deny that the events of Ghadir Khumm actually occurred. Where they differ, and differ significantly, is on the interpretation of the event itself. According to Shi'i doctrine, the above story proves beyond a shadow of a doubt that not only had Muhammad designated Ali ibn Abi Talib and his descendants to succeed him upon his death (which occurred only three months later on 13 Rabi' al-Awal A.H. 11/June 8 A.D. 632), but that he had bestowed his own political and religious authority on them as well. While Sunnis afford Ali a tremendous amount of respect and prestige as an early convert, as Muhammad's cousin and son-in-law, and as the fourth of the Rashidun or "rightly guided caliphs," they simply reject the Shi'i interpretation of the events of Ghadir Khumm altogether.

As things turned out, Muhammad's close companion and father-in-law, Abu Bakr (r. 632–34), became the first caliph. He was followed by two more companions, Umar ibn al-Khattab (r. 634–44) and Uthman ibn Affan (r. 644–56). After Uthman's assassination, Ali ibn Abi Talib (r. 656–61) became caliph/imam. However, the entirety of his caliphate/imamate was disrupted by the first civil war in Islamic history (656–61), ultimately ending in his assassination at the hands of a Khariji dissident. Based on the Shi'i interpretation of the events of Ghadir Khumm, Ali was the first *legitimate* caliph or imam; the first three caliphs—Abu Bakr, Umar, and Uthman—were usurpers.

According to Shi'i tradition, the imamate then passed to Ali's eldest son, Hasan (d. 669). However, Hasan abdicated his claim to the caliphate in 661 and did not oppose Mu'awiya (r. 661–80), who established the Umayyad caliphate (661–750) with Damascus as its capital. Despite Hasan's abdication, there remained a faction (*shi'a*) of Muslims who continued to argue that only someone from Muhammad's house (in particular a descendant of Ali) could legitimately lead the Muslim community.[33] Shortly after Yazid acceded to the caliphate (r. 680–83), Ali's younger son, Husayn (the third imam), was persuaded to leave his home in the Hijaz and to travel to Kufa to lead a revolt and to take his rightful place at the head of the Muslim community. On 10 Muharram 61 (October 10, 680), Umayyad forces routed Husayn and 72 armed men (together with their women and children) at Karbala. The victors beheaded Husayn and his companions and put their heads on pikes as they marched to Kufa. The women and children were taken prisoner, including Husayn's sole surviving son, Ali, who had been too ill to participate in the battle.

As was customary, Husayn's head was sent to the caliph Yazid in Damascus as proof that Husayn was indeed dead. Some reports indicate that Yazid was saddened by the death of Muhammad's grandson. Others suggest that he treated Husayn's head with contempt as he poked at Husayn's mouth with his cane, for which he was immediately taken to task by Abu Barzah al-Aslami, a companion of Muhammad.

Are you poking the mouth of al-Husayn with your cane? Take your cane away from his mouth. How often have I seen the Apostle of God kiss it! As for you, Yazid, you will come forward on the Day of Resurrection, and Ibn Ziyad will be your advocate. But this man will come forward on the Day of Resurrection, and Muhammad will be his advocate.[34]

Husayn's head was returned to his dependants who buried it. But where? His head has a place of honor in the Umayyad Mosque in Damascus. Another tradition says that it was buried in Ashkelon where the Fatimids built a shrine in 1098. During the Crusader period it was disinterred and moved to Cairo (1153) where it is venerated to this day at the Husayn Mosque. There are other traditions that state that Husayn's head was interred in Medina, Kufa, Najaf, Karbala, Raqqa on the upper Euphrates, and even in distant Merv in Afghanistan.[35]

With Husayn's martyrdom, the imamate passed to his son, Ali, and then continued to be passed on from father to son as each imam designated his successor. The most important imam after Ali ibn Abi Talib is Ja'far al-Sadiq (d. 765), the sixth imam. He was renowned for his piety and learning, and many of those who studied at his feet went on to be learned scholars and jurists. Ja'far designated his son, Isma'il (d. 754), to succeed him as the seventh imam upon his death. However, since Isma'il died before his father did, the question of who should succeed Ja'far was contested. One faction contended that the imamate had passed to Isma'il's son, Muhammad. This faction came to be called Seveners or Isma'ilis.[36]

The other faction argued that the imamate should continue through Isma'il's brother, Musa (d. 799), whom they consider to be the seventh imam. The members of this faction (known as Twelvers or Imamis) believe that when the eleventh imam, Hasan al-Askari, died in 873 or 874, he was succeeded by his son, Muhammad, as the twelfth imam. Moreover, the Twelvers believe that Muhammad did not die; rather, he went into occultation; that is, he was and still is present in some hidden form, and that at the appointed time (which of course we cannot know) he will return as the Mahdi (or Messiah).[37] (See "The Twelver and Isma'ili Shi'i Imams" in the "Genealogical and Dynastic Tables.")

While this brief sketch may seem rather long to some, it is necessary to clarify the importance of the role of Imam Ali and his successors in Shi'i theology. For without a basic understanding of the doctrine of the imamate, it is difficult to understand the importance and the meaning of the very public rituals of Shi'i Islam that were part of daily life in the medieval Islamic world, especially in Iraq under the Buyids and in Egypt under the Fatimids. Since Muhammad's designation of Ali as imam at Ghadir Khumm is one of the foundational events in Shi'i Islam, it should come as no surprise that when the Buyids came to power in Iraq they instituted the public commemoration of Ghadir Khumm on 18 Dhu l-Hijja.

Little has survived about the nature of these early celebrations other than that the Buyid ruler, Mu'izz al-Dawla (945–67), issued orders that the city of Baghdad be decorated and that fires be lit at the local police headquarters. More dramatic were the public rituals commemorating the martyrdom of Husayn at the Battle of Karbala on 10 Muharram. (Hence, the name for this festival, Ashura, which means tenth.) Ashura became one of the most important rituals in the Shi'i religious calendar, for it was not only seen as a memorial of Husayn's unjustified death, his was the paradigm of martyrdom that all should emulate.[38] Before we examine the Ashura rituals, let us examine the festival of Ghadir Khumm in Fatimid Egypt.

In 973, a group of people from Fustat and some of the North African troops who had conquered Egypt gathered for the first time to commemorate the festival of Ghadir Khumm with the sanction of the Fatimid state. Information on the early manifestations of the festival remains scanty, but there are enough reports to give us a glimpse of the kinds of things that accompanied it, especially the closing of shops, the wearing of fine clothing, the public mourning and lamenting of Husayn's martyrdom, and the cursing of Muhammad's companions who, according to Shi'i dogma, had betrayed Ali. The themes of martyrdom and suffering suffused the Ghadir Khumm festival and Ashura, which according to the Islamic calendar, occurs some three weeks later.

By the twelfth century, however, Ghadir Khumm had been transformed from a popular festival to a very elaborate celebration at the Fatimid court. The festival had lost much of its Shi'i symbolism and had become one of the public ceremonies that the regime employed to legitimate itself before its subjects—Sunnis, Shi'is, Christians, and Jews. There were special robes for the caliph, his wazir, and the commanders of the infantry and cavalry. The palace gates were bedecked with tapestries. Rams were slaughtered and sumptuous banquets were prepared much like the feasts prepared to celebrate the end of the Ramadan fast and as part of the sacrifices made during the annual pilgrimage.[39]

According to Shi'i doctrine, all of the imams except the twelfth died as martyrs. Some were slain in battle, while others were poisoned or died in prison. The most dramatic martyrdom, of course, is that of Husayn. Since all the imams are seen as the "sinless ones," their suffering and martyrdom is understood to exemplify their willingness to voluntarily take on a portion of the suffering and punishment of mankind. That is, because of their suffering, mankind can be spared the severity of God's justice.

Moreover, the imams' martyrdom qualifies them to serve as intercessors between the faithful and God himself. Such an understanding of redemptive suffering parallels the sacrifice of Jesus Christ for the sins of the world in Christian theology. However, unlike Christian theology, Islamic theology rejects the notion of original sin. Therefore, the suffering of the imams benefits the faithful only for the specific sins they have committed.[40] Since Sunnis reject the Shi'i doctrine of the imamate, they reject the idea that the Shi'i imams play any redemptive role at all.

The faithful can benefit from the imams' suffering and martyrdom by their willingness to become martyrs themselves, but also by visiting the tombs of the imams and weeping over them. There are reports of the faithful weeping over Husayn's grave almost immediately after his tomb was constructed. In 850, the Abbasid caliph al-Mutawakkil had the shrine destroyed in order to put an end to Shi'i pilgrimages to it. His efforts proved unsuccessful as pilgrims continued to go to Karbala even though there was no shrine. The Buyid ruler Adud al-Dawla restored Husayn's tomb at Karbala and Ali's tomb at Najaf in 990.[41]

Over time, elaborate rituals developed as part of the faithfuls' visitation and public mourning at the imams' tombs, whether at Husayn's tomb in Karbala, Ali's tomb in Najaf, or at the tombs of the imams buried in Baghdad, Samarra, Medina, or Mashhad in Iran. According to the thirteenth-century theologian Ta'usi (d. 1266), the faithful expressed their longing for the imams and their suffering as they cried over their graves, "Could I but be your ransom! Since the Lord of the future life takes pleasure in sorrow and since it serves to purify God's servants—behold! we therefore don mourning attire and find delight in letting tears flow. We say to the eyes: stream in uninterrupted weeping forever!"[42]

The most elaborate of the lamentations is for Husayn, and the rituals of the Ashura festival date at least to the Buyid period. Sources indicate that the oldest Ashura ritual is for pilgrims to Husayn's tomb to request a sip of water in commemoration of one of Husayn's final acts prior to his martyrdom. Near the end of the battle, as Husayn pleaded for water for his infant son (whom he held in his arms), an arrow pierced the baby's throat and killed him. Undeterred by his child's death, Husayn continued to fight until he was finally slain.[43] The elaborate passion plays and public processions where mourners beat and cut themselves in identification with Husayn's suffering so common in modern Iran, Iraq, and Lebanon appear to date from the Safavid (1501–1722) and Qajar (1779–1925) periods in Iran, well after the period covered in this book.

While visitation (*ziyara*) to the tombs of the imams did not constitute formal legal substitutes for making the obligatory annual pilgrimage (*hajj*), Shi'is considered their spiritual benefits and rewards to be greater than those of the *hajj*. This is clearly illustrated in a brief exchange in which a certain Shihab ibn Abd Rabbihi was asked how many obligatory annual pilgrimages he had made. When he replied that he had made the *hajj* nineteen times, his interlocutor responded, "Should you complete twenty-one Pilgrimages, they will be counted for you as a *ziyara* to Husayn...."[44]

It should be noted that the public celebration of Ashura and Ghadir Khumm did not go unnoticed by the Sunni populations of Buyid Iraq. In fact, there are reports that in 999, eight days after the Ghadir Khumm festival, Sunnis in Baghdad staged their own counterfestival in commemoration of the day on which Muhammad and Abu Bakr took refuge in a cave during their *hijra* to Medina. Eight days after the Ashura festival in the same year, they commemorated the day on which Mus'ab ibn al-Zubayr (another early hero of Sunni Islam) was killed. At other times, some members of the Sunni population responded to these Shi'i festivals with violence. There are no specific accounts of counterfestivals in Fatimid Egypt, but there is evidence that some of the Sunni population in Fustat responded violently as well.[45]

When Saladin deposed the Fatimids in 1171, state support for Isma'ili Shi'ism and its rituals ended, the name of an Abbasid caliph was invoked in the Friday sermon for the first time in two centuries, and Fatimid institutions of learning were transformed into Sunni ones. Since Isma'ili Shi'ism had never taken deep root in Egypt outside the ruling elite and a few others, it soon withered away.[46] Although the Seljukid conquest of Baghdad in 1055 ended state sponsorship of Twelver Shi'ism in Iraq, this form of Shi'ism did not wither away at all in that region. After all, Iraq was the Shi'i Holy Land of sorts. Karbala and Najaf housed the tombs of Imam Husayn and Imam Ali ibn Abi Talib, while Baghdad and Samarra housed the tombs of other imams as well. Pilgrimage to these shrines continued, though not as freely as had been the case under the Buyids.

The Seljukids were ardent supporters of Sunni Islam and had little sympathy for Shi'ism in any form. In fact, Nizam al-Mulk had many negative things to say about Shi'is. To a certain extent, this stemmed from the fact that in his day the Fatimids in Egypt were the Seljukids' most formidable foe. But more important was the broad Sunni disdain, even contempt, for the Shi'i theology of the imamate, the veneration of the Shi'i imams, and the condemnation of Muhammad's companions as betrayers of Ali. Nizam al-Mulk essentially viewed Shi'is as heretics who represented a potential fifth column that threatened the security of the state itself. His advice to Malikshah was to follow the example of Mahmud of Ghazna, Toghril, and Alp Arslan, who had only appointed upright Sunnis as secretaries, tax collectors, or other government officials. As far as they were concerned, "These men [Shi'is] are of the same religion as the Dailamites [Buyids] and their supporters; if they get a firm footing they will injure the interests of the Turks and cause distress to the Muslims. It is better that enemies should not be in our midst."[47] Nizam al-Mulk advised against appointing any non-Sunni, including Jews, Christians, and Zoroastrians, but clearly his strongest invectives were directed against Shi'is.

OTHER PILGRIMAGES

In addition to the obligatory *hajj*, the praiseworthy *'umra*, and the distinctive Shi'i pilgrimages (*ziyara;* lit. visitation) to the tombs of the Shi'i imams, there were countless local pilgrimages that became part of the fabric of daily life throughout the medieval Islamic world. The tombs of Muhammad's companions, saints, scholars, martyrs, virtuous rulers, even sacred objects such as copies of the Qur'an, or more mundane items that ostensibly belonged to Muhammad himself, were venerated and visited by the faithful hoping to benefit from the *baraka* (divine blessing) they possessed.

Jerusalem and other sacred sites associated with pre-Islamic prophets and patriarchs in Syria, Egypt, and Iraq were especially popular destinations for pilgrims of all types. Understandably, Jerusalem and the Biblical Holy Land (the site of the ancient Jewish Temple and the Church of the Holy Sepulchre) held pride of place for both Jews and Christians. However, Muslims considered Syria to be a holy land (*ard muqaddasa*) as well. Not only was Syria the home of Abraham, Moses, Joseph, David, Solomon, and Jesus, its most holy city, Jerusalem, was the destination of Muhammad's night journey as well as the home of the al-Aqsa Mosque and the venerable Dome of the Rock.[48]

An important subgenre of the merits (*fada'il*) of places literature is the pilgrimage guide or manual, which described important pilgrimage sites in a particular town or province of the medieval Islamic world.[49] One such manual for Syria is Ibn al-Hawrani's (d. 1592) *Guide to Pilgrimage Places*, which draws extensively on earlier sources such as al-Raba'i's (d. 1052) *Merits of Syria and Damascus* and Ibn Asakir's (d. 1176) *History of Damascus.*[50] Like his predecessors, Ibn al-Hawrani praises the merits of Syria and its sacred history, including stories about more than 100 sacred sites in Damascus and Syria such as the location of Moses' (Musa) tomb, the site where Jesus (Isa) will descend to earth at the end of time, the place where John the Baptist's (Yahya ibn Zakariyya) head was discovered, the location of the shrine of Husayn ibn Ali's head, the tomb of Nur al-Din (d. 1174), even the presence of one of Muhammad's sandals, which is buried in the southern wall above the *mihrab* of the *Dar al-Hadith*, near the Citadel of Damascus.

Ibn al-Hawrani emphasizes the importance of visiting the tombs of saints and other holy persons based on hadiths in which Muhammad is reported to have visited the graves of his companions. He concludes his *Guide to Pilgrimage Places* with a section on proper pilgrimage etiquette:

It is customary practice to position oneself facing the face of the tomb's inhabitant, to approach, and greet him. The pilgrim stands near the tomb, comporting himself, humbling himself, surrendering himself, bowing his head to the ground with dignity, God-inspired peace of mind, and awe, casting aside power and chieftanship. He should imagine himself as if he were looking at the tomb's inhabitant and he at him. Then he should look with introspection to what God has granted to the one visited of loftiness, dignity and divine secrets and how God has made him a locus of sainthood, for secrets, closeness, obedience, and divine gnostic truths.[51]

Al-Hawrani further advises the pilgrim to read from the Qur'an and to devote himself to prayer and the remembrance of God. The purpose of these meditations and supplications is to focus the pilgrim's attention on his sins (which prevent him from drawing close to God) and the virtues and spiritual blessing of the saint (which will be rewarded at the end of days).

One of the many holy sites in Syria where Muslims could pray and confidently expect God's blessing is known as the Dome of the Chain (*qubbat al-silsila*), located near the Dome of the Rock. According to legend, when David was king of Israel, God had suspended a chain between heaven and earth at that very spot. Whenever a dispute arose between two individuals, David would tell them to go to the chain and whoever was telling the truth would be able to grasp the chain. If he lied, the chain would retract and he would not be able to take hold of it. How this worked is illustrated by a fascinating tale in which a certain man entrusted a pearl of great price to another. When the first man demanded it back, the second man told him that he had already returned it to him and that they should appeal to the chain to resolve their dispute.

According to a version of the tale in Ibn Asakir's *History of Damascus*, the second man found a staff and made a hole in it, in which he placed the pearl. They then went to see King David, who said, "Go to the chain." So they went. The pearl's owner said, "O My God! Verily, You know that I entrusted him with this pearl, but he never returned it to me. I petition You, that I may take hold of the chain." He then took hold of it. The other said, "Like you, I too will petition. Take this my staff." And he handed it to him. He said, "O my God! Verily, You know that I returned his pearl to him. I petition You, that I may take hold of the chain." He then took hold of it. Then David said, "What is this! Both the offender and the offended take hold of the chain?" Then God revealed to him, "The pearl is in the staff." And the chain was raised.[52]

It should be noted that some Sunni scholars denounced as heretical innovations any pilgrimage other than the obligatory and praiseworthy pilgrimages to Mecca (*hajj* and *'umra*). The famous Syrian scholar Ibn Taymiyya (1263–1328) is representative of such opinion. Based on the practice of Muhammad, Ibn Taymiyya argued that it was permissible for the faithful to invoke God's blessings on the deceased. However, he adamantly opposed the visitation of tombs for the purpose of petitioning a deceased person (or an object connected to him or her) to intercede with God on one's behalf. As far as Ibn Taymiyya was concerned, such supplication was a form of polytheism. Moreover, based on a hadith attributed to Muhammad, Ibn Taymiyya also argued that the veneration of tombs was forbidden because Jews and Christians had originally instituted the practice. "It is for this reason that the Prophet ... said in a [sound] tradition: ʿMay God curse the Jews and Christians. They have taken the tombs of their prophets as places of prayer (lit. prostration). Such behaviour is to be warned against.'"[53]

Condemnation of religious practices and doctrines because of their real or alleged connections to Jews and/or Christians was standard practice in medieval Islamic polemics. Nevertheless, the Middle East and North Africa had been home to saints, ascetics, mendicants, and miracle workers (Jewish, Christian, and others) since antiquity. Holy men, with their divine blessing, special knowledge, and miracles were part and parcel of daily life in the pre-Islamic Mediterranean world centuries before Muhammad's birth.[54] Moreover, as evidenced by Ibn al-Hawrani's *Guide to Pilgrimages* (and despite the objections of Ibn Taymiyya and his ilk), pilgrimage (*ziyara*) to the tombs and shrines of prophets, scholars, mystics, saints, and even some virtuous rulers and others was "the very center and pivot of popular religious life" in the medieval Islamic world.[55]

NOTES

1. Ezzedin Ibrahim and Denys Johnson-Davies, trans., *An-Nawawi's Forty Hadith* (Damascus: The Holy Koran Publishing House, 1976), 34.

2. Dozens of English-language primers on Islam of varying quality have been published over the years. I have listed some of the best in the "Ritual and Worship" section of "Suggestions for Further Reading." For a detailed description of Islamic ritual practices in early nineteenth-century Egypt, see Edward W. Lane, "Religion and Laws" in *An Account of the Manners and Customs of the Modern Egyptians: The Definitive 1860 Edition* (Cairo: American University Press, 2002), 64–110.

3. See Fred M. Donner, "From Believers to Muslims: Confessional Self-Identity in the Early Islamic Community," in *The Byzantine and Early Islamic Near East*, vol. 4, *Patterns of Communal Identity*, ed. Lawrence I. Conrad (Princeton, NJ: Darwin Press, forthcoming).

4. Alfred Guillaume, trans., *The Life of Muhammad: A Translation of Ibn Ishaq's Sirat Rasul Allah* (Oxford: Oxford University Press, 1955), 186–87.

5. Some scholars have argued that the number five was chosen to set the young Muslim community apart from Jews, who observed three prayers, and Syriac Christian monks, who observed seven. See especially S. D. Goitein, "Prayer in Islam," in his *Studies in Islamic History and Institutions* (Leiden: Brill, 1966), 84–85.

6. Guillaume, *The Life of Muhammad*, 258–59.

7. See pp. 60–62 of this book for an account of the fate of these three Jewish clans.

8. See the Biblical creation story in Genesis 1 where each of the six days of creation ends with the phrase, "And there was evening, and there was morning"— the first day, the second day, the third day, and so forth.

9. See S. D. Goitein, "The Muslim Friday Worship," in *Studies in Islamic History and Institutions* (Leiden: Brill, 1966), 111–25.

10. See Michael Lecker, "On the Markets of Medina (Yathrib) in Pre-Islamic and Early Islamic Times," *Jerusalem Studies in Arabic and Islam* 8 (1986): 133–48.

11. Heinz Halm, *Shiism* (Edinburgh: Edinburgh University Press, 1991), 138.

12. The *Fatiha* (lit., opening) is always recited in Arabic, even if the person reciting it is not an Arabic speaker.

13. See pp. 58–60 for a brief discussion of the concept of *jihad fi sabil Allah* (striving in the path of God) in Islamic thought.

14. My discussion of the establishment of Ramadan as the month of Muslim fasting is based on S. D. Goitein, "Ramadan, the Muslim Month of Fasting," in *Studies in Islamic History and Institutions*, 90–110, and K. Wagtendonk, *Fasting in the Qur'an* (Leiden: Brill, 1968).

15. See Brannon Wheeler, *Moses in the Qur'an and Islamic Exegesis* (Richmond, UK: Curzon Press, 2002).

16. Cited in Goitein, "Ramadan, the Muslim Month of Fasting," 100.

17. Cited in James E. Lindsay, "'Ali ibn 'Asakir as a Preserver of *Qisas al-Anbiya'*: The Case of David b. Jesse," *Studia Islamica* 82 (1996): 62. Ibn Asakir, in his biography of David, transforms this rather earthy figure found in Samuel and Kings into the paradigmatic model of Islamic supererogatory prayer and fasting. *Al-Furqan* is one of the names of the Qur'an. It conveys the idea of that which distinguishes between good and evil.

18. Cited in Sachiko Murata and William C. Chittick, *The Vision of Islam* (St. Paul: Paragon House, 1994), 17.

19. On pre-Islamic pilgrimage and other ritual practices in and around Mecca, see Patricia Crone, "The Sanctuary and Meccan Trade," in *Meccan Trade and the Rise of Islam* (Princeton, NJ: Princeton University Press, 1987), 168–99. On the identification of the *hajj* with Abraham, Hagar, and Ishmael, see Reuven Firestone, *Journeys in Holy Lands: The Evolution of the Abraham-Ishmael Legends in Islamic Exegesis* (Albany: State University of New York Press, 1990).

20. Wheeler M. Thackston, trans., *Naser-e Khosraw's Book of Travels (Safarnama)* (Albany: State University of New York Press, 1986), 68. Since the *Safarnama* was written in Persian, Thackston employs the Persian vocalization (*ehram; ezar*) rather than the Arabic (*ihram; izar*). See also Ibn Jubayr's twelfth-century account of the pilgrimage in R. J. C. Broadhurst, trans., *The Travels of Ibn Jubayr* (London: J. Cape, 1952); Ibn Battuta's fourteenth-century account in H. A. R. Gibb, trans. *The Travels of Ibn Battuta A.D. 1325–1354*, 5 vols. (London: Hakluyt Society, 1958–2000), 1:188–248; and F. E. Peters, *The Hajj: The Muslim Pilgrimage to Mecca and the Holy Places* (Princeton, NJ: Princeton University Press, 1994).

21. Thackston, trans., *Naser-e Khosraw's Book of Travels*, 69.

22. See 1 and 2 Maccabees in the Apocrypha.

23. Thackston, trans., *Naser-e Khosraw's Book of Travels*, 75.

24. See Firestone, *Journeys in Holy Lands*, 48–51; 63–71.

25. Thackston, trans., *Naser-e Khosraw's Book of Travels*, 69.

26. Broadhurst, trans., *The Travels of Ibn Jubayr*, 176–77. Also cited in Peters, *The Hajj*, 121–22.

27. For some of the arguments for Isaac and for Ishmael, see al-Tabari, *The History of al-Tabari*, vol. 2, *Prophets and Patriarchs*, trans. William M. Brinner (Albany: State University Press of New York, 1987), 82–97.

28. Individual pilgrims no longer slaughter animals by themselves. Rather, they donate the price of the sacrifice to a fund controlled by the Saudi Arabian govern-

ment, which supervises the slaughter of the animals and then distributes the meat to poor communities all over the Muslim world.

29. Broadhurst, trans., *The Travels of Ibn Jubayr*, 184–85; Peters, *The Hajj*, 126.

30. Broadhurst, trans., *The Travels of Ibn Jubayr*, 185; Peters, *The Hajj*, 126–27. The *bismilla* is the opening sentence of all but one of the 114 chapters of the Qur'an, "In the name of God, the Merciful, the Compassionate." It was customary for an author to write only a few phrases of a Qur'anic passage with the assurance that his reader had the Qur'anic text memorized and would fill in the blanks himself. Qur'an 3:96–97 in its entirety reads as follows, "The first temple [house] ever to be built for mankind was that at Bakkah, a blessed site, a beacon for the nations. In it there are veritable signs and the spot where Abraham stood. Whoever enters it is safe. Pilgrimage to the House is a duty to God for all who can make the journey. As for the unbelievers, God can surely do without them." Bakkah is another name for Mecca.

31. There are a number of introductions to Shi'i Islam, which is far more nuanced than I have space to describe here. I have listed some of the best in the section "Shi'i Islam" in the "Suggestions for Further Reading."

32. Cited in Moojan Momen, *An Introduction to Shi'i Islam* (New Haven, CT: Yale University Press, 1985), 15.

33. On competing theories of legitimacy in early Islam, see Moshe Sharon, "The Development of the Debate around the Legitimacy of Authority in Early Islam," *Jerusalem Studies in Arabic and Islam*, 5 (1984): 121–42; Patricia Crone and Martin Hinds, *God's Caliph: Religious Authority in the First Centuries of Islam* (New York: Cambridge University Press, 1986); Patricia Crone, *God's Rule: Government and Islam* (New York: Columbia University Press, 2004); and Wilferd Madelung, *The Succession to Muhammad: A Study of the Early Caliphate* (New York: Cambridge University Press, 1997).

34. al-Tabari, *The History of al-Tabari*, vol. 19, *The Caliphate of Yazid b. Mu'awiyya*, trans. I. K. A. Howard (Albany: State University of New York Press, 1990), 174.

35. Halm, *Shiism*, 16.

36. On Isma'ili Shi'ism, see Farhad Daftary, *The Isma'ilis: Their History and Doctrines* (New York: Cambridge University Press, 1990).

37. On the doctrine of the hidden Imam, see Momen, *An Introduction to Shi'i Islam*, 161–72. On the parallels between Roman Catholicism and Shi'i Islam, see James A. Bill and John Alden Williams, *Roman Catholics and Shi'i Muslims: Prayer, Passion and Politics* (Chapel Hill: University of North Carolina Press, 2002).

38. It should be noted that Husayn's death at the hands of Yazid ibn Mu'awiyya's agents has never been seen as a good thing by Sunni Muslims either, for no good could ever come from the murder of Muhammad's own grandson.

39. On the importance of the festival of Ghadir Khumm as an official public Fatimid ceremony, see Paula Sanders, *Ritual, Politics, and the City in Fatimid Cairo* (Albany: State University of New York Press, 1994), 121–34.

40. Halm, *Shiism*, 139–40. See also Mahmoud Ayyoub, *Redemptive Suffering in Islam: A Study of the Devotional Aspects of 'Ashura' in Twelver Shi'ism* (The Hague: Mouton, 1978); I. K. A. Howard, trans., *The Book of Guidance into the Lives of the Twelve Imams: Kitab al-irshad* (Elmhurst, N.Y.: Tahrike Tarsile Qur'an, 1981); and Bill and Williams, *Roman Catholics and Shi'i Muslims*.

41. Halm, *Shiism*, 15–16. Some Muslims also believe that Ali is buried in Mazar-i Sharif in Afghanistan.

42. Cited in Halm, *Shiism,* 140.

43. Momen, *An Introduction to Shi'i Islam,* 30.

44. Cited in Josef W. Meri, *The Cult of Saints among Muslims and Jews in Medieval Syria* (New York: Oxford University Press, 2002), 141.

45. Sanders, *Ritual, Politics, and the City in Fatimid Cairo,* 125.

46. Devin J. Stewart, "Popular Shiism in Medieval Egypt," *Studia Islamica* 84 (1996): 35–66.

47. Hubert Darke, trans., *The Book of Government or Rules for Kings: The Siyar al-Mulk or Siyasat-nama of Nizam al-Mulk* (Richmond, UK: Curzon Press, 2002), 159–60.

48. Amikam Elad, *Medieval Jerusalem and Islamic Worship: Holy Places, Ceremonies, Pilgrimage* (Leiden: Brill, 1995) and Paul M. Cobb, "Virtual Sacrality: Making Muslim Syria Sacred before the Crusades," *Medieval Encounters: Jewish, Christian and Muslim Culture in Confluence and Dialogue* 8.1 (2002): 35–55.

49. See Christopher Taylor, *In the Vicinity of the Righteous: Ziyara and the Veneration of Muslim Saints in Late Medieval Egypt* (Leiden: Brill, 1999) and Josef W. Meri, *The Cult of Saints.* Although Taylor and Meri focus on different regions and historical periods, they demonstrate unequivocally the importance of *ziyara* to the religious life of the medieval Islamic world.

50. Josef W. Meri, "A Late Medieval Syrian Pilgrimage Guide: Ibn al-Hawrani's *al-Isharat il Amakin al-Ziyarat (Guide to Pilgrimage Places),*" *Medieval Encounters: Jewish, Christian and Muslim Culture in Confluence and Dialogue* 7.1 (2001), 3–79. See also Josef W. Meri, trans., *A Lonely Wayfarer's Guide to Pilgramage: 'Ali ibn Abi Bakr al-Harawi's kitab al-isharati ila ma'rifat al-ziyarat.* Princeton, NJ: Darwin Press, 2004, which appeared after this book went to press.

51. Ibid., 76.

52. Cited in Lindsay, "Ibn 'Asakir as a Preserver of *Qisas al-Anbiya',*" 70. Ibn Asakir's (d. 1176) contemporary, Usama Ibn Muhqidh (d. 1188), records a version of the pearl story in his entertaining collection of anecdotes about walking sticks called *Kitab al-'Asa,* or *The Book of the Staff.* Paul M. Cobb, "Usama Ibn Muhqidh's *Book of the Staff:* Autobiographical and Historical Excerpts" *Al-Masaq: Islam and the Medieval Mediterranean* 17.1 (2005): 115–16. Naser-e Khosraw (d. ca. 1075) includes a description of the Dome of the Chain in his *Book of Travels.* "Next to this structure [the Dome of the Rock] is another dome called *Qobbat al-Selsela* [the Dome of the Chain], which is where David hung the chain that could not be reached by anyone other than the innocent, for the guilty and unjust could never pull it. This is well known to the learned." Thackston, trans., *Naser-e Khosraw's Book of Travels ,* 32. See also Elad, *Medieval Jerusalem,* 47–49.

53. Cited in Meri, *Cult of Saints,* 131.

54. Peter Brown, *The Cult of the Saints: Its Rise and Function in Latin Christianity* (Chicago: University of Chicago Press, 1981) and idem, *Society and the Holy in Late Antiquity* (Berkeley: University of California Press, 1982).

55. S. D. Goitein, *Jews and Arabs: Their Contacts through the Ages* (New York: Shocken Books, rev. ed. 1974), 188.

6

CURIOUS AND ENTERTAINING INFORMATION

Abu Mansur Abd al-Malik ibn Muhammad ibn Isma'il al-Tha'alibi (961–1038) was born in Nishapur and early on acquired a reputation as a scholar. He was a prolific author whose varied interests earned him the nickname "the Jahiz of Nishapur," in memory of the inimitable ninth-century Basran belletrist. One of al Tha'alibi's many works, *Kitab lata'if al-ma'arif* [Book of Curious and Entertaining Information], is a grab-bag collection of musings on a host of disparate topics, including chapters dealing with curious nicknames, strange coincidences, geography, the first occurrences (*awa'il*) of a wide range of phenomena, and so forth.

This chapter, like al-Tha'alibi's *Kitab lata'if al-ma'arif*, is a bit of a grab-bag as well in that it treats a wide range of themes relevant to daily life not dealt with in the first five chapters, in particular, those that deal with life cycle and family life issues. A propos of the nature of the chapter, I have borrowed al-Tha'alibi's title, though I make no claim to be his literary peer. Topics addressed herein include the traditional Arabic naming system, Qur'anic admonitions on the role and status of women and men in the family and society, children and childhood, circumcision, clothing and modesty, education, entertainments, and death and the afterlife.

TRADITIONAL ARABIC NAMING SYSTEM

One key to understanding Arabian tribal society in Muhammad's day and the importance of kinship to it is the traditional Arabic naming system, which at first glance seems unusual to most Americans—not so much because the names can be incredibly long, but because the very words that make up the names are simply unfamiliar and often unpronounceable. However, once one understands the basic components of a name, it is a fairly simple system to understand. Since this naming system was employed from medieval to early modern times (and is still used in some places today), it is appropriate that we begin this chapter by clarifying how this naming system worked.[1] We will use as our model Abu l-Qasim Ali Ibn Asakir (1105–76), the leading scholar in Damascus during the twelfth century. Abu l-Qasim Ali Ibn Asakir's proper name was Abu l-Qasim Ali ibn Abi Muhammad al-Hasan ibn Hibat Allah Abi l-Hasan ibn Abd Allah ibn al-Husayn al-Dimashqi al-Shafi'i al-Muhaddith al-Hafiz Thiqat al-Din, but he is usually referred to simply as Ibn Asakir because he belonged to the Banu Asakir clan (see "Part Three: *Nasab* or Genealogy," below). In spite of its length, Ibn Asakir's name has only five basic parts.

Part One: *Kunya* or Patronym   Abu l-Qasim literally means "Father of al-Qasim." It was also the prophet Muhammad's *kunya.* In Ibn Asakir's case, al-Qasim was the name of his first son. Since it was customary for men to be known by their *kunya*, that is as "father of so-and-so" after the birth of their first-born sons, Abu l-Qasim is one of the names by which Ibn Asakir's family, friends, and students would have addressed him. According to the same principle, his wife would have been known as Umm al-Qasim or "Mother of al-Qasim" as well. (al-Tha'alibi was known as Abu Mansur.) What if a couple had no sons, as was inevitably the case in some marriages? They would be known by the name of their oldest daughter; e.g., Abu Zubayda (Father of Zubayda) and Umm Zubayda (Mother of Zubayda), respectively. If a man were to have the misfortune of fathering many daughters (however cherished), but no sons, he could be referred to derisively, but more often as an object of pity, as Abu Banat, "Father of Daughters." Since Muhammad was a "Father of Daughters" of sorts (he did father sons, but none of them survived infancy), a Muslim man could always appeal to Muhammad's example as precedent that there is no dishonor in not having fathered any male heirs.

In the context just described, *Abu* literally means "Father of"; however, *Abu* can be followed by the name of some quality or some common noun, which changes its meaning to "possessor of" or "characterized by." *Kunya*s of this type are legion and function as *laqab*s or nicknames (see "Part Five: *Laqab* or Nickname"). Examples include Abu l-Fadl, "Father of Excellence," i.e., "the Excellent" or Abu l-Makarim, "Father of Virtues," i.e., "the Virtuous," or Abu l-Kadha'ib, "Father of Lies," i.e., "the Liar."

Part Two: *Ism* or Name   Ali is the name (*ism*) Ibn Asakir's parents gave him at his birth. Among Arabic speakers, four kinds of names have always been especially favored.

1. Ancient Arabian names of obscure significance such as Ali, Bishr, Marwan, Mu'awiya, Umar, Usama, Uthman, and Yazid. These

names only survived the early Islamic period when they had been the name of some great hero of the first century of Islamic history. Sunnis were proud and eager to name their sons after all of these early heroes. However, while nearly every Shiʻi family includes at least one son, cousin, or uncle named Ali, Hasan, or Husayn (or the name of one of the other Shiʻi imams), names such as Muʻawiya, Umar, Uthman, and Yazid were especially repugnant to them. Umar and Uthman because, according to the Shiʻis, they usurped Ali ibn Abi Talib's rightful place as Muhammad's successor; Muʻawiya because of Muʻawiya's involvement in the first civil war against Ali (656–61). Yazid (Muʻawiya's son) is particularly despised because Ali's son, Husayn, and his followers were slaughtered by Yazid's men at Karbala in 680.

2. Names of the prophets mentioned in the Qurʾan such as Ayyub (Job), Dawud (David), ʻIsa (Jesus), Musa (Moses), Nuh (Noah), Sulayman (Solomon), Yusuf (Joseph), and Zakariyya (Zechariah).

3. Names based on the Arabic root *H-M-D* (praise) such as Ahmad, Hamid, Mahmud, and Muhammad, all of which convey the notion of "Praised" or "Praiseworthy." These names are extremely common.

4. Names that begin with the word *ʻAbd* (Servant of), which theologically should always be followed by the name of God or one of His attributes such as Abd Allah (Servant of God), Abd al-Aziz (Servant of the Mighty), Abd al-Jabbar (Servant of the Almighty), Abd al-Hadi (Servant of the Guide), Abd al-Rahim (Servant of the Merciful), Abd al-Malik (Servant of the Sovereign, al-Thaʻalibi's *ism*), and Abd al-Hayy (Servant of the Living One). Nevertheless, one can still find theologically incorrect examples such as Abd al-Nabi (Servant of the Prophet), Abd al-Husayn (Servant of Husayn), Abd al-Imam (Servant of the Imam), and Abd al-Masih (Servant of the Messiah). Abd al-Nabi tended to be used by both Sunni and Shiʻi Muslims; Abd al-Husayn and Abd al-Imam by Shiʻis; Abd al-Masih by Christians. The theologically meticulous inserted the word *rabb* (Lord) after Abd; for example, Abd Rabb al-Nabi (Servant of the Prophet's Lord). Finally, in Iran and other non-Arabic speaking areas one could even find the grammatically absurd, though euphonious, Abdul (Servant of the).

Women's names follow similar patterns to those of men. Some of the ancient Arabian names such as Hind and Layla were quite common. Pious names that Muslim parents were fond of giving their daughters included Maryam (Mary, the mother of Jesus) as well as the names of Muhammad's wives including Khadija and Aisha or his daughters including Fatima. Finally, women were often named after a precious jewel such as Fayruz (Turquoise) or Zumurrud (Emerald). It was fairly common for male slaves to be named after a precious jewel; for example, Lu'lu' (Pearl). Free men, however, were rarely given such names.

Part Three: Nasab or Genealogy

Needless to say, in societies in which kinship played such a major role, a person's genealogy is extremely important. In Ibn Asakir's case, his genealogy is known for at least four generations—ibn Abi Muhammad al-Hasan ibn Hibat Allah Abi l-Hasan ibn Abd Allah ibn al-Husayn. That is, Ali son of al-Hasan (Muhammad's father), son of Hibat Allah (al-Hasan's father), son of Abd Allah son of al-Husayn. In the case of a woman, her father's name would be preceded by *bint* (daughter of), and then followed by several generations of her father's fathers. In exceptional cases, a female ancestor of great repute might feature in a person's genealogy as well. Given the importance of one's genealogy, it was not uncommon that boys and girls were known by their father's names.

In fact, it is entirely possible that as a child, Ibn Asakir was only occasionally called Ali and may well have been called Ibn Abi Muhammad (Son of Muhammad's father) or Ibn al-Hasan (Son of al-Hasan) by his neighbors, teachers, and friends. After the birth of his first-born son many may have begun to call him Abu l-Qasim, while others continued to call him Ali or Ibn Abi Muhammad or Ibn al-Hasan or all four names depending on the whim of the moment. Obviously, it can be rather difficult to identify someone precisely when only part of a name is used, especially for such common names as Abu Muhammad and Ibn Abi Muhammad. This situation is even more difficult when a person's paternity is uncertain and he is simply called by the rather disreputable name, Ibn Abihi (Son of His Father; essentially, The Bastard).

Finally, *Ibn* (Son of) can refer to the founder of one's clan or family, who may have lived only a few generations back or in the distant murky past. The plural of *Ibn* (*Banu*; Sons of, or Children of) is used to represent the clan as a whole. Thus, Ibn Asakir was not the "Son of Asakir"; rather, he was a member of the famous Banu Asakir clan that had played important roles in the public life of Damascus since the late eleventh century. In fact, he was the leading member of the clan during his adult life. Likewise, the famous fourteenth-century historian and philosopher Ibn Khaldun was not the "Son of Khaldun," he was a member of the clan whose founder was Khaldun; that is, the Banu Khaldun. Other examples of this usage include the Banu Hashim, Muhammad's own clan in Mecca named after his grandfather, Hashim; and the Banu Qayla, named after Qayla, the *mother* of al-Aws and al-Khazraj (the two leading clans of Medina).[2] Then, of course, there are the famous Banu Isra'il (Children of Israel) whose history is recorded in the Old Testament.[3]

Part Four: *Nisba* or Ascription of Some Sort

The *nisba* identifies a person's regional or ethnic origins, his religious affiliation, his occupation, and so forth. One may have several *nisbas*. In fact, Ibn Asakir had at least four—al-Dimashqi, al-Shafi'i, al-Muhaddith, and al-Hafiz. A person's *nisba* does not always refer to him or her personally; it can refer to one of his or her ancestors. For example, a physician in Baghdad could have the *nisba* al-Shirazi because his father had been born in the Iranian city of Shiraz but moved to Baghdad as an adult before he had fathered any children. This imaginary Shirazi/Baghdadi physician could also have the *nisba* al-Saffar because his father had been a coppersmith, al-Kattani because he had been in the linen business, or al-Tha'alibi because he traded in the furs of foxes (*tha'alib*).

So what do Ibn Asakir's *nisba*s tell us about him? Ibn Asakir was called al-Dimashqi because he was from Damascus (Dimashq in Arabic). Had he never left his hometown and had he not been as famous as he was, he would probably not have been called al-Dimashqi. What would be the point? However, since he spent most of his twenties and early thirties traveling and studying in Iraq, the Hijaz, Khurasan, Afghanistan, and Transoxiana (and returned home an accomplished scholar), people in those distant lands recognized him as a Damascene and called him al-Dimashqi.

His other *nisba*s refer to his scholarly accomplishments. The *nisba* al-Shafi'i means that he belonged to the *madhhab* or legal school named after Muhammad ibn Idris al-Shafi'i (d. 820);[4] al-Muhaddith means that he was a hadith scholar; and al-Hafiz is a very prestigious honorific that was restricted to a man who had memorized the entire Qur'an as well as a tremendous amount of religious literature and whose contemporaries recognized him as having made extensive contributions to the preservation and transmission of religious knowledge. (A woman of similar accomplishments would be called by the feminine forms, al-Dimashqiyya, al-Shafi'iyya, al-Muhadditha, and al-Hafiza respectively.)

We see a number of modifications to this ancient naming system beginning in the tenth century in that many rulers and military men began to give themselves designations that are not really formal names or *nisba*s, but

Part Five: *Laqab* or Nickname

*laqab*s (nicknames) that have to do with military or political functions. While *laqab*s had been employed long before the coming of Islam, this change in emphasis among military men seeking to legitimate their seizures of power is significant at this time.

Common political and military *laqab*s include Sayf al-Din (The Sword of the Religion), Nizam al-Mulk (The Good Order of Kingship), Nasir al-Dawla (The Helper of the Dynasty), and Adud al-Dawla (The Pillar of the Dynasty). Despite the Qur'an's admonition not to use pejorative *laqab*s (Qur'an 49:11), we find a host of *laqab*s describing almost everything about a person that would distinguish him from his contemporaries, ranging from his ugliness (al-Qabih, The Ugly) to his odd appearance (al-Jahiz, The Goggle-Eyed) to his intelligence (al-Ahmaq, The Moron) to his physical health (al-Abras, The Leper).

Not all *laqab*s, however, described one's intellectual or physical qualities. In fact, some of the most revered *laqab*s are those that venerate the heroes of Islamic sacred history including Abraham, known as Khalil Allah (The Friend of God); Moses, known as Kalim Allah (The One Whom God Addressed); Jesus, known as Kalimat Allah (The Word of God); Muhammad, known as al-Amin (The Trustworthy); and Abu Bakr, Muhammad's immediate successor, known as al-Siddiq (The Truthful).

Although *laqab*s such as Hujjat al-Islam (The Proof of Islam) referred to a scholar's piety and learning, scholars were not the only ones known by *laqab*s of piety; rulers used them as well. For example, while Ibn Asakir's *laqab* was Thiqat al-Din (The Authority of the Religion), his principal patron was Nur al-Din (The Light of the Religion), who occupied Damascus in 1154 and ruled the Muslim provinces of Syria from there until his death in 1174, after which he was succeeded by his protégé Salah al-Din (The Probity of the Religion, known in the west as Saladin).

Beginning in the tenth century as well, we begin to see a revival of old Iranian names such as Rostam, Feraydun, Jamshid, and Esfandiyar, which were popularized in the great Persian epic the *Shahnameh* (The Book of Kings).[5] The Turkish military elite also used a wide range of Turkish names, including Alp Arslan (Hero-Lion) and Ak Bogha (White Bull). Finally, while Persian and Turkish speakers employed the Arabic system with *Abu* and *Ibn* to indicate their family affiliations, they also used Persian (*zade*) and Turkish (*oghlu*) suffixes to indicate "son of so-and-so"; for example, Mirzade (Son of Amir) and Hasanoghlu (Son of Hasan).

As noted above, once one understands the basic parts of the naming system, it really is not all that complicated. Moreover, as we have seen with Ibn Asakir, a person's full name can provide much valuable information about him or her as well. While neither the nomads of seventh-century Arabia nor the scholars of twelfth-century Damascus had legal family names in the same sense as do modern Americans, the names that were used are very similar to the English names that provide one model for the modern American naming system. All one has to do is look through the phone book of any major American city to find names such as Baker, Cooper, and Smith, or Berlin, Paris, and Rome that have nothing to do with the bearer's occupation or place of birth. In addition, there are many people whose family names are Johnson, Peterson, Anderson, and Knutson who are completely unaware of anyone in their family trees named John, Peter, Andrew, or Knut.

WOMEN AND MEN IN THE FAMILY AND SOCIETY

Few themes in Islamic history cut against the grain of modern American social and cultural values more than the role and status of women and men in the Qur'an. In traditional Islamic thought, concepts that modern Americans take for granted—individual liberty, individual choice, personal fulfillment—necessarily lead to moral chaos because they are not informed by the admonitions and guidance of God's revelation to mankind in the Qur'an. While the Qur'an has very little material that may be considered legal in nature, the bulk of the legal material in the Qur'an

deals with the proper role and status of women and men in the family
and in society as a whole. However, as even a brief survey of the modern
literature on women in Islamic history makes evident, it is very difficult
to discern precisely what women's roles were in early Islamic history, let
alone pre-Islamic Arabia.[6]

In the late nineteenth century, W. Roberston Smith argued that pre-
Islamic Arabia was matriarchal in character; that is, kinship and descent
were traced through the mother's lineage, and that Islam replaced this
system with a patriarchal one in which kinship and descent were subsequently traced through the father's line.[7] Later scholars argued for both
patriarchal and matriarchal tendencies. Other scholars have argued that
the coming of Islam changed very little for women, while still others have
argued that Islam did bring certain improvements for women in Arabia, but left "woman forever inferior to man, placing her one step below
him."[8]

Although the specific status of women in pre-Islamic Arabia and early
Islamic history remains a mystery, it is clear that prior to the coming
of Islam, both patrilineal and matrilineal kinship systems did exist (the
Banu Qayla in Medina). It is also clear that during this transitional period
some women played a variety of very important public roles including
those of caravan merchants (Khadija, Muhammad's first wife), religious leaders, warriors (Hind, wife of Abu Sufyan and daughter of Utba
the helmetless), battlefield nurses (Fatima, Muhammad and Khadija's
daughter), and even instigators of rebellions (Aisha, Muhammad's third
wife).

Rather than rehearse the activities of the exceptional women discussed
in preceding chapters, I will briefly examine some of the Qur'anic passages that speak to the proper relations between women and men, especially with respect to issues of sexual morality, marriage, divorce, and
inheritance. For it is to these passages (and others like them) that Muslim
scholars have long turned for guidance in determining men's and wom-
en's rights and responsibilities according to Islamic law. This idealized
and theoretical discussion intends to clarify what the role and status of
women and men were supposed to be (especially in the context of the
family), at least according to the Qur'an and its later interpreters.

As such, it provides necessary background, context, and general expectations with respect to women's roles in the medieval Islamic world. The
extent to which these expectations were actually fulfilled (or enforced)
is difficult to ascertain, in part because of the problematic nature of our
sources for early Islamic history in general. In addition, while some of
our sources ostensibly record the statements of women, all were authored
by men. Moreover, unlike modern American kiss-and-tell books, it was
simply considered bad form for men to write about the *private* lives of
respectable men, let alone women.

As noted in chapter 1, the formal methodology of the shari'a, or Islamic
law, was developed in Medina and the urban culture of Iraq, Syria, and

elsewhere during the first Islamic centuries. Using the building blocks of the shari'a—the Qur'an, the sunna of Muhammad, and Arabian custom—scholars sought to discern precisely what one's submission (*islam*) to God entailed. In principle, at least, the role and status of women and men in Islamic thought are governed by three concepts that if not explicitly stated in the Qur'an, are certainly implied therein.

The first principle is embodied in the *shahada*—the simple two-part credal declaration that is at the very center of Islamic belief, ritual, and worship—"There is no god but God; Muhammad is the messenger of God (*la ilaha illa'llah; Muhammadun rasul Allah*)." Each man and each woman is personally responsible for making this declaration (*shahada*) and submitting (*islam*) to the one God and acknowledging Muhammad as His messenger. Consequently,

Those who surrender themselves to God and accept the true Faith; who are devout, sincere, patient, humble, charitable and chaste; who fast and are ever mindful of God—on these, *both men and women*, God will bestow forgiveness and a rich reward. It is not for true believers—*men or women*—to take their choice in their affairs if God and His apostle decree otherwise. He that disobeys God and His apostle strays far indeed. (Qur'an 33:35–36) (Emphasis added)

The second principle is that while the Qur'an condemns many of the practices of seventh-century Mecca and Medina including idolatry, polytheism, gambling, drinking wine, the abuse of the poor by the rich, and female infanticide, it accepts the *patrilineal* kinship system of Arabia and many of its values as the natural order of things. "Men have authority over women because God has made the one superior to the other...." (Qur'an 4:34a). The third principle—that a man must provide for every member of his household (wives, children, servants, and slaves) from his own resources—is closely connected to the second, "because they [men] spend their wealth to maintain them" (Qur'an 4:34b).

Although every man and woman is morally responsible before God for his or her beliefs and actions (and despite modern interpretations, polemics, and protestations to the contrary), medieval commentators interpreted the Qur'an as uncompromisingly patriarchal in its description of proper relations between men and women. Of course, the principle that women are subordinate to men was not unique to seventh-century Arabia. It was extremely common throughout the ancient Near East and the Mediterranean world as a whole. While this principle is taken for granted in the Qur'an, many of the modifications to existing practices set forth in the Qur'an do represent what we might call improvements in women's status. Nevertheless, even this improved status can be jarring to many modern Americans whose conceptions of family and individual rights differ considerably from those of the Qur'an.

One of the most important elements of the system of patrilineal kinship is paternal certainty, for without it the entire system would fall apart.

According to this structure, *female* chastity before marriage and fidelity in marriage are essential in guaranteeing *paternal* certainty. Sexual activity by a woman outside of marriage was not a matter of individual choice, but a violation of family honor and the Qur'anic sexual ethic that embraced it:

The adulterer and the adulteress shall each be given a hundred lashes. Let no pity for them cause you to disobey God, if you truly believe in God and the Last Day; and let their punishment be witnessed by a number of believers. The adulterer may marry only an adulteress or an idolatress; and the adulteress may marry only an adulterer or an idolater. True believers are forbidden such marriages. Those who defame honourable women and cannot produce four witnesses shall be given eighty lashes. Do not accept their testimony ever after, for they are great transgressors—except those among them that afterwards repent and mend their ways. God is forgiving and merciful. (Qur'an 24:2-5)

In theory, the Qur'anic requirements of chastity and fidelity applied equally to men and women; however, the physical consequences of sexual activity by a man outside of marriage were less readily apparent and the punishments less strictly enforced. In short, the reason that women were the guardians of the purity and honor of a kin's lineage was related to basic biology. That is, while a child's mother's identity was known to her and the midwives who helped deliver the child, the identity of the father could rarely be attested to by outside eyewitness testimony.[9]

Related to female chastity is the issue of modesty. One practice designed to ensure female chastity was the requirement that women be segregated from men who were not part of their households. Modern Americans ordinarily distinguish between private and public space, or a person's private and his or her public life. While this division between private and public is applicable to the medieval Islamic world, a more accurate distinction would be between appropriate behavior among one's kin and appropriate behavior among those outside of one's kin group. For example, in what we would call the private space of a home, segregation of the sexes could consist of women's actual physical separation from men when unrelated men were guests in the common area of the home. In such instances, women might be segregated in the women's quarters of a dwelling or they could be separated from men who were not their kin by appropriate female dress.

However, neither type of segregation was necessary among men who were close relatives. Segregation of the sexes did not apply to prepubescent girls and boys for the simple reason that they were not considered sexual beings because they were physically unable to reproduce. Likewise, many of these restrictions on women were not applied as strictly to widows or to women whose children were adults. Such women had far greater freedom of activity, especially in the public sphere, for reasons of biology and perceived sexuality. Thus, postmenopausal women were no longer considered to be sexual beings because they could no longer bear children. As such, they ceased to be viewed as sources of illicit temptation (*fitna*) for men, nor could they produce illegitimate offspring, which would bring shame to their families.[10]

According to the Qur'an, Muhammad's wives were specifically commanded to remain in their homes and to separate themselves from men. They were, however, given the option of divorce before they were required to accept these requirements.

Prophet, say to your wives, 'If you seek this nether life and all its finery, come, I will make provision for you and release you honourably. But if you seek God and His apostle and the abode of the hereafter, know that God has prepared a rich reward for those of you who do good works.' Wives of the Prophet! Those of you who commit a proven sin shall be doubly punished. That is easy enough for God. But those of you who obey God and His apostle and do good works shall be doubly rewarded; for them We have made a generous portion. Wives of the Prophet, you are not like other women. If you fear God, do not be complaisant in your speech, lest the lecherous-hearted should lust after you. Show discretion in what you say. Stay in your homes and do not display your finery as women used to do in the days of ignorance [*jahiliyya*]. Attend to your prayers, give alms and obey God and his apostle. Women of the Household, God seeks only to remove uncleanness from you and to purify you. Commit to memory the revelations of God and the wise sayings that are recited in your dwellings. Benignant is God and all-knowing. (Qur'an 33:28–34)

While some scholars argued that seclusion should be applied to women in general on the principle that all Muslim women should follow the practice of the "Mothers of the Believers," it never became an absolute practice in Islamic history. In fact, such universal cloistering of women was nearly impossible for all but the wealthiest of families in the towns and cities. Less wealthy families as well as rural and pastoral communities generally needed the labor of both their male and their female kin.

As noted in chapter 3, Muhammad's third wife, Aisha (one of the "Mothers of the Believers"), certainly did not confine herself to her house. In fact, she was a major player on the losing side in the First Civil War (*fitna*), especially in the Battle of the Camel (656), which is so named because of her presence there on her camel. For this reason, she has been held up as a model for those who argue that women should be able to take part in public life, but more often as an example of the disasters that will befall the community when women become involved in politics.[11]

Nevertheless, the principle of modesty and separation of the sexes was observed in the public sphere; that is, essentially everywhere outside of the home and apart from one's kin. In the most prominent of public spaces, the market, this separation of the sexes consisted of the physical separation of women from men by means of modest dress. This practice was especially important in larger oasis settlements and towns and later in major urban centers where the residents were not all close kin and where the likelihood that women would encounter strangers was a virtual certainty.

Fundamental to family life in any society are the conditions under which new families are established in marriage, how they are dissolved in divorce, and how property should be disposed of in divorce settlements or the event of a family member's death. The Qur'an addresses each of these issues explicitly. In pre-Islamic Arabia, when a man wanted to marry, he paid a dowry, or bride price, to the father or male guardian of the girl or woman to whom he was betrothed, in part as compensation for the loss of her value as a laborer in her father's or male guardian's household.

According to the Qur'an, this bride price became *her* property that she would bring into the marriage, not the property of her male guardian.

Give women their dowry as a free gift; but if they choose to make over to you a part of it, you may regard it as lawfully yours. (Qur'an 4:4)

If you wish to replace a wife with another, do not take from her the dowry you have given her even if it be a talent of gold. That would be improper and grossly unjust; for how can you take it back when you have lain with each other and entered into a firm contract? (Qur'an 4:20)

Since a man was supposed to provide for every member of his household from his own resources, the husband was to have no recourse to this wealth. It became the wife's property solely to dispense with as she saw fit. She could, of course, give a part of it to her husband, but he could not lawfully take it away from her on his own.

Despite the fact that marriage under this Qur'anic scenario became a contract between a man and a woman (not between a man and a woman's male guardian), most marriages resulted from some sort of arrangement between families. After all, each family had a vested interest in the prestige and economic status of the other as well as the success of the union. Unlike in the American ideal of marital bliss, where many believe one's spouse should be one's best friend and soul mate, the purpose of marriage in the Qur'an and the medieval Islamic world was the procreation of children and the strengthening of ties between two extended families. In principle, the man or the woman was able to decline a proposed match, but rarely was there an opportunity for such an arrangement to be initiated on the basis of mutual affection or common interests and certainly not after a period of courtship as in the American ideal of the institution.

Another way in which marriage differs from the modern American model is that according to the Qur'an, a man may take up to four wives at the same time, with the proviso that he treat each wife fairly in order to avoid injustice.

If you fear that you cannot treat orphan [girls] with fairness, then you may marry other women who seem good to you: two, three, four of them. But if you fear that you cannot maintain equality among them, marry one only or any slave-girls you may own. This will make it easier for you to avoid injustice. (Qur'an 4:3)

Scholars interpreted this passage to mean that if a man took more than one wife, he had to maintain each wife equitably in *separate* residences. Given the expense involved, having more than one wife was a luxury that only the wealthy classes could afford.

Whether a man took one wife or as many as four, it is clear from the Qur'an that in return for his protection and provision, he was owed obedience. If a wife was not obedient, her husband was allowed to chastise her and even to beat her into submission.

> Men have authority over women because God has made the one superior to the other, and because they spend their wealth to maintain them. Good women are obedient. They guard their unseen parts because God has guarded them. As for those from whom you fear disobedience, admonish them and send them to beds apart and beat them. Then if they obey you, take no further action against them. Surely God is high, supreme. If you fear a breach between a man and his wife, appoint an arbiter from his people and another from hers. If they wish to be reconciled God will bring them together again. Surely God is all-knowing and wise. (Qur'an 4:34–35)

Not surprisingly, this passage often produces embarrassment among some modern Muslims, especially in the west, where women and men (at least according to the laws in most western countries) are supposed to be equals in a marriage relationship. However, this passage makes it clear that according to the Qur'anic worldview, "men have authority over women because God has made the one superior to the other, and because they spend their wealth to maintain them."

Men of the wealthy classes were able to afford slaves as well as wives. According to shari'a, in exchange for his maintenance and support, the head of the household had the right to obedience as well as sexual relations with his female slave(s). While a concubine was in no position to refuse her owner's advances, there did exist the possibility of winning his affection prior to the onset of a sexual relationship as many poems attest. Moreover, according to shari'a, a concubine did have certain legal protections not afforded to a wife. Once a concubine bore a child she was henceforth classified as an *umm walad* (mother of a child).

Unlike the American slave system, the child of a free Muslim man and a slave woman received the status of the father not the mother. That is, the child was a legally free Muslim and bore no stigma of illegitimacy. Initially, such offspring tended to be seen as inferior (though not illegitimate), largely because their mothers were not of Arabian stock. However, as the importance of Arabian purity began to be contested vigorously in the eighth and ninth centuries, this sense of inferiority waned considerably. In fact, the mothers of many of the caliphs and sultans in Islamic history were *umm walads* (e.g. Khayzuran, mother of the famous Abbasid caliph Harun al-Rashid, r. 786–809).[12] In addition, once a slave woman had borne a child, she could not be put out of the house, she could legally expect maintenance and support, and she had to be granted her freedom upon the death of her owner. A wife, on the other hand, could bear her husband as many children as physically possible and he could divorce her without cause.[13]

The Qur'anic procedures under which a man can divorce his wife are fairly simple—he merely needs to say three times that he is divorcing her and the marriage is dissolved. "Divorce may be pronounced twice, and then a woman must be retained in honour or allowed to go with kindness" (Qur'an 2:229a). The woman does, however, have certain rights and protections should her husband decide to divorce her. Since the property with which she entered the marriage was supposed to remain in her possession throughout the marriage, whatever property she had at the time of the divorce remained hers to do with as she saw fit:

It is unlawful for husbands to take from them anything they have given them, unless both fear that they may not be able to keep within the bounds set by God; in which case it shall be no offence for either of them if the wife ransoms herself. These are the bounds set by God; do not transgress them. Those that transgress the bounds of God are wrongdoers. (Qur'an 2:229b)

A man also owed his wife three months' maintenance after the divorce for the purpose of determining whether she was pregnant.

Those that renounce their wives on oath must wait four months. If they change their minds, God is forgiving and merciful; but if they decide to divorce them, know that God hears all and knows all. Divorced women must wait, keeping themselves from men, three menstrual courses. It is unlawful for them, if they believe in God and the Last Day, to hide what God has created in their wombs: in which case their husbands would do well to take them back, should they desire reconciliation. Women shall with justice have rights similar to those exercised against them, although men have a status above women. God is mighty and wise. (Qur'an 2:226–28)

Muslim scholars devoted considerable attention to the meaning of this passage, and as good lawyers, they spent a great deal of time addressing all sorts of possibilities. Was the waiting period the same for a Muslim man's Muslim wives as it was for his Jewish or Christian wives? What if the marriage was never consummated? What if the woman did not menstruate (either because she was too young or because she had already gone through menopause), but had had sexual relations with her husband? The possibilities are too numerous to be addressed here, but in general, the practice came to be that if a woman was pregnant, her husband was required to support her until the delivery of their child. In addition, he was required to support both mother and child until the child was weaned (generally around age two).

As shari'a developed, provisions were made for women to seek a divorce as well. However, it was much more difficult for a woman to divorce her husband, and the procedure required the services of a court. Legitimate causes for divorce included the husband having some sort of disgusting disease, his intolerable cruelty, and/or his abandonment—ranging from 10 to 90 years depending on which *madhhab* a woman followed. Needless to say, few women lived long enough to be granted a divorce on the grounds of abandonment in those courts where the husband had to have been gone missing for 90 years.

According to American law, one's right to dispose of one's wealth (after estate taxes and outstanding debts have been paid) is entirely discretionary. According to the Qur'an, the bulk of one's estate must go to specified heirs; only about one-third is discretionary. Moreover, the specific percentage of one's wealth owed to female heirs is less than that owed to males.

God has thus enjoined you concerning your children: A male shall inherit twice as much as a female. If there be more than two girls, they shall have two-thirds of the inheritance; but if there be one only, she shall inherit the half.... (Qur'an 4:11)

The actual percentages of an inheritance varied considerably and the math could become complicated based on the number of total children a person might have, the ratio of sons to daughters, whether a person's parents or siblings were alive and thus eligible to inherit, and so forth. Whatever the division of wealth, the reason that females received a smaller percentage of an inheritance than did males is straightforward. Since a man was obligated to provide for every member of his household from his own resources, he simply needed more resources than did a woman, whose maintenance was the responsibility of her male guardian, whether husband, brother, uncle, or cousin.

The preceding discussion of the role and status of women and men in Islamic thought has focused on how things were supposed to be according to the Qur'an and its medieval interpreters. In the medieval Islamic world, as in any society, there were disparities between the ideal and the real in daily life. However, a few general comments about how this ideal was applied in nonurban settings are in order. In the countryside and especially among the pastoral nomadic populations, local custom usually outweighed the dictates of shari'a on these issues, even though they are set forth clearly in the Qur'an.

If a bride price was paid to a guardian or inheritance rights were withheld or divorce protections were not honored, to whom could a woman appeal? Moreover, if a woman decided to contest these issues, her brothers and other male relatives could always coerce her by refusing to find her a husband, much less a suitable one. Faced with the choice of never marrying or worse, many women in such circumstances likely chose to forgo their marriage and inheritance rights, if in fact they knew they had them at all. In a major city, however, a woman—especially an educated upper-class woman—could appeal to a court and have confidence that a judge would rule in her favor. Moreover, she could trust that the judge would not only seek to enforce his rulings, but also have the authority and means to do so with the backing of the ruler who had appointed him judge, even in the face of possible opposition from her husband or other relatives.

CHILDREN AND CHILDHOOD

Childhood in the medieval Islamic world was generally defined as lasting from birth to the onset of puberty. In the absence of any physical signs of maturity, fourteen to fifteen were the generally accepted ages by which the age of majority (adulthood) was defined. Such a determination was important because neither sexual segregation nor the requirements for women to wear the veil applied to prepubescent girls, for the simple reason that girls and boys were not yet considered sexual beings in that they were physically unable to reproduce.

The four stages of childhood were generally defined as 1) from birth to teething; 2) from teething to about age seven, or the age of discernment; 3) from seven to fourteen; and 4) the transitional phase from fourteen to the onset of puberty. Medieval treatises on marriage admonished parents to receive the births of boys with restrained joy, and to avoid demonstrating disappointment at the birth of girls. They also emphasized the importance of breast-feeding, which was the basic right of an infant for the first two years of its life.

Child mortality rates were high in the medieval Islamic world, as they were in all premodern societies. It was common for parents to lose one or more children in infancy or later to childhood diseases as was the case during outbreaks of plague (or Black Death), which hit the medieval Islamic world especially hard during the fourteenth century. Shortly after birth, it was customary to whisper in the child's ear the call to prayer (*adhan*) and the Islamic statement of faith (*shahada*)—"There is no god but God; Muhammad is the Messenger of God." Seven days later, when the child's prospects for survival were more certain, a public feast was held during which the child was named, had some hair cut, and a sheep or goat was slaughtered to express gratitude for the child's birth. The public nature of these ceremonies confirmed the father's parentage and his responsibility to provide for the child.

While children were able to discern between right and wrong, they were generally seen to have certain legal disabilities that parallel those who are mentally deficient. For example, children could not make binding contracts. Nor were they subject to the same punishments for criminal offenses as adults. In addition, most jurists argued that children were not required to fulfill the rituals of Islamic worship—prayer (*salat*), fasting (*sawm*) during Ramadan, paying alms (*zakat*), or making the pilgrimage (*hajj*). Rather, they should be taught these as part of their religious education in preparation for adulthood.

The marriage age for females tended to coincide with the onset of puberty, but it was not uncommon for prepubescent girls to be given in marriage as well. While there is evidence of marriages being arranged between children, most males married after they had entered into adulthood and tended to be older than their brides. It was not uncommon for much older men to marry very young girls. In fact, when Muhammad was in his fifties, he contracted a marriage to his third wife, Aisha, when she was nine years old (some accounts say that she was six or seven years old).[14]

Based on Muhammad's example, the reverse occurred as well. His employer and first wife, Khadija (d. 619), was some 15 years his senior. It was she who initiated the marriage proposal and Muhammad took no other wives as long as she was alive. Despite Khadija's trust in Muhammad as a businessman and her steadfast moral support for him once he began to receive his revelations, it is possible that Muhammad's monogamy may have been motivated by more than his deep affection for his wife. While the specific details of *their* marriage contract remain a mystery, we do know that it was not uncommon for a woman of means to contract a marriage on the condition that her husband take no other wives.[15]

One of the more famous examples of such a restriction in a marriage contract is the oath that the wealthy widow Umm Salamah extracted from the youthful Abu l-Abbas (who later became the first Abbasid caliph al-Saffah). Umm Salamah made him swear an oath that he would neither take another wife nor a concubine. Abu l-Abbas agreed to Umm Salamah's terms and, by all appearances, he kept his vow even after he ascended to the caliphate, despite his aides' advice and encouragement that he should partake of the abundantly rich variety of women at his beck and call.[16]

CIRCUMCISION

The most famous example of circumcision in the ancient Near East is the institution of male circumcision as the sign of God's covenant with Abraham as described in Genesis:

Then God said to Abraham, "As for you, you must keep my covenant, you and your descendants after you for the generations to come. This is my covenant with you and your descendants after you, the covenant you are to keep: Every male among you shall be circumcised. You are to undergo circumcision, and it will be a sign of the covenant between me and you. For the generations to come every male among you who is eight days old must be circumcised.... My covenant in your flesh is to be an everlasting covenant. Any uncircumcised male, who has not been circumcised in the flesh, will be cut off from his people; he has broken my covenant." (Genesis 17:9–14)

Parade prior to a circumcision. *Source:* Lane, *Manners and Customs,* 58.

The early Christian community debated at length whether this physical sign of God's covenant with Abraham should be required under the New Covenant or New Testament. In the end, the Church embraced St. Paul's argument (made in many of his epistles) that "circumcision is circumcision of the heart, by the Spirit, not by the written code" (Romans 2:29).

Despite the fact that circumcision is not mentioned in the Qur'an, classical poetry as well as the biographical literature (*sira*) on the life of Muhammad indicate that both male and female circumcision were practiced in pre-Islamic Arabia. Male circumcision, understandably, was linked to Abraham. According to one account, female circumcision, too, had its origins in the Abraham story—that is, in Sarah's animosity toward Hagar, the mother of Ishmael. After Sarah had sent Hagar away and called her back several times,

She swore to cut something off of her, and said to herself, "I shall cut off her nose, I shall cut off her ear—but no, that would deform her. I will circumcise her instead." So she did that, and Hagar took a piece of cloth to wipe the blood away. For that reason women have been circumcised and have taken pieces of cloth [sanitary napkins?] down to today.[17]

In his famous anti-Christian polemic, "Contra Christianorum," al-Jahiz (777–869) minced no words as to his opinion of the ritual and hygienic merits of both male and female circumcision:

[T]he Christian is at heart, a foul and dirty creature. Why? Because he is *uncircumcised*, does not wash after intercourse and eats pig meat. His wife does not wash after intercourse, either, or even after menstruation and childbirth, which leaves her absolutely filthy. Furthermore she, too, is *uncircumcised*. (Emphasis added)[18]

Four centuries later, the Damascene Shafi'i scholar al-Nawawi (1233–77), summarized the views on circumcision advocated by the various *madhhab*s (schools of Islamic jurisprudence) in a treatise on ritual purity (*tahara*):

Circumcision is obligatory (*wadjib*) according to al-Shafi'i and many of the doctors, *sunna* [tradition] according to Malik and the majority of them. It is further, according to al-Shafi'i, equally obligatory for males and females. As regards males it is obligatory to cut off the whole skin which covers the *glans*, so that this latter is wholly denudated. As regards females, it is obligatory to cut off a small part of the skin in the highest part of the genitals.[19]

While there was general agreement on the procedure itself, there was little consensus as to timing. Some scholars advocated circumcision on the seventh or eighth day; others at around seven years of age (when the boy began his formal education); others forbade it before ten years of age. Still others argued in favor of circumcision even later as a right of passage to mark the onset of puberty and in preparation for adulthood and marriage. At whatever age it was performed, circumcision was understood as an essential act of Islamic ritual purification (*tahara*). In fact, a common colloquial term for the practice is *tahara*.

The circumcision of Muslim boys was very much a public affair. Those parents who could afford to do so paraded their sons through neighborhood streets on horseback, accompanied by family, friends, and other well-wishers. Less-well-to-do parents often scheduled their son's circumcision to coincide with a wedding procession in order to defray costs. When the child and his entourage had finished their procession, the local barber performed the operation.

Public celebrations and festivities did not accompany the circumcision of a girl. Rather, female circumcision was a private affair attended by the women of the family and the woman who performed the operation. In addition to ritual purity, some of the rationales for female circumcision included the preservation of chastity and the inhibition of sexual desire, but it was also thought to promote fertility and to ensure the birth of sons. Despite the admonitions of scholars, female circumcision was apparently not observed in much (possibly most) of the medieval Islamic world. However, in Egypt, where it had long been observed prior to the Islamic conquest, female circumcision was widely practiced among both Muslims and Christians. Finally, despite the scholarly arguments in favor of it, female circumcision (unlike its male counterpart) had a decidedly shameful and secretive connotation attached to it. We see this clearly evidenced by the contemptuous and vulgar epithet, "son of a cutter of clitorises" (*ibn muqatti'at al-buzur*).[20]

CLOTHING AND MODESTY

How modest dress was specifically defined in early Islamic history is yet another contested issue among historians because of the paucity of contemporary evidence as well as the allusive (and elusive) character of many Qur'anic passages. This issue is also vigorously debated among modern Muslims because of the implications that the practice of the early community has for Muslim women and men today. Fundamental to this discussion is the proper interpretation of the concept of modesty as well as the precise meaning of the Arabic words for veil or covering that are used in the Qur'an (*khimar*, pl. *khumur; hijab*, pl. *hujub*).[21]

Enjoin believing men to turn their eyes away from temptation and to restrain their carnal desires. This will make their lives purer. God has knowledge of all their actions. Enjoin believing women to turn their eyes away from temptation and to preserve their chastity; to cover their adornments (except such as are normally displayed); to draw their veils [*khumur*] over their bosoms and not to reveal their finery except to their husbands, their fathers, their husbands' fathers, their sons, their step-sons, their brothers, their brothers' sons, their sisters' sons, their women-servants, and their slave-girls; male attendants lacking in natural vigour, and children who have no carnal knowledge of women. And let them not stamp their feet when walking so as to reveal their hidden trinkets. Believers, turn to God in repentance, that you may prosper (Qur'an 24:30–31).

In modern Muslim countries and among Muslim communities in the west, the meaning of veiling is understood in a variety of ways. [22] Some Muslims, especially in the west or among more westernized communities in the Islamic world, argue that simply covering one's bosom and dressing modestly (usually according to western standards of modesty) meets the requirement. Others argue that, despite the admonition to "draw their veils [*khumur*] over their bosoms," the subsequent admonition not to "reveal their finery except to their husbands, their fathers, ..." requires not only modest dress, but the use of a headscarf or shawl to cover one's hair either partially or completely in the presence of all except kin, servants, slaves, and impotents. Others argue that the proper interpretation of this passage requires the complete covering of a woman's body, hands, feet, hair, and face—even to the point of wearing gloves and a veil with sheer material where a woman's eyes are covered so that she can see, but that nobody can see any part of her body, including her eyes.

But the question that concerns us here is how was modest Islamic dress defined in seventh-century Arabia? The short and rather unsatisfying answer to this question is that the nature of our sources makes it difficult to provide definitive answers. The earliest evidence of what the residents of the Arabian peninsula wore are rock drawings from the second and first millennia B.C. that depict men wearing very little clothing at all—essentially, loincloths and a variety of head dresses. Women are portrayed as scantily clad as well. Both men and women are represented as wearing sandals or slippers. Shirtless statues from the northern Hijaz complement Strabo's observation in the first century B.C. that the neighboring Nabateans "go without tunics, with girdles about their loins, and with slippers on their feet."[23]

The Qur'an makes it clear that the new Islamic ethic of modesty is more in keeping with Biblical standards of modesty than the more lax attitudes that had existed prior to the advent of Islam.

Children of Adam! We have given you clothes to cover your nakedness, and garments pleasing to the eye; but the finest of all these is the robe of piety (Qur'an 7:26).

Modesty and dress are linked explicitly in how the word for clothing (*libas*) was defined by early Arabic lexicographers as well; that is, that which conceals or covers one's private parts or that which is indecent to reveal (*'awra*). Subsequently, *libas* became the common term for undergarments in general and pantaloons in particular.[24] It should be noted that some scholars defined that which is indecent to reveal (*'awra*) as the area between the navel and the knees.[25] Some extended the definition to include everything but a woman's face and hands; still others extended the definition to include even these.

Although many modern Americans understand the veil as a uniquely Islamic form of women's dress, there is evidence that face veiling was practiced in some pre-Islamic Arabian towns as a sign of high social status. According to the biographical literature, Muhammad required his wives to cover their faces. This was in addition to the Qur'anic injunction that they should remain in their homes. In fact, one of the meanings of the phrase *darabat al-hijab* (She took the veil) is "She became one of Muhammad's wives."[26]

Because the earliest complete woman's face veil that has survived— found at Quseir al-Qadim along the Egyptian Red Sea coast—dates to the fourteenth or fifteenth century A.D., it is difficult to ascertain whether Muhammad's wives covered their faces with such a garment.[27] It is also possible that they wrapped themselves so completely with their cloaks or mantles that only one eye was left uncovered in the manner described

Early nineteenth-century veils. Only the veil on the right is represented in its full length. *Source:* Lane, *Manners and Customs*, 50.

by Tertulian in the third century A.D.[28] In addition, while the veil found at Quseir al-Qadim is similar to those that appear in some earlier manuscript illuminations that depict women with veils, there exist a number of illuminations in which women are depicted with their hair covered by some sort of shawl or scarf but without any face veils at all.

All this is to say that it remains unclear when, precisely, face veiling for women became part of broader Islamic practice. Nevertheless, we do know that both seclusion and veiling were practiced as symbols of economic wealth and high social status before the advent of Islam in some parts of Arabia, among the urban upper classes in Byzantium, and in Sasanian Iran. It seems entirely plausible that as these areas and their populations were incorporated into the Islamic empire in the first Islamic centuries, the new Islamic order easily adapted this elite urban custom to its standards of sexual morality and segregation of the sexes.

Finally, whatever the proper interpretation of Qur'anic passages on dress may be for the modern world, it is clear that the dress—especially the public dress—of women and men in early Islamic history as well as throughout much (though not all) of the medieval Islamic world was modest by any modern American standards and included shirts, undergarments, robes, wraps, cloaks, shawls, and mantles as well various types of head covering. That the Quseir al-Qadim style veil continued to be worn in Egypt is evi-

denced by the early nineteenth-century image of a veiled woman in Edward
W. Lane's *The Manners and Customs of the Modern Egyptians,* which is similar
to (though much longer than) the veil found at Quseir al-Qadim.[29]

EDUCATION

For the vast majority of Muslims, the Qur'an is the eternal uncreated
speech of God, flawlessly recited to mankind by His messenger, Muhammad. It should come as no surprise then that the Qur'an was the fundamental building block of education in the medieval Islamic world. Nor
should it come as a surprise that the medieval Islamic world was a world
in which the written word was ubiquitous. In addition to pious and lau-
datory inscriptions on public buildings, coins, swords, textiles, carpets,
ceramics, and lamps, one could find inscriptions, poetry, and belles-lettres
with far less noble themes as well.

Despite the importance of the written word, it was the word that was
committed to memory that was held in highest regard. One could not
claim to have studied the Qur'an, or any text for that matter, unless he had
committed the text to memory. Therefore, beginning around the age of six
or seven, children were taught to memorize the Qur'an (beginning with
the shortest chapters, which are only a few lines) and to study the basics
of Islamic beliefs and practices with their teachers. In addition, students
learned the basics of Arabic grammar, for without a solid understanding
of the Arabic language one could not truly understand the speech of God.
While paper was introduced to the Middle East during the early Islamic
period and eventually made its way to Europe, it was only the wealthiest
who could afford to waste it. Therefore, students did their lessons with
a reed pen and ink on a washable tablet (usually made of wood). Very
young boys and the mentally ill were generally discouraged from learning
to write in a mosque because they "scribble on the walls and soil the floor,
not bothering about urine and other kinds of dirt."[30]

In the early centuries of Islamic history, elementary education was a very
informal affair where young children studied with their fathers, uncles, or
brothers (and occasionally mothers, aunts, or sisters) at home and, as they
matured, with local scholars in the mosque. More advanced students then
moved on to study hadiths (reports attributed to or about Muhammad),
which along with the Qur'an formed the basis of Islamic jurisprudence
and theology. The primary place to study hadith in the early centuries of
Islam was the mosque. Scholars also taught in their homes, which allowed
them to offer hospitality to their students. It also made it easier for some
scholars to charge for their services, despite the fact that it was considered
bad form.[31]

The education of boys received a great deal of attention in medieval
treatises on education. Al-Shayzari (d. ca. 1193) summarizes the sentiments of many in his *Book of the Market Inspector.* Based on a hadith attrib-

uted to Muhammad, all boys who have reached the age of seven should be ordered to pray with the congregation in the mosque. "Teach your children to pray when they reach seven, and when they are ten, beat them if they neglect it."[32] According to al-Shayzari, teachers should employ corporal punishment with what he viewed as moderation:

> The educator should beat them when they are ill-manered, use bad language, and do other things against Islamic law, such as playing with dice, [decorated] eggs, backgammon and all other kinds of gambling. He should not beat a boy with a stick so thick that it will break a bone, nor with one so thin that it will cause too much pain. Rather, the stick should be of middling size. The educator should use a wide strap and aim at the buttocks, the thighs and the lower part of the legs, because there is no fear of injury or harm happening to these places.[33]

According to al-Shayzari, teachers also should teach their charges to honor and obey their parents. They should avoid using their students for their own needs, for performing demeaning chores such as moving manure or stones; they should also avoid any appearance of impropriety with their students.

Of course, medieval Muslim scholars and educators were well aware of the sentiment that "all work and no play make little Muhammad a dull boy." According to the extremely influential scholar al-Ghazali (d. A.D. 1111), "Prevention of the child from playing games and constant insistence on learning deadens his heart, blunts his sharpness of wit and burdens his life; he looks for a ruse to escape them (his studies) altogether."[34] The kinds of games al-Ghazali mentions include puppet theater, games with balls, toy animals, and toy birds on strings.

In a mosque, teachers generally sat on a mat and against a pillar facing the direction (*qibla*) of Mecca. Their students sat in a circle (*halaqa*) in front of them. Some early scholars thought the use of mats an inappropriate innovation and sat on the bare ground. More renowned scholars often sat on cushions or pillows, which elevated them to a place of honor above their students. As one might expect, the better or more popular teachers attracted larger circles of students than some of their lesser colleagues. In such situations, a teacher might sit on a bench so that his audience could hear him better.

Students intent on mastering the material were expected to faithfully copy out a teacher's lectures, which generally consisted of the teacher dictating a text to which he added his own commentary as well as the commentaries of his teachers. This method of learning from a teacher, who learned from his teachers, who learned from his teachers, illustrates the fundamental importance that medieval Muslims placed on direct personal interaction between teacher and pupil. Once a scholar determined that his student had mastered a given text, he granted him (or her) an *ijaza* (diploma) certifying that he (or she) was now qualified to teach that particular text to others. In part because of this emphasis on the interpersonal, we find scholars and students traveling hundreds, even thousands of miles to study with the leading lights throughout the medieval Islamic world.

The relationship between travel and education is illustrated eloquently by a hadith in which Muhammad is reported to have told his followers that they should seek religious knowledge (*'ilm*) even unto China; that is, to the ends of the earth. This desire to travel in order to study with the masters was often coupled with the obligation to undertake the pilgrimage to Mecca at least once if one is able. In addition to being the means for many to fulfill one of the five pillars of Islam, pilgrimage caravans from such distant places as Spain, West Africa, Central Asia, India, and elsewhere functioned as informal traveling universities that continually added new scholars as they made their way to Mecca and back each year. As such, these pilgrimage caravans played a very important role in spreading new ideas and reinforcing old ones throughout the Islamic world.

To cite just one example, between the years 1126 and 1141, Ibn Asakir made two lengthy study trips from his home in Damascus to the centers of Islamic learning in his day: Baghdad (where he studied at the famous Nizamiyya *madrasa*), the Hijaz (where he also made the pilgrimage), Kufa, and Islamic lands further East—Khurasan, Isfahan, Transoxiana, Marw, Nishapur, and Herat. During his travels in Syria, Arabia, Iraq, Iran, and Central Asia, he studied with some 1,300 male teachers and some 80 female teachers. He collected hundreds, if not thousands, of hadiths and other materials for his massive *Ta'rikh madinat Dimashq* [History of Damascus] and returned to his home in Damascus a *hafiz*—an appellation conferred only on those extraordinary and pious individuals who had committed tremendous amounts of religious literature to memory and were held in the highest esteem among the religious scholars of their day.[35] Ibn Asakir is reported to have recited "the entire Qur'an once every week and once every day of the month of Ramadan."[36]

While the overwhelming majority of Ibn Asakir's teachers were men, the fact that roughly 6 percent of his teachers were women clearly demonstrates that there were women as well as men who took seriously Muhammad's admonition to seek religious knowledge—"even unto China." In fact, hadith transmission was the primary field in which women could make their mark as teachers of men. After all, one could hardly argue that women were inadequate to the task of transmitting hadith, since Aisha, Muhammad's third wife, was one of the most important hadith transmitters in early Islamic history. In addition, Muhammad is reported to have praised the women of Medina because of their desire for religious knowledge. "How splendid were the women of the *ansar*; shame did not prevent them from becoming learned in the faith."[37]

Understandably, religious education for girls tended to be strongest within scholarly families. However, despite Aisha's example and despite Muhammad's praise for the women of Medina, educating girls and women was not universally supported. Opponents could even make their case by citing an apparently contradictory statement attributed to Muhammad. "It is said that a woman who learns [how to] write is like a snake given poison to drink."[38] Al-Shayzari warns against teaching women to write as well. "The educator must not teach a woman or a female slave how to write, because this makes a woman worse, and it is said that a woman learning to write is like a snake made more venomous by being given poison to drink."[39]

Nevertheless, it is clear that girls and women could be and were educated, some very considerably. In addition, it is clear that elite women had long played very important roles as endowers of religious and educational institutions as well as charities for pilgrims and the destitute. In the eighth century, Harun al-Rashid's mother, the concubine Khayzuran, purchased Muhammad's traditional birthplace in Mecca and transformed it into the sacred Mosque of the Nativity. She also endowed a drinking fountain in Mecca, endowed a water pool in Ramle in Palestine, as well as a channel west of the city of Anbar in Iraq.[40] Harun al-Rashid's wife, his cousin Zubayda, funded the renovation of Muhammad's mosque in Ta'if near Mecca. But she is most famous for her charitable concern for pilgrims' basic comforts and water needs. She endowed wells, rest areas, and caravanserais along the well-traveled pilgrimage route between Kufa and Mecca, which came to be known as the Zubayda Road. In the Hijaz, she funded the Mushshash Spring in Mecca and a water complex on the Plain of Arafat, which bears her name as well—the Spring of Zubayda.[41]

Five centuries later, Ayyubid princesses vied with their kinsmen in endowing religious architecture as part of the Ayyubid campaign of jihad against the Franks and Shi'is. During the Ayyubid period (1174–1260), some 160 mosques, *madrasa*s (religious colleges; lit. place of study), and other religious monuments were established in Damascus alone, more than the combined total established during the century prior to and after their rule. Women attached to the Ayyubid house endowed 26 of these monuments (16 percent), and half of all royal patrons were women.[42]

Although the *madrasa* existed as early as the late ninth century, by the late eleventh century it had become much more prevalent throughout the Islamic world.[43] Funded by pious endowments (made by private individuals and members of royal families), the *madrasa* was more than a mere change in venue from the mosque (or private residence) and its informal instruction. The better-endowed *madrasa*s provided salaries for teachers and stipends for students. Many were built with apartments for students and teachers as well. One of Islam's greatest medieval scholars, al-Ghazali (d. 1111), taught at Baghdad's Nizamiyya *madrasa*, founded by the Seljukid wazir, Nizam al-Mulk (d. 1092). In addition, Nur al-Din (r. 1154–74), the ruler of Damascus and Ibn Asakir's patron, built a *madrasa* (known as the *Dar al-Hadith*) to serve as the intellectual center of his jihad against Sunni Islam's foreign and domestic enemies—the Christian Crusaders and Shi'i Muslims.

As Ibn Asakir's experience demonstrates, there were opportunities for girls to study, to earn *ijaza*s (diplomas), and to become learned enough that eminent scholars such as he sought them out as teachers. This was especially the case among learned families who often made special efforts to ensure high quality education in the Qur'an and hadith for both their sons and daughters. To cite but one example, Amat al-Latif (d. 1243) was the daughter of the notable Syrian scholar Nasih al-Din Abd al-Rahman al-Hanbali. For many years she served as a close companion and mentor to Salah al-Din's sister, Rabi'a Khatun (d. 1246). This relationship between the scholar and the princess proved to be mutually beneficial, for in 1231, Rabi'a established a *madrasa* specifically for Nasih al-Din in Salihiyya, apparently at Amat al-Latif's prompting.[44]

While women did not enroll as students in formal classes, it is clear that they did attend ad hoc lectures and study sessions in mosques, *madrasas*, and other public places. It should come as no surprise that some men did not approve of women's public participation. The dyspeptic fourteenth-century scholar Muhammad Ibn al-Hajj (d. 1336) was appalled by the behavior of some women who informally audited lectures in his day:

[Consider] what some women do when people gather with a shaykh to hear [the recitation of] books. At that point women come, too, to hear the readings; the men sit in one place, the women facing them. It even happens at such times that some of the women are carried away by the situation; one will stand up, and sit down, and shout in a loud voice. [Moreover,] private parts of her body will appear; in her house, their exposure would be forbidden—how can it be allowed in a mosque, in the presence of men?[45]

As noted above, the Arabic term '*awra* (here translated as "private parts of her body") refers to "that which is indecent to reveal," generally understood to mean anything other than a woman's face and hands. Some extended the definition to include even these as well.[46]

Education in the medieval Islamic world, of course, was not limited to religious subjects—Qur'an, hadith, jurisprudence, theology, and so forth. Ancient Greek, Persian, and Sanskrit works on philosophy, medicine, mathematics, astronomy, geography, and other sciences were translated into Arabic between the eighth and tenth centuries under the patronage of the Abbasids.[47] Muslim (as well as Jewish and Christian) scholars studied these classics and built upon them. Many of these ancient classics were eventually translated into Latin and made their way into the medieval European curriculum. The pantheon of philosophers, polymaths, physicians, and others contains far too many personalities to be addressed here. I briefly mention two merely to illustrate that, building on the work of the ancients, scholars in the medieval Islamic world (Jews, Christians, and Muslims) made important advancements in all areas of science and learning.[48]

The ninth-century mathematician al-Khwarazmi (ca. 800–ca. 847), played a major role in the introduction of "Hindu Numerals" into the Islamic world.

This numbering system was later adopted and modified in the west resulting in what are now known as "Arabic" numerals. Al-Khwarazmi also wrote an important mathematical text, *Kitab al-mukhtasar fi hisab al-jabr wa l-muqabila* (Compendium on Calculation by Transposition and Reduction), in which he developed methods for solving quadratic equations in which words and letters were used to represent numerical values. In 1145, Robert of Ketton began his Latin translation of al-Khwarazmi's *Compendium* (*Liber Algebras et Almucabola*) with the phrase *dixit Algorithmi;* that is, "Algorithmi says." It is from Ketton's transliteration of al-Khwarazmi's title (*Algebras* for *al-jabr;* transposition) that we get our word algebra; from Ketton's transliteration of his name (Algorithmi for al-Khwarazmi) that we get our term for the step-by-step process of working out mathematical problems, algorithm.[49]

Ibn Sina (980–1037) had a tremendous influence on philosophy, theology, and medicine in the medieval Islamic world as well as in Europe. Ibn Sina's proof for the existence of God, based on the distinction between *possible* and *necessary* existence, was equally influential among Jewish and Christian thinkers. The Jewish philosopher and physician Moses Maimonides (d. 1204), a native of Muslim Spain (who relocated to Egypt in the wake of Almohad persecutions), read Ibn Sina's work in Arabic and adapted it to his own theological writings. The Christian theologian St. Thomas Aquinas (d. 1274) studied it in Latin translation and incorporated it into his own systematic theology. Ibn Sina's proof remains the starting point for many rational proofs for the existence of God to this day. I even remember learning a greatly simplified version of this proof as a child in Sunday school.[50]

In addition to his major contributions to philosophy and theology, Ibn Sina is most famous for his comprehensive and systematic medical text, *al-Qanun fi l-tibb* (*The Canon of Medicine*), based in large part on the works of Galen (d. A.D. 203) and his disciples in the medieval Islamic world. After all, when human beings are ill or injured, they tend to be more interested in their immediate physical health than the eternal fate of their souls. About a century after Ibn Sina's death, Gerard of Cremona translated Ibn Sina's *Canon* into Latin. In Europe where he was known as Avicenna, his *Canon* was a favorite of doctors and medical schools until the rise of experimental medicine in the sixteenth and seventeenth centuries. It was translated into Hebrew, was retranslated into Latin in the early sixteenth century, and was the subject of countless commentaries in European and Islamic languages.

ENTERTAINMENTS

Common children's entertainments in the medieval Islamic world included puppet theaters and seesaws as well as games played with balls, dolls, toy animals, and birds. Board games such as chess and backgammon were popular among all sectors of society. So too were card games. Entertainments that involved tests of physical prowess were quite popular, including wrestling, races, polo, mock military competitions, and other displays of horsemanship—a sort of medieval rodeo.

Not all popular entertainments involved toys, puppets, or physical competitions. One of the most popular events at trade fairs in seventh-century Arabia was the poetry competition among the leading poets of the clans present. For to the best poet went not only a financial reward, but his entire clan benefited from the prestige of his poetic prowess. Arabic poetry performances continued to be extremely popular throughout the medieval Islamic world and remain so today, often selling out large auditoriums. Persian re-emerged as a language of literature and administration in the tenth century. Public recitations of Ferdowsi's (ca. A.D. 940–1020) *Shahnameh* (Book of Kings)—one of the earliest and greatest examples of new Persian epic poetry—were quite popular throughout the Persian-speaking world. Turkish poetry began to become popular as well by 1400 after the rise of the Ottoman house in Anatolia and southeastern Europe.

It should come as no surprise that poetry often dealt with themes of honor, glory, and heroism among men, but also the beauty of one's beloved, the passions of unrequited love, and the romantic benefits of wine. Among the ruling elites as well as among the wealthy classes, poetry performances were often accompanied by music and performed by singing girls, many of whom were slaves purchased expressly for their beauty, voices, and dancing abilities.

Hunting in the medieval Islamic world was done for sport as well as for food. It was a favorite entertainment for the wealthy and a necessity for the diet of some of the less well-to-do. Given the specific regulations for butchering domesticated animals in order for them to be *halal,* that is, permitted according to shariʿa or Islamic law, Muslim scholars devoted their attention to determining which game was permissible for consumption and when. Essentially, any wild animal killed by a hunter was considered *halal,* with the notable exception of pigs, which are forbidden under any circumstances. However, it is forbidden for pilgrims to eat game during the annual pilgrimage (*hajj*). Finally, whereas according to the Jewish tradition only fish with fins and scales are considered kosher, all fish and seafood are permissible to Muslims at any time.

Hunting was a common theme in medieval Islamic literature, whether in poetry or in descriptions of a ruler's fondness for spending time on his horse as he and his companions pursued hares, partridges, quail, geese, and other small game with their hunting falcons and hounds. In his memoir, Usama ibn Muhqidh (1095–1188) includes a section about his father's exploits as a hunter near the family estate at Shayzar in the mountains between Hama and the Syrian coast. Since his was a well-to-do family, they had broad access to land on which to hunt. In fact, Usama reports that in Shayzar "we had two hunting fields, one for partridges and hares, in the mountain to the south of town; and another for waterfowl, francolins, hares and gazelles, on the bank of the river in the cane fields to the west of town."[51]

Falcons and hawks are birds of prey that were essential to a successful hunt; so too were hunting hounds. In fact, Usama's father used to dispatch some of his men to distant lands to purchase choice falcons as well as pigeons to feed them. He even sent some of his aides as far as Constantinople, the Byzantine capital, to purchase his falcons and hounds. Falcons and hawks were also purchased from locals who had set up trapping stations nearby in order to meet the demand for the birds. While falcons and hawks were excellent hunters of small game and other birds, cheetahs were often used when hunting larger game such as gazelles, antelopes, deer, wild donkeys, and wild boar.

Falcons, hawks, hounds, cheetahs, and horses were a keeper's livelihood as well as essential to his employer's successful hunts. Hence, a great deal of care and attention was paid to a man's hunting animals. In fact, it was not uncommon for a hunter to keep his birds of prey in his home. Usamah reports that his father even kept his prize cheetah in their house:

He had a special maid who served it. In one side of the courtyard she had a velvet quilt folded, with dry grass beneath. In the wall was an iron staple. After the hunt, the cheetah trainer would bring it to the door of the house in which its couching place lay, and leave it there. It would then enter the house and go to that place where its bed was spread and sleep. The maid would come and tie it to the staple fastened to the wall.[52]

Usamah also reports that gazelles, rams, goats, and fawns were born in the same courtyard, but that the cheetah was so well behaved that it never touched them.

DEATH AND AFTERLIFE

Muslim burial rituals are fairly simple and, if possible, should occur on the day the person dies. First, the corpse is washed and its orifices plugged. It is then wrapped in a shroud in preparation for burial (coffins are not used). The ritual prayer (*salat*) is performed, followed by the recitation of funeral prayers (*janaza*). The shrouded corpse is then carried on a bier or kind of stretcher to the cemetery, where it is placed on its right side with its face towards Mecca in a relatively shallow grave so that the deceased can hear the muezzin's call to prayer. According to most Muslim scholars, cremation was not an acceptable practice because of the importance of the physical bodily resurrection of the dead at the end of time. Traditionally, it had also been unacceptable according to Jewish and Christian scholars for similar reasons.[53]

While the rather modest procedures for properly burying a corpse are important, it is the theology of death itself and the rewards and punishments in the afterlife that are of eternal consequence. One of the most common themes in the Qur'an is the necessity of belief in the One God and the Last Day (The Day of Judgment, or Day of Resurrection). The importance of this theme is made abundantly clear in the seventh chapter of the Qur'an, which describes an event that ostensibly occurred at the beginning of human time when God brought forth Adam's descendants from the loins of his children and made them testify that He was their Lord so that on the Last Day they could not claim ignorance of His Oneness nor could they claim that they were blameless in their polytheism or idolatry because they had learned such false beliefs from their parents (Qur'an 7:171).

Of course, only God knows the moment when each individual will inevitability encounter the angel of death, known as Izra'il. A common belief was that God determined the location of each person's death by commanding an angel to put a speck of the soil from the territory where a person was destined to die into the semen in his or her mother's womb. There are many stories told about people who for some unexplained reason felt compelled to visit a particular place, only to die once they arrived there. According to many scholars, once a person is in the grave, two angels (often referred to as Munkar and Nakir) arrive to conduct an interrogation about the content of his or her faith, after which they mete out rewards to the righteous and punishments to the wicked.[54] As noted above, the grave needs to be shallow enough for the deceased to be able to hear the muezzin's call to prayer; however, it also needs to be deep enough for the deceased to be able to sit up and answer the angels' questions.

As the appointed time and location of one's death is known only to God, so too is the exact moment when another angel, Israfil, will sound the trumpet announcing the resurrection of the dead and the ingathering of souls for the final Day of Judgment. However, there are certain events or signs that are expected to occur prior to the Last Day such as natural disasters, the sun rising in the west, a triple eclipse of the moon, and the arrival of Yajuj and Majuj (the Biblical Gog and Magog) to wreak havoc on the earth. Jesus will also return at the end of days to do battle with the Anti-Christ (al-Dajjal). After Jesus defeats the Anti-Christ, he will die for the first time (according to Qur'an 4:157, Jesus only appeared to die on the cross) and be buried in a tomb near Muhammad in Medina.[55]

In addition, a messianic figure called the Mahdi will come and defeat God's enemies, the world will be destroyed, and a new millennial age ushered in. Most Sunni scholars argue that the Mahdi is a member of Muhammad's family; a minority position is that Jesus and the Mahdi are one and the same.[56] Twelver Shi'is, of course, believe that Muhammad al-Mahdi—the Hidden Imam—is the Mahdi. Prior to the Day of Judgment, the physical resurrection of the dead will occur. The righteous and the wicked will then be summoned before God, their vices and virtues recited by angels who recorded them in special books, and God's final judgment given. Essentially, God's final judgment is a formal, ominous, and public vindication of the reward or punishment that He decreed for each person at the moment he or she died.

According to some Muslim scholars, the Final Judgment will occur in the Valley of Jehosephat to the east of Jerusalem (as it will in Judaism and Christianity) and the Ka'ba will be transported from Mecca to witness it. The reward for the righteous and the punishment for the wicked also parallel those found in Judaism and Christianity. The righteous are rewarded with a garden (*janna*), while the wicked are condemned to the fire (*nar*). According to some commentators, the wicked will access the fire via Gehenna (Hebrew, *gehinom*; Arabic, *jahannam*), Jerusalem's garbage dump that used to smolder south of the city. While the Qur'an speaks of two gardens "for those who fear to stand before God" (Qur'an 55:46) and "two more gardens" beyond them (Qur'an 55:62), some commentators expanded the number from four to seven gardens or "heavens" culminating in the "Garden of Eden."

Whatever the specific number of gardens for the righteous or precise routes to the fire taken by the wicked, the Qur'an makes perfectly clear what is in store for those who obey God and His messenger and those who do not:

This is the Garden which the righteous have been promised. Therein shall flow rivers of water undefiled, and rivers of milk forever fresh; rivers of wine delectable to those that drink it, and rivers of clarified honey. They shall eat therein of every fruit and receive forgiveness from their Lord. Is this like the lot of those who shall abide in the Fire forever, and drink scalding water which will tear their bowels? (Qur'an 47:15)

NOTES

1. For a more detailed treatment of the Arabic naming system used throughout the Islamic world, see Annemarie Schimmel, *Islamic Names* (Edinburgh: Edinburgh University Press, 1989).

2. Alfred Guillaume, trans., *The Life of Muhammad: A Translation of Ibn Ishaq's Sirat Rasul Allah* (Oxford: Oxford University Press, 1955), 713, n. 140. See also p. 51 of this book.

3. According to Genesis 32, after Jacob (Abraham's grandson) wrestled all night with an unknown man, Jacob's name was changed to Israel. Consequently, Jacob's descendants are known as the Children of Israel.

Then the man said, "Let me go, for it is daybreak." But Jacob replied, "I will not let you go unless you bless me." Then the man asked him, "What is your name?" "Jacob," he answered. Then the man said, "Your name will no longer be Jacob, but Israel, because you have struggled with God and with men and have overcome." Jacob said, "Please tell me your name." But he replied, "Why do you ask my name?" Then he blessed him there. So Jacob call the place Peniel, saying, "It is because I saw God face to face, and yet my life was spared." (Genesis 32:26–30)

4. See pp. 22–23 of this book.

5. Dick Davis has translated much of this epic poem of some 50,000 couplets in *Stories from the Shahnameh of Ferdowsi*, 3 vols. (Washington, DC: Mage Publishers, 1998, 2000, 2003). For translations of three cycles of the *Shahnameh*, see Dick Davis, trans., *The Legend of Seyavash* (New York: Penguin Books, 1992); Jerome W. Clinton, trans., *The Tragedy of Sohráb and Rostám* (Seattle: University of Washington Press, 1997); and idem, *In the Dragon's Claws: The Story of Rostam and Esfandiyar from the Persian Book of Kings* (Washington, DC: Mage Publishers, 1999).

6. Much has been written on women in Islamic history in recent decades, but most of it concerns the early modern and modern periods, for which sources are more plentiful. For a broad overview of women in the medieval Islamic world, see the relevant chapters in Leila Ahmed, *Women and Gender in Islam: Historical Roots of a Modern Debate* (New Haven, CT: Yale University Press, 1992); Wiebke Walther, *Women in Islam* (Princeton, NJ: Markus Wiener, 1993); Denise A. Spellberg, *Politics, Gender, and the Islamic Past: The Legacy of 'A'isha bint Abi Bakr* (New York: Columbia University Press, 1994); and Ruth Roded, ed., *Women in Islam and the Middle East: A Reader* (New York: I. B. Tauris Publishers, 1999). For more specific studies of women in premodern Islamic history, see the section titled "Women" in "Suggestions for Further Reading."

7. W. Robertson Smith, *Kinship and Marriage in Early Arabia* (Cambridge, UK: Cambridge University Press, 1885).

8. Nabia Abbott, "Women and the State in Early Islam," *Journal of Near Eastern Studies* 1.2 (1942): 107.

9. As shari'a developed, the Qur'anic punishment of lashing was changed to death by stoning, a punishment that parallels the Biblical practice of execution for all sorts of illicit sexual intercourse described in Leviticus 20 and Deuteronomy 22.

10. *Fitna* is a widely used pejorative, meaning that which upsets the proper order of things. It is used to describe the chaos provoked by women's sexuality, the civil wars of early Islamic history, and any kind of social and/or religious discord. See Fedwa Malti-Douglas, *Woman's Body, Woman's Word: Gender and Discourse in Arabo-Islamic Writing* (Princeton, NJ: Princeton University Press, 1991).

11. See Spellberg, *Politics, Gender, and the Islamic Past*, and p. 68 in this book.

12. Nabia Abbott, *Two Queens of Baghdad: Mother and Wife of Harun al-Rashid* (Chicago: University of Chicago Press, 1946).

13. While the Ottoman period is beyond the chronological scope of this book, it is worthwhile mentioning that in order to ensure an orderly succession, the Ottoman sultans took their right to sexual relations with their slave women to an extreme. That is, for much of early Ottoman history, sultans fathered children almost exclusively by slave women of Russian, Polish, and Slavic origin. The virtue in this from the Ottoman perspective was that since slaves had no families, there could be no kin who might seek a share of political power and authority as would be the case if a sultan produced an heir with one of his free-born wives. See Leslie Peirce, *The Imperial Harem: Women and Sovereignty in the Ottoman Empire* (New York: Oxford University Press, 1993).

14. Spellberg, *Politics, Gender and the Islamic Past*, 39–41.

15. Ahmed, *Women and Gender in Islam*, 76–78.

16. On the story of the marriage between Umm Salamah and Abu l-Abbas, see Abbott, *Two Queens of Baghdad*, 10–14.

17. al-Tabari, *The History of al-Tabari*, vol. 2, *Prophets and Patriarchs*, trans. William M. Brinner (Albany: State University Press of New York, 1987), 72.

18. Jim Colville, trans., *Sobriety and Mirth: A Selection of the Shorter Writings of al-Jahiz* (London: Kegan Paul, 2002), 79.

19. A.J. Wensinck, "*Khitan* [circumcision]," in *Encyclopaedia of Islam*, New Edition, 12 vols. (Leiden: Brill, 1954–2004), 5:20–22.

20. On female circumcision in the medieval Middle East, see Jonathan P. Berkey, "Circumcision Circumscribed: Female Excision and Cultural Accommodation in the Medieval Near East," *International Journal of Middle East Studies* 28.1 (1996): 19–38.

21. See especially Yedida Kalfon Stillman's *Arab Dress: From the Dawn of Islam to Modern Times* (Leiden: Brill, 2000). Stillman's book is by far the best work on the subject of dress in the Islamic world. My discussion of dress here and elsewhere is based largely on this study.

22. See Fatima Mernisi, *The Veil and the Male Elite: A Feminist Interpretation of Women's Rights in Islam* (New York: Addison-Wesley, 1991).

23. Stillman, *Arab Dress*, 7. Herodotus (484–420 b.c.) mentions that Arabs wore a long flowing garment gathered up with a belt. See also Emmanuel Anati, *Rock-Art in Central Arabia*, vol. 1 (Louvain: Institut Orientaliste, 1968).

24. Stillman, *Arab Dress*, 11.

25. Ibid., 37.

26. Ahmed, *Women and Gender in Islam*, 54.

27. Gillian Eastwood, "A Medieval Face-Veil from Egypt," *Costume* 17 (1983): 33–38; it is also included in David Waines, ed., *Patterns of Everyday Life: The Formation of the Classical Islamic World*, vol. 10 (Aldershot, UK: Ashgate, 2002), 233–38.

28. Stillman, *Arab Dress*, 9. One can still find women dressed in this fashion from North Africa to Iran.

29. Edward W. Lane, *An Account of the Manners and Customs of the Modern Egyptians: The Definitive 1860 Edition* (Cairo: American University Press, 2002 [1836]), 50.

30. R. P. Buckley, trans., *The Book of the Islamic Market Inspector: Niyayat al-rutba fi talab al-hisba (The Utmost Authority in the Pursuit of Hisba) by ʿAbd al-Rahman b. Nasr al-Shayzari* (New York: Oxford University Press, 1999), 119.

31. See Christopher Melchert, "The Etiquette of Learning in the Early Islamic Study Circle," in Joseph Lowry, Devin Stewart and Shawkat M. Toorawa, eds., *Law and Education in Medieval Islam: Studies in Honor of Professor George Makdisi* (Cambridge, UK: E. J. W. Gibb Memorial Trust, 2004), 33–44.

32. Buckley, *The Book of the Market Inspector*, 119.

33. Buckley, *The Book of the Market Inspector*, 119–120.

34. Cited in Avner Giladi, *Children of Islam: Concepts of Childhood in Medieval Muslim Society* (New York: St. Martin's Press, 1992), 58.

35. Ibn Asakir, *Taʾrikh madinat Dimashq* [History of Damascus], 80 vols., eds. Umar al-Amrawi and Ali Shiri (Beirut: Dar al-Fikr, 1995–2001).

36. Josef W. Meri, "A Late Medieval Syrian Pilgrimage Guide: Ibn al-Hawrani's *al-Isharat il Amakin al-Ziyarat (Guide to Pilgrimage Places)*," *Medieval Encounters: Jewish, Christian and Muslim Culture in Confluence and Dialogue* 7.1 (2001), 40–41.

37. Cited in Jonathan Berkey, *The Transmission of Knowledge in Medieval Cairo: A Social History of Islamic Education* (Princeton, NJ: Princeton University Press, 1992), 161.

38. Cited in Berkey, *The Transmission of Knowledge*, 161–62.

39. Buckley, trans., *The Book of the Market Inspector*, 120.

40. Abbott, *Two Queens of Baghdad*, 118–20.

41. Ibid., 239–47.

42. R. Stephen Humphreys, "Women as Patrons of Religious Architecture in Ayyubid Syria," *Muqarnass: An Annual on Islamic Art and Architecture* 11 (1994): 35–54.

43. On the importance of the *madrasa* to medieval Islamic education, see especially George Makdisi, *The Rise of Colleges: Institutions of Learning in Islam and the West* (Edinburgh: Edinburgh University Press, 1981) and Richard Bulliet, *Islam: The View from the Edge* (New York: Columbia University Press, 1994), 143–56.

44. Humphreys, "Women as Patrons," 40–41. Some of the colophons at the end of the surviving manuscript Ibn Asakir's *al-Arbaʿin fi al-ijtihad fi iqamat al-jihad* (The Forty Hadiths on the Obligation to Wage Jihad) mention children, including a two-year-old girl, who were brought by their fathers to receive the right—*ijaza* or license—to transmit the text when they grew up and became scholars. See Suleiman A. Mourad and James E. Lindsay, "Rescuing Syria from the Infidels: The Contribution of Ibn Asakir of Damascus to the *Jihad* Campaign of Sultan Nur al-Din," in *Crusades* 6 (2007): 50–51.

45. Cited in Berkey, *The Transmission of Knowledge*, 171–72. Ibn al-Hajj made this observation in his treatise in which he catalogued many of the contemporary practices of which he disapproved, including "those scholars, who, when delivering their lectures, sat on a raised dais or platform. Such behavior, he thought, smacked of conceit and an inappropriate sense of self-importance." Berkey, *The Transmission of Knowledge*, 38.

46. See pp. 190–93 of this book for a discussion of clothing and modesty in the medieval Islamic world.

47. Dimitri Gutas, *Greek Thought, Arabic Culture: The Graeco-Arabic Translation Movement in Baghdad and Early ʿAbbasid Society (2nd–4th/8th–10th Centuries)* (New York: Routledge, 1998).

48. On contributions to science and technology in the medieval Islamic world, see Howard R. Turner, *Science in Medieval Islam: An Illustrated Introduction* (Austin: University of Texas Press, 1995); Donald R. Hill, *Islamic Science and Engineering* (Edinburgh: Edinburgh University Press, 1993); Toby E. Huff, *The Rise of Early Modern Science: Islam, China, and the West.* (New York: Cambridge University Press, 1993); Ahmad Y. Hasan and Donald R. Hill, *Islamic Technology: An Illustrated History* (New York: Cambridge University Press, 1986); and Sayyed Hossein Nasr, *Science and Civilization in Islam* (New York: Plume, 1968).

49. J. Vernet, "al-Khwarazmi," in *Encyclopaedia of Islam*, New Edition. 4:1070–71.

50. A.-M. Goichon, "Ibn Sina," in *Encyclopaedia of Islam*, New Edition. 3:941–47.

51. Philip K. Hitti, trans., *An Arab-Syrian Gentleman and Warrior in the Period of the Crusades: Memoirs of Usamah Ibn-Muhqidh* (Princeton, NJ: Princeton University Press, 1987 [1929]), 228.

52. Ibid., 237.

53. Timothy Insoll, *The Archaeology of Islam* (Malden, MA: Blackwell Publishers, 1999), 166–200.

54. On medieval Islamic scholarship on what happens when one dies, see Jane Idleman Smith and Yvonne Yazbeck Haddad, "Death and Resurrection: Classical Islam," in *The Islamic Understanding of Death and Resurrection* (Albany: State University of New York Press, 1981), 31–61. See also al-Ghazali, *The Remembrance of Death and the Afterlife. Book 40 of the Revival of the Religious Sciences: Ihya ʿUlum al-Din* (Cambridge, UK: The Islamic Texts Society, 1989).

55. On medieval Islamic scholarship on eschatology and the apocalypse, see David Cook, *Studies in Muslim Apocalyptic* (Princeton, NJ: Darwin Press, 2002). See also Smith and Haddad, "The Eschaton, the Judgment, and the Final Dispensation: Classical Islam," in *Death and Resurrection*, 63–97.

56. Suleiman A. Mourad, "Jesus According to Ibn ʿAsakir," in James E. Lindsay, ed. *Ibn ʿAsakir and Early Islamic History* (Princeton, NJ: Darwin Press, 2001), 24–43. See also Tarif Khalidi, *The Muslim Jesus: Sayings and Stories in Islamic Literature* (Cambridge: Harvard University Press, 2001).

SUGGESTIONS FOR FURTHER READING

This bibliography is designed to provide the reader with a broad range of (primarily) English-language reference works, journals, articles, and monographs relevant to *Daily Life in the Medieval Islamic World*. Those interested in a more complete and annotated bibliography should consult R. Stephen Humphreys, *Islamic History: A Framework for Inquiry*, revised edition (Princeton, NJ: Princeton University Press, 1991). Not only is it available in affordable paperback, but it is by far the most comprehensive English-language introduction to the primary and secondary sources for understanding the history of the medieval Islamic world. *Encyclopaedia of Islam*, New Edition, 12 volumes (Leiden: Brill, 1954–2004) is the essential resource for any serious student of Islamic history or religion. Unfortunately, because it is prohibitively expensive, one is likely to find it primarily in college and university libraries. *Encyclopaedia of the Qur'an*, 5 volumes (Leiden: Brill, 2000–2005). It is the best compendium of scholarship on the Qur'an available in English. Finally, while the *Dictionary of the Middle Ages*, 13 volumes (New York: Scribner, 1982–89) emphasizes the European Middle Ages, it also contains many excellent entries on the medieval Islamic world. One is more likely to find it in local public libraries as well.

REFERENCE WORKS

Bacharach, Jere L. *A Middle East Studies Handbook.* Seattle: University of Washington Press, 1984.

Bosworth, C. E. *The New Islamic Dynasties: A Chronological and Genealogical Manual.* New York: Columbia University Press, 1996.

Cambridge History of Arabic Literature: 'Abbasid Belles-Lettres. Julia Ashtiany, T. M. Johnstone, R. B. Serjeant, and G. R. Smith, eds. New York: Cambridge University Press, 1990.

Cambridge History of Arabic Literature: Arabic Literature to the End of the Umayyad Period. A. F. L. Beeston, T. M. Johnstone, R. B. Serjeant, and G. R. Smith, eds. New York: Cambridge University Press, 1983.

Cambridge History of Arabic Literature: Religion, Learning and Science in the 'Abbasid Period. M. J. L. Young, J. D. Latham, and R. B. Serjeant, eds. New York: Cambridge University Press, 1990.

Cambridge History of Arabic Literature: The Literature of Al-Andalus. M. R. Menocal, R. P. Scheindlin, and M. Sells, eds. New York: Cambridge University Press, 2000.

Cambridge History of Egypt, 2 vols. Carl F. Petry, ed. New York: Cambridge University Press, 1998.

Cambridge History of Iran, 7 vols. New York: Cambridge University Press, 1968–91.

Cambridge History of Islam, 2 vols. P. M. Holt, Ann K. S. Lambton, and Bernard Lewis, eds. New York: Cambridge University Press, 1970.

Crone, Patricia. *Pre-Industrial Societies: Anatomy of the Pre-Modern World.* Oxford: Oneworld, 1993.

Dictionary of the Middle Ages, 13 vols. Joseph R. Strayer, gen. ed. New York: Scribner, 1982–1989.

Encyclopaedia of Islam, New Edition, 12 vols. Leiden: Brill, 1954–2004.

Encyclopedia of the Qur'an, 5 vols. Jane Dammen McAuliffe, gen. ed. Leiden: Brill, 2000–2005.

The Formation of the Classical Islamic World, 17 vols. (48 projected). Lawrence I. Conrad, gen. ed. Aldershot, UK: Ashgate, 1998–.

Goitein, S. D. *A Mediterranean Society: The Jewish Communities of the World as Portrayed in the Cairo Geniza*, 6 vols. Berkeley: University of California Press, 1967–93.

Humphreys, R. Stephen. *Islamic History: A Framework for Inquiry*, rev. ed. Princeton, NJ: Princeton University Press, 1991.

Index Islamicus, 1906–1955. J. D. Pearson, ed. Cambridge: Cambridge University Press, 1958, with Supplements at five-year intervals.

Robinson, Chase F. *Islamic Historiography.* New York: Cambridge University Press, 2003.

Udovitch, A. L., ed. *The Islamic Middle East, 700–1900: Studies in Economic and Social History.* Princeton, NJ: Darwin Press, 1981.

JOURNALS

International Journal of Middle East Studies (Middle East Studies Association of North America. New York, volume 1, 1970–)

Jerusalem Studies in Arabic and Islam (Jerusalem, volume 1, 1979–)

Journal of Islamic Studies (Oxford, volume 1, 1989–)

Journal of Near Eastern Studies (Chicago, volume 1, 1942–)

Journal of Semitic Studies (Manchester, UK, volume 1, 1956–)

Journal of the American Oriental Society (New Haven, CT, volume 1, 1843–)

Journal of the Economic and Social History of the Orient (Leiden, volume 1, 1957–).
Al-Masaq: Islam and the Medieval Mediterranean (Leeds, UK, volume 1, 1988–)
Medieval Encounters: Jewish, Christian and Muslim Culture in Confluence and Dialogue (Leiden, volume 1, 1994–)
The Muslim World (Hartford, CT, volume 1, 1911–)
Studia Islamica (Paris, volume 1, 1953–)

GENERAL SURVEYS OF ISLAMIC HISTORY

Abun-Nasr, Jamil M. *A History of the Maghrib in the Islamic Period*. New York: Cambridge University Press, 1987.

Berkey, Jonathan. *The Formation of Islam: Religion and Society in the Near East, 600–1800*. New York: Cambridge University Press, 2003.

Bloom, Jonathan, and Sheila Blair. *Islam: A Thousand Years of Faith and Power*. New Haven, CT: Yale University Press, 2002.

Bulliet, Richard W. *Islam: The View from the Edge*. New York: Columbia University Press, 1994.

Egger, Vernon O. *A History of the Muslim World to 1405: The Making of a Civilization*. Upper Saddle River, NJ: Prentice Hall, 2004.

Esposito, John L., ed. *The Oxford History of Islam*. New York: Oxford University Press, 1999.

Hodgson, Marshall G. S. *The Venture of Islam*, 3 vols. Chicago: University of Chicago Press, 1974.

Hourani, Albert. *A History of the Arab Peoples*. Cambridge, MA: Harvard University Press, 1991.

Lapidus, Ira. *A History of Islamic Societies*, rev. ed. Berkeley: University of California Press, 2002.

Lewis, Bernard. *The Middle East: A Brief History of the Last 2,000 Years*. New York: Simon and Schuster, 1995.

Lewis, Bernard, ed. and trans. *Islam: From the Prophet Muhammad to the Capture of Constantinople*, 2 vols. New York: Walker and Company, 1974.

Robinson, Francis, ed. *Cambridge Illustrated History of the Islamic World*. New York: Cambridge University Press, 1996.

Sicker, Martin. *The Islamic World in Ascendancy: From the Arab Conquests to the Siege of Vienna*. Westport, CT: Praeger, 2000.

THE RISE OF ISLAM AND THE HIGH CALIPHATE (CA. 600–1000):

ʿAthamina, Khalil. "Arab Settlement during the Umayyad Caliphate," *Jerusalem Studies in Arabic and Islam* 8 (1986): 185–207.

Bulliet, Richard W. *The Camel and the Wheel*. Cambridge: Harvard University Press, 1975.

———. *Conversion to Islam in the Medieval Period: An Essay in Quantitative History*. Cambridge: Harvard University Press, 1979.

Cobb, Paul M. *White Banners: Contention in Abbasid Syria, 750–880*. Albany: State University of New York Press, 2001.

Crone, Patricia. *God's Rule: Government and Islam*. New York: Columbia University Press, 2004.

————. *Meccan Trade and the Rise of Islam.* Princeton, NJ: Princeton University Press, 1987.

Crone, Patricia, and Martin Hinds. *God's Caliph: Religious Authority in the First Centuries of Islam.* New York: Cambridge University Press, 1986.

Dafarty, Farhad. *The Isma'ilis: Their History and Doctrines.* New York: Cambridge University Press, 1990.

Daniel, Elton. *The Political and Social History of Khurasan under Abbasid Rule, 747–820.* Minneapolis: Bibliotheca Islamica, 1979.

Donner, Fred M. *The Early Islamic Conquests.* Princeton, NJ: Princeton University Press, 1981.

————. "From Believers to Muslims: Confessional Self-Identity in the Early Islamic Community," in *The Byzantine and Early Islamic Near East,* vol.4, *Patterns of Communal Identity,* ed. Lawrence I. Conrad. Princeton, NJ: Darwin Press, forthcoming.

————. *Narratives of Islamic Origins: The Beginnings of Islamic Historical Writing.* Princeton, NJ: Darwin Press, 1998.

El-Hibri, Tayeb. *Reinterpreting Islamic Historiography: Harun al-Rashid and the Narrative of the Abbasid Caliphate.* New York: Cambridge University Press, 1999.

Gordon, Matthew. *The Rise of Islam.* Westport, CT: Greenwood Press, 2005.

Guillaume, Alfred, trans. *The Life of Muhammad: A Translation of Ibn Ishaq's Sirat Rasul Allah.* Oxford: Oxford University Press, 1955.

Halm, Heinz. *The Empire of the Mahdi: The Rise of the Fatimids,* trans. Michael Bonner. Leiden: Brill, 1996.

Hawting, G. R. *The Idea of Idolatry and the Emergence of Islam: From Polemic to History.* New York: Cambridge University Press, 1999.

Horovitz, Josef. *The Earliest Biographies of the Prophet and Their Authors.* Princeton, NJ: Darwin Press, 2002.

Hoyland, Robert G. *Arabia and the Arabs: From the Bronze Age to the Coming of Islam.* New York: Routledge, 2001.

————. *Seeing Islam as Others Saw It: A Survey and Evaluation of Christian, Jewish and Zoroastrian Writings on Early Islam.* Princeton, NJ: Darwin Press, 1997.

Ibn Ishaq. *Sirat rasul Allah.* See Guillaume.

Ibn Kathir. *al-Sira al-Nabawiyya.* See Le Gassick.

Issawi, Charles. "The Area and Population of the Arab Empire: An Essay in Speculation," in *The Islamic Middle East, 700–1900: Studies in Economic and Social History,* ed. A. L. Udovitch. Princeton, NJ: Darwin Press, 1981, 374–96.

Kennedy, Hugh N. *Muslim Spain and Portugal: A Political History of al-Andalus.* New York: Longman, 1996.

————. *The Prophet and the Age of the Caliphates: The Islamic Near East from the Sixth to the Eleventh Century.* New York: Longman, 1986.

Landau-Tasseron, Ella. "From Tribal Society to Centralized Polity: An Interpretation of Events and Anecdotes in the Formative Period of Islam," *Jerusalem Studies in Arabic and Islam* 24 (2000): 180–216.

Lassner, Jacob. *The Shaping of Abbasid Rule.* Princeton, NJ: Princeton University Press, 1980.

Le Gassick, Trevor, trans. *The Life of the Prophet Muhammad: A Translation of Ibn Kathir's al-Sira al-Nabawiyya.* Reading, UK: Center for Muslim Contribution to Civilization, 1998.

Lecker, Michael. "On the Markets of Medina (Yathrib) in Pre-Islamic and Early Islamic Times," *Jerusalem Studies in Arabic and Islam* 8 (1986): 133–48.

Lindsay, James E., ed. *Ibn 'Asakir and Early Islamic History*. Princeton, NJ: Darwin Press, 2001.

———. "The Fatimid Da'wa in North Africa: Excerpted and Translated from al-Qadi al-Nu'man's (d. 974 A.D.) *Kitab iftitah al-da 'wa*," *Graeco-Arabica*, 7–8 (1999–2000): 283–310.

———. "Prophetic Parallels in Abu 'Abd Allah al-Shi'i's Mission among the Kutama Berbers, 893–910," *International Journal of Middle East Studies* 24.1 (1992): 39–56.

Madelung, Wilferd. *The Succession to Muhammad: A Study of the Early Caliphate*. New York: Cambridge University Press, 1997.

Morony, Michael G. *Iraq after the Muslim Conquest*. Princeton, NJ: Princeton University Press, 1984.

Peters, F. E. *Muhammad and the Origins of Islam*. Albany: State University of New York Press: 1994.

Robinson, Chase F. *Empire and Elites after the Muslim Conquest: The Transformation of Northern Mesopotamia*. New York: Cambridge University Press, 2000.

Rubin, Uri. *Between Bible and the Qur'an: The Children of Israel and the Islamic Self-Image*. Princeton, NJ: Darwin Press, 1999.

Savage, Elizabeth. *A Gateway to Hell, a Gateway to Paradise: The North African Response to the Arab Conquest*. Princeton, NJ: Darwin Press, 1997.

Sharon, Moshe. *Black Banners from the East: The Establishment of the Abbasid State, Incubation of a Revolt*. Jerusalem: Magnes Press, 1983.

———. "The Development of the Debate around the Legitimacy of Authority in Early Islam," *Jerusalem Studies in Arabic and Islam*, 5 (1984): 121–42.

Shoufani, Elias. *al-Ridda and the Muslim Conquest of Arabia*. Toronto: University of Toronto Press, 1973.

al-Tabari, *The History of al-Tabari*, 40 vols. Albany: State University of New York Press, 1985–97.

Walker, Paul E. *Exploring an Islamic Empire: Fatimid History and Its Sources*. London: I. B. Tauris, 2002.

Watt, W. Montgomery. *Muhammad at Mecca*. Oxford: Clarendon Press, 1953.

———. *Muhammad at Medina*. Oxford: Clarendon Press, 1956.

Wink, André. *al-Hind: The Making of the Indo-Islamic World*. Vol. 1, *Early Medieval India and the Expansion of Islam in the 7th–11th Centuries*. Leiden: Brill, 1990.

ISLAMIC HISTORY, 1000–1300

Barthold, W. *Turkestan down to the Mongol Invasion*, 4th ed. London: E. J. W. Gibb Memorial Trust, 1977 [1900].

Bosworth, C. E. *The Ghaznavids: Their Empire in Afghanistan and Eastern Iran, 944–1040*. Beirut: Librairie du Liban, 1973.

Broadhurst, R. J. C., trans. *The Travels of Ibn Jubayr*. London: J. Cape, 1952.

Cahen, Claude. *The Formation of Turkey: The Seljukid Sultanate of Rum: Eleventh to Fourteenth Century*. New York: Longman, 2001.

Constable, Olivia Remie. *Trade and Traders in Muslim Spain: The Commercial Realignment of the Iberian Peninsula, 900–1500*. New York: Cambridge University Press, 1996.

Darke, Hubert, trans. *The Book of Government or Rules for Kings: The Siyar al-Mulk or Siyasat-nama of Nizam al-Mulk*. Richmond, UK: Curzon Press, 2002.

Gabrieli, Francesco. *Arab Historians of the Crusades*. New York: Dorset Press, 1989.

Glick, Thomas F. *From Muslim Fortress to Christian Castle: Social and Cultural Change in Medieval Spain*. Manchester, UK: Manchester University Press, 1995.

Harvey, L. P. *Islamic Spain, 1250 to 1500*. Chicago: University of Chicago Press, 1990.

Hillenbrand, Carole. *The Crusades: Islamic Perspectives*. Edinburgh: Edinburgh University Press, 1999.

Hitti, Philip K., trans. *An Arab-Syrian Gentleman and Warrior in the Period of the Crusades: Memoirs of Usamah Ibn-Muhqidh*. Princeton, NJ: Princeton University Press, 1987 [1929].

Holt, P.M. *The Age of the Crusades: The Near East from the Eleventh Century to 1517*. New York: Longman, 1986.

Humphreys, R. Stephen. "Ayyubids, Mamluks, and the Latin East in the Thirteenth Century," *Mamluk Studies Review* 2 (1998): 1–17.

———. *From Saladin to the Mongols: The Ayyubids of Damascus, 1193–1260*. Albany: State University of New York Press, 1977.

———. "Legitimacy and Political Instability in the Age of the Crusades," in *The Jihad and Its Times*, eds. H. Dajani-Shakeel and R. A. Messier. Ann Arbor: University of Michigan Press, 1991.

Ibn Munqidh. *Memoirs*. See Hitti.

Irwin, Robert. *The Middle East in the Middle Ages: The Early Mamluk Sultanate, 1250–1382*. Carbondale: Southern Illinois University Press, 1986.

Kennedy, Hugh N., ed. *The Historiography of Islamic Egypt, c. 950–1800*. Leiden: Brill, 2001.

Lambton, A. K. S. *Continuity and Change in Medieval Persia. Aspects of Administrative, Economic, and Social History, 11th–14th Century*. Albany: State University of New York Press, 1988.

Lev, Yaacov. *State and Society in Fatimid Egypt*. Leiden: Brill, 1991.

Luther, Kenneth Allin, trans. *The History of the Seljuq Turks from the Jamiʿ al-Tawarikh: An Ilkhanid Adaption of the Saljuq-nama of Zahir al-Din Nishapuri*. Richmond, UK: Curzon Press, 2001.

Morgan, David. *Medieval Persia, 1040–1797*. Longman: New York, 1988.

Mottahedeh, Roy P. *Loyalty and Leadership in an Early Islamic Society*. Princeton, NJ: Princeton University Press, 1980.

Nizam al-Mulk. *Book of Government*. See Darke.

Reilly, Bernard F. *The Contest of Christian and Muslim Spain: 1031–1157*. Cambridge, MA: Blackwell, 1992.

Riley-Smith, Jonathan. *The Crusades: A Short History*. New Haven, CT: Yale University Press, 1987.

Riley-Smith, Jonathan, ed. *The Oxford Illustrated History of the Crusades*. New York: Oxford University Press, 1995.

Scales, Peter C. *The Fall of the Caliphate of Córdoba: Berbers and Andalusia in Conflict*. Leiden: Brill, 1994.

Setton, Kenneth M., gen. ed. *A History of the Crusades*, 7 vols. Madison: University of Wisconsin Press, 1969–89.

Sivan, Emmanuel. *L'Islam et la Croisade*. Paris, 1968.

Taha, Abdulwahid Dhanun. *The Muslim Conquest and Settlement of North Africa and Spain*. New York: Routledge, 1989.

Walker, Paul E. *Exploring an Islamic Empire: Fatimid History and Its Sources.* London: I. B. Tauris, 2002.

Wasserstein, David J. *The Caliphate in the West: An Islamic Political Institution in the Iberian Peninsula.* New York: Oxford University Press, 1993.

———. *The Rise and Fall of the Party-Kings: Politics and Society in Islamic Spain, 1002–1086.* Princeton, NJ: Princeton University Press, 1985.

Watt, W. Montgomery, and Pierre Cacchia. *A History of Islamic Spain.* Edinburgh: Edinburgh University Press, 1967.

Wink, André. *al-Hind: The Making of the Indo-Islamic World, Vol. 2. The Slave Kings and the Islamic Conquest, 11th-13th Centuries.* Leiden: Brill, 1996.

Woods, J. E. *The Aqquyunlu: Tribe, Confederation, Empire.* Minneapolis: Bibliotheca Islamica, 1976.

JIHAD AND MILITARY HISTORY

Amitai-Preiss, Reuven. *Mongols and Mamluks: The Mamluk-Ilkhanid War, 1260–1281.* New York: Cambridge University Press, 1995.

Cheveddin, Paul. "The Invention of the Counterweight Trebuchet: A Study in Cultural Diffusion," *Dumbarton Oaks Papers* 54 (2000): 71–116.

Cook, David. "Muslim Apocalyptic and *Jihad*," *Jerusalem Studies in Arabic and Islam* 20 (1996): 66–104.

Crone, Patricia. *Slaves on Horses: The Evolution of the Islamic Polity.* New York: Cambridge University Press, 1980.

Dajani-Shakeel, H., and R. A. Messier, eds. *The Jihad and Its Times.* Ann Arbor: University of Michigan Press, 1991.

Elgood, Robert, ed. *Islamic Arms and Armour.* London: Scholar Press, 1979.

Firestone, Reuven. *Jihad: The Origin of Holy War in Islam.* New York: Oxford University Press, 1999.

Gordon, Matthew. *The Breaking of a Thousand Swords: A History of the Turkish Military of Samarra,* A.H. *200–275/815–889* C.E. Albany: State University of New York Press, 2001.

Hill, D. R. "The Role of the Camel and the Horse in the Early Arab Conquests," in *War, Technology and Society in the Middle East,* V. J. Parry and M. E. Yapp, eds. London: Oxford University Press, 1975, 32–43.

Humphreys, R. Stephen. "The Emergence of the Mamluk Army," *Studia Islamica,* 45 (1977): 67–99; 46 (1977): 147–82.

Jackson, Peter. *The Delhi Sultanate: A Political and Military History.* New York: Cambridge University Press, 1999.

Kennedy, Hugh N. *The Armies of the Caliphs: Military and Society in the Early Islamic State.* New York: Routledge, 2001.

Kepel, Gilles. *Jihad: The Trail of Political Islam.* Cambridge: Harvard University Press, 2002.

Lev, Yaacov, ed. *War and Society in the Eastern Mediterranean, 7th–15th Centuries.* Leiden: Brill, 1996.

Mamluk Bibliography Online, http://www.lib.uchicago.edu/e/su/mideast/mamluk/. Middle East Document Center, University of Chicago.

Mourad, Suleiman A., and James E. Lindsay, "Rescuing Syria from the Infidels: The Contribution of Ibn ʿAsakir of Damascus to the *Jihad* Campaign of Sultan Nur al-Din," in *Crusades* 6 (2007): 37–55.

Nicolle, David. *The Armies of Islam 7th–11th Centuries.* London: Osprey Publishing, 1987.

———. *Armies of the Muslim Conquest.* London: Osprey Publishing, 1993.

———. *Arms and Armour of the Crusading Era, 1050–1350.* London: Greenhill Books, 1999.

———. "Arms of the Umayyad Era: Military Technology in a Time of Change." In *War and Society in the Eastern Mediterranean, 7th–15th Centuries,* ed. Yaacov Lev. Leiden: Brill, 1996, 9–100.

———. *Early Medieval Islamic Arms and Armour.* Madrid: Instituto de Estudios Sobre Armas Antiguas, 1976.

———. *Saladin and the Saracens: Armies of the Middle East, 1100–1300.* London: Osprey Publishing, 1986.

———. "Saljuq Arms and Armour in Art and Literature." In *The Art of the Saljuqs in Iran and Anatolia,* ed. Robert Hillenbrand. Costa Mesa, CA: Mazda Publishers, 1994, 247–56.

———. *Yarmuk: The Muslim Conquest of Syria.* London: Osprey Publishing, 1994.

Peters, Rudolph, ed. *Jihad in Classical and Modern Islam.* Princeton, NJ: Markus Wiener, 1996.

Pipes, Daniel. *Slave Soldiers and Islam: The Genesis of a Military System.* New Haven, CT: Yale University Press, 1981.

Ruthven, Malise. *A Fury for God: The Islamist Attack on America.* Granta Books, 2002.

Sivan, Emmanuel. *Radical Islam: Medieval Theology and Modern Politics.* New Haven, CT: Yale University Press, 1985.

Toru, Miura, and John Edward Philips, eds. *Slave Elites in the Middle East and Africa: A Comparative Study.* New York: Kegan Paul International, 2000.

CITIES

Abu-Lughod, Janet. *Cairo: 1000 Years of the City Victorious.* Princeton, NJ: Princeton University Press, 1971.

Ashtor, Eliyahu. *A Social and Economic History of the Near East in the Middle Ages.* Berkeley: University of California Press, 1976.

Bates, Michael. *Islamic Coins.* New York: American Numismatic Society, 1982.

Buckley, R. P., trans. *The Book of the Islamic Market Inspector: Niyayat al-rutba fi talab al-hisba (The Utmost Authority in the Pursuit of Hisba) by 'Abd al-Rahman b. Nasr al-Shayzari.* New York: Oxford University Press, 1999.

Cahen, Claude. "Monetary Circulation in Egypt at the Time of the Crusades and the Reform of al-Kamil." In *The Islamic Middle East, 700–1900: Studies in Economic and Social History,* ed. A.L. Udovitch. Princeton, NJ: Darwin Press, 1981, 315–34.

Cobb, Paul M. "Virtual Sacrality: Making Muslim Syria Sacred before the Crusades," *Medieval Encounters: Jewish, Christian and Muslim Culture in Confluence and Dialogue* 8.1 (2002): 35–55.

Cook, Michael A. *Commanding the Right and Forbidding Wrong in Islamic Thought.* New York: Cambridge University Press, 2000.

Elisséeff, Nikita, trans. *La Description de Damas d'Ibn 'Asakir.* Damascus: Institut Français de Damas, 1959.

Hitti, Philip. *Capital Cities of Arab Islam*. Minneapolis: University of Minnesota Press, 1973.

Hourani, A.H., and S.M. Stern, eds. *The Islamic City: A Colloquium*. Philadelphia: University of Pennsylvania Press, 1970.

Ibn Asakir. *La Description de Damas*. See Elisséeff.

al-Khatib al-Baghdadi. *The Topography of Baghdad in the Early Middle Ages*. See Lassner.

Lambton, Ann K.S. *Landlord and Peasant in Persia: A Study of Land Tenure and Land Revenue Administration*. London: I. B. Tauris, 1991.

Lapidus, Ira M. *Muslim Cities in the Later Middle Ages*. Cambridge: Harvard University Press, 1967.

Lapidus, Ira M., ed. *Middle Eastern Cities: A Symposium on Ancient, Islamic, and Contemporary Middle Eastern Urbanism*. Berkeley: University of California Press, 1969.

Lassner, Jacob, trans. *The Topography of Baghdad in the Early Middle Ages: Texts and Studies*. Detroit: Wayne State University Press, 1970.

Lev, Yaacov, ed. *Towns and Material Culture in the Medieval Middle East*. Leiden: Brill, 2002.

Rabie, Hassanein. *The Financial System of Egypt*, A.H. *564–741/*A.D. *1169–1341*. London, 1972.

Raymond, André. *Cairo*. Cambridge: Harvard University Press, 2000.

Rodenbeck, Max. *Cairo: The City Victorious*. New York: Vintage Books, 1999.

Sabra, Adam. *Poverty and Charity in Medieval Islam: Mamluk Egypt, 1250–1517*. New York: Cambridge University Press, 2000.

Sanders, Paula. *Ritual, Politics, and the City in Fatimid Cairo*. Albany: State University of New York Press, 1994.

Schultz, Warren C. "The Monetary History of Egypt, 642–1517." In *The Cambridge History of Egypt*, vol. 1, ed. Carl F. Petry. New York: Cambridge University Press, 1998, 318–38.

Wiet, Gaston. *Baghdad: Metropolis of the Abbasid Caliphate*. Norman: University of Oklahoma Press, 1971.

———. *Cairo: City of Art and Commerce*. Norman: University of Oklahoma Press, 1964.

GEOGRAPHY AND TRAVEL

Bosworth, C.E., trans. *The Lata'if al-ma'arif of Tha'alibi: The Book of Curious and Entertaining Information*. Edinburgh: Edinburgh University Press, 1968.

Broadhurst, R.J.C., trans. *The Travels of Ibn Jubayr*. London: J. Cape, 1952.

Constable, Olivia Remie. *Housing the Stranger in the Mediterranean World: Lodging, Trade, and Travel in Late Antiquity and the Middle Ages*. New York: Cambridge University Press, 2003.

Dunn, Ross E. *The Adventures of Ibn Battuta: A Muslim Traveler of the 14th Century*. Berkeley: University of California Press, 1989.

Fisher, W.B. *The Middle East: A Physical, Social, and Regional Geography*, 7th ed. London: Methuen, 1978.

Gibb, H.A.R., trans. *The Travels of Ibn Battuta*, A.D. *1325–1354*. 5 vols. London: Hakluyt Society, 1958–2000.

Ibn Battuta. *Travels of Ibn Battuta*. See Gibb.

Ibn Jubayr. *Travels of Ibn Jubayr.* See Broadhurst.

Kennedy, Hugh N. *An Historical Atlas of Islam.* Leiden: Brill, 2002.

Lassner, Jacob, trans. *The Topography of Baghdad in the Early Middle Ages: Texts and Studies.* Detroit: Wayne State University Press, 1970.

Le Strange, Guy, trans. *Baghdad during the Abbasid Caliphate from Contemporary Arabic and Persian Sources.* New York: Barnes and Noble, 1972 [1900].

———. *The Lands of the Eastern Caliphate: Mesopotamia, Persia, and Central Asia from the Moslem Conquest to the Time of Timur.* New York: Barnes and Noble, 1966 [1905].

———. *Palestine under the Moslems: A Description of Syria and the Holy Land from A.D. 650 to 1500.* Beirut: Khayats Oriental Reprints, 1965 [1890].

Lev, Yaacov, ed. *Towns and Material Culture in the Medieval Middle East.* Leiden: Brill, 2002.

al-Muqaddasi. *The Best Divisions for Knowledge of the Regions: Ahsan al-taqasim fi maʿrifat al-aqalim,* trans. Basil Collins. Reading, UK: Garnet Publishing, 2001.

Naser-e Khosraw. *Naser-e Khosraw's Book of Travels.* See Thackston.

al-Thaʿalibi. *Lataʾif al-maʿrif.* See Bosworth.

Thackston, Wheeler M., trans. *Naser-e Khosraw's Book of Travels (Safarnama).* Albany: State University of New York Press, 1986.

THE QURʾAN: TRANSLATIONS AND INTRODUCTIONS

Ali, Abdullah Yusuf, trans. *The Qurʾan: The Meaning of the Glorious Qurʾan.* Istanbul: Asir Media, 2002.

Ali, Ahmed, trans. *al-Qurʾan: A Contemporary Translation.* Princeton, NJ: Princeton University Press, 1994.

Ali, Muhammad, trans. *The Holy Qurʾan.* Lahore, Pakistan: Ahmadiyyah Trust, 1951.

Arberry, Arthur J., trans. *The Koran Interpreted.* New York: Macmillan, 1955.

Ayoub, Mahmoud. *The Qurʾan and its Interpreters,* 2 vols. Albany: State University of New York Press, 1984.

Bell, Richard. *Introduction to the Qurʾan.* Edinburgh: Edinburgh University Press, 1963.

Cleary, Thomas, trans. *The Qurʾan.* Starlach Press, 2004:

Cook, Michael. *The Koran: A Very Short Introduction.* New York: Oxford University Press, 2000.

Cragg, Kenneth. *Muhammad in the Qurʾan: The Task and the Text.* London: Melisende, 2001.

———. *Readings in the Qurʾan.* Brighton, U.K.: Sussex Academic, 1999.

Dawood, N.J., trans. *The Koran,* 5th rev. ed. New York: Penguin Books, 1995.

Fakhry, Majid, trans. *The Qurʾan: A Modern English Version.* Reading, UK: Garnet, 1996.

Ibn Warraq, ed. *The Origins of the Koran: Classic Essays on Islam's Holy Book.* Amherst, NY: Prometheus Books, 1998.

Kaltner, John. *Ishmael Instructs Isaac: An Introduction to the Qurʾan for Bible Readers.* Collegeville, MN: The Liturgical Press, 1999.

Kassis, Hanna E. *A Concordance of the Qurʾan.* Berkeley: University of California Press, 1983.

Lester, Toby. "What Is the Koran?" *The Atlantic Monthly* 283 (January 1999): 43–56.

Pickthall, Mohammed Marmaduke, trans. *The Meaning of the Glorious Koran: An Explanatory Translation*. New York: New American Library, 1961.

Rippin, Andrew. "Literary Analysis of *Qur'an, Tafsir,* and *Sira:* The Methodologies of John Wansbrough." In Richard C. Martin, ed., *Approaches to Islam in Religious Studies* (Tucson: University of Arizona Press, 1985), 151–63.

Rippin, Andrew, ed. *Approaches to the History of the Interpretation of the Qur'an*. New York: Oxford University Press, 1988.

———. *The Qur'an and Its Interpretive Tradition*. Aldershot, UK: Ashgate, 2001.

Rippin, Andrew, and Jan Knappert. *Textual Sources for the Study of Islam*. Chicago: University of Chicago Press, 1990.

Sells, Michael. *Approaching the Qur'an: The Early Revelations*. Ashland, OR: White Cloud Press, 1999.

Wheeler, Brannon M. *Prophets in the Qur'an: An Introduction to the Qur'an and Muslim Exegesis*. New York: Continuum, 2002.

ISLAMIC RITUAL AND WORSHIP

Bukhari, *Sahih al-Bukhari*. See Khan.

Denny, Frederick M. *Islam and the Muslim Community*. Prospect Heights: Waveland Press, 1998.

Durán, Khalid, and Abdelwahab Hechiche. *Children of Abraham: An Introduction to Islam for Jews*. Hoboken, NJ: Ktav Publishing House, 2001.

Elias, Jamal. *Islam*. Upper Saddle River, NJ: Prentice Hall, 1998.

Endress, Gerhard. *Islam: An Historical Introduction*. Edinburgh: Edinburgh University Press, 2002.

Firestone, Reuven. *Journeys in Holy Lands: The Evolution of the Abraham-Ishmael Legends in Islamic Exegesis*. Albany: State University of New York Press, 1990.

al-Ghazali. *The Revival of the Religious Sciences: Ihya 'Ulum al-Din,* 9 vols. Cambridge: The Islamic Texts Society, 2002.

Gibb, H. A. R. *Muhammadanism*, 2d ed. New York: Oxford University Press, 1972.

Goitein, S. D. *Studies in Islamic History and Institutions*. Leiden: Brill, 1966.

Ibrahim, Ezzedin, and Denys Johnson-Davies, trans. *An-Nawawi's Forty Hadith*. Damascus: The Holy Koran Publishing House, 1976.

Khan, M. Muhsin, trans. *Sahih al-Bukhari: The Translation of the Meanings of Sahih al-Bukhari,* 9 vols. Riyadh: Darussalam Publishers, 1997.

Martin, Richard C., ed. *Approaches to Islam in Religious Studies*. Tucson: University of Arizona Press, 1985.

Meri, Josef W. *The Cult of Saints among Muslims and Jews in Medieval Syria*. New York: Oxford University Press, 2002.

Meri, Josef W., trans. *A Lonely Wayfarer's Guide to Pilgrimage:'Ali ibn Abi Bakr al-Harawi's Kitab al-isharat ila ma 'rifat al-ziyarat*. Princeton, NJ: Darwin Press, 2004.

Murata, Sachiko, and William C. Chittick. *The Vision of Islam*. St. Paul, MN: Paragon House, 1994.

Peters, F. E. *The Hajj: The Muslim Pilgrimage to Mecca and the Holy Places*. Princeton, NJ: Princeton University Press, 1994.

———. *Islam: A Guide for Jews and Christians*. Princeton, NJ: Princeton University Press, 2003.

———. *Judaism, Christianity, and Islam: The Classical Texts and their Interpretation,* 3 vols. Princeton, NJ: Princeton University Press, 1990.

————. *The Monotheists: Jews, Christians, and Muslims in Conflict and Competition*, 2 vols. Princeton, NJ: Princeton University Press, 2003.

Rahman, Fazlur. *Islam*, 2d ed. Chicago: University of Chicago Press, 1979.

Rippin, Andrew. *Muslims: Their Religious Beliefs and Practices*, rev. ed. New York: Routledge, 2001.

Rippin, Andrew, and Jan Knappert. *Textual Sources for the Study of Islam*. Chicago: University of Chicago Press, 1990.

Rutter, Eldon. *The Holy Cities of Arabia*. New York: G. P. Putnam's Sons, 1928.

Smith, Jane Idleman, and Yvonne Yazbeck Haddad. *The Islamic Understanding of Death and Resurrection*. Albany: State University of New York Press, 1981.

Taylor, Christopher. *In the Vicinity of the Righteous: Ziyara and the Veneration of Muslim Saints in Late Medieval Egypt*. Leiden: Brill, 1998.

SHI'ISM

Ayyoub, Mahmoud. *Redemptive Suffering in Islam: A Study of the Devotional Aspects of 'Ashura' in Twelver Shi'ism*. The Hague: Mouton, 1978.

Bill, James A., and John Alden Williams. *Roman Catholics and Shi'i Muslims: Prayer, Passion and Politics*. Chapel Hill: University of North Carolina Press, 2002.

Cole, Juan Ricardo. *Sacred Space and Holy War: The Politics, Culture and History of Shi'ite Islam*. London: I.B. Tauris, 2002.

Daftary, Farhad. *The Assassin Legends: Myths of the Isma'ilis*. London: I. B. Tauris, 1994.

————. *The Isma'ilis: Their History and Doctrines*. New York: Cambridge University Press, 1990.

Halm, Heinz. *The Empire of the Mahdi: The Rise of the Fatimids*. Trans. Michael Bonner. Leiden: Brill, 1996.

————. *Shiism*. Edinburgh: Edinburgh University Press, 1991.

Howard, I. K. A., trans. *The Book of Guidance into the Lives of the Twelve Imams: Kitab al-irshad*, Elmhurst, NY: Tahrike Tarsile Qur'an, 1981.

Jafri, S. H. M. *Origins and Early Development of Shi'a Islam*. New York: Longman, 1979.

Kohlberg, Etan, ed. *Shi'ism: The Formation of the Classical Islamic World*, vol. 33. Aldershot, UK: Ashgate, 2003.

Momen, Moojan. *An Introduction to Shi'i Islam*. New Haven, CT: Yale University Press, 1985.

al-Mufid, Muhammad. *Kitab al-irshad*. See Howard.

Nasr, Seyyed Hossein, Hamid Dabishi, and Seyyed Vali Reza Nasr, eds. *Shi'ism: Doctrines, Thought, and Spirituality*. Albany: State University of New York Press, 1988.

Sobhani, Ja'far Sobhani. *Doctrines of Shi'i Islam: A Compendium of Imami Beliefs and Practices*. Reza Shah-Kazemi, trans, and ed. London: I. B. Tauris, 2001.

al-Tabataba'i, Muhammad Husayn. *Shi'i Islam*. Albany: State University of New York Press, 1975.

Walker, Paul E. *Exploring an Islamic Empire: Fatimid History and Its Sources*. London: I.B. Tautis, 2002.

Yann, Richard. *Shi'ite Islam: Polity, Ideology, and Creed*. Cambridge, MA: Blackwell, 1995.

ISLAMIC LAW

Calder, Norman. *Studies in Early Muslim Jurisprudence.* New York: Oxford University Press, 1993.

Cook, Michael. *Commanding the Right and Forbidding the Wrong in Islamic Thought.* New York: Cambridge University Press, 2000.

———. *Forbidding Wrong in Islam: A Brief Introduction.* New York: Cambridge University Press, 2003.

Coulson, Noel J. *A History of Islamic Law.* Edinburgh: Edinburgh University Press, 1964.

Dutton, Yassin. *The Origins of Islamic Law: The Qur'an, the Muwatta' and the Medinan 'Amal.* Surrey: Curzon, 1999.

Esposito, John L., with Natana J. DeLong-Bas. *Women in Muslim Family Law,* 2d ed. Syracuse, NY: Syracuse University Press, 2001.

Goldziher, Ignaz. *Introduction to Islamic Theology and Law.* Princeton, NJ: Princeton University Press, 1981 [1910].

Hallaq, Wael. *Authority, Continuity, and Change in Islamic Law.* New York: Cambridge University Press, 2001.

Hurvitz, Nimrod. *The Formation of Hanbalism: Piety into Power.* New York: Routledge, 2002.

———. "From Scholarly Circles to Mass Movements: The Formation of Legal Communities in Islamic Societies," *American Historical Review* 108.4 (2004): 985–1008.

Khadduri, Majid, trans. *al-Shafi'i's Risala: Treatise on the Foundations of Islamic Jurisprudence,* 2d ed. Cambridge, UK: The Islamic Texts Society, 1987.

Lowry, Joseph, Devin Stewart, and Shawkat M. Toorawa, eds. *Law and Education in Medieval Islam: Studies in Honor of Professor George Makdisi.* Cambridge, UK: E. J. W. Gibb Memorial Trust, 2004.

Melchert, Christopher. *The Formation of the Sunni Schools of Law, 9th–10th Centuries C.E.* Leiden: Brill, 1997.

Motzki, Harald. *The Origins of Islamic Jurisprudence: Meccan Fiqh before the Classical Schools.* Leiden: Brill, 2002.

Schacht, Joseph. *An Introduction to Islamic Law.* New York: Oxford University Press, 1964.

al-Shafi'i. *al-Shafi'i's Risala.* See Khadduri.

Tabataba'i, Hossein Modarressi. *An Introduction to Shi'i Law: A Bibliographical Study.* London: Ithaca Press, 1984.

Weiss, Bernard. *The Spirit of Islamic Law.* Athens: University of Georgia Press, 1998.

SUFISM

Arberry, A. J. *Sufism: An Account of the Mystics of Islam.* London: Allen and Unwin, 1950.

Chittick, William. *Sufism: A Short Introduction.* Oxford: Oneworld Publications, 2000.

Ernst, Carl W. *The Shambhala Guide to Sufism.* Boston, MA: Shambhala, 1997.

al-Ghazali. *The Revival of the Religious Sciences: Ihya 'Ulum al-Din,* 9 vols. Cambridge UK: The Islamic Texts Society, 2002.

Homerin, Th. Emil, trans. *Umar ibn al-Farid: Sufi Verse, Saintly Life*. New York: Paulist Press, 2001.

Massignon, Louis. *The Passion of al-Hallaj: Mystic and Martyr of Islam*, 4 vols. Princeton, NJ: Princeton University Press, 1982.

Nasr, Seyyed Hossein. *Sufi Essays*. Albany: State University of New York Press, 1991.

Sells, Michael A., ed. and trans. *Early Islamic Mysticism: Sufi, Qur'an, Miraj, Poetic and Theological Writings*. New York: Paulist Press, 1996.

Smith, Margaret. *Muslim Women Mystics: The Life and Work of Rabi'a and Other Women Mystics in Islam*. Oxford: Oneworld, 2001 [1928].

al-Sulami, Muhammad ibn al-Husayn. *Early Sufi Women: Dhikr an-Niswa al-Muta'abbidat as-Sufiyyat by Abu 'Abd ar-Rahman as-Sulami*, Rkia E. Cornell, trans. Louisville, KY: Fons Vitae, 1999.

Trimingham, J. Spencer. *The Sufi Orders in Islam*. Rev. ed. New York: Oxford University Press, 1998 [1971].

Watt, W. M., trans. *The Faith and Practice of al-Ghazali*. London: Allen and Unwin, 1953.

EDUCATION

Ahmed, Munir-ud-Din. *Muslim Education and the Scholars' Social Status up to the Fifth Century Muslim Era in the Light of Ta'rikh Baghdad*. Zurich: Verlag Der Islam, 1968.

Berkey, Jonathan. *The Transmission of Knowledge in Medieval Cairo: A Social History of Islamic Education*. Princeton, NJ: Princeton University Press, 1992.

Boss, Gerrit, trans. *Qusta ibn Luqa's Medical Regime for the Pilgrims to Mecca: The Risala fi tadbir safar al-hajj*. Leiden: Brill, 1992.

Chamberlain, Michael. *Knowledge and Social Practice in Medieval Damascus, 1190–1350*. New York: Cambridge University Press, 1994.

Conrad, Lawrence I. "The Arab-Islamic Medical Tradition." In *The Western Medical Tradition, 800 BC to 1800 AD*. New York: Cambridge University Press, 1995.

Conrad, Lawrence I., et al., eds. *The Western Medical Tradition, 800 BC to 1800 AD*. New York: Cambridge University Press, 1995.

Dols, Michael W. *The Black Death in the Middle East*. Princeton, NJ: Princeton University Press, 1976.

———. *Majnun: The Madman in Medieval Islamic*. New York: Oxford University Press, 1992.

Dols, Michael W., trans. *Medieval Islamic Medicine: Ibn Ridwan's Treatise "On the Prevention of Bodily Ills in Egypt."* Berkeley: University of California Press, 1984.

Giladi, Avner. *Children of Islam: Concepts of Childhood in Medieval Muslim Society*. New York: St. Martin's Press, 1992.

Goitein, S. D. *A Mediterranean Society: The Jewish Communities of the World as Portrayed in the Cairo Geniza*, 6 vols. Berkeley: University of California Press, 1967–93. (See especially vol. 2, 240–72).

Gutas, Dimitri. *Greek Thought, Arabic Culture: The Graeco-Arabic Translation Movement in Baghdad and Early 'Abbasid Society (2nd–4th/8th–10th centuries)*. New York: Routledge, 1998.

al-Jawziyah, Ibn Qayyim. *Medicine of the Prophet*. See Johnstone.

Johnstone, Penelope, trans. *Medicine of the Prophet*. Cambridge, UK: Islamic Texts Society, 1998.

Lowry, Joseph, Devin Stewart, and Shawkat M. Toorawa, eds. *Law and Education in Medieval Islam: Studies in Honor of Professor George Makdisi.* Cambridge, UK: E. J. W. Gibb Memorial Trust, 2004.

Makdisi, George. *Ibn 'Aqil: Religion and Culture in Classical Islam.* Edinburgh: Edinburgh University Press, 1997.

———. *The Rise of Colleges: Institutions of Learning in Islam and the West.* Edinburgh: Edinburgh University Press, 1981.

Rosenthal, Franz. "The Physician in Medieval Muslim Society," *Bulletin of the History of Medicine* 52.4 (1978): 475–91.

———. *Science and Medicine in Islam.* Aldershot, UK: Variorum, 1998.

Toorawa, Shawkat. "The *Dhimmi* in Medieval Islamic Society: Non-Muslim Physicians of Iraq in Ibn Abi Usayb'iah's '*Uyun al-anba' fi tabaqat al-atibba'* [The Sources of Information on the Classification of Physicians," *Fides et Historia* 26 (1994): 10–21.

Tritton, A.S. *Materials on Muslim Education in the Middle Ages.* London: Luzac, 1957.

WOMEN

Abbott, Nabia. '*A'isha: The Beloved of Mohammed.* Chicago: University of Chicago Press, 1946.

———. "Pre-Islamic Arabian Queens," *The American Journal of Semitic Languages and Literature* 58.1 (1941): 1–22.

———. *Two Queens of Baghdad: Mother and Wife of Harun al-Rashid.* Chicago: University of Chicago Press, 1946.

———. "Women and the State in Early Islam," *Journal of Near Eastern Studies* 1.2 (1942): 106–26.

———. "Women and the State on the Eve of Isalm," *The American Journal of Semitic Languages and Literature* 58.3 (1941): 259-84.

Afsaruddin, Asma. "Reconstituting Women's Lives: Gender and the Poetics of Narrative in Medieval Biographical Collections," *Muslim World* 92.4 (2002): 461–80.

Ahmed, Leila. *Women and Gender in Islam: Historical Roots of a Modern Debate.* New Haven, CT: Yale University Press, 1992.

Berkey, Johnathan P. "Circumcision Circumscribed: Female Excision and Cultural Accommodation in the Medieval Near East," *International Journal of Middle East Studies* 28:1 (1996): 19–38.

Eastwood, Gillian. "A Medieval Face-Veil from Egypt," *Costume* 17.1 (1983): 33–38; it is also included in David Waines, ed., *Patterns of Everyday Life: The Formation of the Classical Islamic World,* vol. 10. Aldershot, UK: Ashgate, 2002, 233–38.

Esposito, John L., with Natana J. DeLong-Bas. *Women in Muslim Family Law,* 2d ed. Syracuse: Syracuse University Press, 2001.

Giladi, Avner. *Infants, Parents and Wet Nurses: Medieval Islamic Views on Breastfeeding and Their Social Implications.* Leiden: Brill, 1999.

Hussain, Freda, ed. *Muslim Women.* New York: St. Martin's Press, 1984.

Keddie, Nikki R., and Beth Baron. *Women in Middle Eastern History: Shifting Boundaries in Sex and Gender.* New Haven, CT: Yale University Press, 1991.

Kimball, Michelle R., and Barbara R. von Schlegell, eds. *Muslim Women throughout the World: A Bibliography.* Boulder, CO: Lynne Rienner Publishers, 1997.

Lichtenstadter, Ilse. *Women in Ayyam al-Arab.* London: Royal Asiatic Society, 1935.

Malti-Douglas, Fedwa. *Woman's Body, Woman's Word: Gender and Discourse in Arabo-Islamic Writing.* Princeton, NJ: Princeton University Press, 1991.

Mernisi, Fatima. *The Veil and the Male Elite: A Feminist Interpretation of Women's Rights in Islam.* New York: Addison-Wesley, 1991.

Peirce, Leslie. *The Imperial Harem: Women and Sovereignty in the Ottoman Empire.* New York: Oxford University Press, 1993.

Roded, Ruth, ed. *Women in Islam and the Middle East: A Reader.* London and New York: I. B. Tauris Publishers, 1999.

Smith, Margaret. *Muslim Women Mystics: The Life and Work of Rabi'a and Other Women Mystics in Islam.* Oxford: Oneworld, 2001 [1928].

Smith, W. Robertson. *Kinship and Marriage in Early Arabia.* Cambridge: Cambridge University Press, 1885.

Spellberg, Denise A. *Politics, Gender, and the Islamic Past: The Legacy of 'A'isha bint Abi Bakr.* New York: Columbia University Press, 1994.

Stern, Gertrude. *Marriage in Early Islam.* London: Royal Asiatic Society, 1939.

Stowasser, Barbara Freyer. *Women in the Qur'an, Traditions, and Interpretation.* New York: Oxford University Press, 1994.

al-Sulami, Muhammad ibn al-Husayn. *Early Sufi Women: Dhikr an-Niswa al-Muta'abbidat as-Sufiyyat by Abu 'Abd ar-Rahman as-Sulami.* Rkia E. Cornell, trans. Louisville. KY: Fons Vitae, 1999.

Walther, Wiebke. *Women in Islam.* Princeton, NJ: Markus Wiener, 1993.

DHIMMIS OR NON-MUSLIMS

Bosworth, C. E. "The Concept of Dhimma in Early Islam." In *Christians and Jews in the Ottoman Empire: The Functioning of a Plural Society,* eds. Benjamin Braude and Bernard Lewis, 2 vols. London and New York: Holmes and Meier, 1982, 1:37–51.

Braude, Benjamin, and Bernard Lewis, eds. *Christians and Jews in the Ottoman Empire: The Functioning of a Plural Society,* 2 vols. London and New York: Holmes and Meier, 1982.

Brody, Robert. *The Geonim of Babylonia and the Shaping of Medieval Jewish Culture.* New Haven, CT: Yale University Press, 1998.

Cohen, Mark R. *Jewish Self-Government in Medieval Egypt: The Origins of the Office of Head of the Jews, ca. 1065–1126.* Princeton, NJ: Princeton University Press, 1980.

Friedman, Yohanan. *Tolerance and Coercion in Islam: Interfaith Relations in the Muslim Tradition.* New York: Cambridge University Press, 2003.

Ghosh, Amitav. *In an Antique Land.* New York: Alfred A. Knopf, 1993.

Glick, Thomas F. *Islamic and Christian Spain in the Early Middle Ages.* Princeton, NJ: Princeton University Press, 1979.

Goitein, S. D. *Jews and Arabs: Their Contacts through the Ages,* rev. ed. New York: Schocken Books, 1974.

———. *Letters of Medieval Jewish Traders.* Princeton, NJ: Princeton University Press, 1973.

———. *A Mediterranean Society: The Jewish Communities of the World as Portrayed in the Cairo Geniza,* 6 vols. Berkeley: University of California Press, 1967–93.

Hoyland, Robert, ed. *Muslims and Others in Early Islamic Society.* Aldershot, UK: Ashgate, 2004.

Lassner, Jacob. *A Mediterranean Society: An Abridgement in One Volume*. Berkeley: University of California Press, 1999.

Meri, Josef W. *The Cult of Saints among Muslims and Jews in Medieval Syria*. New York: Oxford University Press, 2002.

Stillman, Norman A. *The Jews of Arab Lands: A History and Source Book*. Philadelphia: Jewish Publication Society of America, 1979.

———. "The Non-Muslim Communities: The Jewish Community." In *The Cambridge History of Egypt*, vol. 1, ed. Carl F. Petry. New York: Cambridge University Press, 1998, 198–210.

Toorawa, Shawkat. "The *Dhimmi* in Medieval Islamic Society: Non-Muslim Physicians of Iraq in Ibn Abi Usaybʿiah's *ʿUyun al-anbaʾ fi tabaqat al-atibba*ʾ [The Sources of Information on the Classification of Physicians," *Fides et Historia* 26 (1994): 10–21.

Tritton, A.S. *The Caliphs and Their Non-Muslim Subjects: A Critical Study of the Covenant of Umar*. London: Frank Cass, 1970 [1930].

Vryonis, Speros. *The Decline of Medieval Hellenism in Asia Minor and the Process of Islamization from the Eleventh through the Fifteenth Century*. Berkeley: University of California Press, 1971.

Wilfong, Terry G. "The Non-Muslim Communities: Christian Communities," in *The Cambridge History of Egypt*, vol. 1, ed. Carl F. Petry. New York: Cambridge University Press, 1998, 175–97.

FOOD AND WATER

Gelder, Gert Jan van. *God's Banquet: Food in Classical Arabic Literature*. New York: Columbia University Press, 2000.

al-Hassan, Ahmad Y., and Donald R. Hill. *Islamic Technology: An Illustrated History*. New York: Cambridge University Press, 1986.

Hattox, Ralph S. *Coffee and Coffeehouses: The Origins of a Social Beverage in the Medieval Near East*. Seattle: University of Washington Press, 1985.

Rodinson, Maxime and A.J. Arberry. *Medieval Arab Cookery*. Devon, UK: Prospect Books, 2001.

Waines, David. "Bread, Cereals and Society," *Journal of the Economic and Social History of the Orient* 30.3 (1987): 255–85.

———. *In a Caliph's Kitchen*. London: Riad El-Rayyes Books, 1989.

Watson, Andrew M. *Agricultural Innovation in the Early Islamic World: The Diffusion of Crops and Farming Techniques, 700–1100*. New York: Cambridge University Press, 1983.

ART, ARCHITECTURE, AND LITERATURE

Allen, Roger. *The Arabic Literary Heritage*. New York: Cambridge University Press, 1998.

Anati, Emmanuel. *Rock-Art in Central Arabia*, vol. 1. Louvain: Institut Orientaliste, 1968.

Blair, Sheila S., and Jonathan Bloom. *The Art and Architecture of Islam, 1250–1800*. New Haven, CT: Yale University Press, 1995.

Bloom, Jonathan M. *Paper Before Print: The History and Impact of Paper in the Islamic World*. New Haven, CT: Yale University Press, 2001.

Bloom, Jonathan, and Sheila Blair. *Islamic Arts.* London, Phaidon, 1997.

Clinton, Jerome W., trans. *In the Dragon's Claws: The Story of Rostam and Esfandiyar from the Persian Book of Kings.* Washington, DC: Mage Publishers, 1999.

———. *The Tragedy of Sohráb and Rostám.* Seattle: University of Washington Press, 1997.

Colville, Jim, trans. *Sobriety and Mirth: A Selection of the Shorter Writings of al-Jahiz.* London: Kegan Paul, 2002.

Cooperson, Michael. *Classical Arabic Biography.* New York: Cambridge University Press, 2000.

Creswell, K. A. C. *A Short Account of Early Muslim Architecture.* Aldershot, UK: Scholar Press, 1989 [1968].

Davis, Dick, trans. *The Legend of Seyavash.* New York: Penguin Books, 1992.

Ettinghausen, Richard, and Oleg Grabar. *The Art and Architecture of Islam, 650–1250.* New Haven, CT: Yale University Press, 1987.

Falk, Toby, ed. *Treasures of Islam.* Seacaucus, NY: Wellfleet Press, 1985.

Flood, Finbarr Barry. *The Great Mosque of Damascus: Studies on the Makings of an Umayyad Visual Culture.* Leiden: Brill, 2001.

Gonzalez, Valérie. *Beauty and Islam: Aesthetics in Islamic Art and Architecture.* London: I. B. Tauris, 2001.

Grabar, Oleg. *The Formation of Islamic Art,* rev. ed. New Haven, CT: Yale University Press, 1987.

Hillenbrand, Robert. *Islamic Art and Architecture.* London: Thames and Hudson, 1999.

Irwin, Robert. *The Arabian Nights: A Companion.* New York: Penguin Books, 1994.

———. *Islamic Art in Context.* New York: Calmann and King, 1997.

Irwin, Robert, ed. *Night and Horses and the Desert: An Anthology of Classical Arabic Literature.* New York: Anchor Books, 1999.

Kilpatrick, Hilary. *Making the Great Book of Songs: Compilation and the Author's Craft in Abu l-Faraj al-Isbahani's Kitab al-aghani.* New York: Routledge, 2003.

Lyall, Charles J. *Translations of Ancient Arabian Poetry, Chiefly Pre-Islamic, with an Introduction and Notes.* Westport, CT: Hyperion Press, Inc., 1986 [1930].

Michell, George, ed. *Architecture of the Islamic World: Its History and Social Meaning.* London: Thames and Hudson, 2002.

Pellat, Charles, trans. *The Life and Works of al-Jahiz.* Berkeley: University of California Press, 1969.

Rabbat, Naser O. *The Citadel of Cairo: A New Interpretation of Royal Mamluk Architecture.* Leiden: New York: Brill, 1995.

Schimmel, Annemarie. *Islamic Names.* Edinburgh: Edinburgh University Press, 1989.

Sells, Michael, trans. *Desert Tracings: Six Classical Arabic Odes.* Middletown, CT: Wesleyan University Press, 1989.

Stillman, Yedida Kalfon. *Arab Dress: From the Dawn of Islam to Modern Times.* Leiden: Brill, 2000.

Tabbaa, Yasser. *Constructions of Power and Piety in Medieval Aleppo.* University Park, PA: Pennsylvania State University Press, 1997.

———. *The Transformation of Islamic Art during the Sunni Revival.* Seattle: University of Washington Press, 2001.

GLOSSARY

Abbasid Caliphate (750–1258)
The second caliphal dynasty in Islamic history, the Abbasids overthrew
the Umayyads in 750 and ruled primarily from Baghdad (est. 762) until
the Mongol conquest of the city in 1258.

'abd
Slave, generally used for field hands. Also used in conjunction with one of
the names for God as a personal name; for example, Abd Allah (Servant
of God), Abd al-Rahman (Servant of the Merciful).

'abid
Slave; used for slaves from sub-Saharan Africa who were trained as infantry.

adhan
Call to prayer. See *mu'adhdhin* (muezzin).

ahadith
See **hadith.**

ahl al-kitab
People of the Book. See *dhimmi.*

akhbar
See *khabar.*

amir
Military commander; military governor.

amir al-mu'minin

Commander of the Believers; one of the titles for the head of the Muslim community. See also *imam* and *khalifat allah*.

ansar

Muhammad's supporters in Medina after his hijra (migration) there in 622. (Lit., helpers, supporters.)

Aramaic

Semitic language spoken in Syria and Mesopotamia in late antiquity. Continued to be used by some of the Christian populations especially as a liturgical language.

'Ashura

The tenth. On 10 Muharram A.H. 61 (October 10, A.D. 680), Muhammad's grandson, Imam Husayn ibn Ali, was killed with his supporters at Karbala, Iraq. Ashura became one of the most important rituals in the Shi'i religious calendar, for it was not only seen as a memorial of Imam Husayn's unjustified death, his was the paradigm of martyrdom that all should emulate.

atabeg

Guardian of a prince; tutor; commander of the army.

baraka

Supernatural blessing that distinguishes a Sufi saint or friend of God (wali Allah); similar in meaning to how "charisma" is used in the New Testament.

beg

The Turkish equivalent of amir (commander).

Byzantium

The eastern Roman Empire, whose capital was Constantinople.

caliph

See *khalifat allah* and *khalifat rasul Allah*.

caravanserai

Way station along long-distance trade routes; usually comprised of inns and provisions for traders and travelers, warehouses for goods, and stables and fodder for animals.

Coptic

The language of Egypt on the eve of Islam. Continued to be used by Egyptian Christians, especially as a liturgical language.

dar al-harb

Abode of War. Those territories not under Muslim political domination; hence they are fair game for conquest.

dar al-Islam

Abode of Islam; Abode of Surrender. Those territories under Muslim political domination.

darabat al-hijab
She took the veil (*hijab*); that is, she became one of Muhammad's wives.

dhikr
Remembrance; as in remembering the name of God.

dhimmi
Protected religious communities (primarily Jews, Christians, and Zoroastrians) who were afforded certain protections and limited freedoms in exchange for paying a special tax called *jizya* and acquiescing to a range of disabilities imposed on them.

dinar
Gold coin.

dirham
Silver coin.

du'at
Supplications of petitions. Types of prayer distinct from the required ritual prayer (*salat*).

fada'il
Merits or virtues; a common genre of literature extolling the merits of a particular region was known as *fada'il al-buldan*.

fals
Base metal coin, usually copper.

faqih
Jurisprudent; one who practices jurisprudence (*fiqh*). See also **usul al-fiqh** and *furu' al-fiqh.*

fatiha
The first chapter of the Qur'an, which is recited as part of the ritual prayer (**salat**). (Lit., opening.)

fiqh
Jurisprudence.

fitna
A widely used pejorative term that means that which upsets the established order of things.

funduq
Inn.

furu' al-fiqh
Practical application of Islamic legal theory. (Lit., the branches of jurisprudence.)

Geniza
Storeroom. The geniza in the Ibn Ezra synagogue in Fustat, containing some 250,000 documents, was discovered in the late nineteenth century.

Ghadir Khumm
Pool of Khumm. On 18 Dhu l-Hijja A.H. 10 (March 16 A.D. 632), Muhammad
  stopped at a place called Ghadir Khumm on his way back to Medina
  after he had made his final pilgrimage to Mecca. His followers gathered
  in a grove of trees to escape the suffocating heat and to perform the
  noon prayers. At the conclusion of the prayers, Muhammad took Ali's
  hand and said, "Of Whomsoever I am Lord [*Mawla*], then Ali is also
  his Lord. O God! Be Thou the supporter of whoever supports Ali and
  the enemy of whoever opposes him." According to Shi'i doctrine, this
  proves beyond a shadow of a doubt that not only had Muhammad designated Ali ibn Abi Talib and his descendants to succeed him upon his
  death, but that he had bestowed his own political and religious authority on them as well.

ghazi
Holy Warrior.

ghiyar
Compulsory distinctive patch of colored cloth (for example, red, blue, yellow) worn by dhimmis.

ghulam
Boy, servant, slave; used as a synonym for mamluk. Similar to the largely
  defunct American practice of using "boy" to indicate the inferior status
  of black men, whatever their ages.

ghusul
Major ablution performed to restore ritual purity (*tahara*) prior to performing ritual prayers (*salat*).

Gregorian Calendar
The system for reckoning years from the birth of Jesus as A.D., Anno
  Domini (or more correctly, *Anni Domini Nostri Jesu Christi*, meaning "In
  the Year of Our Lord Jesus Christ"), was instituted by the Roman abbot
  Dionysius Exiguus in about A.D. 527. The calendar was further revised
  in a papal bull by Pope Gregory XIII in A.D. 1582; hence, the name Gregorian Calendar. The alternative C.E., Common Era, has recently come
  into fashion for some.

hadith
Report attributed to or about Muhammad and his companions.

hajj
Pilgrimage to Mecca.

halakha
Jewish law. The duties and obligations incumbent on all Jews worked out
  during centuries of debate among the rabbis. See also *shari'a*.

halal
Permitted according to Muslim dietary restrictions.

halaqa
Used for a teacher's students, who often sat at his feet in a semicircle as he taught. (Lit., circle.)

Hanafi
Follower of the *madhhab* named after Abu Hanifa (d. 767)

Hanbali
Follower of the *madhhab* named after Ahmad ibn Hanbal (d. 855)

Hellenism
The humanistic and classical ideals associated with Greek learning and culture.

hijab
Covering, veil. See *darabat al-hijab.*

Hijaz
Region of western Arabia where Mecca and Medina are located.

hijra
Muhammad's migration (*hijra*) from Mecca to Medina in A.D. 622, which marks the year 1 of the Islamic hijri calendar; often denoted as A.H., *Anno Hegira.* (Lit., migration.)

hisba
The Qur'anic injunction to "command the good and forbid the wrong."

'Id al-Adha
Feast of Sacrifice; the feast that is part of the annual pilgrimage to Mecca and commemorates Abraham's willingness to sacrifice his son.

'Id al-Fitr
Feast of Fast Breaking; the feast that marks the end of the Ramadan Fast.

ihram
Two rectangular pieces of unstitched white cloth that pilgrims don prior to entering Mecca when making the annual pilgrimage.

ijaza
Certificate or diploma issued by a scholar permitting a pupil to transmit a text on his authority.

ijma‘
Consensus of the community or of religious scholars.

‘ilm
Religious knowledge.

imam
Used for the one who leads others in ritual prayer (*salat*). Also, one of the titles for the head of the Muslim community (*umma*). For the distinctive Shi‘i definition of Imam, see *Shi‘i.* (Lit., in front of.)

Injil
Gospel.

ism
Personal name. Part of the traditional Arabic naming system.

ʿ*isma*
Doctrine that all of God's prophets and messengers are preserved from gross moral error; that is, they are *maʿsum*.

Ismaʿilism
Branch of Shiʿism that follows the seventh Imam, Ismaʿil ibn Jaʿfar al-Sadiq. Also known as Seveners. The official version of Islam advocated by the Ismaʿili Fatimid Caliphs in North Africa and Egypt (909–1171).

isnad
Chain of authorities who transmitted hadiths.

jahannam
Hell.

jahili
Something that dates to or is characterized by the moral ignorance of the jahiliyya.

jahiliyya
The age of ignorance, especially moral ignorance that defined Arabia prior to Muhammad and the revelation of the Qurʾan.

janna
Garden; Paradise; Heaven.

Jazira
The rich agricultural lands of Upper Mesopotamia; the region between the Tigris and Euphrates rivers north of Tikrit in modern Iraq. (Lit., island.)

Jazirat al-ʿArab
The Arabian Peninsula. (Lit., The Island of the Arabs.)

jihad fi sabil Allah
Striving in the path of God; often incompletely translated as Holy War. Secondary meanings can include the propagation of right religion and suppression of heresy. Some of the more mystically inclined argued that the pious struggle within oneself against evil can be a form of jihad.

jizya
Special tax paid by Jews, Christians, Zoroastrians, and other protected religious communities. See **dhimmi.**

Kaʿba
The black cubical structure in Mecca, which according to Islamic tradition was built by Abraham and his son, Ishmael.

khabar
Narrative report about the events of the early community. (Pl. *akhbar.*)

khadim
Servant; generally used for domestic servants.

khalifat Allah
Head of the Muslim community (umma). (Lit., God's deputy. Caliph.)

khalifat rasul Allah
Head of the Muslim community (umma). (Lit., Deputy or Successor to the Messenger of God. Caliph.)

khamr
Wine; also used to describe alcoholic beverages in general.

khan
Turkish word for autocrat or monarch. See also *shah* and *sultan*.

khanqa
Sufi retreat or convent. See also *zawiya*.

Khariji
See *Khawarij*.

Kharijite.
See *Khawarij*.

Khawarij
For the *khawarij* (sing. *khariji*), the principal criterion for leadership of the community (*umma*) was piety—genealogy did not matter to them nor did the practical consideration of maintaining the unity of the community. Also known as Kharijites. (Lit., seceders.)

khimar
Covering, veil (pl. *khumur*).

khirqa
Cloak that a Sufi master presented to one of his disciples indicating that he had reached a certain level of mystical understanding.

khutba
The Friday sermon in the mosque. Invoking the ruler's name during the khutba is one of the two traditional symbols of political authority; the second is *sikka*.

kiswa
Covering for the *Kaʿba*.

al-Kitab
The Book or The Scripture. The sacred text of Islam; also known as al-Qurʾan (The Recitation).

kunya
Patronym. Part of the traditional Arabic naming system.

laqab
Nickname. Part of the traditional Arabic naming system.

libas
Undergarments, pantaloons, clothing in general.

maʿsum
See *ʿisma.*

madhhab
Movement or school of thought that followed a particular methodology
   for discerning and applying shariʿa.

madrasa
Place of study. Religious school.

Mahdi
One who is rightly guided by God; the awaited messianic figure of Islamic
   eschatology.

Maliki
Follower of the *madhhab* named after Malik ibn Anas (d. 795)

mamluk
Military slave; usually used to describe slaves from Central Asia and the
   Caucasus Mountains who were trained as cavalry.

maqam Ibrahim
Station of Abraham, opposite the Kaʿba in Mecca.

maʿrifa
Gnosis; mystical knowledge.

masjid
Place of prostration, mosque. Building where the faithful performed ritual
   prayer (*salat*) together. See *sajjada.*

maternal
See **matrilineal**

matn
The text of a hadith.

matriarchal
See **matrilineal.**

matrilineal
When kinship and descent are traced though the mother's lineage.

mawlid
Birthday. Important public celebrations were held to mark birthdays of
   Muhammad, the Shiʿi Imams, Sufi saints, and other important figures.

mihrab
Niche or other marker on the wall of a mosque to indicate the direction
   (*qibla*) of Mecca, the proper orientation for Islamic ritual prayer (*salat*).

minaret
A tower of a mosque from which the summons to prayer (*adhan*) is made
   by the muezzin (*muʾadhdhin*).

minbar
Pulpit.

Monophysites
Those churches which adhered to the doctrine that Christ's nature remained altogether divine and not human even though he took on an earthly and human body with its cycle of birth, life, and death. Primarily in Egypt and the Near East.

mosque
See **masjid.**

muʾadhdhin
One who performs the call to prayer (*adhan*). Often spelled muezzin.

muezzin
See *muʾadhdhin.*

muhajirun
The Meccan followers of Muhammad who made the *hijra* to Medina. (Lit., emigrants.)

muhtasib
Market inspector. The person who is charged with maintaining public order and decency.

mujahid
One who is engaged in jihad. Holy Warrior.

murid
Sufi disciple.

murshid
Sufi master.

naft
Pitch. Also used for "Greek Fire."

nar
Fire; Hell.

nasab
Genealogy. Part of the traditional Arabic naming system.

nass
The special designation by which Shiʿi imams named their successors.

Nestorians
Those churches adhered to the doctrines advocated by Nestorius, patriarch of Constantinople (428–431), who preached that the divine and human natures of Christ were one in action but not one in person. That is, that the divine and human persons remained separate in the incarnate Christ. Nestorius was deposed and his teachings were condemned by the Orthodox Church in 431. His doctrine spread widely in Asia, centering in Iran and Asia Minor.

nisba
Adjective denoting tribal affiliation, ethnic origin, profession, religious affiliation, and so forth. Part of the traditional Arabic naming system.

Orthodox Christianity
The official religion of the Byzantine Empire based on the Trinitarian doctrines set forth at the council of Nicea (325) and later at the council of Chalcedon (451).

orthodoxy
Right belief; that is, about God.

orthopraxis
Right behavior; that is, in obedience to God.

paternal
See **patrilineal.**

patriarchal
See **patrilineal.**

patrilineal
When kinship and descent are traced though the father's lineage.

Perso-Islamic Kingship
Theory of political legitimacy that is based on the ancient Persian theory that God appoints the king with the responsibility to maintain order and justice in his kingdom.

qadi
Islamic religious court judge.

qasida
Ode. Principal art form of pre-Islamic Arabia.

qasr
Residential compound made of stone or mud brick. Later used for fortress.

qibla
Direction of ritual prayer (*salat*). Initially towards Syria (Jerusalem), but changed to Mecca in 624 after Muhammad's hijra to Medina.

qubbayt
A preserve made from locust fruit and nuts.

Qurʾan
The sacred text of Islam; (Lit., recitation.)

rafiq
Traveling companion.

rakʿa
Bowing; series of precise bowings and prostrations that constitute a single ritual prayer cycle.

Rashidun caliphs
The rightly guided caliphs—Abu Bakr (632–34), Umar (634–44), Uthman (644–56), and Ali ibn Abi Talib (656–61). The four Rashidun caliphs were close companions of Muhammad and after his death in 632 ruled in succession from Medina until the fourth Rashidun caliph, Ali ibn Abi Talib, moved the capital to Kufa and was assassinated there in 661.

razzia
Raid; common "sport" among the Bedouin of the Arabian Peninsula.

ribat
Inn, frontier fortress, Sufi retreat.

Ridda **Wars**
Wars of apostasy (632–34) after the death of Muhammad, during which rebellions were quashed and Arabia was brought under Muslim political domination.

Sabean
One of the groups mentioned in the Qur'an as People of the Book (*ahl al-kitab*). "Believers, Jews, Christians, Sabeans—whoever believes in God and the Last Day and does what is right—shall be rewarded by their Lord; they have nothing to fear or regret" (Qur'an 2:64). The precise identity of the Sabeans mentioned in the Qur'an is unclear.

sajjada
Prayer rug. (Lit., place of much prostration.) See *masjid.*

al-salam ʿalaykum
Peace upon you. Traditional greeting. Also said as part of the ritual prayer (*salat*).

salat
Ritual prayer. One of the five pillars of Islam; the prayer is performed at five prescribed times each day.

Sasanians
The ruling dynasty of Iran (226–642) that was deposed during the Islamic conquests.

sawad
The rich black (*sawad*) agricultural lands of southern Iraq.

sawm
Fasting. One of the five pillars of Islam is to fast during the daylight hours of Ramadan, the ninth month of the Islamic calendar.

sayrafi
Money changer; the person who determined the value of coins by measuring its bullion content.

Shafiʿi
Follower of the *madhhab* named after Muhammad ibn Idris al-Shafiʿi (d. 820).

shah
Persian for autocrat or monarch. See also *khan* and *sultan.*

shahada
First Pillar of Islam. Muslim statement of faith. "There is not god but God; Muhammad is the Messenger of God."

shariʿa
Islamic law. The duties and obligations incumbent on all Muslims worked out during centuries of debate among the ulama. See also *halakha.*

shaykh
Literally, "old man." Used for tribal elder, Sufi master, teacher, person of religious authority.

Shiʿi
Derived from the phrase *shiʿat* Ali ibn Abi Talib (the faction of Ali ibn Abi Talib). Shiʿis believe that Muhammad designated his cousin and son-in-law, Ali, to be his successor on 18 Dhu l-Hijja A.H. 10 (March 16 A.D. 632) at Ghadir Khumm. There are two basic doctrines that distinguish Shiʿis from Sunnis. First, the rightful imam had to be a lineal descendant of Muhammad, in particular through the line of Ali and Muhammad's daughter, Fatima. The second, and more controversial, is that the caliph or imam was not only the political head of the community, but an infallible religious teacher—guaranteed to be without error in matters of faith and morals. See **Ghadir Khumm.**

Shiʿite.
See Shiʿi.

shura
The Islamic principle of rule by consultation.

sikka
The minting of coins. One of the two traditional symbols of political authority; the second is *khutba.*

Sind
The Indus River plain; Muhammad ibn al-Qasim invaded Sind in 711.

slave
See *ʿabd, ʿabid, ghulam,* and *mamluk.*

Sufism
Islamic mysticism.

sultan
Arabic for autocrat or monarch. See also *khan* and *shah.*

Sunni
Derived from the phrase *ahl sunna waʾl-jamaʿa* (the people of tradition and unity). The vast majority of Muslims define themselves as Sunnis.

tahara
Ritual purity.

Tawrah
Torah; Old Testament or Hebrew Bible.

Transoxiana
The territories north of the Oxus River in Central Asia.

ʿulamaʾ
Islamic religious scholars.

Umayyad caliphate (661–750)
The first caliphal dynasty in Islamic history, the Umayyads ruled from Damascus until they were overthrown by the Abbasids in 750.

umm walad
Mother of a child. Term to denote a concubine who has borne a child to her owner.

umma
The Muslim community.

ʿumra
A pilgrimage to Mecca that is separate from the *hajj* and which can be made at any time of the year. While the *ʿumra* is considered praiseworthy, it is neither obligatory nor is it considered a substitute for the *hajj*.

ustadh
Master. Used to denote the man who purchased, trained, and eventually manumitted his mamluks.

usul al-fiqh
Islamic legal theory. (Lit., the roots of jurisprudence.)

wadi
The bed or the valley of a river or stream that is usually dry except during the rainy season, gully or wash.

wali
Saint. (pl. *awliyaʾ*) *awliyaʾ Allah* (Friends of God).

wuduʿ
Minor ablution performed to restore ritual purity (*tahara*) prior to performing ritual prayers (*salat*).

Zabur
The Psalms.

zakat
Almsgiving. One of the five pillars of Islam.

Zamzam
According to Islamic tradition, at Zamzam the Angel Gabriel miraculously brought forth water for Hagar and Ishmael after Abraham had left them at Mecca and headed into the desert. At the well of Zamzam, pilgrims drink some of the water and perform additional ablutions. Despite the

well's brackish water, the waters of Zamzam are believed to possess special healing qualities.

zawiya
Sufi retreat or convent. See also *khanqa.*

ziyara
Visitation, especially the visitation of the tombs of Sufi saints and the Shi'i Imams.

Zoroastrianism
Founded in Iran by the prophet Zoroaster (6th century B.C.), Zoroastrianism is characterized by worship of a supreme god named Ahura Mazda who requires good deeds for help in his cosmic struggle against the evil spirit, Ahriman. The sacred text of Zoroastrianism is the Avesta. In Islamic law (*shari'a*), Zoroastrians are afforded protected (*dhimmi*) status as People of the Book (*ahl al-kitab*).

zunnar
A distinctive girdle or belt worn by *dhimmis.*

RECIPES

Rather than dividing meals into discrete courses as modern Americans tend to do, in the medieval Islamic world more than one dish (for example, a lamb dish and a chicken dish) would be served at the table at the same time. It was customary that a dish of dates would be present with which to begin the meal. A fruit salad of some type often was eaten to conclude the meal. I have included four recipes here—a lamb recipe (*Ibrahimiya*), a chicken recipe (*Shaljamiya*), a cold dish recipe (*Bahinjan mahshi*), and a date dish recipe (*Rutab mu'assal*). Since specific quantities are rarely given in medieval Arabic cookbooks, one must do some guessing, especially with respect to spices and condiments. Essentially, the cook is advised to season to taste, "God willing" (the formula with which many recipes conclude).

The recipes below are taken from David Waines, *In a Caliph's Kitchen* (London: Riad el-Rayyes Books, 1989). As the title indicates, these are dishes that would be found in the kitchens of the caliphs and other elites of medieval Islamic society. Waines re-creates the medieval recipes into specific western measurements in quantities sufficient to feed four. See also Maxime Rodinson and A. J. Arberry, eds. *Medieval Arab Cookery* (Devon, UK: Prospect Books, 2001).

Ibrahimiya—made with lamb (named after the eighth-century gourmand, Ibrahim ibn al-Mahdi, the brother of Harun al-Rashid)

Cut the meat into medium sized pieces, and place in a casserole with water to cover, salt to taste, and boil until the juices are given off. Throw in a bag of stout cotton containing coriander, ginger, pepper, all ground fine, then add some pieces of cinnamon bark and mastic. Cut up two or three onions very small and throw in. Mince red meat and make into kabobs as usual, and add. When the ingredients are cooked, remove the bag of seasonings. Add to the broth the juice of sweet old grapes or, if unprocurable, of fresh grapes, squeezing in the hand without skinning, or else distilled vinegar. The juice is strained then sweet almonds are chopped fine and moistened in water, the grape juice is poured on them, and the mixture is sweetened slightly with white sugar, so as not to be too sour. Leave over the fire an hour to settle. Wipe the sides of the casserole with a clean cloth and sprinkle with rose water. When settled, remove. (Waines, *In a Caliph's Kitchen*, 33)

Shaljamiya—made with chicken and turnips (*shaljam*, hence the name, *shaljamiya*)

Take the breasts of chicken or other fowl, cut into thin slices and place in a pot with a lot of oil adding water to cover. Remove the scum. Throw in chick peas and olive oil and the white of onion and when cooked, sprinkle on top with pepper and cumin. Next take the turnip and boil it until cooked and then mash it so that no hard bits remain in it. Strain in a sieve and place in the pot. Then take shelled almonds and put in a stone mortar adding to it a piece of cheese and bray very fine. Break over this the whites of five eggs and pound until it becomes very soft. Put this mixture over the turnip and if there is milk in it, put in a bit of nard and leave on the fire to settle. Serve it with mustard. (Waines, *In a Caliph's Kitchen*, 35)

Badhinjan mahshi—cold dish made with eggplant

Take the eggplant and stew it. Cut it up into small pieces after stewing. Next take a serving dish and put into it vinegar, white sugar and crushed almonds, saffron, caraway and cinnamon. Then take the eggplant and the fried onion and put them in the dish. Pour oil over it and serve, God willing. (Waines, *In a Caliph's Kitchen*, 37)

Rutab mu'assal—"Honeyed Dates"

Take freshly gathered dates and lay in the shade and air for a day. Then remove the stones and stuff with peeled almonds. For every ten *ratl*s of dates take two *ratl*s of honey. Boil over the fire with two *ugiya* of rose water and half a dirham of saffron, then throw in the dates, stirring for an hour. Remove and allow to cool. When cold, sprinkle with fine-ground sugar scented with musk, camphor and hyacinth. Put into glass preserving jars, sprinkling on top some of the scented ground sugar. Cover until the weather is cold and chafing dishes are brought in. (Waines, *In a Caliph's Kitchen*, 39)

Measurements used in medieval Arabic cooking

1 *ratl* = 12 *ugiya*s = 16 ounces = 1 pint

1 *ugiya* = 10 *dirham*s

1 *dirham* = 6 *daniq*

GENEALOGICAL AND DYNASTIC TABLES

THE BANU QURAYSH

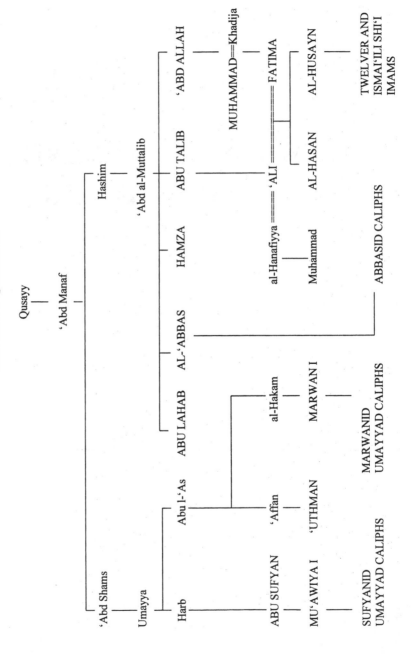

THE RASHIDUN CALIPHS WITH REGNAL DATES

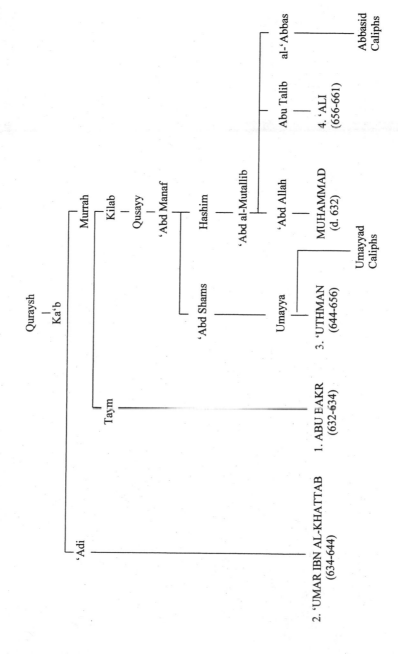

Quraysh
Ka'b

'Adi

Murrah

Taym

Kilab

Qusayy

'Abd Manaf

'Abd Shams

Hashim

Umayya

'Abd al-Mutallib

'Abd Allah

Abu Talib

al-'Abbas

MUHAMMAD (d. 632)

4. 'ALI (656-661)

Abbasid Caliphs

Umayyad Caliphs

3. 'UTHMAN (644-656)

1. ABU BAKR (632-634)

2. 'UMAR IBN AL-KHATTAB (634-644)

THE UMAYYAD CALIPHS WITH REGNAL DATES

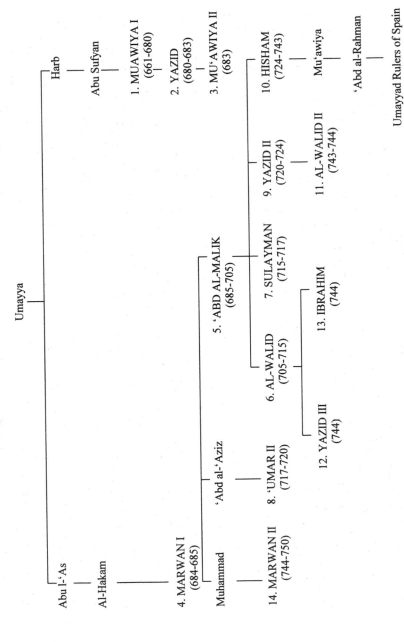

Umayya

Abu l-'As

Al-Hakam

4. MARWAN I
(684-685)

Muhammad

'Abd al-'Aziz

8. 'UMAR II
(717-720)

14. MARWAN II
(744-750)

12. YAZID III
(744)

5. 'ABD AL-MALIK
(685-705)

6. AL-WALID
(705-715)

7. SULAYMAN
(715-717)

13. IBRAHIM
(744)

9. YAZID II
(720-724)

11. AL-WALID II
(743-744)

Harb

Abu Sufyan

1. MUAWIYA I
(661-680)

2. YAZID
(680-683)

3. MU'AWIYA II
(683)

10. HISHAM
(724-743)

Mu'awiya

'Abd al-Rahman

Umayyad Rulers of Spain

THE TWELVER AND ISMA'ILI SHI'I IMAMS

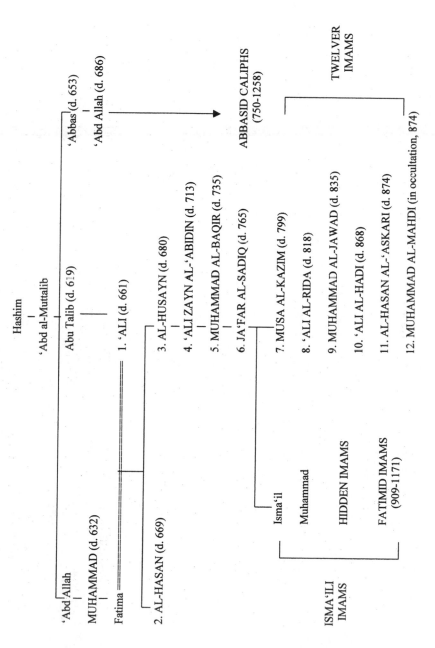

Hashim

'Abd al-Muttalib

Abu Talib (d. 619)   'Abbas (d. 653)

'Abd Allah (d. 686)

ABBASID CALIPHS
(750-1258)

TWELVER
IMAMS

'Abd Allah

MUHAMMAD (d. 632)

Fatima

1. 'ALI (d. 661)

2. AL-HASAN (d. 669)

3. AL-HUSAYN (d. 680)

4. 'ALI ZAYN AL-'ABIDIN (d. 713)

5. MUHAMMAD AL-BAQIR (d. 735)

6. JA'FAR AL-SADIQ (d. 765)

Isma'il

7. MUSA AL-KAZIM (d. 799)

Muhammad

8. 'ALI AL-RIDA (d. 818)

HIDDEN IMAMS

9. MUHAMMAD AL-JAWAD (d. 835)

FATIMID IMAMS
(909-1171)

10. 'ALI AL-HADI (d. 868)

11. AL-HASAN AL-'ASKARI (d. 874)

ISMA'ILI
IMAMS

12. MUHAMMAD AL-MAHDI (in occultation, 874)

THE ABBASID CALIPHS WITH REGNAL DATES

al-ʿAbbas ibn ʿAbd al-Muttalib, Muhammad's Paternal Uncle (d. 653)

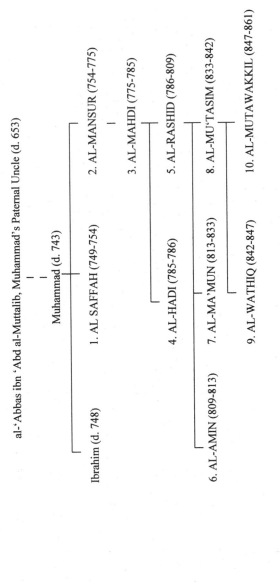

Muhammad (d. 743)

Ibrahim (d. 748)

1. AL SAFFAH (749-754)

2. AL-MANSUR (754-775)

3. AL-MAHDI (775-785)

4. AL-HADI (785-786)

5. AL-RASHID (786-809)

6. AL-AMIN (809-813)

7. AL-MAʾMUN (813-833)

8. AL-MUʿTASIM (833-842)

9. AL-WATHIQ (842-847)

10. AL-MUTAWAKKIL (847-861)

11. al-Muntasir (861-862)
12. al-Mustaʿin (862-866)
13. al-Muʿtazz (866-869)
14. al-Muhtadi (869-870)
15. al-Muʿtamid (870-892)
16. al-Muʿtadid (892-902)
17. al-Muktafi (902-908)
18. al-Muqtadir (908-932)
19. al-Qahir (932-934)

20. al-Radi (934-940)
21. al-Muttaqi (940-944)
22. al-Mustakfi (944-946)
23. al-Muti (946-974)
24. al-Taʾiʿ (974-991)
25. al-Qadir (991-1031)
26. al-Qaʾim (1031-1075)
27. al-Muqtadi (1075-1094)
28. al-Mustazhir (1094-1118)

29. al-Mustarshid (1118-1135)
30. al-Rashid (1135-1136)
31. al-Muqtafi (1136-60)
32. al-Mustanjid (1160-1170)
33. al-Mustadiʾ (1170-1180)
34. al-Nasir (1180-1225)
35. al-Zahir (1125-1126)
36. al-Mustansir (1226-1242)
37. al-Mustaʿsim (1242-58)

THE ISMA'ILI FATIMID CALIPHS WITH REGNAL DATES

ISMA'IL

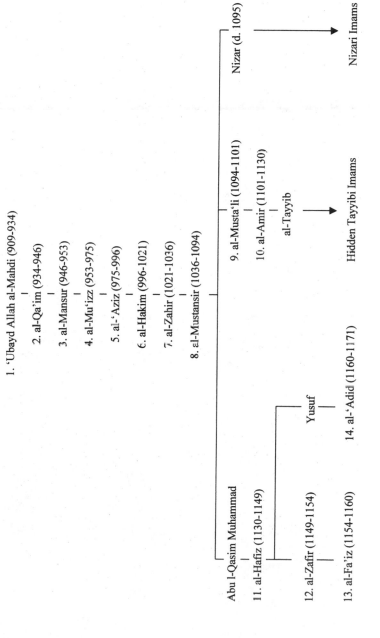

1. 'Ubayd Allah al-Mahdi (909-934)
2. al-Qa'im (934-946)
3. al-Mansur (946-953)
4. al-Mu'izz (953-975)
5. al-'Aziz (975-996)
6. al-Hakim (996-1021)
7. al-Zahir (1021-1036)
8. al-Mustansir (1036-1094)

9. al-Musta'li (1094-1101)
10. al-Amir (1101-1130)

al-Tayyib

Hidden Tayyibi Imams

Nizar (d. 1095)

Nizari Imams

Abu l-Qasim Muhammad
11. al-Hafiz (1130-1149)

Yusuf

12. al-Zafir (1149-1154)
13. al-Fa'iz (1154-1160)

14. al-'Adid (1160-1171)

CHRISTIAN AND ISLAMIC CALENDARS WITH CONVERSION TABLE[1]

The system for reckoning years from the birth of Jesus as A.D., *Anno Domini* (or more correctly *Anni Domini Nostri Jesu Christi,* meaning "In the Year of Our Lord Jesus Christ") was instituted by the Roman abbot Dionysius Exiguus in about A.D. 527. The calendar was further revised in a papal bull by Pope Gregory XIII in A.D. 1582. Consequently, the A.D. dating system is known as the Gregorian Christian calendar. While C.E., Common Era, has recently come into fashion for some, the only thing truly common about the Common Era is that most modern countries now use the Gregorian Christian calendar.

The Islamic calendar is known as the *hijri* calendar, because it begins with the year in which Muhammad (ca. A.D. 570–632) made his *hijra* or migration from Mecca to Medina (A.D. 622). According to Islamic tradition, the *hijri* calendar was instituted in A.D. 638 by the second Rashidun caliph, Umar ibn al-Khattab (r. 634–44). Under this system, A.H. 01/01/01 was calculated as July 16 A.D. 622. Most western scholars employ the abbreviation A.H., *Anno Hejirae,* to distinguish the *hijri* calendar from Gregorian one (A.D.; *Anno Domini*).

The Islamic calendar, like many other calendars, is based on a lunar year of 12 months totaling approximately 354 days, or about 11 days fewer than a solar year's 365 days. In order to keep the lunar months in alignment with the four seasons, most users of lunar calendars periodically add an extra or thirteenth month. In fact, it was customary in seventh-century Arabia to insert a leap month every few years in order to ensure that the sacred months (in which pilgrimages to shrines took place, fighting was forbidden, and trade flourished) occurred roughly at the same time each year.

The Jewish tradition also follows a lunar calendar composed of 12 lunar months. However, since many Jewish holy days and festivals have their origins in the agricultural practices of ancient Israel, they are tied to the seasons of the year as well as a particular Jewish month. Hence, a leap month—called the Second Adar—is added after the sixth Jewish month (Adar) in the following 19-year cycle: third, sixth, eighth, eleventh, fourteenth, seventeenth, and nineteenth years. Thus, a particular holiday such as the Jewish New Year may vary by as many as 28 days from year to year, but it will always occur in the fall, and usually in September.

According to the biographical literature, during his last pilgrimage to Mecca, Muhammad received a revelation forbidding the practice of inserting an extra month.

God ordained the months twelve in number when He created the heavens and the earth. Of these, four are sacred, according to the true Faith. Therefore, do not sin against yourselves by violating them. But you may fight against the idolaters in all these months, since they themselves fight against you in all of them. Know that God is with the righteous. The postponement of sacred months is a grossly impious practice, in which the unbelievers are misguided. They allow it one year and forbid it in the next, so that they may make up for the months which God has sanctified, thus making lawful what God has forbidden. Their foul acts seem fair to them: God does not guide the unbelievers. (Qur'an 9:36–37)

Some scholars have argued that this passage is speaking against the Quraysh leaders' practice of manipulating the sacred months of the year for their own economic and political advantage; how this was done remains a mystery. Others have argued that another reason for this may have been related to the fact that the annual pilgrimage in and around Mecca had been held during the spring season. That is, forbidding the practice of intercalation may have been done specifically to ensure that the new Islamic pilgrimage would no longer coincide with the Jewish Passover and Christian Easter holidays, which also occurred in the spring season. In any case, one of the results of this prohibition is that none of the Islamic religious holidays—including the Ramadan fast and the annual pilgrimage—correspond in any way to the seasons.

Reasons for this prohibition aside, there is no easy way to make the Islamic lunar calendar match up with the Gregorian Christian solar calendar. Subtracting 622 from the Gregorian year can provide a rough approximation of the Islamic year in which an event occurred, especially for the first decades of Islamic history. For example, the caliph Umar conquered Jerusalem in the year A.D. 637 or A.H. 15 (637 – 622 = 15). However, by the time we reach the Crusader period, things are more complicated. The Franks conquered Jerusalem in the summer of A.D. 1099 or A.H. 492 (1099

– 622 = 477, not 492); Saladin reconquered it in the summer of A.D. 1187 or A.H. 583 (1187 – 622 = 565, not 583).

One can calculate the rough equivalents between the Gregorian (C) and Islamic (H) years with the following formulas:

$$H \cdot 32/33 + 622 \approx C$$

$$(C - 622) \cdot 33/32 \approx H$$

In addition, the accompanying conversion table lists the Islamic year in the left column. The equivalent Gregorian date for 1 Muharram, the first day of the Islamic year, is listed in the right column.

A few words of caution are necessary before using any formula or table to calculate the exact Gregorian date for an Islamic date (or vice versa). Formulas and tables can only provide imprecise estimates since the beginning of an Islamic month varies from region to region, depending on when the religious scholars (*'ulama'*) first sighted the crescent moon. For example, the first day of Ramadan A.H. 400 in Cairo may or may not be the same day of the week in Baghdad, or Cordoba, or Delhi, or any other city.

Select Muslim Holidays

- Muharram 1 [*Ras al-sana:* The New Year] is the first day of the first month. It is celebrated throughout the Islamic world, though it is not a particularly religious holiday, nor was it much observed in the medieval Islamic world.

- Muharram 10 [*'Ashura:* The Tenth] is the day on which many pious Muslims fast from dawn to sunset. For Shi'i Muslims this day is of particular importance, as it commemorates the martyrdom of Ali ibn Abi Talib's son, Husayn.

- Rabi' al-Awwal 12 [*Mawlid al-nabi:* The Prophet's Birthday] is a holiday associated with festivities and exchanging of gifts. Often passages eulogizing Muammad are read.

- Rajab 27 [*Laylat al-isra' wa l-mi'raj:* The Night of Journey and Ascent] commemorates Muhammad's night journey from Mecca to the Haram al-Sharif area in Jerusalem and his ascent to Heaven and return to Jerusalem, and then Mecca—all in one night. This night is traditionally celebrated by prayers.

- Sha'ban 14 [*Laylat al-bara'a:* Night of Remembrance] is, according to Muslim tradition, the night God approaches earth to grant forgiveness for an individual's sins.

- Ramadan [ninth month of the Muslim year] is devoted to spiritual purification through the abstinence from food, drink, and physical pleasures from dawn until dusk.

- Ramadan 27 [*Laylat al-qadar:* Night of Power and Greatness] is considered a particularly holy time, as it is the night, by tradition, on which Muhammad received the first revelation.
- Shawwal 1 ['Id al-fitr: The Feast of Fastbreaking; or The Lesser Feast] is the most joyous festival in the Islamic calendar and marks the end of abstinence during Ramadan.
- Dhu l-Hijja 8–13: The period in which Muslims are to undertake a pilgrimage (*hajj*) to Mecca and its environs in imitation of Muhammad's last pilgrimage.
- Dhu l-Hijja 10 ['Id al-adha: The Feast of Sacrifice; or The Greater Feast] is the high point of the pilgrimage and is celebrated by Muslims throughout the world even if not actually participating in the pilgrimage. It commemorates Abraham's willingness to sacrifice his son (Qur'an 37:103–9). The Feast of Sacrifice is most often marked by the slaughtering of lambs and the distribution of meat to the needy.
- Dhu l-Hijja 18 [Ghadir Khumm] is a Shi'i festival commemorating the date when Muhammad bestowed his own political and religious authority on Ali ibn Abi Talib and his descendants at a place called Ghadir Khumm on his way back to Medina after he had made his final pilgrimage to Mecca.

GREGORIAN/ISLAMIC CONVERSION TABLE

The Gregorian/Islamic conversion table below can be used to calculate the approximate Gregorian date for a corresponding Islamic date. First, locate on the table the Gregorian date for the first day (1 Muharram) of a particular Islamic year. Then add the appropriate number of months of the Islamic date to the Gregorian date for a ballpark estimate. The Islamic months are as follows:

1.	Muharram	7.	Rajab
2.	Safar	8.	Sha'ban
3.	Rabi' al-Awwal	9.	Ramadan
4.	Rabi' al-Thani	10.	Shawwal
5.	Jumada l-Ula	11.	Dhu l-Qa'da
6.	Jumada l-Akhira	12.	Dhu l-Hijja

In order to calculate the exact Gregorian date for an Islamic date, more elaborate tables than the one provided here must be used. H. Taqizadeh, "Various Eras and Calendars Used in the Countries of Islam," *Bulletin of the School of Oriental and African Studies* 9 (1937–39): 902–99; and 10 (1940–42): 107–132, is a general survey of the types of calendars found in the Islamic world. G.S.P. Freeman-Grenville, *The Muslim and Christian Calendars* (London: Oxford University Press, 1963), has clear instructions and is easy to use. P. Lemerle, *Traite d'etudes Byzantines* (Paris: Presses Universitaires de France, 1958), has a comprehensive list of medieval calendars, including the Julian, Armenian, Coptic, Sasanian, Mongolian, and Muslim calendars, plus data on comets, eclipses, earthquakes, and so forth to 1453. Finally, the Institute of Oriental Studies at Zurich University has a very easy-to-use conversion calculator posted on its website—http://www.unizh.ch/ori/hegira.html. One can type in a Gregorian day/month/year and the program will calculate the corresponding *hijri* day/month/year (or vice versa).

Islamic Year	Gregorian Date of 1 Muharram	Islamic Year	Gregorian Date of 1 Muharram
1	16 July 622	22	30 November 642
2	5 July 623	23	19 November 643
3	24 June 624	24	7 November 644
4	13 June 625	25	28 October 645
5	2 June 626	26	17 October 646
6	23 May 627	27	7 October 647
7	11 May 628	28	25 September 648
8	1 May 629	29	14 September 649
9	20 April 630	30	4 September 650
10	9 April 631	31	24 August 651
11	29 March 632	32	12 August 652
12	18 March 633	33	2 August 653
13	7 March 634	34	22 July 654
14	25 February 635	35	11 July 655
15	14 February 636	36	30 June 656
16	2 February 637	37	19 June 657
17	23 January 638	38	9 June 658
18	12 January 639	39	29 May 659
19	2 January 640	40	17 May 660
20	21 December 640	41	7 May 661
21	10 December 641	42	26 April 662

Islamic Year	Gregorian Date of 1 Muharram	Islamic Year	Gregorian Date of 1 Muharram
43	15 April 663	75	2 May 694
44	4 April 664	76	21 April 695
45	24 March 665	77	10 April 696
46	13 March 666	78	30 March 697
47	3 March 667	79	20 March 698
48	20 February 668	80	9 March 699
49	9 February 669	81	26 February 700
50	29 January 670	82	15 February 701
51	18 January 671	83	4 February 702
52	8 January 672	84	24 January 703
53	27 December 672	85	14 January 704
54	16 December 673	86	2 January 705
55	6 December 674	87	23 December 705
56	25 November 675	88	12 December 706
57	14 November 676	89	1 December 707
58	3 November 677	90	20 November 708
59	23 October 678	91	9 November 709
60	13 October 679	92	29 October 710
61	1 October 680	93	19 October 711
62	20 September 681	94	7 October 712
63	10 September 682	95	26 September 713
64	30 August 683	96	16 September 714
65	18 August 684	97	5 September 715
66	8 August 685	98	25 August 716
67	28 July 686	99	14 August 717
68	18 July 687	100	3 August 718
69	6 July 688	101	24 July 719
70	25 June 689	102	12 July 720
71	15 June 690	103	1 July 721
72	4 June 691	104	21 June 722
73	23 May 692	105	10 June 723
74	13 May 693	106	29 May 724

Islamic Year	Gregorian Date of 1 Muharram	Islamic Year	Gregorian Date of 1 Muharram
107	19 May 725	139	5 June 756
108	8 May 726	140	25 May 757
109	28 April 727	141	14 May 758
110	16 April 728	142	4 May 759
111	5 April 729	143	22 April 760
112	26 March 730	144	11 April 761
113	15 March 731	145	1 April 762
114	3 March 732	146	21 March 763
115	21 February 733	147	10 March 764
116	10 February 734	148	27 February 765
117	31 January 735	149	16 February 766
118	20 January 736	150	6 February 767
119	8 January 737	151	26 January 768
120	29 December 737	152	14 January 769
121	18 December 738	153	4 January 770
122	7 December 739	154	24 December 770
123	26 November 740	155	13 December 771
124	15 November 741	156	2 December 772
125	4 November 742	157	21 November 773
126	25 October 743	158	11 November 774
127	13 October 744	159	31 October 775
128	3 October 745	160	19 October 776
129	22 September 746	161	9 October 777
130	11 September 747	162	28 September 778
131	31 August 748	163	17 September 779
132	20 August 749	164	6 September 780
133	9 August 750	165	26 August 781
134	30 July 751	166	15 August 782
135	18 July 752	167	5 August 783
136	7 July 753	168	24 July 784
137	27 June 754	169	14 July 785
138	16 June 755	170	3 July 786

Islamic Year	Gregorian Date of 1 Muharram	Islamic Year	Gregorian Date of 1 Muharram
171	22 June 787	203	9 July 818
172	11 June 788	204	28 June 819
173	31 May 789	205	17 June 820
174	20 May 790	206	6 June 821
175	10 May 791	207	27 May 822
176	28 April 792	208	16 May 823
177	18 April 793	209	4 May 824
178	7 April 794	210	24 April 825
179	27 March 795	211	13 April 826
180	16 March 796	212	2 April 827
181	5 March 797	213	22 March 828
182	22 February 798	214	11 March 829
183	12 February 799	215	25 February 830
184	1 February 800	216	18 February 831
185	20 January 801	217	7 February 832
186	10 January 802	218	27 January 833
187	30 December 802	219	16 January 834
188	20 December 803	220	5 January 835
189	8 December 804	221	26 December 835
190	27 November 805	222	14 December 836
191	17 November 806	223	3 December 837
192	6 November 807	224	23 November 838
193	25 October 808	225	12 November 839
194	15 October 809	226	31 October 840
195	4 October 810	227	21 October 841
196	23 September 811	228	10 October 842
197	12 September 812	229	20 September 843
198	1 September 813	230	18 September 844
199	22 August 814	231	7 September 845
200	11 August 815	232	28 August 846
201	30 July 816	233	17 August 847
202	20 July 817	234	5 August 848

Islamic Year	Gregorian Date of 1 Muharram	Islamic Year	Gregorian Date of 1 Muharram
235	26 July 849	267	12 August 880
236	15 July 850	268	1 August 881
237	5 July 851	269	21 July 882
238	23 June 852	270	11 July 883
239	12 June 853	271	29 June 884
240	2 June 854	272	18 June 885
241	22 May 855	273	8 June 886
242	10 May 856	274	28 May 887
243	30 April 857	275	16 May 888
244	19 April 858	276	6 May 889
245	8 April 859	277	25 April 890
246	28 March 860	278	15 April 891
247	17 March 861	279	3 April 892
248	7 March 862	280	23 March 893
249	24 February 863	281	13 March 894
250	13 February 864	282	2 March 895
251	2 February 865	283	19 February 896
252	22 January 866	284	8 February 897
253	11 January 867	285	28 January 898
254	1 January 868	286	17 January 899
255	20 December 868	287	7 January 900
256	9 December 869	288	26 December 900
257	29 November 870	289	16 December 901
258	18 November 871	290	5 December 902
259	7 November 872	291	24 November 903
260	27 October 873	292	13 November 904
261	16 October 874	293	2 November 905
262	6 October 875	294	22 October 906
263	24 September 876	295	12 October 907
264	13 September 877	296	30 September 908
265	3 September 878	297	20 September 909
266	23 August 879	298	9 September 910

Islamic Year	Gregorian Date of 1 Muharram	Islamic Year	Gregorian Date of 1 Muharram
299	29 August 911	331	15 September 942
300	18 August 912	332	4 September 943
301	7 August 913	333	24 August 944
302	27 July 914	334	13 August 945
303	17 July 915	335	2 August 946
304	5 July 916	336	23 July 947
305	24 June 917	337	11 July 948
306	14 June 918	338	1 July 949
307	3 June 919	339	20 June 950
308	23 May 920	340	9 June 951
309	12 May 921	341	29 May 952
310	1 May 922	342	18 May 953
311	21 April 923	343	7 May 954
312	9 April 924	344	27 April 955
313	29 March 925	345	15 April 956
314	19 March 926	346	4 April 957
315	8 March 927	347	25 March 958
316	25 February 928	348	14 March 959
317	14 February 929	349	3 March 960
318	3 February 930	350	20 February 961
319	24 January 931	351	9 February 962
320	13 January 932	352	30 January 963
321	1 January 933	353	19 January 964
322	22 December 933	354	7 January 965
323	11 December 934	355	28 December 965
324	30 November 935	356	17 December 966
325	19 November 936	357	7 December 967
326	8 November 937	358	25 November 968
327	29 October 938	359	14 November 969
328	18 October 939	360	4 November 970
329	6 October 940	361	24 October 971
330	26 September 941	362	12 October 972

Islamic Year	Gregorian Date of 1 Muharram	Islamic Year	Gregorian Date of 1 Muharram
363	2 October 973	395	18 October 1004
364	21 September 974	396	8 October 1005
365	10 September 975	397	27 September 1006
366	30 August 976	398	17 September 1007
367	19 August 977	399	5 September 1008
368	9 August 978	400	25 August 1009
369	29 July 979	401	15 August 1010
370	17 July 980	402	4 August 1011
371	7 July 981	403	23 July 1012
372	26 June 982	404	13 July 1013
373	15 June 983	405	3 July 1014
374	4 June 984	406	21 June 1015
375	24 May 985	407	10 June 1016
376	13 May 986	408	30 May 1017
377	3 May 987	409	20 May 1018
378	21 April 988	410	9 May 1019
379	11 April 989	411	27 April 1020
380	31 March 990	412	17 April 1021
381	20 March 991	413	6 April 1022
382	9 March 992	414	26 March 1023
383	26 February 993	415	15 March 1024
384	15 February 994	416	4 March 1025
385	5 February 995	417	22 February 1026
386	25 January 996	418	11 February 1027
387	14 January 997	419	31 January 1028
388	3 January 998	420	20 January 1029
389	23 December 998	421	9 January 1030
390	13 December 999	422	29 December 1030
391	1 December 1000	423	19 December 1031
392	20 November 1001	424	7 December 1032
393	10 November 1002	425	26 November 1033
394	30 October 1003	426	16 November 1034

Islamic Year	Gregorian Date of 1 Muharram	Islamic Year	Gregorian Date of 1 Muharram
427	5 November 1035	459	22 November 1066
428	25 October 1036	460	11 November 1067
429	14 October 1037	461	31 October 1068
430	3 October 1038	462	20 October 1069
431	23 September 1039	463	9 October 1070
432	11 September 1040	464	29 September 1071
433	31 August 1041	465	17 September 1072
434	21 August 1042	466	6 September 1073
435	10 August 1043	467	27 August 1074
436	29 July 1044	468	16 August 1075
437	19 July 1045	469	5 August 1076
438	8 July 1046	470	25 July 1077
439	28 June 1047	471	14 July 1078
440	16 June 1048	472	4 July 1079
441	5 June 1049	473	22 June 1080
442	26 May 1050	474	11 June 1081
443	15 May 1051	475	1 June 1082
444	3 May 1052	476	21 May 1083
445	23 April 1053	477	10 May 1084
446	12 April 1054	478	29 April 1085
447	2 April 1055	479	18 April 1086
448	21 March 1056	480	8 April 1087
449	10 March 1057	481	27 March 1088
450	28 February 1058	482	16 March 1089
451	17 February 1059	483	6 March 1090
452	6 February 1060	484	23 February 1091
453	26 January 1061	485	12 February 1092
454	15 January 1062	486	1 February 1093
455	4 January 1063	487	21 January 1094
456	25 December 1063	488	11 January 1095
457	13 December 1064	489	31 December 1095
458	3 December 1065	490	19 December 1096

Islamic Year	Gregorian Date of 1 Muharram	Islamic Year	Gregorian Date of 1 Muharram
491	9 December 1097	523	25 December 1128
492	28 November 1098	524	15 December 1129
493	17 November 1099	525	4 December 1130
494	6 November 1100	526	23 November 1131
495	26 October 1101	527	12 November 1132
496	15 October 1102	528	1 November 1133
497	5 October 1103	529	22 October 1134
498	23 September 1104	530	11 October 1135
499	13 September 1105	531	29 September 1136
500	2 September 1106	532	19 September 1137
501	22 August 1107	533	8 September 1138
502	11 August 1108	534	28 August 1139
503	31 July 1109	535	17 August 1140
504	20 July 1110	536	6 August 1141
505	10 July 1111	537	27 July 1142
506	28 June 1112	538	16 July 1143
507	18 June 1113	539	4 July 1144
508	7 June 1114	540	24 June 1145
509	27 May 1115	541	13 June 1146
510	16 May 1116	542	2 June 1147
511	5 May 1117	543	22 May 1148
512	24 April 1118	544	11 May 1149
513	14 April 1119	545	30 April 1150
514	2 April 1120	546	20 April 1151
515	22 March 1121	547	8 April 1152
516	12 March 1122	548	27 March 1153
517	1 March 1123	549	18 March 1154
518	19 February 1124	550	7 March 1155
519	7 February 1125	551	25 February 1156
520	27 January 1126	552	13 February 1157
521	17 January 1127	553	2 February 1158
522	6 January 1128	554	23 January 1159

Islamic Year	Gregorian Date of 1 Muharram	Islamic Year	Gregorian Date of 1 Muharram
555	12 January 1160	587	29 January 1191
556	31 December 1160	588	18 January 1192
557	21 December 1161	589	7 January 1193
558	10 December 1162	590	27 December 1193
559	30 November 1163	591	16 December 1194
560	18 November 1164	592	6 December 1195
561	7 November 1165	593	24 November 1196
562	28 October 1166	594	13 November 1197
563	17 October 1167	595	3 November 1198
564	5 October 1168	596	23 October 1199
565	25 September 1169	597	12 October 1200
566	14 September 1170	598	1 October 1201
567	4 September 1171	599	20 September 1202
568	23 August 1172	600	10 September 1203
569	12 August 1173	601	29 Aug 1204
570	2 August 1174	602	18 Aug 1205
571	22 July 1175	603	8 Aug 1206
572	10 July 1176	604	28 July 1207
573	30 June 1177	605	16 July 1208
574	19 June 1178	606	6 July 1209
575	8 June 1179	607	25 June 1210
576	28 May 1180	608	15 June 1211
577	17 May 1181	609	3 June 1212
578	7 May 1182	610	23 May 1213
579	26 April 1183	611	13 May 1214
580	14 April 1184	612	2 May 1215
581	4 April 1185	613	20 April 1216
582	24 March 1186	614	10 April 1217
583	13 March 1187	615	30 March 1218
584	2 March 1188	616	19 March 1219
585	19 February 1189	617	8 March 1220
586	8 February 1190	618	25 February 1221

Islamic Year	Gregorian Date of 1 Muharram	Islamic Year	Gregorian Date of 1 Muharram
619	15 February 1222	651	3 March 1253
620	4 February 1223	652	21 February 1254
621	24 January 1224	653	10 February 1255
622	13 January 1225	654	30 January 1256
623	2 January 1226	655	19 January 1257
624	22 December 1226	656	8 January 1258
625	12 December 1227	657	29 December 1258
626	30 November 1228	658	18 December 1259
627	20 November 1229	659	6 December 1260
628	9 November 1230	660	26 November 1261
629	29 October 1231	661	15 November 1262
630	18 October 1232	662	4 November 1263
631	7 October 1233	663	24 October 1264
632	26 September 1234	664	13 October 1265
633	16 September 1235	665	2 October 1266
634	4 September 1236	666	22 September 1267
635	24 August 1237	667	10 September 1268
636	14 August 1238	668	31 August 1269
637	3 August 1239	669	20 August 1270
638	23 July 1240	670	9 August 1271
639	12 July 1241	671	29 July 1272
640	1 July 1242	672	18 July 1273
641	21 June 1243	673	7 July 1274
642	9 June 1244	674	27 June 1275
643	29 May 1245	675	15 June 1276
644	19 May 1246	676	4 June 1277
645	8 May 1247	677	25 May 1278
646	26 April 1248	678	14 May 1279
647	16 April 1249	679	3 May 1280
648	5 April 1250	680	22 April 1281
649	26 March 1251	681	11 April 1282
650	14 March 1252	682	1 April 1823

Islamic Year	Gregorian Date of 1 Muharram	Islamic Year	Gregorian Date of 1 Muharram
683	20 March 1284	715	7 April 1315
684	9 March 1285	716	26 March 1316
685	27 February 1286	717	16 March 1317
686	16 February 1287	718	5 March 1318
687	6 February 1288	719	22 February 1319
688	25 January 1289	720	12 February 1320
689	14 January 1290	721	31 January 1321
690	4 January 1291	722	20 January 1322
691	24 December 1921	723	10 January 1323
692	12 December 1292	724	30 December 1323
693	2 December 1293	725	18 December 1324
694	21 November 1294	726	8 December 1325
695	10 November 1295	727	27 November 1326
696	30 October 1296	728	17 November 1327
697	19 October 1297	729	5 November 1328
698	9 October 1298	730	25 October 1329
699	28 September 1299	731	15 October 1330
700	16 September 1300	732	4 October 1331
701	5 September 1301	733	22 September 1332
702	26 August 1302	734	12 September 1333
703	15 August 1303	735	1 September 1334
704	4 August 1304	736	21 August 1335
705	24 July 1305	737	10 August 1336
706	13 July 1306	738	30 July 1337
707	3 July 1307	739	20 July 1338
708	21 June 1308	740	9 July 1339
709	11 June 1309	741	27 June 1340
710	31 May 1310	742	17 June 1341
711	20 May 1311	743	6 June 1342
712	9 May 1312	744	26 May 1343
713	28 April 1313	745	15 May 1344
714	17 April 1314	746	4 May 1345

Islamic Year	Gregorian Date of 1 Muharram	Islamic Year	Gregorian Date of 1 Muharram
747	24 April 1346	779	10 May 1377
748	13 April 1347	780	30 April 1378
749	1 April 1348	781	19 April 1379
750	22 March 1349	782	7 April 1380
751	11 March 1350	783	28 March 1381
752	28 February 1351	784	17 March 1382
753	18 February 1352	785	6 March 1383
754	6 February 1353	786	24 February 1384
755	26 January 1354	787	12 February 1385
756	16 January 1355	788	2 February 1386
757	5 January 1356	789	22 January 1387
758	25 December 1356	790	11 January 1388
759	15 December 1357	791	31 December 1388
760	3 December 1358	792	20 December 1389
761	23 November 1359	793	9 December 1390
762	11 November 1360	794	29 November 1391
763	31 October 1361	795	17 November 1392
764	21 October 1362	796	6 November 1393
765	10 October 1363	797	27 October 1394
766	28 September 1364	798	16 October 1395
767	18 September 1365	799	5 October 1396
768	7 September 1366	800	24 September 1397
769	28 August 1367	801	13 September 1398
770	16 August 1368	802	3 September 1399
771	5 August 1369	803	22 August 1400
772	26 July 1370	804	11 August 1401
773	15 July 1371	805	1 August 1402
774	3 July 1372	806	21 July 1403
775	23 June 1373	807	10 July 1404
776	12 June 1374	808	29 June 1405
777	2 June 1375	809	18 June 1406
778	21 May 1376	810	8 June 1407

Islamic Year	Gregorian Date of 1 Muharram	Islamic Year	Gregorian Date of 1 Muharram
811	27 May 1408	843	14 June 1439
812	16 May 1409	844	2 June 1440
813	6 May 1410	845	22 May 1441
814	25 April 1411	846	12 May 1442
815	13 April 1412	847	1 May 1443
816	3 April 1413	848	20 April 1444
817	23 March 1414	849	9 April 1445
818	13 March 1415	850	29 March 1446
819	1 March 1416	851	19 March 1447
820	18 February 1417	852	7 March 1448
821	8 February 1418	853	24 February 1449
822	28 January 1419	854	14 February 1450
823	17 January 1420	855	3 February 1451
824	6 January 1421	856	23 January 1452
825	26 December 1421	857	12 January 1453
826	15 December 1422	858	1 January 1454
827	5 December 1423	859	22 December 1454
828	23 November 1424	860	11 December 1455
829	13 November 1425	861	29 November 1456
830	2 November 1426	862	19 November 1457
831	22 October 1427	863	8 November 1458
832	11 October 1428	864	28 October 1459
833	30 September 1429	865	17 October 1460
834	19 September 1430	866	6 October 1461
835	9 September 1431	867	26 September 1462
836	28 August 1432	868	15 September 1463
837	18 August 1433	869	3 September 1464
838	7 August 1434	870	23 August 1465
839	27 July 1435	871	13 August 1466
840	16 July 1436	872	2 August 1467
841	5 July 1437	873	22 July 1468
842	24 June 1438	874	11 July 1469

Islamic Year	Gregorian Date of 1 Muharram	Islamic Year	Gregorian Date of 1 Muharram
875	30 June 1470	907	17 July 1501
876	20 June 1471	908	7 July 1502
877	8 June 1472	909	26 June 1503
878	29 May 1473	910	14 June 1504
879	18 May 1474	911	4 June 1505
880	7 May 1475	912	24 May 1506
881	26 April 1476	913	13 May 1507
882	15 April 1477	914	2 May 1508
883	4 April 1478	915	21 April 1509
884	25 March 1479	916	10 April 1510
885	13 March 1480	917	31 March 1511
886	2 March 1481	918	19 March 1512
887	20 February 1482	919	9 March 1513
888	9 February 1483	920	26 February 1514
889	30 January 1484	921	15 February 1515
890	18 January 1485	922	5 February 1516
891	7 January 1486	923	24 January 1517
892	28 December 1486	924	13 January 1518
893	17 December 1487	925	3 January 1519
894	5 December 1488	926	23 December 1519
895	25 November 1489	927	12 December 1520
896	14 November 1490	928	1 December 1521
897	4 November 1491	929	20 November 1522
898	23 October 1492	930	10 November 1523
899	12 October 1493	931	29 October 1524
900	2 October 1494	933	8 October 1526
901	21 September 1495	934	27 October 1527
902	9 September 1496	935	15 September 1528
903	30 August 1497	936	5 September 1529
904	19 August 1498	937	25 August 1530
905	8 August 1499	938	15 August 1531
906	28 July 1500	939	3 August 1532

Islamic Year	Gregorian Date of 1 Muharram	Islamic Year	Gregorian Date of 1 Muharram
940	23 July 1533	972	9 August 1564
941	13 July 1534	973	29 July 1565
942	2 July 1535	974	19 July 1566
943	20 June 1536	975	8 July 1567
944	10 June 1537	976	26 June 1568
945	30 May 1538	977	16 June 1569
946	19 May 1539	978	5 June 1570
947	8 May 1540	979	26 May 1571
948	27 April 1541	980	14 May 1572
949	17 April 1542	981	3 May 1573
950	6 April 1543	982	23 April 1574
951	25 March 1544	983	12 April 1575
952	15 March 1545	984	31 March 1576
953	4 March 1546	985	21 March 1577
954	21 February 1547	986	10 March 1578
955	11 February 1548	987	28 February 1579
956	30 January 1549	988	17 February 1580
957	20 January 1550	989	5 February 1581
958	9 January 1551	990	26 January 1582
959	29 December 1551	991	25 January 1583
960	18 December 1552	992	14 January 1584
961	7 December 1553	993	3 January 1585
962	26 November 1554	994	23 December 1585
963	16 November 1555	995	12 December 1586
964	4 November 1556	996	2 December 1587
965	24 October 1557	997	20 November 1588
966	14 October 1558	998	10 November 1589
967	3 October 1559	999	30 October 1590
968	22 September 1560	1000	19 October 1591
969	11 September 1561	1001	8 October 1592
970	31 August 1562	1002	27 September 1593
971	21 August 1563	1003	16 September 1594

Islamic Year	Gregorian Date of 1 Muharram	Islamic Year	Gregorian Date of 1 Muharram
1004	6 September 1595	1029	8 December 1619
1005	28 August 1596	1030	26 November 1620
1006	14 August 1597	1031	16 November 1621
1000	19 October 1591	1032	5 November 1622
1001	8 October 1592	1033	25 October 1623
1002	27 September 1593	1034	14 October 1624
1003	16 September 1594	1035	3 October 1625
1004	6 September 1595	1036	22 September 1626
1005	28 August 1596	1037	12 September 1627
1006	14 August 1597	1038	31 August 1638
1007	4 August 1598	1039	21 August 1629
1008	24 July 1599	1040	10 August 1630
1009	13 July 1600	1041	30 July 1631
1010	2 July 1601	1042	19 July 1632
1011	21 June 1602	1043	8 July 1633
1012	11 June 1603	1044	27 June 1634
1013	30 May 1604	1045	17 June 1635
1014	19 May 1605	1046	5 June 1636
1015	9 May 1606	1047	26 May 1637
1016	28 April 1607	1048	15 May 1638
1017	17 April 1608	1049	4 May 1639
1018	6 April 1609	1050	23 April 1640
1019	26 March 1610	1051	12 April 1641
1020	16 March 1611	1052	1 April 1642
1021	4 March 1612	1053	22 March 1643
1022	21 February 1613	1054	10 March 1644
1023	11 February 1614	1055	27 February 1645
1024	31 January 1615	1056	17 February 1646
1025	20 Jaw 1616	1057	6 February 1647
1026	9 January 1617	1058	27 January 1648
1027	29 December 1617	1059	15 January 1649
1028	19 December 1618	1060	4 January 1650

Islamic Year	Gregorian Date of 1 Muharram	Islamic Year	Gregorian Date of 1 Muharram
1061	25 December 1650	1093	10 January 1682
1062	14 December 1651	1094	31 December 1682
1063	2 December 1652	1095	20 December 1683
1064	22 November 1653	1096	8 December 1684
1065	11 November 1654	1097	28 November 1685
1066	31 October 1655	1098	17 November 1686
1067	20 October 1656	1099	7 November 1687
1068	9 October 1657	1100	26 October 1688
1069	29 September 1658	1101	15 October 1689
1070	18 September 1659	1102	5 October 1690
1071	6 September 1660	1103	24 September 1691
1072	27 August 1661	1104	12 September 1692
1073	16 August 1662	1105	2 September 1693
1074	5 August 1663	1106	22 August 1694
1075	25 July 1664	1107	12 August 1695
1076	14 July 1665	1108	31 July 1696
1077	4 July 1666	1109	20 July 1697
1078	23 June 1667	1110	10 July 1698
1079	11 June 1668	1111	29 June 1699
1080	1 June 1669	1112	18 June 1700
1081	21 May 1670	1113	8 June 1701
1082	10 May 1671	1114	28 May 1702
1083	29 April 1672	1115	17 May 1703
1084	18 April 1673	1116	6 May 1704
1085	7 April 1674	1117	25 April 1705
1086	28 March 1675	1118	15 April 1706
1087	16 March 1676	1119	4 April 1707
1088	6 March 1677	1120	23 March 1708
1089	23 February 1678	1121	13 March 1709
1090	12 February 1679	1122	2 March 1710
1091	2 February 1680	1123	19 February 1711
1092	21 January 1681	1124	9 February 1712

Islamic Year	Gregorian Date of 1 Muharram	Islamic Year	Gregorian Date of 1 Muharram
1125	28 January 1713	1157	15 February 1744
1126	17 January 1714	1158	3 February 1745
1127	7 January 1715	1159	24 January 1746
1128	27 December 1715	1160	13 January 1747
1129	16 December 1716	1161	2 January 1748
1130	5 December 1717	1162	22 December 1748
1131	24 November 1718	1163	11 December 1749
1132	14 November 1719	1164	30 November 1750
1133	2 November 1720	1165	20 November 1751
1134	22 October 1721	1166	8 November 1752
1135	12 October 1722	1167	29 October 1753
1136	1 October 1723	1168	18 October 1754
1137	20 September 1724	1169	7 October 1755
1138	9 September 1725	1170	26 September 1756
1139	29 August 1726	1171	15 September 1757
1140	19 August 1727	1172	4 September 1758
1141	7 August 1728	1173	25 August 1759
1142	27 July 1729	1174	13 August 1760
1143	17 July 1730	1175	2 August 1761
1144	6 July 1731	1176	23 July 1762
1145	24 June 1732	1177	12 July 1763
1146	14 June 1733	1178	1 July 1764
1147	3 June 1734	1179	20 June 1765
1148	24 May 1735	1180	9 June 1766
1149	12 May 1736	1181	30 May 1767
1150	1 May 1737	1182	18 May 1768
1151	21 April 1738	1183	7 May 1769
1152	10 April 1739	1184	27 April 1770
1153	29 March 1740	1185	16 April 1771
1154	19 March 1741	1186	4 April 1772
1155	8 March 1742	1187	25 March 1773
1156	25 February 1743	1188	14 March 1774

Islamic Year	Gregorian Date of 1 Muharram	Islamic Year	Gregorian Date of 1 Muharram
1189	4 March 1775	1222	11 March 1807
1190	21 February 1776	1223	28 February 1808
1191	19 February 1777	1224	16 February 1809
1192	30 January 1778	1225	6 February 1810
1193	19 January 1779	1226	26 January 1811
1194	8 January 1780	1227	16 January 1812
1195	28 December 1780	1228	4 January 1813
1196	17 December 1781	1229	24 December 1813
1197	7 December 1782	1230	14 December 1814
1198	26 November 1783	1231	3 December 1815
1199	14 November 1784	1232	21 November 1816
1200	4 November 1785	1233	11 November 1817
1251	24 October 1786	1234	31 October 1818
1202	13 October 1787	1235	20 October 1819
1203	2 October 1788	1236	9 October 1820
1204	21 September 1789	1237	28 September 1821
1205	10 September 1790	1238	18 September 1822
1206	31 August 1791	1239	7 September 1823
1207	19 August 1792	1240	26 August 1824
1208	9 August 1793	1241	16 August 1825
1209	29 July 1794	1242	5 August 1826
1210	18 July 1795	1243	25 July 1827
1211	7 July 1796	1244	14 July 1828
1212	26 June 1797	1245	3 July 1829
1213	15 June 1798	1246	22 June 1830
1214	5 June 1799	1247	12 June 1831
1215	25 May 1800	1248	31 May 1832
1216	14 May 1801	1249	21 May 1833
1217	4 May 1802	1250	10 May 1834
1218	23 April 1803	1251	29 April 1835
1119	12 April 1804	1252	18 April 1836
1220	1 April 1805	1253	7 April 1837
1221	21 March 1806	1254	27 March 1838

Islamic Year	Gregorian Date of 1 Muharram	Islamic Year	Gregorian Date of 1 Muharram
1255	17 March 1839	1288	23 March 1871
1256	5 March 1840	1289	11 March 1872
1257	23 February 1841	1290	1 March 1873
1258	12 February 1842	1291	18 February 1874
1259	1 February 1843	1292	7 February 1875
1260	22 January 1844	1293	28 January 1876
1261	10 January 1845	1294	16 January 1877
1262	30 December 1845	1295	5 January 1878
1263	20 December 1846	1296	26 December 1878
1264	9 December 1847	1297	15 December 1879
1265	27 November 1848	1298	4 December 1880
1266	17 November 1849	1299	23 November 1881
1267	6 November 1850	1300	12 November 1882
1268	27 October 1851	1301	2 November 1882
1269	15 October 1852	1302	21 October 1884
1270	4 October 1853	1303	10 October 1885
1271	24 September 1854	1304	30 September 1886
1272	13 September 1855	1305	19 September 1887
1273	1 September 1856	1306	7 September 1888
1274	22 August 1857	1307	28 August 1889
1275	11 August 1858	1308	17 August 1890
1276	31 July 1859	1309	7 August 1891
1277	20 July 1860	1310	26 July 1892
1278	9 July 1861	1311	15 July 1893
1279	29 June 1862	1312	5 July 1894
1280	18 June 1863	1313	24 June 1895
1281	6 June 1864	1314	12 June 1896
1282	27 May 1865	1315	2 June 1897
1283	16 May 1866	1316	22 May 1898
1284	5 May 1867	1317	12 May 1899
1285	24 April 1868	1318	1 May 1900
1286	13 April 1869	1319	20 May 1901
1287	3 April 1870	1320	10 April 1902

Islamic Year	Gregorian Date of 1 Muharram	Islamic Year	Gregorian Date of 1 Muharram
1321	30 March 1903	1354	5 April 1935
1322	18 March 1904	1355	24 March 1936
1323	8 March 1905	1356	14 March 1937
1324	25 February 1906	1357	3 March 1938
1325	14 February 1907	1358	21 February 1939
1326	4 February 1908	1359	10 February 1940
1327	23 January 1909	1360	29 January 1941
1328	13 January 1910	1361	19 January 1942
1329	2 January 1911	1362	8 January 1943
1330	22 December 1911	1363	28 December 1943
1331	11 December 1912	1364	17 December 1944
1332	30 November 1913	1365	6 December 1945
1333	19 November 1914	1366	25 November 1946
1334	9 November 1915	1367	15 November 1947
1335	28 October 1916	1368	3 November 1948
1336	17 October 1917	1369	24 October 1949
1337	7 October 1918	1370	13 October 1950
1338	26 September 1919	1371	2 October 1951
1339	15 September 1920	1372	21 September 1952
1340	4 September 1921	1373	10 September 1953
1341	24 August 1922	1374	30 August 1954
1342	14 August 1923	1375	20 August 1955
1343	2 August 1924	1376	8 August 1956
1344	22 July 1925	1377	29 July 1957
1345	12 July 1926	1378	18 July 1958
1346	1 July 1927	1379	7 July 1959
1347	20 June 1928	1380	25 June 1960
1348	9 June 1929	1381	14 June 1961
1349	29 May 1930	1382	4 June 1962
1350	19 May 1931	1383	25 May 1963
1351	7 May 1932	1384	13 May 1964
1352	26 April 1933	1385	2 May 1965
1353	16 April 1934	1386	22 April 1966

Islamic Year	Gregorian Date of 1 Muharram	Islamic Year	Gregorian Date of 1 Muharram
1387	11 April 1967	1420	17 April 1999
1388	31 May 1968	1421	6 April 2000
1389	20 March 1969	1422	26 March 2001
1390	9 March 1970	1423	15 March 2002
1391	27 February 1971	1424	5 March 2003
1392	16 February 1972	1425	22 February 2004
1393	4 February 1973	1426	10 February 2005
1394	25 January 1974	1427	31 January 2006
1395	14 January 1975	1428	20 January 2007
1396	3 January 1976	1429	10 January 2008
1397	23 December 1976	1430	28 December 2008
1398	12 December 1977	1431	18 December 2009
1399	2 December 1978	1432	8 December 2010
1400	21 November 1979	1433	27 November 2011
1401	9 November 1980	1434	15 November 2012
1402	30 October 1981	1435	5 November 2013
1403	19 October 1982	1436	25 October 2014
1404	8 October 1983	1437	15 October 2015
1405	27 September 1984	1438	3 October 1016
1406	16 September 1985	1439	22 September 2017
1407	6 September 1986	1440	12 September 2018
1408	26 August 1987	1441	1 September 1019
1409	14 August 1988	1442	20 August 2020
1410	4 August 1989	1443	10 August 2021
1411	24 July 1990	1444	30 July 2022
1412	13 July 1991	1445	19 July 2023
1413	2 July 1992	1446	8 July 2024
1414	21 June 1993	1447	27 June 2025
1415	10 June 1994	1448	17 June 2026
1416	31 May 1995	1449	6 June 2027
1417	19 May 1996	1450	25 May 2028
1418	9 May 1997		
1419	28 April 1998		

1. Adapted from Jere L. Bacharach, *A Middle East Handbook* (Seattle: University of Washington Press, 1984). Used by permission.

Biblical and Qur'anic Citations

INDEX

About the Author

James E. Lindsay is the Associate Professor of History at Colorado State University, Fort Collins.